Isaac J Wistar
Colonel 71st Regt. Pa. Vols.
1863. Age 35.

AUTOBIOGRAPHY

OF

ISAAC JONES WISTAR

1827–1905

HALF A CENTURY IN WAR AND PEACE

ILLUSTRATED

HARPER & BROTHERS PUBLISHERS

New York and London

CONTENTS

ILLUSTRATIONS

PREFACE

These notes have been written almost entirely from recollection as other occupations permitted and the memory of events long forgotten or confused could be recalled and arranged.

Motives are complex and difficult to trace, but besides that insidious modicum of vanity which being common to all mankind cannot safely be denied, I am only conscious of two: the desire to sort out, marshal, and arrange the recollections which in the lapse of time and events had become confused, and the wish to leave some record to kinsmen perhaps unborn, of a long life during an eventful period affording glimpses of the lives of all classes of Americans during a stirring part of the nineteenth century.*

Many circumstances not now recalled with sufficient clearness have been omitted, but those related are true, though no doubt inaccuracies respecting names, dates, and the sequence of small events, may in some cases have imposed themselves as the recollections of occurrences many of which are now so remote.

Isaac J. Wistar

Philadelphia, 1892

* This paragraph, although omitted in the first confidential printing for some unknown reason, appears as written in the original manuscript.

CHAPTER I

When one not inordinately addicted to discoursing of himself begins to contemplate a lapse from such negative virtue, though he can easily find plenty of reasons to satisfy a conscience quite ready to yield, a second person is sure to discover among them some few grains of vanity more or less speciously concealed. Nevertheless, there are all sorts of vanity, useful, indifferent and offensive, and if in that broad variety we are to include such foibles as love of approbation, desire to please, or a wish to convey information amusing or useful, in our view, then it must be acknowledged that few intelligent acts of our lives are entirely free from the quality we are all so ready to disclaim.

It may therefore be admitted that it is one of the Protean forms of that all-pervading weakness that leads us to regard our own period as peculiarly eventful or important. It is not unnatural and I hope not unbecoming, that when one discovers little that is remarkable in his own career, as must always be the case with most of us, he should find a certain complacency in the reflection that he has at least lived among remarkable persons, or during a specially eventful period.

Possessing no doubt a full share of the common weakness, I nevertheless cannot help thinking that posterity with all its accumulated wisdom will find something peculiarly interesting in that portion of the nineteenth century which has seen such new forces as steam and electricity hunted down, captured and harnessed into the daily service of man, has reconstructed every branch of human knowledge, created a new chemistry, physiology, biology, geology and physics, has substituted rational and systematic inquiry for the old dogmas of supernaturalism and authority, and has applied each conquest thus

11

obtained over nature and ignorance to such practical purpose
as to revolutionize the life of man and separate him farther
than ever before from other animate beings and from all other
known forms of existence. It is scarcely too much to insist
that by the useful application of the new knowledge gained
during this comparatively short period, nearly every human
habit has been modified and to a great extent changed. We
gain our livelihood differently, we work, trade and travel, eat,
fight and amuse ourselves differently, are ill and use medical
and surgical remedies differently, have immeasurably increased the activity, comfort and average length of our lives.
It is only when arrived at the final article of death that we
continue to traverse the identical road of our fathers and sink
to rest very much as they did, in the same old way, unchanged
since the beginning of life in the world.

The economic changes in production and distribution during
the present generation have of themselves modified nearly all
our daily habits, and would require a volume to enumerate and
describe. During a period almost momentary, compared with
the long centuries of human history, every adult man has had
conferred upon him by the new mastery of the several natural
forces before referred to, and previously unknown or mischievous, the equivalent of a certain number—perhaps a score
—of willing and obedient slaves requiring no food, wages,
amusement, or police restraint, always cheerful, willing, ready,
who never quarrel over their share of the product, and never
offend any moral sense or charitable scruple of their bene-
ficiaries. The augmentation and cheapness of production thus
gained, in rendering life easy to the workers, and luxurious to
all as consumers, has pushed far back the barrier of the subsistence limit, for expounding which Malthus was so long derided,
and aided by important medical and sanitary discoveries, has
increased the population of the civilized races beyond any
former experience or prediction. Under such influences, that
steadily increasing accession has overflowed into all previously
unknown or unused portions of the world, pushing back or
exterminating inferior peoples, tending to substitute the more
advanced races throughout all continents and islands and

converting all available territory everywhere into farms, mines and workshops sustaining and inviting still denser populations.

Even with the knowledge now possessed, it seems as though the process must go on till within a short time the races who know how to avail themselves of these new agents, and perhaps to discover more, will displace or destroy all others and themselves occupy every useful corner of the world. It is a significant fact, that all these advances react and interact upon each other without cessation and with rapidly accumulating force. Every acre reclaimed from the wilderness in Africa, India or Dakota, makes life easier and therefore more abundant in London, Berlin, New York; and every new facility, every new-found cheapening of production and distribution in these old centers of population, renders life easier, safer, happier and more abundant in the newest lands won for industry and civilization. Thus even if our civilization has already reached its maximum—which there seems little reason to believe—the new forces already set in motion must go on operating, until in a short time—perhaps within one lifetime—the world as the seat of industry and population must become as unrecognizable to us who are about to leave it, as our existing world would now be to the men of a former century.

When I was born and for some time afterwards, there was no coal, natural gas or petroleum used in America. There were no railroads, electric telegraphs or telephones, no steamships, no anaesthetics, no knowledge of microbic causes and phenomena of disease. Chemistry and metallurgy as now applied to industrial production were almost unknown, and many of the most necessary and cheapest substances now in daily use, like aluminium and Bessemer steel, were either not to be had or only in minute quantities as a curiosity for cabinets. The greatest cities of our country were unimportant provincial towns occupying small fractions of their present areas, and with no greater proportion of their existing populations. Florida and the vast territory then known as Louisiana, now occupied by numerous great commonwealths, had but recently been acquired. California, Oregon, Texas and Arizona had not been acquired at all and the Mississippi river was with trifling exceptions the western limit of American population. Wood was everywhere the chief or only fuel. Grain was cut and harvested by hand, and badly ground by small water-powers adjacent to its place of growth. Manufacturing production was mostly by individuals at their residences and only on the minute and costly scale of which such a system was susceptible, and while the requital of labor was infinitely less than at present, the cost of everything in which it was a principal ingredient was so high as to keep out of use many articles now thought essential for ordinary comfort in the humblest households. Owing to the relatively great cost of the modes of transportation then in use, the areas of local distribution were small, and the advance of population clung closely to rivers and natural waterways. Domestic slavery was the social condition of a large part of the country and not only tinged all its domestic habits and foreign relations, but was considered such an indispensable economic and social advantage that even scholars and economists were scarcely permitted to criticize or discuss it.

Making full allowance for the natural tendency to magnify the importance of our own times, it can scarcely be doubted that the great changes which have thus occurred during a single life not yet spent, although so gradual and insensible as scarcely to command full appreciation without comparing one distant period with another, have been greater, and have established more radical modifications in domestic and individual life than those of any equal period in former times. But while the average length and comfort of individual life has been sensibly increased, it is yet doubtful whether a corresponding advance has been gained in political knowledge, and it now seems as though the life of nations—or rather of governments—is tending to even greater instability, notwithstanding the general opinion of the eighteenth century publicists that political stability was dependent on popular content, and popular content on popular comfort. Though the prevailing system of gratuitous education does not seem to have accomplished much of real value either in the repression of criminal depredation, or by increasing public contentment, yet popular intelligence due to the activities of surrounding life, has undoubtedly increased, and with augmented public comfort has tended at the same time to render the half-educated masses more critical of political forms, and to supply readier means for demolishing and changing them. Whether for instance, the modifications effected in our federal constitution—mostly for ephemeral partisan objects—either by deliberate amendment, or by legislative or judicial usurpation, will tend ultimately to augment public contentment or rational liberty, seems at present improbable to me, but must be for another generation to determine.

Be that as it may, it is for the reasons thus imperfectly sketched, that notwithstanding the well-known tendency to magnify the events of our own times, I must venture the opinion that whatever triumphs of knowledge await our race in the future, and to whatever further modifications in life and habits these may lead, yet posterity, however it may despise our attainments, cannot fail to distinguish the nineteenth century as the beginning at least of the new knowledge and the modern life, and will study its thought, methods and development with the same philosophic interest that we bestow on the times and the discoveries of Galileo, Copernicus, Harvey, Newton, Watts, Stephenson and Morse.

It is therefore rather for these considerations than for mere vanity, that having passed the age of greatest activity and being in a measure restricted by wounds and infirmities from some of the pursuits still agreeable to many at my period of life, I have thought myself privileged to look forward to a less active life than heretofore and to occupy some leisure hours from time to time in setting forth for younger members of my family something of the march of knowledge and empire in America as it has seemed to one individual during what this generation regards as a stirring period in both war and peace. For simplicity's sake I propose to do this in a plain autobiographical manner, notwithstanding the necessary frequency of the personal pronoun, perhaps catching a glance at some contemporaneous persons and events as they attracted my attention by the way, but for the most part withholding names except in the case of public characters or where I feel entire confidence in the accuracy of my memory. As I never kept diary or notes, with the very few exceptions which will appear, I may sometimes be uncertain or erroneous in dates or even in the sequence of small events, for I have little to reinforce my recollections except the notes above mentioned, some old letters and accounts, and a very incomplete series of official military orders, papers and telegrams of the civil war period.

As respects the vast territory traversed forty years ago in the far Northwest, I may claim some excuse for possible omissions or errors of a minor character in geographical or other details. My business there was trading, hunting and trapping, my only companions were wholly unlettered, and for a period of some years I never saw a book, map, or indeed even a roof except some few and widely scattered posts of the Hudson Bay Company. For months together I heard no language but voyageur French or Indian, and little contemplated any future attempt to give a narrative of the adventures that seemed simple enough at the time. But notwithstanding distance of time, absence of notes, and nearly half a century of subsequent occupations of totally different character and associations, I have sufficient confidence in my memory to believe that by omitting all events not remembered with clearness, I may attain substantial accuracy, with some of the minor exceptions mentioned.

As I have no expectation or intention that these notes shall go beyond the members (in esse or in futuro) of my own family, I will begin by setting forth some items of family history of interest to no one else, in the hope that they may be worth an effort to rescue from the oblivion which surely overtakes at last all things resting principally on scattered papers or oral tradition. I will therefore make no further apology for inserting here some items of family history in more connected form than, so far as I know, they exist elsewhere. In order to facilitate their being easily skipped they shall all be put together in this place.

I was born on the 14th of November, 1827, at Number 184—

now 726—Arch Street, Philadelphia, being the oldest of the ten children of Dr. Caspar, and Lydia Jones Wistar, all of whom lived till maturity.

My mother was the oldest daughter of Isaac Cooper, and Hannah Firth Jones, and was descended on both sides from old colonial families of English and Welsh stock. Her lineal ancestors include the Carpenters, Coopers, Prestons, Hills, Lloyds, Firths and others, distinguished in early colonial annals, some now extinct in name, but none in blood. It is useless for me to try to enumerate her countless virtues as daughter, wife and mother. Beautiful in person, cultivated in mind, gentle in heart, sober and sure in judgment, she was to me an incarnation of the qualities which the mothers of the all-absorbing Anglo-Teutonic race have almost unconsciously developed and transmitted to the best and noblest of its sons. She was companion and friend, joy, solace and delight to every member of her family, and when in 1878, after a long life devoted to their happiness, at the ripe age of seventy-four, she died surrounded by her children, calm, fearless and triumphant, something was taken from their lives which changed the tenor of their thoughts forever.

The nearest common ancestor of all the American Wistars and Wisters, was *Johannes Caspar Wister*, sometimes called in the church records Herr Johannes, and occasionally Hans, which is a common abbreviation of Johannes. He was born at Hilsbach, Baden, April 15, 1671, and died at the same place January 13, 1726–27, leaving surviving him four children aged in the following order, viz.: Caspar, Catharine, John and Ann Barbara. Caspar arrived in Philadelphia September 16, 1717, and John and Catharine not until September, 1727, having remained near their father till his death. Catharine married in America into the family of Heister, and settled on a large tract of land in the Tulpehocken Valley; becoming ancestress of a large and influential body of descendants of that name. Ann Barbara married in Germany a councillor named Bauer and had issue, of whom a daughter married in Germany a gentleman of Dutch descent named Keppele, with whom she came to Philadelphia, where she left numerous descendants of that name. All the American *Wistars* are descended from Caspar, while John is the ancestor of the Wisters.

Caspar Wistar arrived in Philadelphia the 16th of September, A.D. 1717, and at once proceeded to apply his capital and earnings to the purchase of land in the city, in New Jersey, and in the parts of Pennsylvania now covered by the counties of Chester, Berks, Centre, Clinton, Northumberland and Bradford, in all of which he acquired large tracts which were transmitted to his descendants. In the year 1738, as fixed by articles of agreement now in my possession, he constructed near Salem, N. J., the first glass works in America, which were successfully operated by himself and his oldest son, Richard, principally by the labor of 'redemptioners,' of whom they imported a large number. I possess a goblet made there for his own use and carrying his monogram, which in style and ornamentation would be quite creditable to a later period.

Caspar had come to America very much against the wish of his father, who had offered without avail to resign office in his favor if he would remain, and I cannot discover that he afterwards maintained much intercourse with his family in Germany. The numerous personal traditions which have come down respecting him indicate a vigorous and original character. One of them which has been published in various forms was committed to writing from the dictation of his grandson by the latter's daughter, Mary Wistar Brown, as follows:

He was appointed with a number of other persons among whom was a clergyman named Peters,[1] the Secretary of the Governor's Council, to make or attend an Indian treaty in the interior of Pennsylvania. It being the trout season they expected to be well provided with that favorite fare, but on arriving at their destined inn and summoned to table, were exceedingly disappointed in seeing but one small dish of inferior trout with a single good sized one placed on the top. The divine hurried to his seat and sticking his fork into the only desirable fish, transferred it to his own plate. This being secured, with closed

[1] Rev. Richard Peters, 1704-1776. Studied law at the Inner Temple, London. Ordained Clergyman 1730. Came to Philadelphia in 1735, where as Secretary of the Land Office during twenty-five years he acquired a large fortune. Was rector of Christ Church from 1764 to 1775.

eyes and uplifted hands, he said *now* let us pray—and rehearsed the usual form. While he was thus engrossed, his facetious friend (C. W.) being seated near him, quietly removed the coveted dish—and when the surprised dignitary opened his eyes to the fact, he was thus pleasantly accosted, "Parson Peters, men ought to *watch* as well as *pray*."

Though during after life he obtained great wealth, his early struggles with poverty in a strange country of different language from his own were not unlike those of other early immigrants under similar circumstances. When he declined his father's offer to resign office in his favor, his sire was greatly displeased and remarked that "a son who would not be satisfied with such a proposal, was not worth caring for," whereupon the youth paid his passage and embarked for the New World, then so little known, landing safely in Philadelphia with rifle in hand and ninepence in his pocket. Among his first employments was said to be wheeling ashes from a soap boiling establishment which gave rise to an amusing circumstance in his later years. Having assumed an active political part on the side of the Proprietary Government, in favor of which his great influence among the Germans was of considerable importance, certain political opponents conceived the brilliant idea of reminding him of the humble labors of his youth by hiring a common fellow to wheel a barrow of ashes back and forth before his door. But these worthy predecessors of some of our modern demagogues made a bad mistake in their man. As soon as the crowd attracted his attention he went out to the barrow wheeler saying, "Thee doesn't know anything about wheeling ashes; give me the barrow and let me show thee how it should be done," at the same time taking hold of the barrow and wheeling it back and forth for a time himself, thus signally triumphing over his assailants and spoiling their intended mirth by the practical demonstration that such *little things* are only great to *little minds*.

Caspar Wistar and Katharine Johnson, a member of the Society of Friends, having duly declared their intentions at the Monthly Meeting of Abington, according to the good order of that Society, were married in the Friends' Meeting at Germantown, on March 25th, 1726, Caspar having been admitted to

Membership in the Society of Friends for that purpose. The bride was of English Quaker parentage and the connection, while introducing him to membership and communion with that religious society, doubtless tended in other respects to promote his English associations—and it is worthy of remark as shedding some light on the important subject of the assimilation of the early emigrants with the then predominating English stock, that every one of his male descendants having, like him, married with persons of that race, there is a very minute fraction of German blood now remaining in the present generation, and they have thus gradually come to possess, along with the old Teutonic name, a more unmixed English lineage than many families bearing names of English origin. On the death of Johannes Caspar at Hilsbach in 1726, his brother John and his older sister, Catharine, followed Caspar to Philadelphia. The former settled at Germantown, where he left many descendants, who followed him in the spelling of his name. Caspar died of dropsy in Philadelphia March 21, 1752, leaving surviving him two sons, Richard and Caspar, and four daughters, Margaret W. Haines, Rebecca W. Morris, Catharine W. Greenleaf, and Sarah, who died unmarried.

Richard was born July 6, 1727, married Sarah Wyatt at Salem, N. J., on November 27, 1751, and became a prominent citizen of Philadelphia, remarked in Watson's Annals as one of the few who then possessed a carriage. Like most persons of property and standing, he adhered stoutly to the king's side and as appears from numerous Whig squibs and doggerel of the time, became sufficiently obnoxious to the rebel canaille. On the 17th of June, 1778, Sir Henry Clinton in obedience to instructions, evacuated Philadelphia, and with an army numbering over 17,000 effectives crossed the Delaware and abandoned Pennsylvania—the key of the struggle—to the rebels. The reasons have since been abundantly disputed and discussed, but whatever cogency they may have had at the time, the measure was fatal to the king's cause. Little was it realized by the scanty forces then contending along the extreme littoral borders of the great American wilderness, that such a casual act of war, by assuring speedy defeat to the royal cause, was to surrender half the world to popular institutions, so-called, and ultimately to ruin everywhere the hereditary principle.

Yet such far-reaching results are distinctly traceable to that great military and political error, as we must now regard it. The vast area, and unequalled virgin resources of North America must have attracted population and accumulated wealth and power under any system, but as its development under peculiarly stimulating circumstances surpassed any similar national growth of ancient or modern times, and coincided so closely with the great popular victory, democratic institutions have usurped the credit, and received an irresistible impulse among the optimistic and superficial of all lands.

Little could Washington and the well-descended, land-owning, colonial gentry of whom he was the type, have foreseen that their success was to lead to the destruction of their class in the new continent, and to vest its government and law-making exclusively in the hands of the least interested and the least qualified. Yet it now seems as if that is about what 'self-government' has accomplished in the United States, since every observant person must admit that the educated and well-born, though hardly to be regarded as unfit or criminal on account of those advantages, are habitually distrusted by the democracy and, as a rule, excluded from popular favor and public affairs.

What remedies the future may bring forth to elevate the judgment and taste of the democracy, relieve it from stupid prejudices, and render its rule compatible with independent statesmen, honorable officials and intelligent government, cannot be foreseen, but it is certain that its tendencies at present are not such as to enlist the best ability and integrity of the country in public affairs, and there is reason to believe that many thoughtful persons regard administration by 'manhood suffrage' as a demonstrated failure, incompatible with order, offensive to sentiment, and even revolting to good sense. The majority in every populous community includes and always must include, the poor, the ignorant, the vulgar, the depraved; and common observation shows that their numbers increase more than proportionally with the growth of the social organism. That the ignorant should by noise and numbers govern the wise, the improvident make laws and taxes for the industrious and enterprising, the vulgar set standards of taste and the depraved, of virtue—such is surely a condition inconsistent with salutary progress under any but abnormal conditions and cannot endure after our country shall have become fully populated and the competitive struggle of life severe.[2]

Be that as it may, the fatal act of Clinton—or his superiors —brought prompt disaster to many staunch Pennsylvania loyalists, and our own family did not escape. Before the king's troops were out of the city, mobs of bawling 'patriots' attacked the houses of prominent conservatives, and among others that of Richard Wistar on the south side of Chestnut above Third street. The front had been closed and barred by his children and servants, but Richard, who according to tradition was of no very submissive temperament, seized a cane and rushed out to remonstrate, probably not in the gentlest tones. He was set upon by the crowd, knocked down, trampled and beaten and would have been killed on the spot, but for a retiring rearguard of the royal troops who charged and dispersed the mob, rescued its victim half-killed as he was, and placed him in a baggage wagon in which he was carried with the retreating troops to Rahway, N. J., where he died of his injuries on the 4th of August.

My grandfather, Thomas, third son of Richard, was born on St. Patrick's day, March 17, 1765, and was therefore about seventeen at the time of the peace. From the time of his marriage May 24, 1786, to Mary, daughter of Richard and Elizabeth Waln, of Wainford, N. J., his principal interest was in religious subjects, and he became, in sharp contrast with an unusually gay youth, a plain and devoted member of the

[2] I think it was the wise Gouverneur Morris who said, there are but two governments—monarchy and aristocracy—democracy being no government at all, but simply a disorderly and stormy passage from one of the two forms to the other— and in due time, back again. History no less than inclination seems to give confirmation to his thought.

Society of Friends, with whom as an elder he acquired great influence and respect. Like many of his sect and generation he became passively reconciled to the new government though with little enthusiasm for it, and still less admiration for the innumerable demagogues and professional patriots who rose with and fattened upon it. In fact, although his long life only ended in 1851, he never voted under the Republic, but on a single occasion, which was to oppose the new and more radical Pennsylvania State Constitution of 1838.

Caspar, an elder and more distinguished brother of Thomas, born September 13, 1761, seems to have been endowed with a less devotional and more social temperament, and being less absorbed in religious exercises and pursuits, devoted himself to the cultivation of his profession, and to the kindred study of the natural sciences, especially that of comparative anatomy. After a classical training at the Penn Charter School in Philadelphia, so thorough that throughout his life he was able to use the Latin for conversational purposes, he graduated at the University of Pennsylvania as Bachelor of Medicine in 1782. Having during the same year become involved as principal in a celebrated duel, which the Quakers, whose peculiar views still retained great power in Philadelphia, regarded as little better than felony, he determined to prosecute his studies in London and Edinburgh for which object he sailed for Bristol in 1783 on the *Mildred* packet. After spending a year in England he went to Edinburgh, then a distinguished seat of medical science, where after a time he was elected President of the Royal Medical Society, and later President of the "Society for the Further Investigation of Natural History." Referring to these distinguished honors, Chief Justice Tilghman has said, "These honors conferred by a great, a learned and proud nation on a youth, a stranger, one whose country had but just risen into existence, are the surest testimonies of uncommon merit." He received his medical degree at Edinburgh in 1786 and returning to Philadelphia, commenced practice there in the following year, rapidly taking high rank in the profession. He was elected Professor of Chemistry in the College of Philadelphia in 1789, became a physician of the Philadelphia Dispensary in 1787, and in 1793, of the Pennsylvania Hospital. In 1788 he married Isabella Marshall who died without children in 1790. He became a censor of the College of Physicians in 1793, holding that position till his death.

He married in 1798, Elizabeth Mifflin—niece of General Thomas Mifflin, first Governor of Pennsylvania under its Constitution and the newly adopted Constitution of the United States—by whom he had three children who survived him but themselves subsequently died without issue. In 1815 he succeeded his friend, Thomas Jefferson, as President of the American Philosophical Society, and he occupied the chair of Anatomy in the University of Pennsylvania from 1808 till his death, during which period he founded the great Museum now known as The Wistar Institute of Anatomy and Biology —attached to the University of Pennsylvania. He was the first anatomist to discover and figure the pyramidal protuberances still called after his name 'Wistar's pyramids' of the ethmoid bone, and was the author of six papers contributed to the Transactions of the American Philosophical Society, and of numerous other learned and scientific essays, besides ''A System of Anatomy for the use of Students of Medicine'' (2 vols., Philadelphia, 1817) which was long the principal text-book in use throughout the United States. At the time of his death, January 22, 1818, in the 57th year of his age, he had instituted a correspondence with Cuvier, Sommering, and other distinguished foreign naturalists, and was fast rising in European reputation as a comparative anatomist. Having long been in the habit of entertaining at weekly social meetings at his house his medical friends and other learned and scientific men, his friends after his death organized an Association called after his name, which except for a few years' interruption during the Civil War, has ever since continued to exist, its entertainments having now been known for nearly a century as 'Wistar parties.'

My father, Caspar, born June 5, 1801, was the second of three sons of Thomas who survived their father, and influenced, no doubt, by the successful career of his uncle, like him devoted himself to the medical profession. Like him he inherited a sufficient competence, but either that fact, which had not relaxed the ardor of the uncle, or the extreme religious tendencies inherited from his father, seemed to render the nephew fastidious in his practice and indifferent to the numerous professional resources by which success and profit are usually sought and attained. In common with many of his professional contemporaries and friends, I think he possessed the qualities of quick and correct diagnosis, sound judgment, and knowledge of resources which if accompanied by the spur of necessity, must have carried him to the front rank of his profession. Notwithstanding the absence of that inestimable stimulus, which in my judgment no other circumstance or quality can fully replace, he nevertheless acquired a considerable practice, and inspired so much confidence and affection that he found much difficulty in terminating many of his professional relations, even after adopting the practice of living during a large part of each year in the country.

Though devoted to his large family, and deeply interested in their culture and education, his earnest religious sentiment and intense desire to instil it in his children, rendered him a closer domestic disciplinarian than would in these days be thought most judicious for the direction of young lads not to any great extent under the same controlling influence. As the oldest child, and possessed of a much more worldly mind, it fell to my lot to take the first brunt of his early domestic theories before greater experience brought modification. Always a sincere admirer of my father and deeply attached to him—for with his wide range of reading and love of knowledge he was in more demonstrative moments one of the most cultivated and delightful companions I ever knew—I have now to recall with regret that my numerous disobediences and rebellions were mostly traceable to an impatience of control which it was my duty to have restrained, and it was perhaps the best practical solution, that much of my youth came to be passed at boarding schools, by which domestic collisions were softened or avoided.

In the year 1839, when I had scarcely passed the age of ten,

I was sent to the Friends' boarding school at Westtown, in Chester county, Pennsylvania, where with plenty of room, and knocked about among a large number of boys mostly older than myself, I soon learned with immense benefit that the world was pretty large and contained many other persons and wills besides one's own, that had to be regarded. The education was elementary and practical, the living plain, the morals good, and the association in work and play with older and larger boys supplied a struggle and emulation both physical and intellectual, which is of priceless value at that early period of life. I spent a most useful eighteen months at Westtown, and after a year or two at the Friends' Select School—so called— in Philadelphia, where I derived lasting advantage from the excellent mathematical teaching of that good man and judicious teacher, Samuel Alsop, to whom so many of my generation owe, like myself, an unappraisable debt, I was sent in or about 1842 to Haverford School—now Haverford College—where I remained a year and a half, till the completion of the junior year. Daniel B. Smith, a learned and distinguished man was then President, a position which he had accepted at some sacrifice to himself on account of his love of literature, and his great interest in the successful inauguration of that school, which had been instituted by the more liberal class of Friends, and was intended to supply a more advanced education to the youth of the Society, than some of the more zealous members then approved. He was a man not merely learned, but of original mind and cultured taste, and took keen pleasure in expanding and leading the opening minds of appreciative youth. To his broad views and fine taste in letters, and to the conversations which he seemed to take a pleasure in holding with me, I owe a benefit of which I have since been more sensible than at the time. Notwithstanding numerous revolts against the narrow priggism of some of the other authorities and an ardent inclination for mischief and adventure which frequently and justly provoked his rather passionate tempera- ment, I have since perceived that my own tastes and ideals came during that period—by assimilation with his—to take a higher level, which, however depressed sometimes by adverse surroundings, they have afterwards been able to resume when more favorable circumstances presented.

It was under the dominion of Dr. Smith's intellectual influence that I learned to admire the best sentiments of the British poets, and the noble acts and actors of Roman and English history, an admiration which no lad can truly feel without some faint and humble desire to emulate. Those priceless and immortal standards of greatness and nobility, with his well-selected English poetry and fiction, though perhaps since widened and developed in my appreciation by more extended reading of books and men, have remained a more or less constant and beneficial influence throughout a life which has not always been without surroundings of a contrary tendency. It is difficult to exaggerate the beneficial effect of high ideals honestly admired and firmly lodged in the plastic mind of youth. They may be for long periods disregarded and apparently forgotten, but once implanted they can never perish, but are always tending to influence nobler and better thoughts and acts. Man is weak and unstable, but though he grovel on the ground, even from thence he must needs look upward to the planets he has once admired, and I believe none need fear that lofty ideals are wasted upon the young because these fail to come quite up to the mark. It may be, and sometimes certainly is, better to possess high standards and fall short of them, than to enjoy the negative virtues of a sinless prig with no higher ideals than the tattling platitudes of his kind. Virtue is good, but like other goods is better conquered than inherited, and when it proceeds without effort from mere vacuity of mind, it may possess less real moral and intellectual value than a smaller measure conquered by the struggling efforts of more generous but erring souls.

Wister

Isaac Jwiston
Philad. 1845
Age 17.

CHAPTER II

1844–1849

My education, such as it was, being now 'finished,' about the year 1844, much against my inclination I was placed in a Market street dry goods 'store,' under tutelage of a couple of thrifty New England Quakers whose conventional dress, sanctimonious deportment and godly nasal twang indicated an amount and pressure of piety which it was hoped might overflow plenteously on me and fill me to the extent of emulation with admiration of commercial holiness. But with an unaccountable perversity I hated the business and wickedly despised those devout men, notwithstanding their scrupulous —not to say ostentatious—mixture of weekday meetings and other devotions with more carnal efforts to work off their wares on the godless Egyptians of the country districts. Truth obliges me to confess that though I received no pay, even at that price I must have been superfluous to them, and after a year of disappointments which were probably mutual, I could endure it no longer and withdrew my inestimable services as sweeper, folder, and messenger, from the exemplary pietists whom my sinful mind was incapable of appreciating. But the larger world did not seem the least eager to secure the benefit of my talents, and in fact when it appeared that my father was indifferent and inclined to regard me as a failure, it seemed disposed to turn its back on me altogether. In vain I marched from store to store, describing with enthusiasm my talents and capacity; I seldom got any attention, and when I did, an interview with my depressed parent seemed to deprive such unwilling converts of all further desire for my services.

29

Idleness, disapprobation, and dependence were hard to bear and after a course of failures on shore, I thought business might be combined with adventure and turned my efforts toward the sea, as thousands of disappointed lads had done before me. Up and down the wharves I trudged, hunting down all the long voyaging skippers I could find and setting forth the priceless services I could render as a cabin boy.

But even that humble endeavor led to no success, and at last when so depressed that I was willing to shovel coal or sweep the streets or anything but remain idle, I agreed with a hearty young farmer of Montgomery county to work for him a year at anything I could do, or learn to do, in exchange for my lodging, board and washing. Thus having got down to pretty near the bottom, this humble enterprise, though not extremely remunerative, proved successful, for I learned really to support myself, in which I never afterward found any difficulty. Put on my mettle by previous failures, and the very low opinion which prevailed of me at home, I went at this job as though I expected to make a fortune the first year. I learned every kind of farm work, and worked like a horse from dawn till dark, doing a man's work and keeping up with the rest at mowing, cradling and all other work, soon finding myself surrounded with a hearty appreciation which by contrast was doubly inspiriting.

When the season's work was over, near the end of the year 1846, I agreed with a friend of my own age, a lad in a neighboring country store who was then being pampered on the munificent salary of six dollars a month, to spend the winter on a pedestrian and exploring tour through the back counties, and as he possessed a capital of twenty-five dollars, while I only mustered five, he agreed to my peremptory but unbusiness-like requirement that his surplus wealth should be left behind, that we might start on an equal footing. It was about the end of November when I left the place which had furnished such useful and agreeable quarters, with the kind interest of all its inmates and with a certain amount of self appreciation, the fruit of conscious usefulness. L. and I with a shot gun and one small blanket each then started to walk from the old inclined plane, now converted into a rustic path in the park, up the state railroad which then had its western terminus eighty miles distant at Columbia, where it had traffic connection with the state canals extending up the several branches of the Susquehanna. The traffic was then small and the trains few and slow, but by watching at adverse grades where the freight trains toiled slowly, we obtained numerous lifts till detected and put off by the train hands. At the present day when thousands of miles of railroads cover the country and their administration is conducted by scientifically trained specialists, our mode of travelling would be stigmatized as 'beating one's passage,' but that did not trouble our reflections when we could thus avoid a few miles walking. In one way and another, riding and walking, we reached Columbia late one evening, and walked up the canal after dark to Marietta where we tried to sleep in a boardyard. The night though clear was very cold, and notwithstanding the ingenious device of depositing ourselves between two boards placed on edge, with another for covering, the boardyard as a sleeping accommodation proved a failure.

The cold was keen, the frost was heavy, our sleeping troughs were continually breaking down and tumbling in on us, and I have a recollection of sundry language used from time to time which I am confident would not have received the approbation of my father and his pious friends. As soon as it was light enough to see, we left the inhospitable quarters, made a toilet in the canal and started up the towpath, cold hungry and cross. We soon found a boat tied up to the bank, and woke up the skipper who was rather drunk, and alone, all his hands having deserted him, probably for a better or less pugnacious brand of whiskey. The boat was empty on its last return to Bellefonte for the season, and the captain was alarmed at the ice on the canal which threatened to close up and keep him away from home all winter. We therefore found little difficulty in agreeing with him for board and passage to Bellefonte in return for our services. Everyone has heard of the Irishman who worked his passage on the canal by walking on the towpath and driving the mules. It cannot be denied that our contract had a strong family resemblance to his, except that in addition

to the privilege of walking and whacking the mules we were
to be fed. But as soon as our jolly skipper found we could
be trusted, one steering and the other driving, both being in
quite as much of a hurry as he was, he lost no time in resuming
his incipient and interrupted intoxication, and kept continually
and conscientiously drunk during the entire voyage. In that
happy state he required little solid food, and as (like the
famous Mrs. Gilpin) he combined a certain thrift with his
pleasures, he failed to see with the same perspicacity that we
did the advantage of disbursing for our necessities. The
consequence of this dullness of perception on his part was,
that whenever we required money for a loaf of bread or any
other small article we had to scuffle for it and even take it from
his pocket by strategem or force, and as our appetites grew
with the difficulty of satisfying them, there was a continual
alternation of starvation and war. Nevertheless, his tipsy
suspicion and semi-hostile watchfulness did not seem to curtail
his general friendliness and appreciation during the intervals
when we wanted nothing from him, and he trusted us implicitly
against all the outside world.

In the course of a few days, passed in a constant state of
semi-starvation and fighting for food, we arrived opposite a
fine large farm somewhere not far from the place called
Selin's Grove, abounding with poultry and all sorts of agricultural abundance. I regret to have to say that before that
charming vision of rustic wealth and food, all of our carefully
instilled principles of morality and honesty broke down together in confused and tumbling ruin. After mature reflection
on the best way of utilizing that tempting opportunity so as
to fill our stomachs without helping to fill the jail, we tied up,
fastened our tipsy governor in the cabin, and procuring plenty
of corn from some belated field shocks near by, scattered it
along the bank, across the gang plank and down in the empty
hold, and after a little while shut down the hatches on the
entire flock of poultry and started off with chickens enough
for breakfast, dinner and supper, through a long and cheerful
vista of future plenty.

Those State canals constructed by the Commonwealth of
Pennsylvania between 1826 and 1848, were sold in 1857 to

sundry corporations organized for the purpose, and in 1867, long after this not very creditable adventure, I was elected President of the one in question which was known as the West Branch and Susquehanna, and after several years of negotiation ultimately got them all reconsolidated as the Pennsylvania Canal of which I have since been, and am now, the President. I have often since traversed it on foot and horseback, by boat and steamer, and have curiously looked for and endeavored to find the scene of that nefarious operation, not omitting many cautious inquiries from elderly foremen and officials, but have been unable to hear any tradition of it or to identify the place, and like many another offender have hitherto gone unwhipped of justice.

Many years after that event, when L. and I—having long since sowed the last of our wild oats and become substantial and sober citizens, when time had whitened our thinning locks, and sobered all our views of affairs and men—were sitting together on a Municipal Committee (famous in its day) in the vain effort to construct a decent administration of public business from such material as was afforded by greedy demagogues, venal officials, purchased voters, and in short all the dirty paraphernalia of 'universal suffrage,' I took the opportunity of relating this story, taking care to give L. sole credit for the scheme. He manfully acknowledged the main charge, or I might have had some difficulty in obtaining credence from that assemblage of sober venerable and upright burghers.

At Milton the boat's cabin had got to be such a disgusting place that L. and I, after taking care of the mules, started out to find more agreeable sleeping quarters and finding the upper window over a stable unfastened climbed in with the aid of a pole and spent the night in the hay, resuming charge of our craft early next morning. At last after a voyage which I think must have occupied nearly three weeks, by the end of which we had become accomplished canallers, we arrived at the boat's destination on the Bald Eagle Branch near Bellefonte. Here we proceeded to sober up and groom down our worthy skipper, having first thrown the remainder of his whiskey overboard to prevent his falling into worse hands, and bidding him a friendly adieu which was quite affectionate on his part, we struck out on foot across Centre and Clearfield into the mountains of Elk county, a large territory now divided into several populous counties, but then only sparsely settled by hunters and log cutters. Near where the village of Caledonia now is, we hired ourselves for fifty cents a day and 'board' to help cut out a road over the mountains which, according to my recollection, was designed to connect Erie with the town of Jersey Shore. The 'board' consisted of deer and pheasants shot by ourselves, corn meal occasionally brought in on a pack horse, 'tea' made from the young shoots of spruce boughs, and plenty of trout taken every morning and evening from our own traps set close by the house, not forgetting the privilege of sleeping in front of the fire in a log house of our own construction.

After a month or two of hard work which yielded us a very minute amount of wealth, we resigned this brilliant opening, and started out hunting with a wily old mountaineer who, with his solitary pack horse, made a living by hunting deer for their hides, and wolves and other vermin for the bounty then allowed on their scalps, to which the State with remarkably good judgment, required *both* ears to be attached. Snow lay on the ground, mostly to considerable depth, but with a good log fire, plenty of hemlock boughs to lie upon, and entire freedom of movement according to our own sweet wills, we were on the whole very comfortable, and maintained unbroken health without house or tent. One might reasonably hope for immunity from fire in the depth of woods and snow, and yet it was the cause of our principal adventure which it may as well be stated for the benefit of insurance companies, came about as follows: Our blankets being too short to cover both ends simultaneously, we had sewed them up into sleeping bags usually keeping the tow linings on the outside. One cold night with deep snow all 'round, I was waked from a sound sleep by a feeling of unusual warmth about the nether extremities, and discovered that the tow lining had taken fire from a spark and was blazing up into a conflagration. As each had his loaded gun inside his sleeping bag, the work of hurried extrication caused some confusion and considerable damage to clothes, tempers and blankets.

Another night we partially passed in trying to interview a panther who was so much interested in us and our affairs that he spent an hour or more in the investigation of the camp, walking all 'round it and from time to time either expressing his oral disapproval or calling his mate to come and help him examine us, we did not understand which. He kept at a respectful distance and we failed to get even a glimpse of him. I have seen and shot many of them since, but never knew one to linger around so long and exhibit so much curiosity. They are cowardly beasts, like all of our American cats, and unless they think themselves securely concealed, their main object is usually to get quietly away, the only exception being the female in her lair with young, in which position nearly all wild animals prefer a fight to a close inspection.

After a month or two, as it was evident we had not yet found the road to wealth, we dissolved partnership with our old hunter, who of course took care that the heavy deer skins should fall to our share of the effects. These we packed compactly and fastened upon a small raft, which we constructed by burning wind-fallen trees to proper lengths and fastening them together with poles and withes, having no means for making holes for pins and wedges in the usual manner. Securing our guns and all other effects, not forgetting some extra setting poles, upon this precious craft we started down a large creek supposed to be one of the numerous branches of the Sinnemahoning, on our way to Coudersport, a place represented by the retiring member of the firm as a large and thriving seat of the deerskin trade. The water was low and the creek was well supplied with timber, jams, rocks, falls, rapids and all the various sorts of obstacles fitted to elicit language of dubious propriety. The raft was constantly coming to grief, and once in going over a rocky fall, half the logs were torn out and L. jerked overboard in the boiling rapid below, being hauled back upon the remains of the raft with considerable delay and difficulty. After, according to our estimate, we had enjoyed about forty miles of this exciting navigation we abandoned the raft, and struck across the mountains by a well marked foot-trail to find our destination. As the hills were numerous and steep and we had considerably over a hundred pounds of skins, we divided them in four packs and carried two forward a mile or two, returning for the others. In this manner we at last reached the gay metropolis we were searching for, which we found contained three or four houses, all told, one only of which was a general 'store.' We did not observe any signs of the wild competition among skin purchasers which we had been led to expect, and found an immense difference prevailing between cash and trade prices. As only cash was of any use to us we were glad to get twelve cents a pound for our skins, after lugging them on our backs at least seventy-five miles, as we guessed it, mostly over a rough and unsettled country.

Entirely convinced now that no large or immediate fortune was to be had by hunting, we started east on the main wagon road which led through Wellsboro to Towanda, working a little in saw-mills by the way. At the last-named place on the North Branch of the Susquehanna we found a large lumber raft with eight or ten hands, about to start down the river, upon which we agreed to work our passage to Wilkesbarre. At a point a few miles above that place the raft grounded near midnight on the opposite side of the river. As the skipper had already repudiated his undertaking to land us at Wilkesbarre on the alleged ground of this same danger we were now for taking advantage of the opportunity to get ashore and take the chance of being able to get across to the town, but he begged so piteously that we would not leave him in this plight, with the danger of losing his raft, that we remained working, prying and tugging with the rest, sometimes in water up to our middles, till at last the raft was got afloat. When we passed Wilkesbarre, soon after, the skipper pretended to fulfil his promise by bawling for a boat, but as none came, we were in a fair way of being carried on and past the Nanticoke dam, but for the kindness of the pilot and crew who, in spite of the owner's bad faith, skillfully swung the after end inshore so that we could jump off into the slack water of the pool.

In that manner we got ashore about two in the morning, thoroughly wet, with several inches of snow on the ground and a freezing temperature. Making the best of our way back to Wilkesbarre, some three miles distant, we could not find any person awake or a single house open. In trying to wake up the inmates of a tavern where a fire-light shone cheerfully through the window, we pushed the sash loose, which fell in with a tremendous clatter, and feeling that we were strangers in an extremely suspicious position, we foolishly ran away, never stopping till we reached a tavern at the extreme end of the town where we finally obtained admittance. As the snow kept on falling we lay in bed till dinner-time next day, after which we still more foolishly took advantage of an intermission of the storm to start out for the walk of twenty-five miles over the Broad or Wilkesbarre mountain to Whitehaven on the Lehigh.

The snow soon recommenced, and all traces of the single wagon road being obliterated we went astray and when it became dark, found ourselves hopelessly lost in a storm of wind and snow on a wild mountain which then boasted but one house between Wilkesbarre and Whitehaven, a small cabin occupied by an old man engaged in making shingles. We climbed up and tumbled down ravines and precipices, and waded over and through the brush covered deep with snow, the storm seeming to increase in violence, and it was not till near midnight that in a lull of the tempest we dimly perceived the fire-light shining through the old woodcutter's single window, far off across a deep ravine. We got there at last and obtained shelter, but for which lucky chance, inexperienced as we were, we might very probably have ended our careers then and there. On the next day we got down to Whitehaven and following the good wagon-road down the Lehigh to Lehighton, below Mauch Chunk, there crossed the river and mountain to Easton, whence we walked down the Bethlehem turnpike to Philadelphia.

During the year 1847 my paternal grandfather having in consequence of increasing age, abandoned his habit of summer retirement to the country—always so prevalent in Philadelphia, my father received from him his country-seat known as Hilton, near Foxchase, ten miles from the city though within the municipal limits as now fixed, where he had spent his summers since the year 1790. My father then in his turn commenced residing there during the summer months, and being like all citizens, an agricultural enthusiast, required my services not merely to aid in the invention of new theories, but in the practical work of restoring and remodelling the farm and buildings, which were extensive and had been somewhat neglected.

Having inherited a share of bucolic enthusiasm, I worked hard at this business during the season, and though not fully cured of my rural propensities at that time, may say that the experience then acquired, strongly reinforced by some more of later date, has amply satisfied me that agricultural diversions are much better adapted for the extravagance of the rich than for the advancement of the poor. This conclusion, it is true, did not dawn on me all at once, nor in fact till after later and exhaustive experiments in various places and under different conditions; but I am now none the less satisfied, as well from experience as observation, of the solid mass of truth underlying the conclusion of my Aunt Sarah W. Cope—an intellectual and observant woman—that I once thought so prejudiced and narrow, namely, that agriculture as a means of livelihood, so vaunted by sentimentalists and poets, is in all countries the dernier resource of the failures in more active and ambitious pursuits. The theme no doubt admits of discussion and invites a long explanatory essay which, however, I will not indulge in, being satisfied with my conclusion as the result of a long and gradual revolution of opinion. I can well understand how great minds can despise mere pecuniary results and derive keen pleasure from the constant presence of nature and her marvels, but I fail to see how such minds can contentedly waste themselves during the vigorous period of life in mere sentiment and study, without some object better calculated to call forth their active and combative qualities than continuous sowing and mowing, ploughing and digging, eating and sleeping.

Of course such strictures apply only to farming for revenue. For a man of easy fortune, a country life of thought and study or activity in public affairs, with taste and means for intelligent experiment and practice, is replete with all the occupation, usefulness, and intellectual pleasure that any reasonable person could desire. But as such was by no means the kind of rural life that I could aspire to, I proceeded to engage myself, in 1848, to a Philadelphia map publisher who undertook to teach me how to keep his accounts, for which I was to receive the compensation of three dollars a week. As I did not prove an inapt scholar, this was soon increased to four, and then to five dollars, upon which I managed to pay board and live till November, when my cousin, Dr. Mifflin Wistar, who with his wife was about to travel in the South for health, invited me to accompany them, and though my master offered a partnership interest, and did actually print my name on some of his maps, the temptation was much too strong to be resisted.

We sailed from New York on the *S. S. Northerner* some time during November, and had a stormy and inclement voyage to Charleston, in which both quarter-boats were lost and some other damage sustained. Though the passage was not long, it furnished an incident which, though small in itself, served to reveal a new and somewhat amusing page in the opening book of my individual experience. For fear of accidents and separation my cousin had supplied me with the sum of one hundred dollars in the form of ten gold eagles, which for greater security my dear mother had sewed up in my trousers watch-fob to be used only in emergency. Now my stateroommate was not an ornamental person, nor—as I too late remembered—calculated to inspire much confidence. Though numerous peculiarities fully established the descent he claimed from the Pilgrim Fathers, he now hailed from Georgia, and belonged to that second-hand variety of the Puritans there familiarly known as 'galvanized Yankees.' Each night of the voyage on removing my trousers, I placed them under my head, after carefully feeling that the contents of the fob were all right. When the vessel had arrived alongside the dock and after many passengers had left, to render assurance doubly sure, I ripped open the fob, but instead of the bright golden eagles found the same number of old fashioned copper cents! As it was the largest amount I had ever possessed and the catastrophe reflected deeply on my ability to take care of myself, much less to assist anyone else, I made an awful fuss, but my bird had flown and except the sympathy of my cousins, all the satisfaction I ever got was plenty of good round nautical abuse from the Captain for not placing in his charge what I was so evidently unable to take care of myself. But though my cousin lost the money, I think perhaps I gained its value in experience.

As we were abundantly supplied with letters and credentials and found the southern people hospitable and kind, I did not fail to enjoy myself keenly and made many delightful acquaintances in Charleston and Savannah. About the first of February we went in search of a yet milder climate to St. Augustine, then a small and entirely Spanish town still surrounded by its ancient walls, and containing but one shop supplied by one annual schooner from New York. Very little or no English was spoken, except among the few northern visitors who congregated at the only public-house, a small frame building called like its present splendid successor, the Magnolia. Leaving this place after a few weeks by stage for Picolata on the St. John's, we went thence by a small-decked steam launch to Enterprise, then simply a sugar farm recently started on Lake Monroe by Dr. Wurdeman of Charleston with twenty or thirty of his negroes. The plantation having failed as such, the house and negroes had been let to one Henning, who kept it open as a boarding-house for northern people in search of health or sport.

With the exception of a small cabin a mile or two distant, belonging to a hunter named Damaster, it was the only house on the lake and in fact the only inhabited place above Palatka, more than a hundred miles below. The neighboring woods were then full of game, deer and turkeys frequently coming close to the house. Black bass of large size abounded in the lake and all neighboring waters. Alligators swarmed in the rivers and along every sunny bank, and nothing was wanting to complete the happiness of a lad fond of hunting and adventure. But though nothing could exceed my enjoyment of that delightful period so full of novelty to me, I was sensible that it did not tend to much advancement in those practical pursuits which in the absence of fortune, were so essential to me, and I hailed with joy the summons I there received which led to a resumption of the hard work of life, by a novel sort of route, which though for many years it involved privation, toil and peril, served as a useful introduction to the work of maturer years, and which I have never since in the least regretted.

In Savannah and St. Augustine I had become acquainted with a number of more or less educated but impecunious youths of my own age and equally fond of adventure, all like myself with their own fortunes to seek. To us had come like fire to tow the celebrated report of Col. Mason to the War Department, confirming to a certain extent the stories of the discovery of gold in great quantities, far away across the mountains, plains and deserts in the then unknown and almost mythical land of California. Here was offered a combination of fortune-hunting and adventure unequalled since the days of the buccaneers, and well-nigh irresistible—not alone to us, but to the adventurous and ambitious youth of the whole country, who, in fact, swarmed in tens of thousands by every route known and unknown, possible and impossible, to the promised land. Across and through the wild fastnesses of the continent, around Cape Horn, through the unknown interiors of Mexico and Central America, along every route and by every conceivable method pushed forth swarms of adventurers who, leaving thousands to perish by the way, failed not to press onward despite all obstacles, to the long-sought spot; and the splendid Anglo-Saxon empire they have there reared is now well known to all mankind, and already begins to constitute a fascinating page of history.

The movement struck me in a susceptible spot, for I had always been hankering after the adventures of the plains and mountains. Letters had gone forth in all directions from Savannah and St. Augustine for a muster of kindred spirits who were to follow me to Enterprise when the undertaking should have been got into practical shape. Meantime I had at Enterprise, formed acquaintance with Mr. Warren D. Gookin, an American who having abandoned a successful business of sugar planting in Cuba on account of domestic bereavement, had engaged himself with persons in New York to go out in the following spring to Para, Brazil, to take charge of a rice mill near that place. With him I had conditionally arranged that after crossing the continent by land, if I found the condition of affairs in California exaggerated, as was somewhat expected, I was to work my way by vessel down to Truxillo, or some other favorably situated Peruvian port, and thence, crossing the Andes and descending the Amazon, join him at Para, bringing actual personal knowledge of that vast, teeming interior and its products. Affairs being in this expectant condition, the poking semi-monthly mail from St. Augustine at last brought the promised letter, from which I learned of my friend's success in organizing a party of twelve—including myself—who had now scattered to their various homes in Georgia and Florida, pledged to rendezvous as early as possible after the middle of March (1849) at Independence, Missouri, there to obtain animals and outfit, and start thence whenever the young prairie grass should be sufficiently grown to sustain animals. Each was to be possessed of at least a hundred dollars, besides the necessary arms, ammunition and blankets.

Fortunately for my part of the scheme, my cousins had concluded to start North earlier than first contemplated, and toward the end of March we reached Aiken, S. C., whence I preceded them to Philadelphia, arriving there April 2, 1849. My father, family and friends were all, of course, averse to the project and used every effort to dissuade me, my grandfather even offering to advance some capital for me to commence business with, at home. But the long-cherished fascinations of the prairies and mountains, not to mention the golden prospects beyond, had got my mind into a condition proof against all sober reason, and when fully convinced of it, my father presented me with a hundred dollars, another friend, with a fine half ounce calibre rifle, and in company with Dr. William Gambel, assistant curator of the Philadelphia Academy of Natural Sciences, a young naturalist and author already of some distinction, I started at 11 P.M., April 5, 1849, on an expedition which led me during many years through much wild and precarious adventure, and directly or indirectly shaped all my future life and career.

From the old station at Eighth and Market streets, Gambel and I traveled by rail via Baltimore to Cumberland, then the western terminus of the Baltimore and Ohio R. R., and thence by stage-coach over the national turnpike, through one of the

most varied and beautiful portions of the United States, to
Wheeling. The coach was well-filled, and we had an opportunity of walking up the numerous hills, and admiring that
fine scenery, but little of which can be leisurely enjoyed by the
railroad travelers of the present day. We took a steamer to
Cincinnati, where the uncertainty of the steamboats obliged
us to remain a day or two, and where I purchased a wagon
actually in street use, which struck my fancy as a light, strong
shortcoupled vehicle adapted to the purpose. I was not without
experience with wagons, having hauled many a load of hay
from, and of manure to, my father's farm, and in this instance
I made no mistake, for that wagon proved to be one of the only
two of our entire outfit which survived the searching trials of
the rocks and mountains, of alkali plains and desiccating
deserts, and actually reached the Pacific coast.

Between Cincinnati and St. Louis we had the novelty, to us,
of a long and exciting race with a rival steamer, both carrying
hard crowds of California emigrants. Several times we barely
escaped collision and on each occasion rifles and pistols were
flourished, but not discharged. At St. Louis—guided by letters
from the party at Independence—I purchased flour, bacon and
other necessary articles, and took passage with them by
steamer up the Missouri, Gambel remaining a day or longer
for some purposes of his own or because he preferred more
leisurely traveling. The very first night out, the cholera—then
raging throughout the country—broke out on board with
virulence, and as under the unfavorable circumstances of irregular diet and a crowded and dirty steamer, its effects were
quick and deadly, a great panic ensued and many of our
noisiest braggarts became suddenly endowed with a lamblike
meekness. Some eighteen or twenty poor fellows died and
were laid out on deck till enough corpses accumulated, when
they were buried, wrapped only in their blankets, in shallow
holes hastily dug by the deck-hands on river islands, the boat
barely stopping long enough for the purpose. I had a severe
though short attack, but as my bunk-mate was unwilling under
the circumstances to share my bunk, and could get no other, he
had leisure to look after and give me much necessary attention,

and when five or six days later we arrived at Independence landing, three miles from the town, I was already sufficiently recovered to go about my affairs after a fashion.

After no end of trouble and running about, in which I received the willing aid of many others who had passed through similar experience, the party was at last found encamped on the farm of Colonel Ralston, a short distance from the town. This gentleman was himself formerly an emigrant from Kentucky, now a prosperous resident of this place with a large farm, plenty of stock, and quite a large number of negroes, for a frontier farmer. He gave us much aid and advice which we badly needed. I have since heard that one of his numerous small children then running about the premises, many years afterwards became the wife of the celebrated Jesse James, who still later acquired a certain notoriety of the Robin Hood variety, which during the six or seven years of his career, spread widely over the country and penetrated every corner of the United States. I was not long in taking up my abode at the camp, where I was joyfully received. A detachment had just returned from the Ozark country in southern Missouri with some thirty wild, unbroken two-year-old mules, the best to be had, but of whom only five or six had ever felt a collar. We all fell at once to work on these ferae naturae, and had a high old time breaking them to harness and hauling stores from the landing, four miles distant. They were lassoed, thrown, harnessed, and dragged into place by sheer and simple force, to which only they were in the least amenable. Then the most experienced or ambitious driver proceeded to seat himself on the tamest mule, selected for the wheel, and the other preparations being completed, the circus began. Each animal had a rope with a choking-noose around his neck, at the other end of which was a mad and excited individual who walked, ran, jumped, fell, swore, and was dragged alongside, as long as the procession continued to move. When it stopped to repair damages and pick the tangled men and mules out of the heap, we all had time to count our bumps and bruises, while the least-damaged or the best-tempered got things straightened out for a new start.

Independence and its vicinity was a strange and peculiar place to eastern eyes. It had been for many years the favorite seat and outfitting place for the great packmule and wagon trains engaged in the Santa Fé trade, by which Chihuahua, Durango and the northern and least-known parts of Mexico, were then and until the later days of railroads, supplied with manufactured commodities. This once-famous trade had made the place rich and populous, and though within twenty miles of the Indian frontier, beyond which not a house or a settler was allowed by the general government, and within a few days' ride of actively hostile Indians, it had become a large and wealthy place. Nevertheless, as every man in it, of any standing, was or had been a New Mexican trader, Indian fighter or some other kind of adventurer, its whole population from the successful and wealthy traders down to the people who herded their animals and drove their teams, bore a rather tough reputation. Even its peculiar appearance indicated the unique character, interests and occupation of its inhabitants. Some of the wealthiest citizens, millionaires even, then when fortunes were so much smaller than at present, were considered the most dangerous and lawless, and if they did not take a pride in such reputations, were not in the least averse to them, and never slow to earn and maintain them. In winter when they came in from their various errands on and beyond the far-reaching plains, there was gathered a population amounting to several thousand, with plenty of leisure and taste for pleasure, as there understood.

But during the temperate portion of the year, its adventurous people were scattered about over thousands of miles of territory, some on long and dangerous journeys occupying years of time, and the place was comparatively deserted. In some low-lying ground and meadows adjacent, at least fifty or more acres of old and worn-out Santa Fé wagons were falling to decay, and in and around it were at that time encamped several thousand strangers, comprising emigrants, hunters, trappers, Indian and fur traders, besides stock dealers, gamblers, teamsters and all sorts of loafers and desperados, including many of wide frontier renown. Fights and homicides were of frequent occurrence and though always entertaining to the spectators, caused little other sensation. It was perhaps as well for us who were much inclined to see—if not to emulate—these novelties, that the breaking and working of our wild mules gave us plenty of employment elsewhere. Sublette, Hudspeth, 'Peg-leg' Smith, and other famous 'mountain men' were then at Independence and never wanted an admiring and inquisitive crowd about them. These were the first of the celebrated trappers or 'mountain men' whom I had seen, the type of others with whom it was later my lot to associate during long periods, far from men and civilization.[5]

On both sides of the British border-line their race has long since disappeared with the fur trade, though while it continued to exist, they were no ignoble types of the men developed by the perils and exigencies of the mountains and the wilderness. Carrying their lives in their hands, rarely encumbered with baggage or provisions but trusting to a thorough understanding of all the resources of nature, alone or in pairs they penetrated every known and unknown corner of the continent, trading, trapping, fighting or concealing themselves even from the keen-eyed Indian, as occasion required, and there remains today no country or condition in the world to develop or breed

[5] At this time occurred a famous fight which may perhaps still be remembered in the stirring annals of Independence. The celebrated mountain man, 'Peg-leg' Smith, possessed a wooden leg as a substitute for the original—which he had himself amputated with his hunting knife, taking up the arteries with a bullet mould—when it had been irremediably smashed by an Indian bullet, at some solitary spot in the mountains. Now 'Peg-leg' was as timidly modest and retiring as a young girl, when he was sober but not being proof against the festive attractions of Independence, he had on this occasion become pretty drunk and all the bar-rooms were locked against him till he should resume his usual peaceful disposition. He therefore blew off the lock of one of them with his rifle and entered upon four border-desparadoes, deep in the fascination of 'poker,' who instantly opened fire. 'Peg-leg's' gun being empty, he promptly jerked off his hickory leg and at one blow extinguished all the candles on the table and began feeling for the enemy. The general net result of the engagement was—two men killed by the wooden leg, another hors de combat, and the fourth, shot with a captured weapon as he was making his way out. Having been variously wounded in the encounter, 'Peg-leg's' blood was now up, and he was for remaining to fight the town, but his friends applied the 'similia similibus curantur' and with the aid of more whiskey, managed to get him away among the Kaw Indians across the boundary and no one in Independence hankered for the job of capturing this famous character on the open prairie.

a similar race. Though ready for any adventure and shrinking from no peril, these men were habitually silent, grave and gentle-mannered, sharply contrasting with the professional rustlers and bullies who infested the frontier, loudly boasting of their exploits, but quickly punctured and exposed when they ventured a contact with those quiet but resolute characters of modest voice but determined action.

The far-reaching trade of the several great fur companies, bred up many of those famous characters, most of American birth on our side of the boundary line, but beyond it, of Canadian, French or Scotch descent, including many half-breeds of all those races.

The Hudson Bay Company though always managed by its London and Montreal directors with consummate skill, and a humane tact toward its native population which has unfortunately found little imitation on our side the line, nevertheless owes a large proportion of its long-continued prosperity to its Canadian French and Scottish governors, agents and factors and their half-breed descendants—the famous metis. These have for generations constituted the major part of its agents, clerks, traders and trappers, who penetrated its remote territories, conducted its trade, located and held its posts, and though often illiterate, have been without exception as far as I ever heard, honest, enterprising, brave and faithful. In the altered circumstances of the Company, which since parting with its rights of sovereignty to the Dominion, now devotes its attention principally to farming, cattle-breeding, fisheries, and miscellaneous trading, it is probable that most of the unique class referred to have disappeared, and perhaps little now survives of them except the quaint and expressive names, either translated from the Indian or commemorating some once famous fight or adventure, that still lingers about obscure and distant streams and summits, and even these are being fast supplanted with the less pertinent but more familiar names of Smith, Jones and Robinson, by Washington politico-scientists who know or care not for the sentiment and poetry of their origin and associations.

We gradually and with much tribulation reduced our mules to a condition that might be called hostile subjection, that is

to say, where the subject, while in the main yielding to force
and necessity, maintains a noble and gallant spirit of subdued
revolt, always watchful and ready to seize every opportunity
for liberty, if possible—if not, for vengeance. We supplied our
wagons with spare poles and axles, double covers, water casks
and other necessities, and with all such preparations complete,
struck tents and made a start on April 25th. But the first essay
proved a continuous mule fight, aggravated by slippery hills,
countless mud holes, and a steady industrious rain which defied
all reasonable prognastications by coming down almost as
soon as we had started. After making but five miles we encamped, covered with mud, wet, disgusted and worn-out. The
first night of such expeditions—as I have often since had
occasion to know—is always discouraging. The men have not
found out each other's real qualities, the teams are 'soft,' and
soon become exhausted or devilish, or both, the things most
wanted cannot be found, and on this initial occasion we found
ourselves in anything but a joyous mood. To find water and
wood, take care of the animals and harness, set a guard and
prepare supper, all that is never very attractive occupation,
after dark and in the rain, but for our brand-new and inexperienced party—of whom the oldest was but twenty-two—tired,
wet, hungry, and discouraged, it was particularly disagreeable.
However, it was done, and when we waked in the morning with
a glorious sun gilding and glorifying everything with his warm
and joyous beams, our spirits promptly came back to par.
Even the fervent desire to kill his favorite mule which had
pervaded every breast the day before, yielded to more genial
feelings, though soon to be revived with redoubled ardor.

From the diary which I kept after leaving the State Line,
I find that we started sixteen in all, with thirty-five mules and
a few Indian ponies belonging to individuals of hunting proclivities, for riding purposes. Dr. Gambel had joined himself
to five Virginians who with their one wagon and eight mules
traveled with us. For provisions we had at first flour, hardtack, bacon, beans, coffee, sugar and salt, and for other lading
two wall tents, some extra harness, mule shoes and nails,

cooking utensils, carpenter's, digging and pioneer's tools, as well as some simple medicines and other necessaries. For private property each had blankets, arms, ammunition and tobacco, and Seaborn Jones also possessed an excellent young negro who had acquired some useful experience during the late Mexican war, as servant to his elder brother, a voltigeur officer in General Scott's campaign. The experience of the first day's march admonished us that some additional preparation might not be wasted, so we remained a few days longer at our first camp, and it was not till May 2nd that we at last crossed the State Line into the Indian country, and—as the sailors say—'took our departure.'

A country beautifully undulating, and bursting everywhere with the buds of early spring, nevertheless furnished us with a hilly, uneven and sometimes slippery road, with deep, muddy sloughs in every intermediate hollow; and with our raw drivers, untamed mules, overloaded wagons, and continual April showers, our tribulations and difficulties were at first quite disheartening to many. As if to cap the disagreeables, S. J., who had remained behind to look after his negro Milton, who was ill, now overtook us with the alarming intelligence that the disease had been identified as smallpox, which was not particularly encouraging to the rest of us, who had been living in such close association with him. Jones had been obliged to leave Milton in charge of an old negro woman belonging to Colonel Ralston, who promised to look after him and ship him home to Georgia, in case of his recovery. It was not till several years afterward that I learned that the negro did recover, and was shipped by express with a label sewed to his breast, from Independence to Paulding county, Georgia, and arrived there safely! In these days of railroads and continental express companies, that may not seem so very remarkable, but at that time there were few or no railroads west of the Alleghenies, and the whole distance, which must have been at least 1200 miles, could only be traversed by stagecoach and steamboat, or on foot.

For the purpose of conveying a fresh or contemporaneous idea of the long and weary, but interesting journey now fairly commenced, I cannot do better than copy here my diary written at the time, considerably abbreviated, but otherwise nearly in the language then used.

May 3rd. The first day out from the State Line, dawned with a steady, soaking, business-like rain. I tried to sleep under the wagon last night—for which places there was a lively competition as the tents were not pitched—but soon crawled out from a puddle collected in the depression made by my body in the mud, and sat on my rolled-up blanket under the wagon, but as the howling wind blew the rain everywhere, I took little benefit from the shelter. Nothwithstanding the condition of the weather, the roads and ourselves, all hands agreed that it was no wetter moving along than sitting in the mud, while the former offered a chance of finding some other place to camp with more shelter and some fuel, so we harnessed up after a breakfast of wet hardtack and raw bacon, and pulled out. The country in any decent weather would be beautiful, being rolling and well-timbered in the hollows with fine hickory, oak, and walnut, and as far as the Line, shows a few settlements, fences and houses. West of the Line the country belongs to the Indian Territory, and is uninhabited except by wandering Indians. In this vicinity, these are Pottawatomies, who with remnants of other removed tribes, all friendly but thievish, extend for a hundred miles or more, which distance will bring us to the Pawnees, who are counted intractable and hostile. Grass, though as yet little grown, is abundant, and all the hollows at this time of the year contain water. No doubt the country must some day become the seat of a dense and wealthy population. With a little more comfort and less work to do, one might even now enjoy its lovely grassy hills, and richly-timbered creek-bottoms full of deer and turkeys.

May 4th. Rain, with intermissions, constantly emphasized by plenty of thunder and lightning. This morning it was hard to get ourselves limber enough to water and repicket the mules, who notwithstanding the bitter hatred they justly inspire, must be preserved. After carrying some scarce and green wood over a mile, it took the whole water-soaked party two hours to coax it into a fire, after which we took our coffee, hardtack and bacon standing round the fire, well soaked by the falling rain. After a series of desperate and gallant mule fights we 'caught up' in the afternoon and 'rolled on.' After sticking in numerous mud holes, digging, prying and in some cases doubling teams, we were at last brought to a stand by an impassable slough, not much over a mile from our last camp.

May 5th. Raining most of the night and morning with the same hearty, honest steadiness as ever. But the place was too comfortless to stop at, and by filling the slough with brush and putting three teams to a wagon, we at last got across, and tugging over slippery hills and sticking in countless mud holes, covered about five miles, and are encamped on a high roll of the prairie, which sinks away behind us a short distance to the Big Blue, a fine stream skirted with good timber. The sky has cleared, and the moon lights up a far-stretching series of round grassy hilltops in front. There is plenty of wood, and around some generous fires all the wet clothes and blankets are sending up clouds of steam while every one is cheerful with the prospect of a better time tomorrow. The river is high and may give trouble, but notwithstanding the good rule, to camp always on the far side of a stream, we were too much used up to try it tonight.

May 6th, Sunday. We had hardly suspended our execrations of the weather, when the rain began again this morning, with increased vigor, as if under conscientious obligation to make up for the valuable time lost. But now we have the tents set and plenty of wood and are comfortable ourselves, while as for the mules, we hope they are suffering as much as is compatible with their duties tomorrow. The road may now be called impassable for loaded wagons. The mules cannot maintain a footing on the slippery hills, while each intermediate little valley is a bottomless morass in which the wagons plump to the axles. But the mules are perceptibly tamer, and it is now possible to go within stone's-throw of them without open war; and they even seem to be taking in the notion that it is easier to give a good pull altogether, than to jump over each other's backs and kick and bite at everything within reach. Two of our men have had fun enough, and have concluded to go back, but the rest, including the Virginians, are staunch and will stick, come what may. When the mules get tame and can be managed by two men to a wagon, it is thought we have men enough for labor and guard detail, but at present, affairs go hardly, because although the Indians give no trouble, the mules must nevertheless be well guarded to prevent their running back to the settlements, a direction they much prefer. There is a large camp below us on the Blue, badly afflicted with cholera, of which five have died, two of them last night.

May 7th. The train rolled out at daylight leaving S. J., myself and A. as rearguard to gather up the loose mules. In returning separately from that job, I passed the deserted camp which the crows and buzzards were beginning to examine, and seeing a buffalo-robe, as I supposed, forgotten, I tried to pick it up but my Texas pony would not approach it. After discussing the matter with him warmly but fruitlessly, I dismounted, rolled it up compactly and securied it to my riata, the other end of which was fast to the saddle. Then remounting, I dragged it to me, but when it came under the horse's nose he voted decisively against the scheme, every time. Finally, after considerable circus-riding, he fell over backward, giving me just time to slip from under, but as I was bruised and confused, he got away and ran off careering over the prairie with the obnoxious object dragging behind. After a while it got detached, and he fell to grazing, but was always prompt to start again as soon as I approached, and as by this time the train was out of sight, I began to fear seriously that I might have to leave him. But after long and wily manoeuvering I at last got hold of the riata, and my temper by this time not being in its sweetest condition, I determined to break or kill him, and after some more fighting, succeeded in the former, and putting him to a gallop, forded the river and came up to the train just as it came to camp some miles beyond. Here on indignantly throwing down the innocent cause of the commotion I had the satisfaction of learning that, having belonged to the negro Milton, it had been purposely abandoned as probably infected with smallpox! Though I had hugged it closely during a gallop of several miles while in a profuse perspiration, I was never troubled with the disease, though cholera or fatal diarrhoea is prevalent among the emigrant trains, which are numerous, not having had time yet to get much scattered. There is quite a populous graveyard at the crossing of the Blue, and numerous single graves along the trail. Today we sent back J., who has been ill since the first exposed rainy night. He was left with his friend G. to care for him at Lipscombe's—the 'last house.' There is a good deal of discouragement but much of it is due to the weather, which can hardly be a fair sample. We must surely have an improvement sooner or later, and with dry roads, tame mules and more practical experience, things must go better after a while. We made nine miles and camped, to see how it goes with J. We passed a rough stone monument of dry masonry, ten feet high, on an eminence on the right, with a smaller one near by, and another half a mile distant on an opposite hill. By whom or for what purpose erected, there is no means of knowing, but we guess they commemorate the departure of some former Oregon-bound emigrant train. We also saw some deer on the distant ridge near a projecting point of timber, but had no time to go after them. We are camped on a rich, well-timbered bottom, and had for supper a heterogeneous mass, boiled together in the camp kettle, of rabbits, grouse, snipe, curlew, etc. It is to be hoped that the splendid opportunity now offering may ultimately develop a cooking talent in some one, for which there is a rare and brilliant opening.

CHAPTER III

May 8th. Waiting in camp on J.'s illness. If it should be smallpox we will be in a bad way, as we could neither carry him on, nor expect Lipscombe to keep him in his one-roomed log-cabin. To empty a wagon and haul him back to Independence would cause delay that might have serious results, in case we should arrive at the Sierra too late to cross this year, about which our fellows are already nervous.

May 9th. Rode back last night and left two spare mules at Lipscombe's for J. and G. to overtake us with, in case the former should recover. They can easily do it for several days yet, as the wagons move slowly. This morning we rolled out early and in good spirits—except for J.—the blue sky and bright sun reflected in every face, and looking as if they had come to stay. The prairie is covered with lovely flowers brought out by the sun, making some of the little sheltered valleys sheets of beautiful colors. Hitherto we have followed the old well-beaten Santa Fé trail, but now bend off to the north, being encamped tonight at its junction with the Oregon emigrant trail, with wood scarce, but good grass and water not far off. The country is beautiful, being a succession of high, round, grassy ridges with running water in the hollows, and distant points of timber nearly always in sight. We made seventeen miles and passed numerous fresh graves, besides many dead cattle and mules. At noon we passed the 'lone elm,' standing by a chain of water pools, a famous landmark for east-bound Santa Fé trains. How it came to grow here alone, and why no other tree or even bush has joined it in its isolation, none of our scientists can explain.

May 10th. Leaving camp at an early hour, we plodded on over very much the same kind of country as yesterday, but

54

encountered two or three mud holes with nearly vertical banks, which even after considerable pick and shovel work, stalled all the teams. The worst was at the crossing of an insignificant stream about ten miles from the Santa Fé fork, where the bottom was so miry, and the banks so steep and high, that the crossing of our five wagons detained us more than two hours. At 4 P.M. we struck the Wakarusa, a fine running creek of about twenty yards' width, in a timbered bottom half a mile wide, the shade and whispering verdure of which was a delightful thing to our eyes, already somewhat tired of the bare monotony of the illimitable grassy prairie. The bluff on the west side, though no more than thirty or forty feet high, was so steep that it required doubled teams and all hands at the wheels to pull out. Fortunately it was neither muddy nor slippery. In fact, we like the Wakarusa, which besides its lovely marginal forest, is a beautiful swift-flowing stream with a bold ledge of exposed limestone on our side—carved into fantastic shapes by water and ice action, and a steep wooded bluff on the other. Though now running full, from the frequent rains, it looks favorable for fish, but in two hours honest trial I only got one weak nibble, and returned to my bacon.

May 11th. On the road by 7 A.M. today, having turned out before daylight for an early start. Two hours brought us to a singularly shaped hill. It is plainly of natural limestone formation, but from its shape, presenting bold projecting salients all around, and a succession of terraces, due to the more rapid weathering of the upper and more exposed strata, it looks like a great fortification with successive walls, gradually retiring as they rise one above the other. The wagon trail breasts it boldly and leads directly over the top. From the summit there is a superb view of rolling prairie, stretching interminably in every direction from its base to the far edge of the saucer-like horizon. Looking back over the thin, faint line of road we have just passed, Bryant's train of 170 pack mules was just coming into view, straggling along far, far beneath us, like an army of mice. Shouts and whoops came faintly up to us, and so cheeringly dry was the prairie, that the dust from their 700 hoofs hung over them like a moving canopy. Far southward appears another bend of the timber lining the Wakarusa, which stream after a long detour to the right of the trail, here sweeps away again to the southwest, bound for the Kaw river, we suppose. The march today has been, as usual, over a perpetual series of gently undulating hills, one rising beyond another on all sides, through and among which we are perpetually winding to avoid steep ascents. We seem confined in a deep, vast, green bowl, whose encircling sides we are constantly striving in vain to surmount. The horizon presents the illusion of rising higher than ourselves on all sides, and even when we gain a hilltop, it only discloses an illimitable succession of others, without distinctive landmarks, and with views, vistas, landscape and scenery, so precisely alike, that except for the sun and compass and our tired muscles, it would be hard to realize any movement.

B. produced a few curlew and cowbirds tonight, the product of his shot-gun, unfortunately the only one in the party, and these varied pleasantly the usual hungry rush to slapjacks and bacon. Notwithstanding, the rain has followed us and commenced drizzling again after the unusually liberal allowance of two days' sunshine.

May 12th. J. and G. overtook us last night, the former much worse for his ride, though considered nearly recovered when they left Lipscombe's. After a hard march we camped tonight on a small tributary of the Kaw, or Kansas, and within a few miles of that river, which must be crossed tomorrow. The camp has been made near a dead ox, which doesn't enhance its attractions, but the rain has ceased and we are all agog to put the Kansas behind us tomorrow. A large train is camped nearby, waiting for the same purpose, which has lost several men from cholera and still has some bad cases in the wagons. Two heavy ox-trains came up in the rear, passed, and camped ahead of us.

May 13th, Sunday. Rolled out early to reach the crossing, if possible, in advance of the large trains near us. As we passed these, some were burying a man just dead of cholera, while the others were catching up their teams. The five or six miles of road leading to the crossing was bad, and we stalled and had to double teams several times, but reached the place by 8 A.M. to find still other trains ahead, all squabbling for precedence. Some enterprising emigrants preferring a bird in hand to several in the California bush, had built a small scow capable of transporting a single wagon without the team, and naturally every one wanted to be the first. We rushed our wagons in, simultaneously detaching a mule guard to drive the mules up stream to find a good swimming place. The bulk of our men—including our best fighters—closed in round the wagons, in the narrow passage leading to the landing and allowed no teams to pass. Words were high, the weapons were drawn, but as our party though not one third as numerous, were fairly organized, and had agreed to leave our talking to a captain and obey him closely, system, firmness, and discipline prevailed over numbers, and we got and kept the *pass*. We worked hard most of the day, in crossing our wagons and stores, and repacking them on the other side, and in making our initial mule crossing. The mule ford was narrow and crooked, with swimming depth in the middle, and a rapid current; but by leading with mounted men, and crowding the rest in by force over a steep bank which we did not allow them to reclimb, we finally got all across safely, though with considerable excitement to the mulish nervous system. A strong contrast to the laborious energy and effort with which the white man pursues his aims, was afforded by a squad of indolent Pottawatomies, who sauntered about, splendidly dressed in white deerskins ornamented with black cloth, small sleigh bells, ribbons, feathers, and so forth, intensely amused at our tribulations and highly delighted at the excellent promise of a shindy among the white men. Their horses, though not apparently of much value, were richly caparisoned with scarlet cloth, and similar ornaments. One well got up fellow, who most probably had visited the settlements in person to get so much finery, was delighted at a mishap of mine in falling into the water, and concealed his hilarity with difficulty as he gleefully felt me down to see how wet I was. B. caught a catfish at least two feet long, which made supper for our entire party. It was unkindly suggested that he had cheated some guileless Pottawatomie, but as he indignantly denied the imputation on his skill, and everyone was glad to enjoy the change from the everlasting bacon, we agreed not to discuss too closely the mode of acquisition. We found deep, dry sand on the other bank of the river, and after getting clear of it about a mile, we encamped at the edge of the prairie.

May 14th. Spent this day in camp owing to the serious illness of H. which Gambel now pronounces to be pneumonia, and no great wonder considering the bad weather, labor and exposure we have had. It has been severe on all of us, and a provoking consideration is the conviction that with more experience and less haste, we might have avoided a considerable part of it. The rain has recommenced as perseveringly as ever.

May 15th. A steady, beastly downpour kept us in a camp of very indifferent merits all day till 4 P.M. when, the rain having moderated and H's condition improved, we 'caught up' and proceeded about two miles, when we were stopped by a creek with bad banks, and deep muddy approaches. The stream is a pretty one about twenty-five yards wide, with a little poor timber, but as its passage is hopeless at present, we moved down it about half a mile and camped. Two pretty well-mounted Pottawatomies rode into camp, to whom we gave about a bag and a half of flour, by way of reducing our loads, but though they received it, and will surely find a way to make it useful, not a word or sign acknowledged the gift.

May 16th. About an hour after dark last night, as all except the guard were seated round the fire, a single mule, frightened at something, drew his picket and started on a run, but soon brought up among the herd grazing at their pickets, who declined to take part in his scare. We had scarcely finished congratulating each other when suddenly and without the slightest warning, another scare occurred, followed by a wild rush of mules, amounting to a stampede. The night was dark and rainy and the ground soft, but only about half succeeded in drawing their picket pins. We all scattered out, ringing vigorously the mare's bell, while the guard mounted and galloped off, guided by the noise, to head and turn them back. After an hour or more of strenuous exertion and not a little anxiety, we secured them all and allowed them to crowd around the bell mare to get quiet. Divers surmises were offered respecting the cause of this sudden and dangerous freak, some attributing it to Indians, some to wolves, and others to 'natural devilment,' the last theory receiving immediate and general adherence. There was no further alarm, probably because of the increased guard and extra vigilance, and at 2 A.M. all hands were called up by order to prepare for crossing the creek in front. After several hours' hard labor with pick and shovel by relays of men, the approaches were considered fit for trial, and doubling teams and putting all unemployed men at the wheels, we got our five wagons across by 10 A.M. and moved forward. We crossed a number of smaller creeks, gullies and mud holes, some of which gave much trouble. These ditches, or water courses, are much alike. They are mostly ten or twelve feet deep with vertical banks, and of all widths from six to fifty feet, with a trifling runlet at the bottom, converting the latter into a soft quagmire. After picking down the banks somewhat, the team is doubled, which, provided the mules themselves can scramble across, brings the leaders to the top of one bank before the wagon makes its plunge from the other. Consequently, some of the numerous mules are always expected to have good footing, and to be in condition to haul out the rest. But sometimes when the stream is larger and contains considerable water, the mules get entangled with each other in the bottomless mud, and to save them from being carried down and drowned, it is necessary to run in and loose or cut them out. In bad cases it is necessary to unload the wagons, carry everything over, haul out the empty wagon, and reload it, which process, repeated as it must be for each wagon, consumes much time and temper. Taking my turn at driving today, and seated half-asleep on the wheel mule of the rear wagon, which thus fell considerably behind the others, my team suddenly came to a halt which waked me with a start. What was my astonishment to see the two leaders of my six-mule team, poking their noses in the doorway of a quite civilized-looking log cabin, wherein were some twenty or more Indian children, in partly civilized costume, with some French Catholic priests, who had a mission here, and were teaching school. The mules I think, were as much surprised as I was, and seemed quite disinclined to leave a scene so suggestive of corn and comfort. However, as the other wagons were a long way ahead, I had to decline the polite invitation of the fathers, and travel on. Here also, was an American woman from Baltimore, married to a half-breed Pottawatomie with a cabin and an enclosed field. We camped tonight on the wrong side of another apparently impracticable creek.

May 17th. During my watch, last night, the wolves in considerable numbers were barking and howling round the wagons, indicating an increasing distance from the settlements. The mules endured their presence and noise pretty well, but did not seem to hanker after them like long-lost friends. After the usual digging, pulling, hauling and swearing, we got all our wagons over the creek and made a good morning march to the Little Vermillion, over the bad bluffs of which we crossed with difficulty and halted a mile west of it for a noon rest. One of the wagon companies being too indolent to unharness their team, suffered it to graze about with the wagon attached, intending to watch it. But as might have been expected, the watchers went to sleep, with the result of a short turn, an upset, with broken pole, axle, and hounds. In lightening up our wagons a few days ago, we threw away our spare poles and axles, so we seemed in a bad mess. Several went off to search for hickory or white oak in the creek bottom, while I rode back to see if I could meet an ox train and buy some material. Fortunately, I found Waldo's large train from Jackson county, Missouri, and after some trouble, being warmly seconded by Waldo, I got from one of the wagons an excellent piece of seasoned timber, which was lucky, as our men found no growing timber fit for such use. We soon had a blazing fire, around which all our mechanics and amateurs got at work with as many carpenters' and smiths' tools as could be mustered, and we expect to have it finished by morning.

May 18th. Our artisans—expert and amateur—finished the repairs of the fractured wagon before daylight this morning, and the guard then called all hands for an early start. A fair march was made till shortly after noon, when J., another of our invalids, suddenly became so much worse that Dr. G.

advised a halt, to let him die in peace. As signs of the utmost extremity were visible, we came to camp at once on the top of an extensive stony knoll, with neither wood nor water within sight. The consequence was thirst and hunger, as a little cold coffee and half-warmed dough was all the refreshment we could get, after the greater part of two days' and one night's hard work, with the pleasing prospect to half of us, of watching the mules all night. The Doctor says both men must surely die, though when, no one can certainly tell. In the low condition of spirits prevailing, we have time to reflect that, with all our privations and labor, and the probable loss of two of our number, we have scarcely averaged over eight miles per day from Independence, and this over what we suppose to be the best part of the route, furnishing most grass and water. This poor beginning of a long journey, which will become more difficult and over a less known country the farther we advance, must be attributed to several causes—bad weather and roads, unbroken mules, excessive loads, inexperience in driving and managing mule teams, and most of all, a want of better system and organization. All of these can be cured or would cure themselves, if we had some one person of such manifest superiority in qualities or even in age, as to reconcile everyone to a supreme authority. But unfortunately there is none such, and there seems little use in calling this one captain, and that one wagon-master, etc., when no one will obey anyone else without a fight. Some of the men who expected to enjoy a fine hunting-trip, with little discomfort or privation, are bitterly disappointed. For myself, though I did anticipate more leisure and less hard work, yet I did not expect to have adventure without some privations, and am willing to take it as it comes, even the results of our own defects, since they can't be cured. The route has recently been over a constant succession of prairie rolls, which really amount to considerable hills, though the soil is hard and good except in the hollows and at the numerous creek crossings, which are certainly exasperating. The country previously fertile, is becoming thin and rocky, and the grass thinner and inferior. Having little or no wood tonight, it was proposed to draw on our one can of alcohol. But as there doesn't seem any emergency to justify using what may be more necessary as fuel or stimulant by and by, it was warmly opposed, and by a slim majority, defeated. J. and H. the Doctor says, are both dying, and G. also is very ill, thus increasing our labor, while seriously reducing our effective force. However, the Virginians came nobly to the breach, in regard to the extra guard duty .

May 19th. Contrary to all expectations, and with the most unfeeling disregard for the Doctor, J., the sickest man, concluded to get better during the night, and we made an early start and accomplished a good distance of excellent road, interspersed with exasperating mud holes, before 10 A.M., when we were overtaken by a tremendous storm of wind and rain. The former, unchecked for long distances over this bare treeless country, amounted to a tempest, sending the wagons forward with slacked traces. While enduring it according to the best of our several abilities, we suddenly found our leading team at the brink of one of the deepest, steepest and muddiest crossings we had yet encountered. Blinded and soaked by the rain, we went to work at smoothing down the banks, and doubling teams, and then went at it. The first wagon pitched headlong over, the whole front running-gears disappearing in a sea of mud, the wagon standing for an instant on its front end. But the forward team drivers were staunch and ready, the tackle held firm, the wagon was dragged through to the opposite bank and with a yell—up she went. This was encouraging; so packing the three sick men in the rear wagon with all the blankets, and lashing them down solid, we got everything over safely, or with trifling damage, and reached the banks of the Big Vermillion early in the afternoon. This is a wide and considerable stream, but with a hard bottom, and not too deep to ford now, though evidently rising. Under these circumstances we decided to cross at once. We soon cut some blocks on which we raised the wagon beds about fifteen inches, being as much as the standards would bear. Then chaining together the two wheels on each side, we lowered the wagons down the long and steep but straight descent, and got them safely through the river, which came up to the raised wagon bodies, and found an easy, good, straight ascent on the other side. We moved on a mile and camped, to give our fishermen a chance to try the stream, but the freshet prevented successful fishing, though we made an honest effort till dark, by which time the river had risen to an impassable height. We are surely improving, since for the first time when there were two different courses to be pursued, we took the best. Hurrah!

May 20th, Sunday; 18th day out. Sunday brings no rest today. We are so elated at our good conduct yesterday, in camping on the right side of the obstructive stream, and the weather is so threatening, that we decided to push on with a train of ten Indiana and seven Mississippi wagons, by whom we camped last night, twelve or fifteen miles to the Little Blue so as to cross it today, if possible. We reached and crossed it about 1 P.M., descending the eastern side with the aid of ropes and surmounting the far bank without much difficulty. At our crossing, it was about four feet deep and eighty yards wide, with a large island in the middle, and a rapid current. Both trains camped together not far beyond, and one mess caught four fine cats, but mine went fishless, for which I received plenty of sarcasm and abuse, especially from those who had never yet caught, or tried to catch, a fish. Thus is unsuccessful merit apt to be rewarded. The deep solitude and monotony of this region has become oppressive to some, but there is little chance of relief unless from the still more undesirable incident of a dash from some Pawnee war party. So it has been agreed all round, without a dissenting voice, to lay over tomorrow, for the purpose of joining and organizing with the Indiana company, which seems to be composed of rather agreeable fellows, and to have mule teams as good as ours.

May 21st. From daylight till 9 A.M. was spent in general council by all hands of both companies not on actual duty. We elected for captain, Woods,[6] of Indiana, and also a doctor, a wagon-master, a secretary, etc. We also adopted a few plain rules for traveling, keeping the peace, dividing labor, guard duty, etc. A detail of one man from each wagon was then

---

[6] Woods with three companions was killed by the Pitt River Indians, near the head of the Sacramento River in California in 1851, as I learned some years afterwards.

started down the bottom to procure timber for spare poles, axles, and so forth, as this is said to be the last place where timber of any value can be procured. Some very doubtful specimens were brought in, looking much better adapted for back logs than axletrees. About noon we rolled out, made twelve miles, and encamped.

May 25th. Owing to a painful and troublesome return of the Missouri River cholera—or diarrhoea, I have been for the last four days confined to a wagon, with about as much suffering as the wagon could conveniently hold. The weather has been very unpleasant, as on the rare occasions when it doesn't rain, a cold blast is searching the wagon covers, and there is a white frost nearly every night. I don't find things so bad when in health, but there is not much fun in jolting over the stony plains in a freezing gale, racked by a compound of ague, fever, diarrhoea, cholera and headache, with the consciousness that some other fellow is not blessing one for having extra duty to perform. However, I am today much better and able to get some variation from the misery of that infernal wagon by an occasional relief on horseback, which is a most agreeable change. We have been making a steady progress of eighteen to twenty miles a day, following the course of the Little Blue. The joint company numbers seventy-six men (exclusive of four who have died since leaving Independence) and one hundred and thirty animals, including six yoke of oxen driven along loose by Wood's men, and intended for passing mud holes otherwise insurmountable, and ultimately for food. Antelopes, which were first seen on the 22nd, near the crossing of the Blue, are now becoming abundant. In fact they are in sight pretty much all day.

May 26th. In spite of the guard, a stampede occurred last night about midnight, the entire 'mulada' suddenly breaking out of the corral and rushing off over the plain with a thundering tread that turned everyone out at once. The new rules, however, worked well; all the posted men were quickly at their designated posts, rifle in hand, the remainder rushing out after the mules. The bell mare being secure, her bell was well rattled, and inside of an hour the truants were all back in the corral, and everything safe. Nevertheless, as we are now in the hostile country of the Pawnees, who are doubtless watching all our movements, one can't help thinking what a mess we would be in, if the mules did get fairly away from us. We have therefore determined to use some extra care and precaution. During the day our fifteen wagons are, of course strung out in a long line, interspersed with foot- and horsemen, the rear covered by the guard driving the loose stock. But it is night attacks or alarms that we have most to apprehend, so hereafter the Captain will, about camping-time, send a few men ahead to look out a good place, combining as far as possible such advantages as grass, wood, water, shelter from wind, and a reasonable view of the surrounding country. On coming into camp, the wagon-master will take his station at the spot designed for the leading wagon, each succeeding wagon filing off alternately to right and left and taking position outside and rear of its predecessor, to constitute the first half of the corral, and conversely, by drawing them together for the last half, thus making a large circular or oval enclosure. The wagons are then connected by poles and track chains, leaving the only opening at the rear, which constitutes post No. 1 of the guard.

The mules are turned out to water and grass under charge of the retiring or day guard till after supper, when the new guard takes charge. Such tents as have not been thrown away, are pitched round the outside, where also fires are made and cooking conducted, the inside of the corral being reserved entirely for the animals. The men unprovided with tents sleep in or under the wagons with weapons accessible. In the morning those not on guard, gather up and pack away baggage, lay the harness in place, and stand ready for the arrival of the mules. These, after being watered, are driven in through the rear opening, and all available hands proceed to select, harness, and attach their respective teams. When all is ready the night guard is relieved, the new one taking charge of the rear, including loose stock. At the signal for 'rolling out,' the lead wagon remains stationary, the others pulling out on each side alternately, to their allotted positions in line, the leader of yesterday dropping to the rear today, thus giving each its fair proportion of front and rear. At every halt by day or night, the bell mare is securely picketed, and in the event of an alarm, is immediately seized by the Captain of the guard, and either mounted, or fastened to a wagon inside of the corral, the guard hustling the other mules in after her. The mare is white—for easy recognition both by men and mules. She is about eight years old, which is quite venerable compared with her adoring followers, and she has nothing to do but carry the bell and exert her fascinations on the mules, who, judging by their constant condition of terror when separated from her, must have been born scared and remained so ever since. Notwithstanding her immunity from work, however, the bell mare has a pretty hard time. Being always picketed and closely surrounded by her admirers, her grazing is by no means the best. By night or day, as soon as the mules have filled their bellies, their next object is to crowd in and fight for positions close to the mare. If a scare occurs, they watch her, rather than the supposed cause. If she remains unconcerned, as she generally does, they soon quiet down, but if she begins to stretch her neck and prick her ears, there is going to be trouble.

The Little Blue, notwithstanding its name, seems to be much larger than the Big Blue. We followed its general direction all day, mostly in sight of its timbered bottom, and encamped at the edge of the latter, which is said to be the last timber until we reach the mountains, and also the western limit for turkey, which cannot, or does not, exist far from timber.

May 27th, Sunday. We laid over in this delightful camp, all this lovely day, but I personally had an alarming adventure which came within a hair's breadth of ending my travels for good. During the last few days we have seen abundant signs of last year's buffalo, and know they cannot be far off, so this morning when those off duty commenced the usual holiday amusements of washing clothes, mending, bathing, turkey-hunting, and so forth, I determined to distinguish myself by finding first buffalo. Selfishly wishing to monopolize the honor, I quietly got my arms in order and mounting my horse, whose strength had been carefully spared and nursed for this purpose, away I started due north, loaded for buffalo and only buffalo. The day was lovely and the country charming, but

for many miles I did not see a living thing larger than a cow-
bird, except from time to time some distant antelope, which are
innumerable and everywhere. The profound silence was
almost oppressive, and unbroken solitude extended far as the
eye could range over a continuous succession of green, rolling
hills, rising cup-shaped from the traveler to the far horizon
on every side. More than ever I was impressed with the
grandeur and majesty of the boundless solitude, and my mind
had come to be more occupied by such thoughts, than by the
game I was looking for, when, having attained a distance of
several miles from camp, I perceived afar off a column of
dust ahead, that seemed much like signs of the desired buffalo.
Fortunately, I had been impressed with the necessity of
economizing my horse's powers for the expected run, so after
another look at my arms, I trotted moderately forward, descending a long roll of the prairie, crossing the valley and
ascending the next roll, from which the dust column seemed
considerably nearer and distinctly approaching. As I watched
it closely, considering through which depressions I could best
make a hidden approach, I began to discern bright spots
flashing from out the dust. This looked less like buffalo, and
I was not very long in making out a large band of mounted
Indians, with shining white shields and glistening lanceheads,
coming directly toward me at a leisurely gait. Even then my
stupidity was so inconceivable that I was completely taken in
by their slow and careless advance and never once thought of
Pawnees, taking the apparition for some hunting party of
friendly Sioux or Pottawatomies, who are as hostile to Pawnees
as we are. As I never before saw a large band of any Indians,
I excuse myself for not knowing a war from a hunting or a
traveling party, but as we have been constantly fearing
Pawnees for a week past, cannot account for not suspecting
them when actually before me.

I had a good horse under me and, as I supposed, an open road
in the rear and did not feel at all alarmed, but on the other
hand, I "had not lost any Indians," and had no use for such a
large party, so far from home, so when they had approached
within half a mile or less, I waved my hand politely and
turned to ride back, with the intention of regulating my speed
by theirs, so as to avoid closer acquaintance. It was not a

second too soon. In the very act of turning, I caught sight of two small parties in my rear, galloping at full speed from either hand to cut off my retreat, and my discovery of them was soluted by a savage yell that burst from all three gangs when further concealment was useless. While the main body had continued to monopolize my attention by advancing slowly and conspicuously, the two detachments had taken advantage of the undulating nature of the ground to diverge, and by wide circuits attain my rear, I—greenhorn as I was—never thinking of such an ordinary strategem, while stupidly gazing at the imposing and leisurely approach of the main body. I cannot deny that I was badly scared. The total surprise, the sudden dash from three directions, the consciousness of being outwitted, with the savage and exultant war whoops, as the warriors lay forward on their horses' necks and plied whip and spur for all they were worth, were all so alarming that I don't reproach myself for being badly rattled for a moment. It is a very different thing to face death with resolution calmly and leisurely matured, from seeing it spring suddenly upon one without a second of warning or reflection. One may need an instant or two to clinch the determination and close hard the teeth, without being a coward. At least, I hope so. Cold chills and profuse perspiration and quick breath all came at once, and yet I solemnly believe I am not a coward. There was, plainly enough, but one chance of escape. Both detachments were closing in to cut me off from camp, and the main body was charging down with whoops and yells doubtless counting me as good as bagged. I put spurs to my horse—which by the way, though Indian himself, was nearly as frightened as I was—and made a dash for the interval upon which the flanking parties were rapidly closing. Fortunately I had still rather the shortest distance and as it turned out, much the best horse. When I rushed between them, the yelling warriors were laying on with whip and heel, within a hundred yards on either hand, and commenced shooting arrows, all of which, as far as I know, fell short.

The flankers thus safely evaded, the affair settled down to a square race for the best horse and most careful rider, my lead being unpleasantly small for the distance before us. Though my horse was the best, a good many contingencies may happen in seven or eight miles of strange country, and it remained to be seen how his bottom and endurance would compare with those of the hardy coursers of the plains. I gathered up my belongings and took my best position, well aware that a failure of even a misstep of my horse, meant death in a hopeless fight against numbers or torture at the stake. Though two or three guns were fired at this time, my hostile friends could not have possessed many, and hadn't time to take much aim. It was not long before they were stretched out in a long string, according to the speed of their several horses, the yelling subsided, and all parties settled down to steady work, the Indians beating their horses at every jump and evidently taking out all the run there was in them, while mine was at a good steady lope, but after the first burst, by no means at the top of his speed. I reckoned half the distance passed, and was descending at an easy gallop, a long and moderate inclination toward a level valley that spread out a couple of hundred yards wide to the base of the opposite rise. My pursuers were momentarily concealed behind the ridge just passed. I reached the foot of the hill at good speed, my horse sprang forward on what seemed firm ground, and plunged to the shoulders in a treacherous morass concealed by the long grass! A triumphant yell burst from the exultant warriors as they successively topped the ridge behind and came tearing down the hill. The swamp seemed to extend a long distance to right and left, and not being quite so scared as at first, I reflected that if I could once get my horse across, it must delay them as much as me.

Dismounting quickly, I led, pulled, and lifted with the utmost care, and was making good progress, when they began to fire a few shots from the hill while the foremost horsemen abandoned their horses and tried to reach me on foot. But I was through the bog first, and while my horse recovered his breath, had a fine chance for pot shots with gun and both pistols at the foremost footmen struggling in the swamp. Then I had time to ride moderately up the hill while my friends were hauling their ponies through the mud, so that the distance between us was not much diminished, while my horse, though covered with mud and breathing heavily, had been well studied and handled.

I began to feel pretty safe if the course was only correct. From this hill I could make out the long, thin blue line of timber on the Little Blue, but was very uncertain of the locality of the camp. Soon the foremost of the riders—widely scattered—began to appear at the brow of the last hill. I still had a good lead, but my horse trembled and breathed heavily and began to need the spur, while the gaunt ponies seemed no worse for all the running and beating they had had. As I neared the top of another hill, it was for me an anxious moment. If it failed to disclose some sign of camp, I might as well turn and make the best fight I could. Another bound and we were over, and flying down another long inclination which seemed to sweep away in gentle undulations to the line of timber, still a mile or two ahead, I strained my eyes from left to right along the base of the timber, and soon made out with increasing certainty far, far away, but right ahead, the white circle of wagon tops, apparently no bigger than prairie chickens, but which held all there was of hope, safety and life.

Now it was my turn to shout. One after another the baffled warriors came bounding over the ridge, pressing on with perseverance worthy of a better cause, but their practiced eyes no doubt recognized the wagons as soon as, or before, I did. Nevertheless, they chased me right up within gunshot of the camp, where all was confusion, some of the turkey hunters and fisherman being still absent. The mules were, however, quickly corralled, the wagon wheels and intervals manned, and the enemy, after prancing around at a safe distance with insulting gestures, rode off and soon disappeared in some inexplicable manner as though they had sunk into the ground. So sudden was their effacement when they got among the slight inequalities of surface at the edge of the bottom, that where and how they went, and even the direction, still remains a mystery. They may be hovering round tonight, for anything we know, and at any rate having now shown themselves, are pretty sure to make trouble for us at some bad crossing during the next few days. When the boys' siesta was broken up in such an exciting manner, everything about the camp was in confusion. The wagons were unloaded to air the contents, blankets and clothing hanging everywhere to dry, and men lying about, many of them asleep. But the gratifying speed with which the condition of affairs was changed, showed the stimulus of a charge of hostile Indians. The way the cargo was pitched into the wagons and under them, mules run in, corral chained up, rifles overhauled, and everyone in his place, was a marvel that one could hardly realize till it was done.

CHAPTER IV

DIARY OF JOURNEY CONTINUED

May 28th. Contrary to expectation, all passed quietly last night, and turning out early we 'caught up,' and leaving the Little Blue for the last time, struck out across a wide, low divide for the Platte, said to be twenty-five miles distant without water. Two mountain men coming from the west with several pack horse loads of peltry, joined us last night, having seen our fires. They were bound in for the settlements and seemed little concerned about the proximity of the Pawnees who hunted me yesterday, saying they were certain to go no further east, and had probably gone west to lay for us at some convenient opportunity. These men were without blankets, utensils or provisions, except saddle skins and a saddle of antelope, and said our coffee and bread were the first they had seen for many months. Notwithstanding this assumed indifference about the Indians, whom they pronounced a war party with designs either on an emigrant train, or on some Delaware or other friendly village south of us on the Kansas, they took care to start some hours before daylight and keep to the timbered river bottom. Our men do not think they really fear the Indians, as the mountain men have the credit of being on good terms with all the tribes, except a few hostile races like Blackfeet, while they hate emigrants as tending to embroil them with those they are nominally friendly with. Be that as it may, these would not admit any friendly relations with Pawnees, though inclined to be taciturn. With the exception of a few questions about the horses, arms and ornaments of the Indians, they scarcely uttered a word except in monosyllables, retired early to sleep, and were gone before daylight. This day's march, being on the divide between two large river systems, is more level and the ground hard and good but ascending. Failing to make the whole distance we camped on high ground by a small pool of rain-water but without a stick of wood in sight. It was after dark or we could probably see the timber on the Platte. Coffee was made with wood and water brought with us from the Little Blue.

May 29th. Started early from the poor camp, and reached the big river by noon, winding down a narrow, crooked, precipitous ravine through lofty and barren bluffs to the river bottom, which on our side the river is about three miles wide, flat, and bare of anything but grass, which is good. We struck it opposite Grand Island which is several miles long, mostly covered by short, stunted and floodworn cottonwood of no use to us since we cannot get at it. The channel on our side is not much over a hundred yards wide, but that on the other side the island must be over a mile. The water is a rapid, rolling torrent with apparently more mud than water and not inviting to sight or taste. Though more cautious about hunting at a distance, this wide bottom is so flat that a dog could not hide on it, so I borrowed a horse—mine being bandaged and laid up—and rode out to to the bluffs after antelope. I saw some single ones and one monstrously large rabbit or hare but could not get a shot. I, however, saw an animal resembling a large shaggy dog, lying by a large stone near the bluff and rode within sixty yards before it got up. Its doggy appearance was so innocent that I hesitated to shoot till it moved to run. It then went off on three legs with an angry yelp, and I knew it from description for a gray wolf. Omitting to load up in compliance with the good old rule, I gave chase and had him cut off from the bluff, when he suddenly and savagely turned at bay, scaring my strange horse, which bolted and wheeled suddenly, almost throwing me. However, with the aid of spurs I got near enough to break the wolf's backbone with a single-barrelled pistol. As we had load enough in the wagons, I did not skin him, but contented myself with his fine brush.

Our camp is on the site of a former one, and close by are three freshly-made graves, showing that the cholera is ahead of as well as behind us.

May 30th. Adventures seem to be coming thick and fast. At half-past two this morning, in a heavy rain some new deviltry got into our infernal mules, and in an instant without any warning, the entire mulada—bell mare and all—broke and ran in a wild stampede. We were afraid to scatter off in small parties, but more than half the men took the trail, leaving the others to defend the camp. The mules struck the bluff at a bad point for ascending, and being very tired, slackened their gait and began to scatter. Several individuals were recovered in the cañons of the bluff, but the main body, with the mare, were found fully twenty miles south on the high prairie, to which point they had run in their panic, and were now slowly returning for want of water. We cannot, therefore, charge our Pawnee friends with this mischief. The camp guard had unloaded all the wagons during our absence, throwing aside for abandonment every superfluous article, with the design of reducing our entire loads to 250 pounds per man to increase speed and save the stock. As bacon, therefore, was plentier than wood we made our fires from it tonight, trusting to a small reserve, with the expected buffalo, for meat. We did not spare it and are keeping up splendid fires, around which we are discussing what would have had happened if the Pawnees had found the mules before we did, or had cut off some of our search parties, which were thinned out during the search so as to cover a front of several miles.

May 31st. Started early and plodded up the Platte bottom, enjoying the result of the reduced loads, but occasionally annoyed by the steep bed of some creek running down from the bluffs, every one of which must, of course, be crossed within a comparatively narrow space without affording much room for choice. The rain continues and is accompanied by a cold gale of wind. The road is soft and slippery, and sixteen miles were enough for us. That distance, however cleared us of Grand Island, and gave us the whole width of the river to look at, but as it is the ugliest one I ever saw, the view is not an unmixed joy. It seems about a mile and a half wide, and thick enough with mud to cut into chunks. There is plenty of wood on the other side, out of reach, but not a stick as large as a walking cane on this side.

June 1st, thirtieth day out. We made twenty miles today over bad ground, but under a bright sky, which is an unaccustomed phenomenon for it seems to be always raining along here, and whenever the rain gives out, we are sure to have a hurricane to fill up the time. Wood is scarce, water is bad, and the grass though plenty in quantity, seems of a watery, unnourishing kind on which the stock is getting thin. Nevertheless, our course lies for some hundreds of miles up this river and its forks, and we must make the best of it, hoping it may improve towards its source. During the march, a well-mounted Indian man started out toward the bluff after a single antelope, and gave us a splendid view of a fine chase over the level bottom. The antelope strained every nerve to gain the bluff, but could not help stopping occasionally to gratify his curiosity. Owing to these delays and the well-chosen diagonals steered by the horseman, the antelope seemed several times cut off, but at last, becoming seriously alarmed, put forth his strength, leaving the horse with little difficulty, and disappeared among the deep winding ravines of the bluff. The chase occupied over half an hour, giving us all a fine, clear view of every move, and a more adequate conception of how and why this graceful animal has no equal in speed. His curiosity also was very amusing. Whenever the horseman, instead of going directly for him, steered a course to cut him off, the antelope immediately stopped and gazed with ears up, till the cutting off process seemed to strike his apprehension, when he would take a new course to be followed by a similar result. The hunter was completely deceived, and would not give it up, till the antelope disappeared altogether, when he came in with a knocked-up horse, which he will have the pleasure of nursing on foot for a week or two, as I am doing now. I have led my horse all the way from the Little Blue, and he is still not fit to ride if I am to have any buffalo-hunting out of him.

June 2nd. Made another march of twenty miles. Gambel being desirous of traveling more leisurely and comfortably, left us today and joined the large ox train led by Captain Boone of Kentucky, who is anxious to have him and will dispense with any aid from him in driving or working, in return for his medical services. We gave him a mule with his proportion of the tools and provisions. He is an amiable, excellent fellow and very pleasant in conversation, having formerly made a similar journey to the Ratone Mountains and Santa Fé for the Philadelphia Academy of Natural Sciences, of which he is a prominent member. But he is averse to camp duty and hard work, and fond of taking things easy, and there is no doubt that Boone's large train with plenty of men and animals, and leisurely rate of traveling will suit him better than our headlong methods, especially as he has formed a warm friendship with Boone. (I never saw Gambel after that separation, and may as well state here what I did not learn till long afterward, and then only by heresay. Boone's train after losing many teams and wagons in the Humboldt River desert, arrived late in the season at the Sierra, where they encountered more obstacles and losses, reaching California after the beginning of the rains. Gambel personally made his way as far as Rose's bar on Feather River, where he died almost immediately from typhoid fever resulting from the extreme privations suffered during the latter part of his journey. Either Boone himself or some of his party, among whom Gambel was a great favorite, were with him at the time of his death.)

The river and bottom continue to present the same appearance, which is so monotonous that if one were suddenly let down in it from above, he probably could not tell within hundreds of miles what part of the valley he was in. Antelope are plenty but troublesome to approach, in consequence of such entire want of shelter. The whole train had another superb view of a chase after a small band by two mounted men, the hunters trying to cut them off from the bluff; but when the antelope became really alarmed and put forth their speed, there was little real contest, as they can when they will run ten feet to one against grass-fed horses. I got one today by still-hunting, or stalking, but by a chance shot, much longer than could be counted on with certainty. We passed through a prairie-dog town several miles long, so undermined that we had some trouble in steering our wagons among their excavations. The animals though numerous, dodge down their holes so quickly that we only got about a dozen of the thousands in sight.

June 3rd, Sunday. The day was so fine we kept right on, and as there has been so much uncertainty in our estimates of distance, two of the boys measured the route with a four-rod line, and found we covered exactly eleven and a half miles by noon, which was an agreeable surprise to all. There are so few objects by which to estimate distance, that it is habitually underrated; several who have started after antelope supposed to be half a mile distant, have found them nearer four times that distance. As we start early and keep moving all day, we are satisfied by this test that we are averaging at least twenty miles daily.

June 4th. A long march covered today, which I personally at least, doubled in hunting. Results, one antelope attracted within a long shot by a rag on the end of a ramrod; one large grey wolf; one rattlesnake. Tom B. turned up some time after dark with the hind-quarters of a black-tailed deer, shot in the bluffs, the first we had ever seen. He says the bluff ravines and gorges are full of them. The road is now dry and good and game plenty, and if it were not for the want of wood and good water, we would not have much to wish for. There are lots of last year's "bois des vaches" or buffalo chips, which in the dearth of other fuel cause a keen and funny contention just before camping-time by the representatives of the several messes. No sooner is the harness off, than the whole bottom is covered with earnest searchers. It burns well when dry, but if damp or wet, it is smokey and almost fire-proof. As for water, the puddles of rain water are preferred to the river, which latter is also very inaccessible, owing to its under-washed and vertical banks. There has been a vast cloud of smoke in front all day, which is red and luminous tonight. We can't account for it by the burning qualities of the short green grass of the bottom, and suppose it is last year's grass on the high and dry prairie. Rolling off in vast volumes before a strong easterly wind, the masses of fiery smoke make a magnificent and imposing display.

June 5th. Came up with and passed the fire, which is far off to the left of the river valley on the high plateau, doubtless fired by Indians. The sky is fine, but a howling easterly gale makes it necessary to secure the wagon tops with ropes round the beds. Last year's buffalo skulls and bones are almost countless everywhere, and all eyes are on the watch for the living animal. Three lost hunters refuged with us tonight, having seen our fires from the bluff. They have been lost for three days from a train thought to be ahead of us, and have been rioting among buffalo in great droves. When camped last night twenty-five miles to the south, towards the head of the Republican River they were surprised by Indians, but had time to leap on their ready-saddled horses and escape, abandoning blankets, boots, and everything except arms. Today they have ridden all day through vast herds of buffalo moving to the northwest, which we should converge with in a few days. They owe their lives to these herds, which doubtless destroyed their trail and confused their pursuers. I spent today hunting black-tailed deer in the bluffs, and got a fine white-tailed doe, but not what I was hunting for. The bluffs average about three miles from our line of march, at which distance inequalities are softened and they seem merely a high range of hills. But when one gets fairly in them, they offer a great variety of wild and beautiful scenery, with plenty of fine clear rivulets and springs, and abundance of short timber, which rests the eye delightfully after the flat monotony of the grass plains. The rocky scarps and precipices are often really sublime; game various and abundant, and but for the haunting fear of Indians, and one's duties with the wagons, I would like to hunt there for a week. One cannot go amiss for deer, elk and antelope. The best plan is to climb cautiously up one of the knife-like ridges, keeping a lookout on the windward side for the beautiful little secluded dells with wood, water and grass, which are hidden among them. There is sure to be game in any of these glens, and it is easily shot from above. There are also some big bear tracks in those retired valleys which afford plenty of awkward places for meeting one unexpectedly, but Bruin himself has not yet appeared.

We camped above the Platte forks, and will try to cross the South Fork tomorrow, if we find a good place, though it looks quite like rain and high water tonight. One of the hunters brought in a young antelope, but as we have no way of taking care of him, he was allowed to go, though he seemed so much inclined to stay with us that he had to be fairly driven away. Poor little fellow, if his mama doesn't find him, the wolves will.

June 6th. A rainy night, saturating the buffalo chips and making trouble in the housekeeping, but we have successfully put the great obstacle of the Platte behind us. Wagon-master Davis,[7] having carefully reconnoitered and selected the best place—not without plenty of amateur advice—we geared up early and with care, blocked up wagon beds, and reached the ford by 8 A.M. While 'catching up,' four buffalo walked down out of the bluff, grazing leisurely along toward the river without paying the slightest attention to us and all the noise we were making. Four mounted men went for them, but they took to and crossed the river nearly at right angles, notwithstanding the powerful current. The river where we were to cross is pronounced over a mile wide, with a strong current quite red with mud. Nothing about its appearance was encouraging, and to plunge the wagons into it was a strong act of faith, as from its looks it might well be a hundred feet or any other depth. But it had to be crossed, and the mounted men scattered out with a wide front to feel the way, and plunged in, the wagons in a long line following close. The bottom was sandy and shifting, making constant motion necessary to prevent settling down in it, besides incessant attention to the team leaders which alarmed by the swirling current, rushing noise, unstable footing, and deep holes, were with difficulty prevented from being swung round and forced down stream. It was an exciting scene, the long train half submerged in the wide expanse of water, the splashing and floundering of the mules, the whoops and yells of the men, and the foam and roar of the dashing waters. Owing to various mishaps of wagons, mules and men, the crossing occupied three hours, and everybody being wet, cold and exhausted, we camped nearby in another tempest of wind and rain, to repair wagons and harness and dry and preserve the loading, two wagons having been upset in the river, besides numerous breakages of poles, hounds, etc. We were now between the two forks, at no great distance

---

[7] Murdered by Mexicans in Calaveras County, California, about the year 1854.

from either, the place being not at all promising for game. But being in rollicking spirits over our success, as soon as the rain slacked, several of us started our hunting, but only obtained one very youthful antelope, which, had he been older, would have known better.

June 7th. Met numbers of Sioux this morning who though nearly naked, were well mounted, armed with long lances besides bows and arrows, and very friendly, owing partly perhaps to our strength and good order. Three of us started on horseback to visit their village, but when it came in sight, with the crowd about it, my companions thought better of the project and returned. But I had more faith in them, and being desirous of seeing their domestic arrangements at home, and seeing a lot of boys without arms coming to meet me, I kept on till I came among a lot of squaws digging roots, who screamed and broke for the town. As I did not want to have the appearance of chasing them, I waited till the unarmed boys and men came to meet me. The first fellow shook hands, and I handed him my lighted pipe, of which he took a whiff and politely returning it, invited me to proceed. I was conducted to a large tepee or lodge of nicely-tanned skins in front of which a few lances with shields suspended were stacked in tripod fashion. An old chief came out and by motions invited me to dismount and enter, but as half a dozen young fellows had hold of my gun which they were bent on examing, I was so busy holding on to it, with considerable friendly pulling on both sides, that I concluded not to dismount. Besides, the train was passing out of sight, evening was coming on, and I did not care to tempt them too much. Inside the tepee I could see two or three rather good-looking squaws sitting on buffalo robes, who would not have been there if any mischief was intended. Nevertheless, I did not wish to be too presuming on a first acquaintance, so when the chief at my request dispersed the crowd around me, I shook hands and took my leave, working my way through pretty much the entire male population, who were loudly discussing me or some other interesting object. The lodges were well laid out in lines, with lances and shields in front of each. A big lodge, colored red—perhaps a council house—

occupied a prominent place. No obstacle was offered to my departure and several half-grown lads, unarmed, jumped on horses and accompanied me half-way to our camp. There can be no doubt of the friendliness of these people, and that their excessive desire to examine my gun was mere honest curiosity. There are several tribes of this great Sioux nation, and without their aid in keeping off the Pawnees, Cheyennes and Arapahoes, no whites could get through this country without a big army.

June 8th. Large numbers of buffalo in sight on both sides of the river, on the north side in immense herds. S. J. and I were in some hilly ground a mile from the train, when three cows jumped out of the brush and ran for the river. I ran mine by a circuitous route as she doubled about for several miles, emptying gun and both pistols into her from within a few feet but she rushed down a high and nearly vertical bluff where I dared not risk my horse, and got clean away. J. had about the same luck and came back in a towering rage, swearing that lead would not kill them. The fact is, the old hunters say, you may fire lead into them all day unless you can hit a vital spot, which is not so very easy to do at top speed, over rough ground, with a chance of the ugly brute turning on one suddenly. We are following up the North Platte, which we must stick by for some 300 miles. There is little or no wood, and no water but the wretched stuff in the river, but the grass is plenty and good.

June 9th. Made a detour which occupied the entire day, returning to the river through a long, steep, winding ravine, called Ash Hollow, where we suddenly came upon B., who had been lost since we crossed the South Fork. He had walled up a lovely spring in the cañon, had plenty of meat, and being certain we had not passed, was very contentedly waiting for us. Now, we are anxious about the three men sent to look for him. This is a lovely place and a white trapper, with two or three Sioux lodges, evidently admires it as much as we, for they are camped at the foot of the hollow and revelling in variety as well as abundance. Nearly all sorts of game abound in the cañons of the bluff, while the hunter's staff of life, buffalo, are grazing in all the open valleys in innumerable multitudes. On the north side they absolutely crowd the bottom, down to the very river bank, and look across at us with such lazy and provoking indifference that B., H., and I were induced to try to cross the mile or more of river between us. But after steering a changing and zigzag course nearly across, we found an eighty-yard channel of deep water under the farther bank, with a current of not less than ten miles an hour. In trying to return, we had bad luck in finding the bars and shoal places, and were obliged to swim a dozen or more narrow but deep and rapid channels, and after spending several hours in the river, were glad to get out at all, wet, tired and shaking with cold.

June 10th, Sunday. Grass being poor, we moved on about twenty miles, passing the famous 'Castle Bluff.' Here the big river bluff has been hollowed out by the rains of centuries, into all manner of fantastic shapes, castles, cathedrals, forts, and structures of all sorts, the so-called 'castle' being the most remarkable.

June 11th. Twenty miles more covered today. Though the grass is quite poor, there is any quantity of buffalo, but no fuel except twisted grass—not even 'chips,' except the fresh ones that won't burn.

June 12th. Passed another curiously washed bluff called the 'Court House,' with a vast domed top and cupola. Also 'Chimney Rock,' another famous landmark, opposite which we are encamped at the estimated distance of half a mile, a guess which after walking to it and back, is unanimously increased to three miles. Distances are much underestimated on these wide level bottoms, and when hunting, it requires both experience and calculation to avoid shooting under. After constantly finding my bullets striking short, I now double the distance first estimated, and thus have better luck still-hunting than in shooting from horseback. One of our Indiana men had an adventure this morning. When harnessing up, about daylight, a solitary bull came down from the bluff and walked leisurely toward the river, passing by the camp within a few hundred yards. Two of the mounted guard having no work to do at the wagons, started after him and when within fair rifle shot, one dismounted and broke one of the bull's forelegs.

Very much to the hunter's astonishment, the bull instantly charged him on three legs, and as his horse promptly bolted and got away, it looked at first rather bad for the hunter. But his companion came to the rescue, the rest of the guard rushed out, and the bull was soon killed, though his meat proved tough and worthless. As all this occurred in everyone's sight, in fact almost in the camp, the Indiana hunter whose game turned the tables on him, will not soon hear the last of it.

June 13th. Chimney Rock is a large stratified mound of hard clay, about sixty feet in height and diameter, from the rounded top of which rises a chimney-shaped column, considered a hundred feet higher, tapering slightly toward the top. It is in sight far off over the plain before one can distinguish what it is, looking like the dead trunk of a gigantic tree, though in a country where to all appearance, no tree ever existed. From this point, S. J. and I, who have the best horses, left the train by general request to ride on to Fort Laramie, a Hudson Bay post near the mouth of Laramie's Fork, about seventy-five miles distant, to make arrangements to exchange wagons for more mules and pack saddles. We were all the afternoon sinking the conspicuous landmark of the Chimney, passing Scott's Bluff near evening, a place where some trappers, pressed by Indians, were once obliged to abandon to his fate, a wounded man of that name whom they were unable to carry with them. Rising here from the river valley over a high spur which intersected it, we simultaneously caught sight from the summit of an object new to both of us and pulled up in speechless admiration. Far away in front, in the ever widening west, its top gilded by the vanishing sun, was plainly distinguishable the white, snowy summits of Laramie's Peak of the Black Hills, distant, as we calculate, fully 100 miles or more.

June 14th. Slept with an Illinois train last night, and rode fifty miles today, not making out the snowy peak till nearly noon, since when we have scarcely removed our eyes from it. It is superb and grand, getting finer as we near it. We are hiding ourselves and horses tonight in a brush thicket without fire.

June 15th. Saw an occasional Indian—Cheyenne or Arapahoe—watching us from the distant hilltops, and one or two smoke columns, doubtless connected with their observations.

So we pushed on our tired horses hoping to put Laramie's Fork between us and those undesirable acquaintances, but on reaching it, found it swelled to a turbulent river, coming down from the mountains cold as ice and with a rushing current, the channel full of slippery, round boulders.

However, as the Indians had seen us, and the fort was in sight a few miles distant across the river, it had to be crossed. We both stripped for swimming, and securely fastened clothes and arms to the saddles, tying the ammunition on our heads. Selecting a favorable-looking rifle, we drew straws for the first essay, which, with my usual bad luck, fell to me. By this time, stripped as we were, we were in no fighting condition, and not a minute could be wasted. So I jumped my horse off the vertical bank, found swimming water almost immediately, and quartering down stream, made the opposite bank some 100 yards below. J. having a smaller horse, thought he could not make it, and tried a new place, which was worse, as the current rolled his horse over, forcing him to dismount and get dragged out a long distance below, by clinging for all he was worth to the horse's mane. As there was considerable brush on both banks, affording good shelter for Indians, we were not many minutes in shaking ourselves dry, pulling ourselves together and striking out for the fort. This is a good-sized square enclosure of whitewashed adobe, with projections for flank fire at two opposite angles. Two entrances on opposite sides, crowned with loop-holed gate-heads, give admission to the place, which is surrounded inside the walls by a range of small, square adobe apartments, used for storage, fur-pressing, and quarters for man and beast. It is a rough and primitive-looking place, but no doubt when well held, an effective strong-hold against Indians, who visit it for trading purposes in large numbers at the proper season.

A large number of dilapidated wagons are standing about, abandoned by previous emigrants, and whatever their value at home, quite worthless here. Many have been broken up for material for pack saddles. The garrison now holding the place for the Fur Company consists of a 'clerk'—as its officers are modestly called—and six or eight others, all French or half-breeds. They must have horses or mules somewhere, but none are in sight and they profess to have none, at all events, not for American emigrants. Our mission being therefore a failure, we lounged round the fort, looking at the trading and store rooms, fur presses and other arrangements novel to us, till near evening, when, being assured by the people that Indians would not molest us in sight of the fort, we moved three or four miles across the level plain to the Platte, where there was good grass, and had an opportune success in killing a young antelope, on which, with coffee made in a tin cup, we made a good supper and proceeded to enjoy a sound sleep, unmolested by guard duty, stampedes, or any of the usual bedevilments.

June 16th. A man and several head of stock were drowned last night from a large emigrant train, while crossing Laramie's Fork. Tonight our own train came rolling in with men and teams well battered by the forced marches they have been making. The Fork having gone down very much, all hands went right to work blocking up wagon beds, doubling teams, lashing fast cargoes, etc., and after some hard work, crossed everything without loss. Later a U. S. Government train of one company of dragoons under Major Saunders, with wagons, stock and belongings, arrived and crossed, the stream having still further fallen. Their business is to take charge of the fort for a government post. This fine clear evening a long row of the lesser snow summits of the Laramie Range of the Black Hills became plainly visible, stretching in magnificent and splendid succession far away to right and left of our course. By sundown they had disappeared and we may not soon see them again, as they must be a long distance away.

June 17th. The stars and stripes went up on the fort this morning, receiving our hearty cheers. We moved but a short distance and camped, to rest the mules and consider what to do. Since we can get no more animals and there is no other inhabited place nearer than Fort Hall, on Snake River, many hundred miles distant, it is evident we must carry our wagons through, or do worse; so we conclude to nurse our failing teams and make the best of it. There is plenty of evidence of a great lightening of loads here by previous parties, and we still farther reduced ours to the estimated weight of about 200 pounds per man. This work, with washing, mending, reloading and cooking for some days ahead, occupied all hands today, and tomorrow bright and early, away we go.

June 18th. At 4 A.M. we struck out into the Black Hills, leaving the river for a time. Laramie's Peak is in constant view ahead, about forty miles distant, though apparently not more than an hour's ride, so splendid and conspicuous is its white summit and so clear the atmosphere in this dry, elevated region. An Indiana wagon broke its pole this morning but having a spare one along, a detachment of all the amateur mechanics was left with it, and it overtook the train in good shape at the noon halt, the fuel afforded by the broken pole having served to fit the irons on the new one. We passed a warm spring today, and the appearance of the country has much changed. The hills are higher, more rocky and abrupt, and the soil is dry, barren and stony, with little good grass at any one place. The wild sage or artemisia is getting more abundant, and buffalo much scarcer, though we can still get enough for our wants and even add to our stock of jerked meat. Some scattered pines in the rocky valley of a large creek made our hearts glad, it is so long since we have seen any. A large cottonwood on the same stream contains at least fifty Indian bodies, suspended with all their belongings in the branches, that being the fashionable mode of disposing of their dead with these tribes. The swinging about of the decaying remnants of these objects overhead, and the thick crop of fallen remains on the ground, makes this a wierd and ghastly spot. Poor fellows! I suppose, after all, their object is about the same as ours, i.e., to get the perishing bodies out of the way, and launch the departed spirit toward the happy hunting grounds.

> "Their souls proud science never taught to stray
> Far as the solar walk or milky way,
> Yet simple Nature to their hope hath given
> Beyond yon cloud capped hills an humbler heaven."

Among the other peculiarities of this region, the days are exceedingly hot, while the nights are frosty. The fact is, we have about crossed the great Mississippi Valley, and judging from the rapid current of all the rivers, must have very much increased our altitude. We traveled all day without water, passing many large water courses entirely dry, and when tonight we struck a rapid creek of cold mountain water, it was almost impossible to keep the suffering mules out of it, and there was a terrible jam of teams and wagons. The banks on both sides were rough and high and it is hard to see how we got off with so little damage. We traveled several miles up this stream in search of grass, and camped.

June 19th. The whole landscape is now arid and barren and affords little or nothing that is familiar, the chief vegetation being sage, cactus, and yuccas of various kinds. Trees and shrubs do not exist, and grass is scarce and thin. The surface is decidedly mountainous, though known by the modest name of the 'Black Hills.' But it is very odd that both buffalo and antelope are more numerous on these barrens than on some of the much finer grass farther east. Four lone buffalo, apparently lost or confused, came down from a rocky ravine and crossed the trail between the wagons, which were well strung out in consequence of the rough road. Several of us who were mounted, after a short but breakneck gallop and wasting considerable ammunition, killed two. There must surely be some good grass valleys concealed among the hills, but as we get all the meat we want, close by, it is not worth while to look for them. Perhaps it is the Indians who have driven the game away from the better and more extensive pastures below. They even seem less wild here, and it is no trouble to get a forty or fifty yard shot on foot, and quite a matter of pride to kill with one bullet. This naturally causes a tendency to prevarication with our most truthful hunters, which it is hoped will disappear with the unusual temptation.

June 20th. Passed today several small cold-water streams, our course being parallel with, but several miles from, the Platte, now much reduced in width and improved in color, but more rapid than ever. Large or small bunches of buffalo are constantly in sight, and on surmounting a high divide with an extensive view, J. and myself, who were riding ahead, stopped in surprise at seeing the country in the far distance apparently covered with timber, and it was only after close examination that we recognized the dark color prevailing over an area of many square miles, to be buffalo in countless masses. Some of our hunters saw large numbers of dead ones floating down the Platte, and it is hard to tell how these immense herds live on the thin and scattered grass. And yet though not fat they are in excellent condition. Passed today some wagons camped on the Rivière de la Bonté, whose cattle were stampeded last night in the bottom of that lovely stream, by a panther which jumped on and badly clawed one of the oxen. The cattle were recovered after a long chase, but were so scared that when yoked up, all the teams wanted to run away, and one overset the wagon and broke an axle, which they have stopped to repair. It seems that oxen are slower to take a bad fright than mules, but do not get over it so soon.

June 21st, fiftieth day out. Game is more abundant than ever. A small band of antelope galloped right through the train today, and did not seem much alarmed till after they had got by, when they kicked up their heels in astonishment at their own temerity. We came down out of the hills to the Platte, now closely confined by precipitous banks and much reduced in width, though deep, clear and rapid. It must soon be crossed, and fording is out of the question.

June 22nd. Overtook the Missouri train of 47 wagons and 200 men, guided by Hudspeth, the famous mountain man, which left Independence several days before us. They are crossing on rafts of cottonwood and a kind of Noah's Ark—half raft, half scow. We camped nearby, and while engaged in cutting off the end of our heaviest wagon, and shortening the coupling, a large swan sailed down the river at steamboat speed, receiving a running fire from most of our fellows, with entire impunity. The balls struck and splashed all around him but he went tossing along on his way, unhurt. The Missouri pikers of Hudspeth's train, who shoot squirrels in the head with rifles, laughed loudly at our misses, but when their turn came, their shots were no better, and they now swear it was no swan at all but a 'Rocky Mountain witch.'

The soil has become so gravelly and gritty, that our bare-footed mules have worn their hoofs to the quick. Some we are shoeing, but the worst cases we are putting into buffalo hide moccasins, till they can bear shoes. It is fortunate we heeded the mountain men's advice in Independence, in providing shoes and nails, or we should now be in a fine mess. As with few exceptions, none of our mules were ever shod before, and as not one of us had ever shod one, our process of shoeing would probably astonish a blacksmith as much as it does the mules. It is counted cowardly to throw the animal, and the favorite method is to lash him up, head, body and legs, alongside a wagon. The tools are a drawing knife, with a sharp Bowie for the finer touches, a hatchet, and an axehead for clinching.

June 23rd. Commenced crossing at noon today, and finished after dark, without serious accident; then kindling a beacon for the mules, and starting them in a long distance above the coming-out place on the other side, we swam them all without loss, and sent them off, under guard, about three miles for grass.

June 24th, Sunday. Started early, followed the river about four miles over a bad hill and through heavy sand, and then bearing off through an easy depression to the right, we looked our last on the turbid and rushing Platte. We have followed it from near its mouth to this remote and solitary spot, where it is almost overhung by the stupendous snowy chain, in some of whose wild and unknown solitudes it has its birth. We are now passing over the high and considerable divide which separates it from the Sweetwater, which stream we shall follow to its source, and then look out for the Pacific waters. Here on these arid, rocky, sandy and barren expanses, we find numerous white alkaline deposits, the remnants of dried-up lakes and ponds. About twenty-two miles from the Platte, passing through a depression in a ridge of naked rocks, we picked up plenty of coal, lying on the surface, but had no time to look for the vein. There is no water on this divide, which is over forty miles across, consequently there is no game but a few antelope, which I doubt not can travel 100 miles for a drink. One followed us for several miles, keeping a parallel course alongside, a few hundred yards distant. The men say it is from curiosity, but I don't wonder at his wanting company in this arid desert. Not knowing we were to find no wood nor water, we brought neither, and had to camp without, after a sixteen-hours' march. There was considerable language used, but so far as I could ascertain, none of it consisted exclusively of hymns.

June 25th. Disconsolately we caught up at daylight, and proceeded, the mules bawling pitifully for water. About ten, we got the customary water signal from a man sent off to examine a greenish spot at a distance. We found the green tint to be due to an extensive patch of dwarf willow scrub, among which was some scarce and bad water. However, both mules and men were about this time willing to drink 'anything that will run.' After passing numerous bare rocky ridges, we camped within sight of the Sweetwater, the guard taking the mules down into its bottom, which though pretty sterile, has very fair grass on the immediate banks.

June 26th. Daylight revealed 'Independence Rock' within a short distance. It is a rectangular mass of bare rock about 600 by 300 feet, and perhaps sixty feet high, hard to climb but accessible in some places. The repeated echoes and reverberations from the neighboring mountains, of my pistol fired on the summit, were grand and imposing. Five miles above it, is a celebrated place known to mountain men as 'Devil's Gate,' a wonderful chasm yawning deep and dark between vertical or overhanging walls of rock many hundred feet deep and but a few feet across at the surface. The eye is lost in the black depths except only for the white ribbon discernible far down, apparently in the very bowels of the earth, but the abyss is so deep that not a sound comes up from the tossing white ribbon, which is the Sweetwater. Entangled and hanging on a sharp ledge fifty feet below the opposite edge, lay the dried carcass of a bighorn which from some cause or other, had failed to make his jump. This chasm is truly a wonderful place. Being entirely of naked rock, it is simply an earthquake split or cleft, carrying about the same width from top to bottom, suggesting no idea of its having been gradually cut out by water, as is plainly the case with most cañons.

This river heads in the Wind River Range not far from the top of the 'South Pass.' It is bright, clear and cold, and full of salmon trout. The valley is generally two or three miles wide with plenty of small side streams and good grass. The main range of the Rocky Mountains rises on each side to snow peaks, stretching away north and south in endless succession, spotless and shining in virgin white, seen by few and trodden by none. A sharp thunderstorm toward evening produced results unspeakably grand and awful. The black clouds hovered below and in strong contrast with the white shining summits, and their detonations were so confused with reverberations that one only perceived a continuous roar in which reports and echoes were indistinguishable. I think the dullest minds took in some new impressions of power and grandeur.

June 27th. Passed today what looked like an immense frozen lake, but was pure, spotless saleratus, deposited in considerable thickness by dried-up waters. Though we are getting farther into the heart of the mountains, the valley widens rather than narrows. Water, grass and antelope are plenty, but no wood. The variations of day and night temperature are excessive. The sand gets heated by the sun to a temperature which the bare hand can hardly endure, while ice forms in the camp kettles every night, though in this northern latitude daylight lasts till 9 P.M.

June 28th. Trying to make a 'cut-off' today, we got the train involved in a bad cañon and had to cross the river three times in as many hundred yards. The crossings were bad and dangerous for wagons—especially the last—where the current and deepest channel were immediately under the near bank, and notwithstanding the many tons of rock thrown in to level up, the mules were swimming from the start, the wagons taking a headlong plunge after them. On the opposite bank the teams were hauled out with ropes, the leaders soon getting footing enough to help yank out the rest. When the mules were swum back to double teams, they had to be hauled by main force up the nearly vertical, rocky bank, with ropes passing over extemporized shears. But no pen, pencil or tongue can adequately describe the splendor of the scene from the camp, which was made immediately after the last crossing. The rude amphitheatre was closely hemmed in by vertical walls of split and shivered rock, the floor was covered with the finest grass, the dashing river made continuous music, the last rays of the sun peeped in through cracks of the western wall, and on every side, far above and beyond the immediate rocky boundary, towered the superb Wind River peaks, shining white and pink from top to bottom with snows that never melt. It is the unanimous voice that all our tribulations to this time are amply compensated by this single view. Even this secluded mountain glen is penetrated by antelope, who if not overcome like ourselves by the scenery, are at least very tame, and are to be seen all round, watching us from the near foothills. A considerable bunch of bighorn, including some young ones, also came down and watched us with intense interest for a long time from a rocky and inaccessible though not distant ridge, and not liking our looks, went off at last slowly and with seeming reluctance. All the sentimental theory freely indulged in about their apparent wish for our company and closer acquaintance, was cut short off by B., who after listening to it awhile, remarked, "Boys, I wouldn't gush anymore about them bighorn; what's the matter is, they're too bashful to come right into camp, and there's no other place round here where they can get water handy."

June 29th. This morning's march was over sensibly rougher ground, but every step disclosed new and different views of the great ranges of snow-peaks now on every side of us. At noon we sewed together some wagon covers and dragged a river pool about five feet deep for salmon trout. Probably no such net was ever used before, but we had plenty of men for dragging, as well as to form wing or guiding weirs. The river was full of fish and with any proper net we could have had a wagon-load, but the net, being so impervious, could not be quickly handled and the slow process of hauling in the entire river gave the fish a chance to dart between our legs, and we only caught a few. Snow is now abundant even along the trail and at the noon halt we found a green, grassy valley of 100 acres or more, entirely underlaid with hard crystal ice, lying but a few inches below the grass. We dug four feet into it at one place without finding the end of it. Though clear and transparent to the eye, it had a decidedly sulphurous smell and taste.

June 30th. Ice froze two inches thick in the camp kettles during the night, and at daybreak the ground was hard frozen but soon thawed as the sun rose. A train of forty-two wagons with forty men of Colonel Loring's rifle regiment passed us today, being what is left of three companies, the rest of whom have died or deserted. They are on the way to receive possession of Fort Hall, another H. B. Company post on Snake River of the Columbia. The major commanding (Sanderson, it is said) has two daughters along, a sort of ornament rarer than beaver or bighorn in these parts. On this day, memorable in our journey, we crossed the continental back-bone divide, and are now on the down-grade for the Pacific. Having followed the Sweetwater for 120 miles and crossed it eleven times, we left it at nine this morning, and after taking a last look at the Atlantic waters, began a steady though easy ascent, which by noon brought us to the highest part of the pass. The precise summit is not easy to identify. It lies somewhere on a high, arid, barren expanse nearly level, and furnishing a better road than we have seen for hundreds of miles. We, however, fixed upon a spot lying between two conical hills on the right, and had the satisfaction of halting to rest a short time on the summit of the continent, the view from which, however, is not nearly as fine as many we have seen, a large part of the snowy range being here obstructed by rocky foothills clear of snow. With three cheers and several more, we rolled on downward toward the setting sun, not forgetting to carry a little water destined by nature for the Atlantic, to be poured into the first west-flowing water for transfer to the western ocean. This is Pacific Spring, which gives rise to a small rivulet that by way of the Little and Big Sandys, Green River and the Colorado, ultimately reaches the Gulf of California. How near together the solitary mountain sources of these little streams, and yet with half the world between them, how widely severed their ultimate destinations!

CHAPTER V

July 1st, Sunday, sixtieth day out. In a joyous mood at having placed the great continental divide behind us, we pushed on twenty-two miles over a sterile country to camp on the Little Sandy, where fuel, grass, antelope and everything but water is scarce.

July 2nd. Made only six miles to Big Sandy, a fine swift-flowing creek, fifty yards wide and up to the wagon beds, with a good smooth bottom. We camped here to rest the stock and prepare to cross the '*Jornada del Muerte*,' a waterless desert extending fifty miles or more to the Green River of the Colorado. Repacked wagons, filled every vessel that would hold water and overhauled the mules' shoes and harness.

July 3rd. Rolled out on the desert at 3 P.M. yesterday. Road of hard sand, level and good but barren as a brick yard. At sunset the vastness, solitude and desolation were most impressive. No living thing, animal or vegetable, scarcely even a roll or inequality of surface, relieved the monotony of this wide flat desert perched almost on the top of the mountains. Far in the rear, beyond the dreary waste, the distant snowy summits were still visible when night came down. At ten we halted a few minutes to wet the mules' mouths and our own, and then resumed the lonely and depressing march. The night was bitterly cold, and all were glad to walk who could. Daylight disclosed the same cheerless landscape, the snowy summits, the only landmark, apparently not far distant behind. Halted half an hour at daybreak and then pressed on, the ground, dry as it was, being hard frozen. Soon another snowy range became gradually visible ahead, being that of the high mountains beyond Green River, a spur of the Wahsatch, I suppose.

From our intermediate position on the wide level desert between, these two massive and snow-capped ramparts took on an additional and imposing grandeur. At 3 P.M. we commenced winding down a steep and rocky ravine through lofty river bluffs, frequently having to lower the wagons with ropes, and by 5 P.M. stood on the banks of the Green River of the Colorado, after twenty-six consecutive hours of marching, looking up with awe and wonder at the lofty and apparently inaccessible bluffs through which we had nevertheless just descended. There was no grass near, on our side of the river, and while the guard went off with the mules, we commenced unloading wagons and caulking the beds, fastening these together in couples. Some stunted cottonwood from which to make oars, was found a few miles down the river, and by night the preparations were nearly ready for a hard day's work tomorrow. The river is wide and deep, with a rushing current and icy cold.

July 4th. This is a holiday, but not for us. For myself, I stood guard all last night except two hours, which last supplied all the sleep I have had in fifty hours. At daylight the ice in the kettles was an inch thick and the ground white with heavy frost. After much contention with the mules, who objected to take water, we got them huddled together on the bank with a rope drawn round them and so forced them in. But they no sooner struck the main current, than most, including the bell mare, were rolled over, got their ears filled, and came back in spite of us. The others got on the other shore, strung out for a mile or two down stream. A second lot crossed with difficulty in the same way, but as this would soon exhaust the returning mules as well as ourselves, Chamberry stripped, put the bell on his own neck, and undertook to swim over on the mare. He is a fine horseman and a good swimmer and did very well as far as mid-river, when the powerful current rolled the mare over, and the frightened mules commenced piling on him. For a time it looked as though it were all over with C. who, dressed only in a cow bell and a pair of spurs was beyond reach of help in the midst of an icy current of fifteen miles an hour, with a hundred terrified mules crowding over and around him.

But C. was equal to the occasion. Turning over on his back he kicked the water into their faces till he got some room, and then seizing the mare's tail, he guided her quartering down stream ahead of the crowd, and got her safely landed about three miles below. Three mules and two horses were drowned, and seven landed on an island, while one horse got footing several miles below, under an overhanging bluff, on the side he started from. At last, however, all the survivors were got across and we all went to work on the wagons transformed into boats. A number of men crossed first with some harness, not forgetting the clothes of C., who was jumping about in a lively and entertaining manner, to avoid freezing. A team of mules on the other side, and of men on our side, was soon rigged, and thus when the loaded and returning boats, after being carried far down by the current, got within casting distance, they were quickly towed up again abreast of the starting point. The wagon beds being well dried, mostly held the caulking well, and with frequent bailing, answered the purpose. By 9 P.M. everything was across, and the most difficult obstacle yet encountered, was behind us.

July 5th. The mules had a day's rest, today. In the evening two mountain men, east-bound, came in from Salt Lake, where the Mormons, driven out by mobs from Missouri and Illinois, are now settling. They give fine accounts of that vicinity, but say we cannot get our wagons to California on account of the entire absence of grass this season on the Humboldt, where an unmitigated desert impassable for stock, now stretches for 250 miles. *Nous verrons.*

July 7th. Made eighteen miles yesterday, and the same today, over a rough country, from which large game is absent, but there are plenty of a kind of large hawk which are fair eating, and also, in the sage brush, large numbers of a small brown ground squirrel, and some grey grouse called by the trappers, 'cock of the plains.' Water and grass in the bottoms, but high grounds dry and sterile. Snow is in sight on all hilltops, and the snow-capped chain of the Bear River Mountains in full view ahead. During several hours, today, the ground was so completely covered with vast multitudes of large black wingless crickets, that the wagon wheels left long black streaks behind them.

July 8th, Sunday. Crossed and left Ham's Fork of Bear River, today, and are now within the great central basin of the continent, on waters which reach no ocean, but drain into the Great Salt Lake. After crossing the river it required the whole morning to ascend a long, rough and difficult mountain, but from the bleak and rugged summit a superb and majestic view unfolded itself in front, though winter howled around us. Fields of snow lay far below, every ravine and gorge being piled full. One hundred and fifty miles to the east, beyond the barren rocky waste we have been traversing, rose the Main or Wind River Range still dominating everything in that direction in distant but undiminished grandeur. To the south was the massive snow-covered chain of the Wahsatch, and in front stretched an endless series of rough hills, the hollows and intervals mostly filled with dark forests of the fir which at home is called 'Balm of Gilead,' whose dark masses appear by contrast quite black. We camped by the edge of such a forest which was entirely impenetrable, the trees branching to the ground and the interstices filled, six-feet deep with old snow. Here we enjoyed an unaccustomed luxury in the shape of bounteous log fires. The 'cock of the plains,' sage hen, or grouse as it is variously called, having been abundant all day, everyone had as much as he could eat, an agreeable variety from bacon and jerked buffalo beef. The mules soon filled themselves with grass, growing around the edge of the timber, and collected in a dense mass round our fires, whether for warmth or from love of our society, we cannot tell.

July 9th. Leaving our delightful but rather wintry camp, we traversed an elevated and very rough country, crossed the high divide by noon, and descended a long, difficult, and, for the wagons, dangerous mountain to Bear River, flowing through a fertile and delightful valley.

July 10th. A village of Snakes, or Shoshonees, came down out of the mountains and camped close by us, after we turned in last night. Soon after, the mules, now usually quiet enough, stampeded with a wild rush and stopped at the foot of a high inaccessible bluff, several miles distant. Of course we were up all night, not knowing whether the Indians or only the wolves, caused the stampede. The former profess to be friendly, but our men are suspicious and keep them out of camp, which makes them inclined to be quarrelsome, and as we have plenty of hot tempers among ourselves, several altercations have occurred, and been fairly patched up.

July 11th. No attack last night, but a squally time this morning. Just as the train rolled out after daylight, one of the guard shot what he took for a wolf partly concealed in the brush, but which turned out to be a Shoshonee dog. Out rushed the Indians, forming in battle array as they advanced. We had just time to run the wagons into corral, when 150 of the Indians were in line, bawling for vengeance at the top of their voices, with bows bent and arrows drawn to the head. We had about sixty rifles in line, ready and extremely willing, but two chiefs advanced unarmed, with hands held up, and negotiations were commenced which resulted in our paying an old blanket for the dog, they agreeing to move off first, and not follow us. We made a few miles, but seeing many small parties of Indians watching from the hills, and finding a good defensive position, encamped early.

July 22nd, Sunday. From the camp on the 12th, five of us with a few pounds of flour each, left the train and rode southwards to visit the Great Salt Lake. Here on this great inland ocean—across which no land can be seen—were encamped many Mormon wagons, the people being about to form a permanent settlement in this rather uninviting place. There is good timber, however, in the hills, and running water, which can be easily conducted through the valley. The soil in the valley seems good, but the hills are arid, rocky and barren. I should think they might have found better places for settlement, but perhaps none more secluded, and seclusion seems to be what they principally want. After remaining one day at Salt Lake we started north with the intention of overtaking the train either at Soda Springs, or between there and Fort Hall, by successfully dodging the Shoshonees. But as bad luck would have it, the very night we started, I was attacked with headache and the symptoms of a severe bilious attack, which riding by night and hiding in the brush by day, with slim diet and only a saddle blanket for covering, did not tend to alleviate. The suffering was so intense that for some days I was semi-delirious and pretty much indifferent to life. But fifty miles a day must be covered, to overtake the train, even if any single individual had to abandoned, and in some way or other—I am sure I can't tell how—my comrades succeeded in dragging me along. We passed the great natural curiosities of the Soda and Steamboat Springs, finding a note from our train at the former, and about the 19th, found the wagons camped on Snake River, marked on the maps as Lewis' Fork of the Columbia, a lovely stream with clear, bright, cold water and a rapid current.

On the 20th Fort Hall hove in sight across the level river bottom and once more our hearts were gladdened by the sight of a roof. The fort is a concentrating post of the ubiquitous H. B. Company, receiving furs every spring from the wandering trappers who then come in from their winter resorts in the mountains, and also from the smaller posts scattered at wide distances through the adjacent mountains, dispatching its accumulations annually, to Fort Vancouver, a thousand miles distant. The dragoon train has not arrived yet, but is daily expected. The enclosure and buildings are larger but precisely similar to those at Fort Laramie, with the agreeable addition of a delightful location on the bank of this lovely mountain river. It seems necessary to get outside of the Mississippi Valley, on one side or the other to find clear, cold, sparkling streams, those of the great valley being muddy, dirty, and unattractive. Below the fort on the main river, there are considerable falls and rapids, but whether rolling green, clear and deep between rocky banks, or foaming white over black basaltic rocks, it is everywhere beautiful and refreshing to those who have become accustomed to the muddy and unlovely streams of the prairies. But there seem to be few attractions without drawbacks, and here these are the mosquitoes, which swarm in clouds at evening. Fortunately their industry is necessarily confined to the period of an hour or two after the great heat of the mid-day sun, and before the nightly frost which rarely fails to follow later, but their numbers and activity during that time are beyond all former experience. One can hardly open one's mouth to eat or speak without trapping several. The mules huddle together in a close crowd with tails waving overhead, and probably agreed with us that even the extreme heat of the sun is easier to bear than the ceaseless persecution of these marauders, who have to get plunder enough in an hour or two to last them during the rest of the twenty-four.

July 26th, eighty-fifth day out. Descending Snake River some miles, before reaching the mouth of Goose Creek, a tributary from the south, we made a cut-off to strike the latter higher up, and then ascended it steadily to its source, and are crossing the high dry divide which separates its drainage system from that of the Mary's, or Humboldt, some of whose waters we should reach soon. F. C. died on the night of the 24th, and was buried while darkness still shrouded the operation, in a rocky cleft of the Goose Creek bluffs, which was afterward filled with the largest stones we could move. Today we passed a group of boiling springs emitting clouds of steam visible at a long distance, both ground and water of bright scarlet color, attributed to iodine or cinnabar, or both. On the divide the country is an arid desert from which the train raises clouds of dust indicating by a motionless canopy our recent course for miles.

July 27th. Though the snowy masses of the Humboldt Mountains glisten within a few miles on either hand, the day's journey has been hot, dusty and waterless. Near noon, several springs or wells of clear, but badly impregnated water were found, the water being several feet below the surface, and the bottom so deep as to be invisible. Guards had to keep the thirsty mules from pushing each other in, while we hoisted water out for them.

July 28th. Struck and crossed what is taken for a fork of Humboldt, upsetting and damaging one of the best wagons, which, however, was soon patched up.

July 29th. Having discussed for some days the policy of dividing our large train. It was resolved upon and executed today. The reasons were: first, the difficulty of finding grass for so many mules together; second, our diminishing provisions. Our company having sacrificed more of our lading at various points, our teams are now able to travel faster, and the necessity for it becomes daily more apparent, as we have barely a month's provisions left, while the Indiana wagons have twice as much, besides other comforts which we long since abandoned. It is true the Indians here are hostile, but only in a sneaking way, such as hiding among the sage brush and shooting arrows at the men and mules at night. But they seem such poor devils that they inspire little fear and if they should want to fight, we had rather take the chance of handling them by ourselves, than exhaust our provisions before getting over the Sierra. So at or before daylight, our three remaining Georgia wagons pulled out of the corral alone, the 'Old Dominion' declining to join us. No one liked the separation from our old companions, though believing it safest and best, all things considered. Relieved from the long dusty train, our three light wagons covered thirty miles before night, and camped by a big ox train which was attacked last night by 'Diggers.' They had most of their cattle run off by the Indians into the mountains, whither most of the men, reinforced by some friendly 'Snakes,' had gone to try and recover them. Our own little party is now equally divided, one half standing guard half of each night, which is not a nice amusement after a hard day's work.

July 30th. At daylight, though there had been no special alarm during the night, and the mules were all right, H. of the night guard, was found dead and cold with several arrows sticking in him. He had evidently been still-hunted, his gun being undischarged, and as his body was otherwise undisturbed, the marauders were plainly reserving that pleasure till we should roll on and leave the coast clear. To frustrate such designs, the body was buried in the corral, and the mules herded over it for an hour, to destroy the traces. We made a long march, crossing and leaving the river which here flows through an impassable cañon, our route winding among rocky hills and gorges, with a prospecting party ahead. Late at night again we struck the bottom and rushed for the water, which shows a constant deterioration both in quality and temperature.

Nevertheless we supped on trout, duck, and sand-hill crane, all boiled together in the camp kettle, the culinary professors valuing their repose much more than their professional reputation. We purchased today from some Shoshonees, a lot of finely dressed deerskins for an equal number of charges of powder and lead, and all hands are busy tonight making trousers to replace our old rags.

July 31st. Thick ice is in the camp kettles this morning, notwithstanding the intense heat of this cañon by day. We again had to leave the river, the only cheerful object in the landscape, on account of its narrow cañons, debouching again upon it late tonight. The road through the cheerless rocky gorges was dismally depressing, though the desert par excellence, is still many miles ahead.

August 1st. Except some bad muddy sloughs to be crossed, the road today was quite fair. The river, though without tributaries, varies little in dimensions, but the water is nastier and warmer every day. It is too deep to wade, with little current, keeping mostly near the center of its valley, which varies from two to five miles in width, bounded by rocky, dismal and barren hills, without vegetation. The immediate banks are often underwashed and vertical, almost everywhere inaccessible for stock without assistance.

August 2nd. The water gets still worse and more impregnated with mineral. Grass has nearly disappeared, being only found in small patches in the river bends, where it has to be diligently searched for by advance parties. The mules look badly, some of them showing signs of failure. While looking for grass ahead of the wagons, tonight, three of us flushed, rode down, and caught a Digger. He was short, stout and naked except for a small grass bonnet on his ugly head. He had secreted his arms, if he had any, and displayed in a split stick a small eel, doubtless reserved for a family feast. As the miserable wretch stood with lariat round his neck, rolling his longing eyes from us to the free but distant hills, it seemed hard to take his worthless and joyless life, notwithstanding his undoubted proclivity for potting men and mules in the darkness. Yet one man voted for his death, and when outvoted, insisted that he should be "tied up and whipped a little anyhow." I am happy to say his philanthropic view was not allowed to prevail. When released, the rogue walked off slowly—though doubtless momentarily expecting a shot in the rear—for a few yards, when he suddenly disappeared among the sandy ripples of the desert as though the earth had swallowed him.

This afternoon as I was climbing a stony hill in search of sage-hens for the pot, the boys down in the camp yelled and pointed beyond me with excited gestures, but not distinguishing their words, I only thought of Diggers. As the hillside was perfectly bare and open, without much chance of an ambush, I kept on upward, when suddenly from behind a small red boulder, not as big as a wheelbarrow, out skipped a fine sleek panther not twenty yards distant. Having a stern shot, I hit him as he ran, pretty badly I think, upon which he turned and snarled for an instant as I was hastily reloading and then ran the faster. Not being willing to go out of sight of the wagons, I therefore lost him, but must say I should have given him credit for making a better fight.

August 3rd. Passed a train today, whose mules were run off by the Diggers, after they had killed two of the guard. Most of the men have gone after the mules in a desperate hope of recovering them, for life itself here depends on the all-important help of that indispensable but hated animal. All our men are savage by sympathy, and it is lucky for our yesterday's captive that he was not caught today.

The only grass—such as it is—being on the other side of the river, we had to swim the mules over tonight, with some extra care for them and ourselves, as the Diggers have a way of hiding in the low sage and willow scrub along the river, and taking their chance of potting a mule or a guard, whom they can afterwards utilize at their leisure.

August 5th, Sunday. Yesterday and today, the same monotonous plod down the river, water and grass constantly getting scarcer and worse. There is no wood except some short trifling willow brush, and as that is infested with Diggers, whose deadly arrows make no noise and give no alarm, it is as much as one's life is worth to step into it alone. The heat is intense, the bottom is becoming deep and sandy, and everything indicates the vicinity of the 'jumping off place.'

August 6th. The guard ran the mules in before daylight this morning, shouting 'Diggers,' when up came everyone to a rally at the wagons. As soon as the mules were in, Seab Jones ran forward, shouting, "Forward boys, spread out wide and charge 'em. Don't let the d—d rascals think we have to fight behind wagons." About this time a gun on our side was discharged, but not much attention was paid to it, as all hands charged into the brush after S. The Diggers ran, affording a glimpse only of two or three, who were fired at, but as far as we know, none were bagged. But a sad sight awaited us on returning to the wagons. The dead body of P. lay on the ground, his discharged gun beside him. The gun had been hanging in the wagon and in pulling it out hastily, muzzle foremost, it had been discharged, the bullet passing through his heart. P. had been liked by all. He was a good worker and an excellent driver, never backward in doing his full share. Under the circumstances it was perhaps best for all that he had been killed outright, rather than wounded. There was nothing to be done now but to wait for daylight by which to bury him, which we did with sadness and sorrow, and travelled on as we could not afford to lose any time. The mules are evidently failing. On a cut-off of fourteen miles without water, today, one dropped in harness. Another was substituted and the wagons passed on, but the defunct being lifted up revived, and followed the train. Many whirling dust columns were seen today, probably caused by air currents coming out of the gorges and meeting others on the plain. The mirage also now begins to be seen, and as in these dry deserts the thoughts of all run constantly on water, these usually take the form of beautiful blue lakes with waving trees; one even distinguishes a lovely ripple on the water, and white foam along the shore, where, alas, all is dreary barren sand. Tonight two men stopped with us, of the party who went after the stock stolen by the Diggers on the 3rd. They became separated from their party far among the desert mountains of the north, where they came on a mounted Indian concealing himself among rocks. They ran him several miles through cañons and gorges, and over precipices, thinking he would make for the locality of the lost stock. He gained on them, however, sufficiently to light a signal fire, shortly after which they saw a dozen more stealing upon them through the rocks. It was now their turn to run, and though chased till night, they escaped. Today they surprised a single redskin on foot, who, being cornered and either misunderstanding or refusing all terms, attacked them boldly with bow and arrows, but was of course killed.

August 7th. Grass seems now to have disappeared; stunted willow brush and some water rushes constitute the only mule food tonight, except a few bundles brought along with us from a small patch discovered across the river this morning, which we cut with our knives, after swimming the river. It may at least serve as sauce for the willows.

August 9th. We are now traveling mostly by night, lying by during the day, partly by reason of the intense heat, and partly because it is easier to guard the mules from the Diggers, during daylight. The mirage is visible daily, and knowing its falseness, it is only tiresome and tantalizing. But then as one of the fellows awfully suggests, "Boys you are getting to know too much. Perhaps one of those we passed today was a real lake." This thought, though indignantly repelled, rankles! Tonight we have reached several thousand acres of meadow lying adjacent to the large but shallow pond known as the 'Sink of the Humboldt.' Here this river which we have followed for some 300 miles, sinks into the ground, and an absolute desert, said to be 80 miles across without grass or water, extends to the Salmon Trout or Truckee River, coming down from the Sierra Nevada and also disappearing in this great desert by a sink of its own. This desert cannot be avoided. It must be crossed, and our mules are in poor condition for it, having had little nourishing food for the last 300 miles.

August 10th. We employed today cutting and curing grass, which, though coarse, is all the fodder there is. The mules had a fine rest and filled themselves well with tough grass and water, as well they may, for some, at least, will never see any more. Three Piutes, one of whom spoke some Spanish, came into camp tonight, pretty well used up, having just crossed the desert. They give joyful accounts of the gold diggings, but terrible stories of the desert ahead, where they say numerous wagons are left standing, abandoned by preceding trains. They also say that a fair trail is marked out by dead stock. They however told us of some boiling springs, which if we can find, may be very useful.

August 13th. During the last three eventful days we have successfully passed the most dreaded barrier between the two oceans, the Great Desert. On the 10th we carefully repaired and readjusted everything, filled all the water vessels, filled up wagons with dried grass, and at 3 P.M. rolled out into the waste. After leaving the grass and rushes at the Sink, nothing but bare, arid sandy desert meets the eye as far as it can range. At first a few stunted sage-brushes relieve somewhat the bare expanse, but even they soon disappear, after which the only unusual objects are the occasional white patches of alkali. We cleared the Sink before dark, and got rid of its nasty, fetid exhalations, having traced the Humboldt from its mountain sources through 300 miles of desert only made passable by its stream, to its ignominious end, where the desert finally overcomes and destroys it. The Sink is a pond several hundred yards in diameter with stagnant surface looking as if it had received several coats of lead-colored paint, and with indefinite, shallow, marshy borders, where the water enternally contends for existence with the enveloping sand. No living thing is visible about or near it, except some coarse grass and a few rushes in the shallows.

As night shut down on the cheerless waste, even the mules became depressed and bellowed mournfully along the line. The sand, however, was at first hard, making a good smooth road. At twelve the moon rose in a huge distorted pyramidal shape of greenish red hue, but gradually recovered its proper form and color, and became a cheering aid to our forlorn march. We had determined to halt half an hour every four hours, to rest the mules, wet their mouths, and grease the wheels when necessary. The 12th was intensely hot, with whirling dust columns careering over the desert and with an occasional bed of loose and difficult sand, but at 3 P.M., guided by columns of steam, we found the boiling springs, a curious place where the ground seems hollow under a large space supplying numerous springs, varying from a minute jet of steam to a mass of violently boiling water several yards across. The crust seemed cracked and dangerous, especially as the mules were so crazy to reach the water that one got quite badly scalded. To cool the water, we dug a long ditch, but a bare taste was enough for most. When disguised with coffee we managed to swallow some, and my horse drank a little of the coffee, though he declined the water with decision.

At this delectable place, we took a longer rest than usual, during which we were overtaken by a mule abandoned some miles back. When he fell, his mouth was moistened and a mouthful of hay placed by him, and when he actually realized that he was left absolutely alone in that dismal desert, he made fresh efforts and hobbled after us. The train plodded on all night, resting a short time each four hours. During a few minutes of sleep at one such halt near daylight, my horse and G.'s which were tied together, wandered away in search of water, and when the wagons started G. and I took their trail following it six or seven miles to the south where we found them standing in a barren hollow, exhausted. Leading the horses, we struck out on foot W. N. W. to intercept the train which we overhauled about noon. From this place the view to the west had been for some time limited by a high sandy ridge, above and far beyond which, loomed up the long range of shining white summits of the Sierra Nevada. As we toiled painfully over the brow of the ridge, we suddenly discerned, scarcely six miles distant, nestling gracefully under the base of the giant and long sought range, a long line of cottonwoods, whose waving branches and exhilarating verdure seemed to beckon us onward to the cool waters that we knew bathed their roots. A universal bray of joy from the mules showed that they too understood the joyful apparition, and notwithstanding thirst and fatigue, the few miles were quickly passed, the loose mules taking a running lead. Even the teams broke into a run, and just before dark, in a promiscuous rush, we reached a fine stream four or five feet deep and forty yards wide, of bright, rushing, cold water, fresh from the snow peaks. Every one hurried bodily into the stream and drank all he could, while urging the others to be careful and not drink too much. Fortunately Spanish mules never founder, and after drinking all they could hold, they lay down and rolled in the stream mixing up teams and harness in joyous confusion.

Our luck had all come at once. Although the barren desert continued right down to the water's edge, yet on the far side was a lovely grassy bottom, overhung with such splendid cottonwoods as had not gladdened our eyes for 1000 miles. Among these we immediately camped, and after enjoying for a few minutes the delight of the mules, all hands went to sleep without setting any guard. The march except for the half-hour halts, had been continuous for fifty-two hours and we scarcely touched the ground before we were asleep.

August 14th. No one without some such experience as ours can understand the delight with which we turned out this morning and enjoyed the delicious contrast of our surroundings with the recent stern environments of the Humboldt desert. The mules, yesterday so wretched, fairly laughed with content, their round barrels swelled with their fill of grass and water. Even the unaccustomed and almost forgotten whispering of the breeze among the branches overhead was a novelty and delight, producing a curious apprehension of something about to fall on our heads. After enjoying all these new-found pleasures all the morning, including the hunting down by all hands of a large wolf detected almost inside the camp, we caught up in the afternoon and moved twelve miles up the river, which comes down through a rapidly ascending and narrow valley, requiring constant fording. It soon changes its character to that of a rushing mountain torrent, tearing down a rocky channel and foaming over and through numerous obstructions. We suppose we struck it but a few miles above its sink in Pyramid Lake, and shall now follow it to its source. Indeed the nature of the cañon is such that we can no longer leave it if we would, the rocky precipices on both sides, fast rising into inaccessible mountain walls. Our camp tonight is in a minute valley, filled with fine grass and a delightful red berry, growing in abundant clusters on a bush six to eight feet high, which our boys call 'buffalo cherries.' We used our last sugar tonight, in making a stew of them, which was not a success, the fresh ones being much more agreeable. Bighorn are abundant on the bluffs, and deer in the bottom. We are in a paradise, so far, but an upward glance indicates a squally time for wagons tomorrow.

August 15th. We were compelled to ford the stream constantly, today, each ford becoming more difficult in consequence of the large and slippery boulders which the rushing torrent conceals till the wagons are upon or against them. Bighorn are constantly in sight on all commanding points, seeming deeply interested in our proceedings. G. and I killed two, and also a fine panther, who after being wounded too badly to get away, made a good fight, for such a cowardly beast. We also had a fine rain, the first since leaving the Rocky Mountains, the thunder reverberating grandly among the high mountains around.

August 16th. I came on guard at midnight and had six out of twenty-seven mules turned over to me, the others not being found till near morning. On driving them in, my attention was drawn to a mysterious noise finally traceable to a bunch of brush, which I was afraid to enter alone, for fear of arrows. As it continued, however, and as I was adverse to alarming the sleeping camp, I closed in cautiously, when, instead of an Indian, out bounced a big grey wolf, which I did not fire on for fear of hitting a mule. We still follow the Salmon Trout (or Truckee), much smaller in size, having become a roaring torrent tumbling over lovely cascades of all sorts and dimensions, though sometimes opening out into diminutive mountain glens filled with grass and game, and wide enough to disclose the snowy peaks which now hem us round about. In these valleys the stream is crowded with trout, which are easily caught in willow traps made on the simple plan of the numerous old Indian traps lying about. One fine valley, narrow and steep but several miles long, was covered with splendid grass, full of deer and abounding in old Indian camps. Here we bade farewell to the cottonwoods and struck pine timber growing down to the stream.

August 17th. A pull of two hours brought us to the twenty-seventh and last crossing of the river, now a small though turbulent stream. Leaving it here we took up the mountain side through a rough and rocky, but at first not very steep, ravine. Large pines, firs and cedars abound, especially the first, some of which are fully six feet through. At the head of a fine spring branch we came on a secluded valley teeming with black-tail deer, its mountain sides showing three several bands of bighorn. This is surely a wonderful game country, which is fortunate, as our provisions are about gone. Today we surprised and caught two Indians, both as naked as they were born, and without even arms, which they had probably concealed. These are very different in appearance from the Humboldt Diggers, and remembering their kindness to the Donner party in 1846, we treated them gently and gave them a little of our vanishing hardtack which they swallowed obediently as though it were part of their sentence, or an unpleasant duty to oblige us. When released, a few steps took them into the brush, where they disappeared without a sound, like rabbits, perhaps expecting to be shot from the rear.

August 18th. Last night we came upon a lone wagon with five Baltimore men, one of whom lay in the wagon, shot through the thigh by the Humboldt Diggers. Their train had been disorganized by death, loss of stock, and all sorts of accidents and they were trying to cross the mountain alone, and were delighted to fall in with us. We made a noon halt in another delightful mountain valley, where the black-tail deer almost crowded us. An ominous stench from one of the wagons led us to overhaul it, when we found our only remaining bag of biscuit a mass of rotton green mould, owing to an unnoticed wetting at some of the numerous crossings of the Salmon Trout. This is a very serious fact, as all the flour is gone, and we were depending on this supply to carry us in. Hitherto we have been fairly supplied with game by volunteer hunters, but now we must make a business of it by detailing every evening, a hunting party of three to start after game at daylight before it gets alarmed by our advance. This afternoon a pack-train of forty men passed us, under Lieutenant Pleasanton, who left Fort Smith, Arkansas, March 25th and have come *via* Santa Fé and Fort Bridger, under guide of two mountain men. They have but three days' provisions left, and being unencumbered with wagons, are rushing their mules. Their guides pretend to know these mountains, and say we cannot get our wagons across here, and had better abandon them quick and save the mules. But we have heard that sort of talk before.

August 19th.   Hurrying on today, we came suddenly on the 1846–47 camp of the ill-fated Donner party, where over eighty persons from Illinois were caught in the early snows and mostly starved to death that winter. On the left-hand side of the gorge we are following on a small plateau among heavy timber, stands a large cabin roofed with ox hides, and a considerable quantity of human and cattle bones lying about. This can be nothing else but the relics of the Donners, and here, then, is the place of which we heard in the States, where they were caught and held in September 1846, by the increasing snows. Their cattle all died; they could find no game, or were unable to traverse the snow after it. A small party, that undertook to cross the mountains under guidance of friendly Indians, perished in the snow. The rest all died of starvation, except one man, who in the summer of 1847 was found here living on the bodies of the others, by a relief party that came from California as early as the Sierra became passable, on the report of two Indian guides who alone had got in to tell the tale. We had heard this story in Independence, and here before us was its shocking confirmation. The stumps of trees cut off many feet from the ground, showed the depth of the winter snows which shut them in from all escape or relief; and here lay their bones, just as the mountain wolves had left them.

It was said in Independence, that General Kearney had found two cabins, which he burned with all the bones and remains he could find. But if that be true, he must have found the remains of another detachment or another party, for here was the unmistakable débris of a large ox-train, including remains of ox wagons, old camp kettles, ox hides, etc. Whatever the facts of this ghastly catastrophe, our short supply of provisions gave us no time for investigation, and hurrying by, we left them as we found them. By 10 A.M. we found ourselves at the base of a naked rocky ridge which, in this bad and difficult pass, is the final ascent, the backbone of the Sierra.

For some miles we followed a winding and rocky gorge, over the abrupt ledges of which the wagons had to be lifted and dragged. At the top of this opens out a small but grassy plateau, where a small rivulet flowing out from the melting snow affords plenty of cold, delightful water. Here our hunters awaited us with a goose and a fat deer, and hence a practicable but extremely difficult route up a bare rocky slope as steep as one can well stand on, leads to the summit of the far-famed 'Truckee Pass.' The road being first carefully examined, we took one wagon at a time and loading the contents on the left-hand side to counteract the sidelong declivity toward the right, and attaching all the teams able to draw, we started up with a man at each hind wheel to 'scotch.' But finding the wagon still dangerously inclined to slide off over the right-hand precipice, ropes were attached to the top, and all who were not working at the wheels held it up toward the left, by clambering along the rocky cliff as best they could. In this laborious way, the men doing more effective work than the mules, all the wagons, including Baltimore, were at last got safely to the summit of the pass. This is a deep notch in the mountain barrier, itself wind-swept and free of snow, but with snow peaks towering above it on both sides, and immense masses filling the hollows far below, being the highest spot of the 4000 miles or more of trail which separate the two oceans.

While the mules were resting and being readjusted in the pass, I undertook to reach the summit of a high (not the highest) peak on the right, in which there was no great difficulty till near the top, where it was necessary to 'coon it' on hands and knees up the sharp corner of a mass of naked rock clear of snow. It was bitterly cold, but from the almost pointed summit, the grandeur and wild, confused desolation of the prospect was sublime indeed. North, east and south, peak rose beyond peak in endless succession while in the west the eye looked far down into a chasm where every ravine and gorge shone and glistened with the spotless white of vast snow-fields, and beyond, instead of the expected Sacramento Valley, nothing broke the magnificent expanse of the mountain chains. Thousands of feet down in the chasm—but by no means at the bottom—shone an emerald valley of brightest green, surrounded with snow-fields and intersected by a lovely stream, sparkling from afar on its way through these fastnesses to the golden Sacramento. Probably no human foot had ever before rested on the spot where I stood, but the wind roared and howled, the day was drawing to a close, and, nearly frozen, I hastened down to mark out the beautiful valley below for camp, where I found the train had nearly arrived, but had unfortunately stopped short of it in a worse place.

August 20th. Early this morning we moved on into *my* valley, where we laid by to rest the mules and hunt provisions. Four of us bagged two black-tailed deer, two bighorn, and three geese. Two of the latter I killed with one ball on the loveliest little secluded lake imaginable. This lay in a deep hollow among the eternal hills so that it could only be reached at one spot, and was covered with geese, many of them followed by long trains of goslings. The water was of a deep emerald green, and apparently very deep. The deer here are all single bucks, who leave their families below and seek the high peaks at this season and feed about the edge of the snow, where they get a mass of fat several inches thick about the kidneys, and the meat drips before the fire like fat bacon. With our contented mules browsing around, big pitch pine fires blazing, plenty of meat, and the consciousness that we were across the summit—this was an ideal camp.

August 21st; one hundred and eleventh day out. Knowing we were over the summit, we started in high spirits this morning, expecting a short, easy down-hill road, but were rudely disappointed, finding ourselves involved in a wild labyrinth of mountains and chasms, with no visible way out. The whole day has been employed in the hardest labor, dragging the wagons over rocky ledges, and hoisting and lowering them over 'jump-offs' by 'Spanish windlasses' and other mechanical means. At dark we found ourselves at the top of, and looking down into, a deep, rocky gorge with impassable precipices on either hand. Without knowing what might be at the bottom, we undertook to get the wagons down over the huge boulders which choked the gorge. In lowering the second wagon the rope parted, the wagon flew around and rolled over, bringing up among some small pines many feet below. The entire top was irretrievably demolished, but the important parts seem reparable. The harness is badly broken up, and the wheel mules considerably cut and bruised. The driver saved himself in a somewhat damaged condition, by jumping over the off-mule and alighting in a bunch of chaparral. We had to camp, strung out along the rocky cleft, just as the catastrophe found us, and by the light of some big fires went to work at the repairs. Occasional guns were discharged as a signal to the water hunters who, notwithstanding the ugly precipices and dense darkness, returned after a long absence in no very joyous humor but with water enough for the men and none for the mules, whose only refreshment tonight is the tough and miscellaneous brush growing among the rocks.

August 22nd. With the earliest dawn we recommenced lowering the wagons, finally getting down into a narrow, dark ravine with water which must be the head of some branch of the Yuba. All day has been consumed in getting over another great mountain chain, constantly unloading and in some cases taking apart the wagons and carrying the pieces and contents on our backs. One of the wagons, fortunately the most damaged one, was smashed to pieces and abandoned, its few contents being distributed between the others. On the crest of the mountain we became involved in a chain of lovely, but almost inaccessible, mountain lakes whose deep green waters were the summer home of innumerable geese with long trains of half-grown goslings, which supplied the men well, though the mules have been thirty-six hours without grass.

August 23rd. With W. and J. I started off hunting at daylight, and soon struck a lovely grassy valley a mile long and three or four hundred yards wide. A creek lined with willows and similar brush, ran through the middle. Here we killed a deer, and fastening my horse near it, separated to hunt down the valley, W. and J. taking the west side and I the other, intending that each party should shoot the deer flushed by the other. In this manner we soon killed two more, and snapped at others, the guns missing fire as it was raining smartly, rather a novelty to us by this time. About half-way down the valley, I heard a shot from the other side, followed by a shout and another shot and then loud and exciting yells to me. It was useless to take up the open mountain side where I could be plainly seen by Indians from both sides of the valley, so, running to the central fringe of brush, I waded the creek and cautiously peeped out beyond. The very first thing I saw was W. making his best speed directly toward my position, with a monstrous grizzly a few feet behind and pressing him hard. J. was gallantly following the bear, loading as he ran, and trying to draw off the enemy by shouts. Quickly taking a good tree rest, I fired at about forty yards, hitting the bear, who halted, shook his head, and looked viciously behind, thinking the insult had come from that direction where there was just then certainly the most noise. His hesitation gave us each another good shot, and, in short, after a good deal of yelling and running about by all parties, Bruin succumbed after receiving eight balls, every one of which struck him somewhere. Though we had seen and shot at the smaller grizzlies of the Rocky Mountains, this was the first of either kind that any of us had actually killed and we could hardly admire him enough. He was twice as large as any of our Rocky Mountain acquaintance, and though rather poor in flesh, we could not estimate him at less than 1500 pounds gross.

We made a big fire, notwithstanding the rain, and after putting away several pounds apiece of roast ribs, packed as much of the remainder on my horse as he could carry, and abandoned the deer. My fellow hunters both agree that my first shot came at a critical moment when it looked much more like our bringing up inside the bear than having him inside of us. That shot struck and pierced his lower lip, passing through his big jowl, then came out to, but not through the skin, and following it, entered the breast and actually tore off the point of the heart, after all of which he was still able to carry on the fight for a time. If it had struck even an inch more to the right, it would have been deflected harmlessly from his massive jaw, and W. at least, would have been caught and killed. We found the train camped in a fine little valley with good grass, the men tired out with the continuous work at the wagons.

August 24th. Another hard day's journey with no grass
tonight but what was brought from the last camp, notwithstanding the country teems with all sorts of game which must
find grass somewhere. We have now struck oak timber on the
lower levels mixed with the gigantic pines many of which
have trunks thick enough to conceal at one time the entire
length of a passing wagon. Snow has disappeared except in
the deepest ravines, and in low and damp places many new
varieties of trees, shrubs and plants appear. Among other
new trees is a very curious bush or small tree which is common
on all the hillsides. The trunk and large branches are apparently without bark and are of a bright but dark crimson
color, polished like ivory. They bear an abundance of clusters
of red berries as large as peas, filled with a dry, sweet, white
powder very pleasant to the taste.[8]

August 25th. Being delayed by hunting for stray mules, this
morning we got off late and were brought up at the brink of a
long, precipitous descent which at first seemed like an effectual
bar for wagons in that direction. Nevertheless, it was the
termination of a long leading ridge the whole of which would
have to be retraced to search for a more practicable descent;
so we determined to try it and went to work. Commencing
with my Cincinnati wagon, which is the smallest and best, we
chained the wheels, took out the four lead mules, leaving only
the wheelers, cut and chained to the rear axle as large a tree
as we could handle for a drag, put all hands on the back ropes,
and lowered away. The descent was two miles long, with some
bad turns and 'jump-offs,' but it was at length thus successfully accomplished with both wagons. In climbing up
again to get the loose stock, I hastily pulled my rifle out of a
bush where I had concealed it about half-way up, when it discharged itself in my face, the ball piercing my hat in three
places, giving my hair a smart wrench and scorching both hairs
and eyebrows.

At the bottom of this mountain we found a small branch
running to the left through a narrow but grassy bottom, and the
water being considerably discolored, W. and I took our rifles

[8] Manzanita.

and walked up into the cañon to ascertain the cause. There we found a small camp of overlanders washing successfully for gold. They called the creek 'Greenhorn,' and showed us quite a lot of bright shining, yellow scales such as I had never seen before, but we had no difficulty in recognizing it as the attractive bait that had brought to this distant wildnerness ourselves and the many thousands coming on behind us. The gold bearing gravel is contained and only found in a small 'bar,' rarely more than a few feet wide and not over two feet deep to the solid or bed rock, and is so filled with boulders or detached rounded masses of all dimensions, that the wash-gravel is probably less than a fourth or fifth part of the mass. These men had just arrived and were washing the gravel in flat Indian baskets, and already had plenty of gold in small grains and scales, drying on leaves in the sun. Some of them had gone with the best team in search of provisions, which are not to be had about here, and they do not expect to find any on this side of Sutter's Fort, on the Sacramento, which must be quite a hundred and fifty miles distant. As we are pretty tired of living on meat alone, this is not cheering news, since we cannot eat gold. After hearing the little they had to tell us, we geared up and pushed on over a much better road till 9 P.M. when we hastily camped at a creek-crossing in the dark, on the rough banks of a creek where we had to chock ourselves against trees to prevent rolling into the water.

CHAPTER VI

August 26th, Sunday; one hundred and sixteenth day out.
Our journey is done, and we hardly know what to do with
ourselves, and whether to be glad or sorry. No one took the
trouble to stand guard last night, and as we cannot have much
more use for the mules, we bore with calmness and fortitude
their almost entire deprivation of grass. There will be no
more Indian alarms, no more stampedes, no more pulling,
carrying and hauling at wagons. Notwithstanding ragged
clothes and empty stomachs, we are all in an exhilarant and
joyous mood. The gold is here sure enough, for we have seen
it, and we can raise the color ourselves everywhere, even on
this very creek. Our census counts ten men, twenty-four mules,
three horses and two wagons of our original party and outfit.
On the other hand, we are in rags, almost barefooted, without
provisions and almost without tools, nearly all of which have
been broken to pieces or abandoned. But however sad for
the fate of the poor fellows who fell by the way, we are glad
to have got here at all. This creek is a large, or main branch
of the Greenhorn, which runs into Bear River at a little
distance. Bear River is a tributary of the Yuba, whose waters
it must have been that we have followed down from the high
Sierra. The Yuba empties into the Feather and that into the
Sacramento.

We have been down to see the fifteen or twenty men who are
mining at the mouth of this creek on Bear River, and all are
doing well, making from one to three ounces each, per day,
some even more. We killed two deer, tonight, which postpones
the evil day of actual hunger, but they are less numerous here
than above and are likely to be well hunted by the hungry
emigrants; so gold, or not, we must soon starve or get

118

provisions.   They can only be had here in minute quantities, at the following rates: flour 75 cents, bacon $1.25 and coffee $1.00 per pound; molasses $1.00 a quart, whiskey $2.00 a quart, or fifty cents a drink.   But Sutter's Fort cannot be much over a hundred miles distant, where a town is being started by emigrants who have come 'around the Horn,' called Sacramento City.   It is on the Sacramento at the mouth of the *R. De los Americanos,* and since it is accessible for large ships from the sea, food can no doubt be had there.   But there is no use going after it without money, so the first thing to do is to find a good place and go to work to make a 'raise.'

With the end of that journey, and absorption in the ordinary struggle of life, my diary naturally came to an end.   I have drawn on it at considerable length, scarcely changing the words written so long ago, because however marked by the crudity of youth, it may best serve to convey an appreciative idea of the labor, difficulty and anxiety incident to carrying wagons over that long and scarcely known route at a time when the present methods of travel and transportation had hardly crossed the Alleghenies, and the Mississippi was practically the western limit of agricultural settlement.   Except the worthless deserts between the Wahsatch and the Sierra Nevada—now occupied by the fraudulent State of Nevada, which contains less population than the smallest ward in Philadelphia—the whole of the country thus traversed, is at the present time more or less settled, much of it enclosed and supplied with the conveniences of social and domestic life.   In the part of Kansas where I had such a narrow escape from Pawnees, the country has for years past been closely populated, enclosed and probably well mortgaged.   The solitudes of the Wind River and Big Horn Mountains have long been filled with miners, their works and towns, and partially occupied by the National Park.   Even the dreary deserts of Nevada have yielded millions of wealth from the mines and river-side pastures.   The day will perhaps come when even such a plain statement of ordinary events in traversing those regions, will read like a wild romance to the generation of steady untraveled farmers who will then inhabit them.

Most of the surviving members of our traveling-party proposed to remain and mine together, sending a wagon and
party down to Fort Sutter for supplies. But I, being unsettled
in my projects, preferred to try my fortune alone for the
present. In the division of effects, two mules and a few tools
fell to my share, and stopping only long enough to make pack-
saddles, I packed all my worldly belongings on the former, and,
mounted on the horse which had done such good service, started
down to the nearest considerable mining settlement on Bear
River. Scattered in several camps along this river, were some
fifty men—all just arrived overland like myself—who though
in great want of provisions, were doing well in mining.
Associating myself with two of them (Lovett and Cook) from
Michigan, I turned my stock out to find their own living, and
we went to work to get what knowledge we could of our new
occupation.

Both my new comrades were farmers, the former perhaps
fifty, the latter nearer my own age. Having got out some
clap-boards we soon constructed a 'rocker,' for which the
necessary sheet-iron was obtained by flattening out and
punching holes in an old camp kettle. Lovett dug the material,
I carried it to Cook, who rocked the cradle and ladeled in the
water. Though we constantly peeped into the machine, we
saw little gold, but being determined to have a fair trial, toiled
on all day till the sun, having mounted over one ridge and
glared down into our cañon with scorching heat, had passed
from sight behind the opposite mountain. Food being scarce,
we had few distractions from cooking or other details and
doggedly stuck to our work till dark, when we made a fire
and gathering expectantly round the rocker, emptied its contents into our one remaining tin pan. Cook insisting on his
talent for washing-out, was entrusted with bringing to light
the result of the day's labor. Eagerly we all watched the
lessening contents of the pan as it was whirled about in his
sinewy grasp, till a minute yellow pile revealed itself, worth
about quarter of the value of a day's provisions at prevailing
prices. We could have earned twice as much husking corn at
home. Was it then for this pitiful result we had traversed
mountains and deserts, only to beg our way home by tropic
shores or perish during the coming winter in these inhospitable
mountains?

Silence and gloom was our lot that night, but next day after a scanty breakfast, we put in some more hard work and washed out at night perhaps twice as much of the coy and tantalizing metal. On the third day we set our rocker differently and at night gathered again in desperate silence round Cook, as pan in hand he sought out a quiet pool. Round and round flew the pan with its momentous secret, but as the revolving gravel slowly disappeared, we almost held our breath as a shining, yellow residuum of gold and black sand gradually revealed itself to our doubting eyes. At the gait of a quarter-horse we rushed up to camp, where old Lovett's scales (homemade, with leaden weights) determined the quantity at three or four ounces, worth about twenty-four dollars an ounce, but passing here in currency at sixteen. The fault had evidently been our own, and after all, there was considerable joy in the lonely cañon on that eventful night. Not that we were so very greedy; for us it was not so much a question of wealth as of food—the alternative was, gold or starvation. Now we knew the gold was there, and perceived how much we had been wasting. The next evening revealed a still larger quantity, but there was yet scarcely enough to warrant a journey to the trading-post of Sutter's, although we were now reduced to a game diet, with a few spoonfuls of dried apples from Lovett's store, and were panting to see some one from 'the other side.' It was therefore determined to consume another day in accumulating a more commanding capital with which to start Cook with all our pack animals in search of 'grub.' Our good luck continued and increased, and he soon started with two companions, all the animals and the entire treasury.

About this time, the men of Lovett's train, who had till now remained camped on the main emigrant-trail prospecting through the mountains, concluded to move their camp and join us. Their cattle were accordingly hunted up and driven in, staring with astonishment at the sudden resumption of their labors. Plenty of hands cut out a road down to our bar, which in gratitude for the dried apples, we called 'Lovett's,' and which soon had a population of forty or fifty men. The site was a deep cañon shut in by mountain walls on both sides, with a sloping bar of a few feet width on either bank, from which the overhanging masses shot up apparently to the stars. Overhead a blue streak of sky spanned the chasm, while the larger part of the valley floor was occupied by the rushing river, fresh and sparkling from the neighboring snows. Up and down the curving stream a few hundred yards bounded the prospect, apparently shutting out all the world beyond. Our increasing wealth afforded more time for hunting, the proceeds of which were fairly divided, and though all were constantly and chronically hungry, we were waiting with what resignation we could assume, for Cook's return, when very late one evening, we were all aroused by shots and shouts, and in marched a string of laden mules, with our anxiously expected emissaries. These on their long way to Sutter's had met, not very far below, some trading wagons from that place, which had supplied their most pressing wants and caused an immediate return. Flour, pork, coffee and sugar were the staples, and though the prices were alarming to hungry men, our agents had wisely judged that time was more important to us than money.

Although by the time all was unloaded, distributed and tested it was past midnight, all hands spent the rest of the night in hearing the news, being the first that had reached us since passing the frontier line of Missouri. Though Cook had not been able to obtain a newspaper and had never made any professions as an orator, he had the floor until daylight, and had no reason to complain of the inattention of his audience.

There is little to tell of the month that followed. Two or three times a week it was necessary to herd up our fattening animals, on which occasion I rarely failed to bring in a deer or two. The work was steady and monotonous, but our little pile grew larger from day to day. One prepared breakfast at daylight while the others went to work at 'the hole.' Dinner was managed the same way and when too dark to work, we lit our evening fire and while one cleaned up the day's proceeds, another procured fuel and shook out the blankets, while the third prepared the common supper. All meals alike were of coffee, deer meat or pork, with either fried 'slapjacks' or bread, baked in a frying pan propped up before the fire. The best of water was always at hand, clear and sparkling as its snowy sources.

The work consisted in removing and washing about two feet in thickness from the surface of our bar. Three-fourths or more of the material consisted of rounded boulders of all sizes firmly packed into the auriferous gravel. There was no temptation or means of spending the proceeds, which were kept by the old man in buckskin sacks, in some secret place known only to himself. The drinking and gambling dens which later infested every part of the mines, were yet unknown, as was theft and crime of all sorts. Less careful persons than our old man, left everything unguarded in tents, when they had any, and under a tree when that luxury did not prevail. The general honesty—probably largely due to the richness of the mines—was usually attributed to the prompt and severe punishment always ready for offenders. In the few cases of theft that occurred—mostly of horse-stealing—the committee of miners that sat for court and jury, neither knew nor cared about forms of trial or rules of evidence. Facts were what they wanted, and were accepted from any source. Arrest, trial and punishment rarely occupied more than a few hours. Any mining-camp where the prisoner might be caught or brought, was ready to take jurisdiction. No warrants, indictments or appeals delayed the proceedings. Both parties told their story. Witnesses, if there were any, were quickly heard. The miners were anxious to get back to their work, and the prisoner was not kept long in suspense.

Whether or not the miners' plan of preventing crime by exterminating the criminals, be the best, no other was then practicable. Criminals, deserters, beachcombers and vagabonds soon swarmed from all the shores of the Pacific, and in the absence of any ordinary machinery of justice, it seemed quite just to the honest and industrious, that such exasperating nuisances should be stamped out by the shortest process. At all events the method was not without substantial advantage while it lasted, and it may be worth the while of philosophers to note that novel judicial phenomena need not necessarily fail because worked out by practical men, not much given to speculation on remote consequences.

Be that as it may, the seclusion and monotony of mining-life soon became intolerable to me. Curiosity constantly grew to know what was going on below, and what had become of the shiploads of adventurers who had sailed from eastern cities. Rumors of the rapid transformation of Sutter's old Indian-hold into a bustling city, and of a great seaport growing up at 'the Bay' had even penetrated our secluded cañon, and it was not long after the following adventure, that I decided to abandon our lonely camp in search of a broader world. We had been at work and accumulating its rewards for perhaps a month, when I left camp one morning at daybreak, to herd up the animals as usual. But after searching all accustomed haunts in vain, I at length found myself on their trail, leading north far beyond their usual range. Not expecting such delay, I was without provisions, blanket, or even a coat, and far beyond the limits of our friendly Indian neighbors; but hoping to come upon the truants every moment, I followed their track for twenty miles or more over a rough and apparently unvisited country. Day was beginning to wane when I got sight of an object which, on cautious approach, proved to be a roving mountain man or trapper, named Hunt, who having struck the mules' trail, was following it back for information. He readily agreed to help in my search, and as he had passed many years in wandering over the continent, sometimes in a fur company, and at others as a free trapper, and was careless of his time, he was no mean acquisition.

Night was falling fast as from the top of a lofty ridge we discerned a large meadow, traversed by water and abounding in grass. The animals could surely not have passed such a tempting place, and after getting such a night's rest as the frosty mountain air might permit, we should certainly find them in the morning and hurry them back to camp. But just then Hunt's practiced eye made out a dim column of smoke hardly distinguishable from the evening mists, rising from the far end of the valley, and his instant verdict was, 'Indians.' Should these strangers—probably hostile—find the mules before we did, they would be sure to take their back-trail to find the owners, and if discovered, we were too few to fight, and too far from camp to run. Nevertheless, not being willing yet to abandon the animals, we concluded to gain the edge of the valley, find a suitable place to hide during the night and see what could be done next day. Creeping into a dense thicket in the dark, not without fear of disturbing some prior occupant, we lay down, without fire, supperless, to sleep. Early in the morning we separated in search of food and information. But the season was too late for berries and too early for kamas, and a few of the former was all that rewarded my search. With these I was glad to get back to the friendly shelter of the thicket, where Hunt soon joined me with part of a deer that came so temptingly in his way in a distant side valley, that he could not help risking our scalps by a shot. The grass of the valley being very high, it both facilitated our search, and contributed to our safety, and toward mid-day we came upon a fine creek, full of trout. These seemed beyond our reach as we had no fishing tackle and there was no suitable willow for making a fish basket. The old mountaineer, however solved that difficulty by making one of grass, which soon produced more than we could comfortably carry.

Not long after, we found the mules and not liking such a dangerous vicinity, abandoned the rest of our deer and laid a straight course over the mountains for Bear River camp. Riding hard (bareback) till long after dark, we made a fire in a deep cañon, secured the mules, cooked some supper, and betook ourselves to sleep. Next day we reached camp before dark, and described to eager listeners our creek—then and there christened Deer Creek—with the promising appearance of its vicinity, not forgetting Hunt's interview with a grizzly, during the afternoon. He was riding some yards in advance of me, both of us descending across a precipitous ravine, when as he approached the bottom, his mule snorted and wheeled suddenly throwing him over its head—he having neither saddle nor bridle—into the little rivulet at the bottom, which was well-concealed by thick brush. Simultaneously, and from the same spot arose a formidable grizzly, which, frightend out of its wits at the sudden assault, dashed up the opposite mountain, leaving the terrified mule crowding up to me for protection, and Hunt lying in the creek, not knowing exactly what had happened. Being above the scrimmage, I had a good view of the whole, and have never yet been able to decide which was the most astonished—the bear, the mule, or the man.

I never afterwards returned to Deer Creek, but Hunt soon after found an old comrade of his, Captain Sears by name, who was mining some miles below us with a number of tame American River Indians; he conducted over there the entire party, where, on the banks of Deer Creek and Gold Run— as they have ever since been called—they struck some of the richest and most famous diggings ever known in California; here soon after was started the flourishing city of Nevada, which is yet, as I am told, a populous and wealthy town, distinguished for its successful quartz mills.

Some time in the early part of October, my finances having been satisfactorily reinforced, I saddled up and pulled out for the 'Fort,' as Sutter's was then called, but on coming out of the mountains at Gillespie's (or Hoyt's) ranch, I found one Yeldell, a Missourian, engaged in herding emigrant cattle on Lower Bear River in the Sacramento Valley and could not resist his invitation to stop a few days to hunt wild cattle, the emigrant theory being that unbranded cattle were public property, or at least lawful prize. Here I was not long in learning something new, and in some respects more exciting than grizzly or buffalo hunting. Y.'s object was to shoot fat yearlings for jerked beef for winter provisions, but while stalking a small band of cattle for this purpose on foot, an old bull assuming the responsibility for his numerous family, chose to get insulted, and commenced to approach us, bellowing and lashing his tail with every indication of war. He came deliberately, but with such unhesitating directness that even a greenhorn could entertain no doubt of his firm intention to have what in California is termed a 'difficulty.' Y.'s weapon was a 32 calibre cavalry carbine, but my trusty rifle had recently been lost by lending it to a rascal who liked it so well that he ran away with it, so that my only firearms were the two old single-barrelled pistols, which though from their calibre very effective in case of a hit, were only reliable at close quarters.

As there was no tree or bush in sight, and not even a gully or arroyo to hide in, I began to feel nervous. "Shall we run?" said I; "he is coming for us." "Run? no; that bull will chase ye five mile. Did ye never hunt wild cattle afore?" When

I acknowledged the negative, said he, "Well, what a d—d fool to come out and hunt cattle, the fightingest animile they is, when ye don't know nothing about it. Well, you take this carbine and I'll get along with the pistols. You get in line behind me and jump when I do, and not any sooner or you will get us both killed." The arrangement was soon made, but further explanation of intentions was cut short by the bull, who was by this time at no great distance, increasing his gait, lashing his tail, and tossing his head with vicious bellows. Soon he broke into a run, Y. standing fast till in another second it would have been all over with him. But when the bull, not five yards distant, lowered his head for the last deadly rush, Y. stepped quickly but quietly to one side and as the infuriated animal rushed by, placed a single one-ounce pistol ball behind his shoulder at arm's length. It was enough for the bull, who belched out a cataract of blood and came headlong to the ground. The facts when understood are simple enough. When the bull has made his final calculation and commences his last desperate rush, he shuts his eyes. If one steps aside after that, he is safe, but if even a second too soon he is lost, for the bull can still rectify his direction, and it is too late for further maneuvering. "Now, young feller," said Y., "that is the way how a white man kills a bull. Any sneakin' Spaniard or Injun can rope a bull and let his horse throw him but this is the way for a man what ain't afraid."

The wild bull—that is, the one who has never been herded up, rounded in, lassoed or branded—is, I think, the noblest game in America, with possibly the single exception of the large, or California, grizzly. He knows no fear, and shrinks from no enemy, having been accustomed all his life to fighting his rivals and other formidable wild animals, and when surrounded by his family is always spoiling for a fight. He will come a mile for his enemy, and will as lief charge a hundred men as one. To kill him in the manner described, involves no special skill or difficult pursuit, but it requires the highest quality of a virtue not too common even among brave men—cool, dauntless presence of mind. At that time thousands of cattle, many of which had never seen a human form, had wandered far from the few and widely separated ranches, and roamed through the foothills and the secluded valleys they enclose, pasturing by day far out in the great plains of the Sacramento and retiring to the hills at night; but as all that territory has long since been settled and enclosed, cattle really wild, are, I presume, long since extinct within the limits of the United States.

Knowing from recent experience, the scarcity of beef in the mining districts, and understanding that the settlements on the upper American were more populous than those I had last come from, I purchased here a few head of branded but half wild cattle, and leaving my animals with Y., started on foot to drive the cattle to Auburn on the American, a couple of Indian vaqueros undertaking to assist in getting them fairly into the mountains, after which I thought I could manage them alone. In order to get them well tired and docile, my vaqueros ran them fully forty miles the first day, giving me an occasional lift behind them, and helped watch them through the night, but as soon as they left me in the morning, notwithstanding we were now well in among the foothills, my troubles began. The animals were frantically determined to get back to their accustomed pastures on the plain, and kept me on the jump to prevent it through the entire day, when fortunately the people of an arriving emigrant train helped me make a small corral in which they were shut up for the night.

The next day, by running my refractory charges hard all day and giving them no time to concert mischief, I got them at last to Auburn, where I borrowed a rifle and having with the aid of numerous volunteers just then quitting their work on the bar, got them into a suitable place, shot them all, hiring some miners to hang, skin and butcher them during the night. By noon of the next day I had sold out at a handsome profit, and spent the night with two brothers named Thomas, from New York, whom though I had never seen before, I knew of, and was collaterally connected with, and accidently discovered here working on a claim. I have never seen them since that chance meeting. One later became district attorney of the same vicinity and was soon after killed in a duel, and the other after some moderate success returned to New York, where he became a successful broker. The following morning at day-light with as much of golddust as I could conveniently carry in the pockets of my scanty apparel, I started on foot for my animals at Y.'s. After I had walked some forty miles and it was getting dark enough to look for a camping-place, safe from the numerous robbers who, notwithstanding the prompt vigilance of 'miners' juries,' already infested that part of the country, I left the beaten wagon-trail and turned into a small narrow valley, when before I had left the road fifty yards I found myself face to face with three large grizzlies, who quietly sniffed and eyed me, as much as to say, "Why don't you keep to the road? What do you want here?"

It was fast getting dark and my only firearms were two single-barrelled pistols. It was evidently only a question of how to retire most gracefully. The narrow valley was bare of shelter, and the smallest of the great pines on the mountain-side was several feet too large to climb. I thankfully solved the etiquette of the occasion by backing slowly out to the road, and soon as I got timber between us, taking to my heels, the bears continuing while in sight, to gaze intently at the impertinent intruder with some suspicious sniffing but no other active sign of displeasure. From later experience I should say it was probably a family party of a she-bear and her grown cubs, which in that country where their subsistence is so abundant, often remain with their mother till they are several years old and larger than the parent. After this rencontre, I swung along down the road but had not gone far, when, it getting to be pretty dark, I suddenly met another bear squarely in the wagon road, but having the wind of him saw him first and took up the mountain out of his way. Now I was well aware of and keenly looking out for the danger of being followed by robbers, who had seen at Auburn what I carried, and whose usual method is to shoot from ambush, giving a man no chance; but I was by no means counting on so much bear, so I camped on the mountain, then and there, well content to dispense with both fire and water, under the circumstances. Next morning the thick red dust in the road was absolutely full of bear tracks, looking much like that of an immense widened negro foot; but I arrived at Y.'s in due course and after indulging with him in a little more wild calf hunting, quieting the bull's objections in the same way—which is really easy enough when once well learned—I started for Sutter's across the wide Sacramento plains.

Fording the American a short distance above its mouth, and leaving the Fort on the left, I advanced a couple of miles to the Sacramento through a miscellaneous collection of abandoned tents and wagons, in many of which men lay dying and dead, just as their friends had abandoned them! Those yet alive were mostly suffering from dysenteric complaints and were in every form of extremity, but mostly unconscious and moribund. I looked into a number of tents and gave some trifling aid, but many occupants were dead, others speechless and dying in filth, solitude, thirst and misery, so that I was glad to get away to the lively camp at the river already called Sacramento City. It was then but a camp of tents and wagons disposed in two long rows called 'H' and 'J' streets, interspersed with an occasional shanty of muslin stretched on poles. Several large vessels lay tied up at the banks, having brought emigrants 'around the Horn,' and were a delightful feature to one so long buried in the far interior. In the confusion and excitement of this unique crowd, where for the first time in their lives the drawling butternut-colored backwoodsman of the West, knocked against the keen Yankees arriving from an opposite direction, I passed a few days, during which I sold my mules and had my horse stolen, lying at night in my only blanket, pistols in hand, concealed in a gully or arroyo at some distance on the plain.

Here I soon became acquainted with one Moore, a man scarcely over forty, though an old Missouri River steamboat captain, and made camp with him beyond the American, where he possessed a couple of wagons and twelve or fourteen yolk of good cattle, and with whom were eight young fellows who had come with him from Missouri, they providing their own food and arms and he finding the teams and other necessaries for the journey. M. had come in later on our trail, and stopping on the main branch of the Greenhorn, had drained a deep natural hole in its bed, and from a small space at the bottom, not larger than a small dinner table, had taken $40,000, over which one of his faithful 'pikers' now stood guard by day and night. I was not long in acquiring a great liking for this party, and added my own smaller pile to the 'bank' which was all M.'s property, his young men having preferred to work for him on the wages of five dollars a day, certain, and double that 'if he got anything.' There was considerable chagrin at the way the bargain had turned out and being a jovial lot they were never done chaffing each other about it, but not being covetous or greedy, they expended their jokes on each other and looked up to M. with a faith and admiration that knew no bounds. And in fact he well deserved it. Taking up a spot which a more numerous party, after vainly working at for several weeks had abandoned as impossible to clear of water, he had in three weeks, almost without tools, and with little provisions but the proceeds of each morning's hunt, built a dam, constructed two flumes along the vertical rock walls of the cañon, made two pumps operated by flutter wheels in the flumes, and had pumped out an irregular crevice some forty feet in depth, and secured the above reward for his ingenuity and good luck, for it must be admitted that such opportunities were not numerous even then. After a few days' acquaintance and mutual confidences, M. confided to me his wish to build a sawmill somewhere adjacent to the mining-camps above, where lumber was worth a dollar a foot, with great demand and no supply. His men, willing to be settled for the winter, had agreed to work for him at five dollars per day, and his present business was to find the necessary mill-irons. He knew nothing about sawmills, but had a general idea he could make one work, while on the contrary, from my experience in handling slabs and logs in the Pennsylvania backwoods in 1846–47, I felt confident I could contribute some special though superficial knowledge to the project. I therefore promptly accepted his proposition to put my capital and efforts into the enterprise, proposing Bear River as the site, and we forthwith entered upon a regular search for mill-irons.

The arriving vessels had disgorged masses of machinery, comprising all sorts of gold-washing contrivances, which in the wild and frantic rush to the mines, had been abandoned on the banks for want of transportation, and most of which were entirely useless for the original or any other purpose. This trash, which seemed to include nearly everything except what we wanted, lay in piles along the river, and although it contained nothing designed for such purposes as ours, we at length discovered a thirteen-inch crank which was the most essential, for possessed of that it was possible to make all the other parts of wood. As some fancy price would have been demanded for this article had we disclosed our necessities, I opened negotiations for the entire pile of iron 'to start a blacksmith shop'—which indeed was a necessary part of our design, and purchased it for one hundred ounces, equivalent to $1600, as golddust was then rated, which was but little over two-thirds its bullion value. We carried off the crank, part of a rag-wheel, some gudgeons, and other small articles which might be of use, abandoning all the rest of the heap, greatly to the vendor's surprise, as there was considerable wrought iron among it, quite suitable for a blacksmith's use. We lost no time in loading the wagons with provisions for six months, axes, saws, a grindstone and other tools, and I took the opportunity of obtaining from an emigrant an excellent small bore rifle.

It must have been on one of the first days of November that we pulled out from Sacramento, pushed through the terrible Golgotha that lay between the rivers, forded the American, and camped a few miles beyond in a fine grove of live-oaks. On that very night commenced the rains of that unusually inclement season, which is still remembered as the worst for rains, floods and inundations, in all California annals. It rained all night and the next day, and though it showed no signs of abating, the ground was already so soft, and the sloughs so full, that we were glad to get our stuff back to the river with much difficulty, by dividing up our loads and making several trips, camping on the highest ground to be found on the banks of the American, which was already impassable by ford. Knowing little then of the climate with its protracted droughts and long-continued rains, we waited several days, but as the rain kept on, streams and sloughs overflowed, and the entire valley seemed likely to become inundated—as in fact it did— it was plain we must find some other way of transporting our effects to the mountains.

After considerable reflection and discussion, we therefore went to work, hewed out planks and built a scow, eight by forty feet, on which we loaded the goods, starting off three good men with the stock and empty wagons to pick their way along the banks of the streams—which being highest, are usually the last ground to be overflowed—and meet us where Bear River debouches from the mountains, and hard ground might be looked for. The rest of us, after considerably increasing our outfit of provisions, made oars from the best material we could find, and a large square sail from the wagon covers, and undertook to navigate the Sacramento, Feather and Bear Rivers to the same vicinity.

Dropping down the rushing turbid current of the American, though rather exciting, offered little difficulty, but when we swung out into what had now become the sweeping torrent of the Sacramento, the progress up stream was slow, laborious and dangerous, especially in consequence of the large quantity of driftwood. The rain seemed almost incessant, and it was only occasionally that the prevailing high winds gave us an auxiliary push against the rushing current of the swollen river. I remember that on one occasion after toiling all day with oar and pole, we were not out of sight, across a point, of our last camp. Immense tracts of the level valley were under water, in many places almost as far as the eye could range, and but for the fringe of trees along the immediate river banks, a narrow strip of which was mostly free from water, we might have missed our way altogether, and found ourselves far out in the middle of the wide valley. Large numbers of elk, with an occasional deer and coyote, driven from the tule beds, were frequently seen and killed along the margin of the river proper, and several deer were seen swimming the river, in search of

> Some safer world in depth of woods embraced;
> Some happier island in the watery waste.

The instinct of the deer, though sufficient to remind him of his great hunger and discomfort where he was, apparently failed to inform him that the other side was no better, and accordingly there was about an equal number crossing in each direction.

Finally, after many days of exposure and hard work, rowing, poling, cordelling and warping from the banks, we at last arrived with the scow and its seven tons of lading at a place on Bear River where long and dangerous rapids, obstructed by rocks and logs and overhung by the low branches of trees, seemed to forbid all further navigation even at the present high stage of water. Here therefore the boat was unloaded, the cargo carried piece by piece to a dry knoll not far distant, where it was compactly piled on logs cut for the purpose, and covered with the sail, well secured from animals by heavy logs. From here M. and the men started on foot to make connections with the wagons, while I took the empty boat down alone, and in two days with the steering oar alone, covered the route which up stream had cost us so many days of hard labor, landing the boat safely at Sacramento, where I had no difficulty in disposing of it for $420, to be used somewhere up river as a ferry boat. After making up for lost sleep by a long bear's nap at Sacramento, and devoting several days to the exposing and laborious journey back, which was mostly made by wading along the tree-covered river banks, tumbling into and swimming the concealed sloughs and so forth, I rejoined M. at the provision depot. He had found the wagons, but it was impossible to get them to the provision camp. He had therefore placed them in corral at the foot of the mountains, about twenty miles distant, setting the men to work making pack-saddles, with instructions, when finished, to bring the cattle down with yokes and chains without wagons, on the first fine day. After witnessing my safe return, M. started back to the wagon camp, and the weather settling in bad again, I remained solitary for a week or two, surrounded by water, though with plenty of wood and all the ducks I chose to shoot, but for the most part seeing no other living thing.

Yet even in this lonely situation a rencontre occurred which shows how narrow is the world we live in. About dusk one evening, a mounted man, endeavoring to get down from the mines to Scramento by following the comparatively high and tree-marked banks of streams, stopped at my camp, got some supper and passed on without recognition. Shortly after, hearing shouts, I ran down through the shoal water to a deep slough I knew of, into which his horse had wandered and was swimming about at random in the darkness, with a good chance for final exhaustion and drowning. Aided by my voice, horse and man found their way out. I insisted that he remain with me till daylight should make traveling safer. We therefore lit our pipes, and in the leisurely conversation which ensued, it appeared that my guest, though considerably older than myself, had been born in the same block of the same street, had attended the same church or 'meeting' and gone to the same school. I never met him before nor since, and have no knowledge what became of him afterward, but surely the accidental interview during a single night in that solitary place, may be set down among the most remarkable of coincidences.[9]

After my long and tiresome vigil, I was not sorry one fine morning to see our whole party come splashing into camp with all the horses, and the best-behaved oxen. M.'s plan was to pack them quickly and return immediately, taking advantage of every good day to make a round trip, the bad weather being likely to give plenty of time for resting between trips. The quiet oxen were to be packed on saddles, the others were to be yoked and were expected to carry from 150 to 200 pounds on the yoke. In the course of time we thus got all our stuff to firm ground where the wagons could receive it, the crank being carried by four men on a stretcher or hand-barrow.

One could hardly go astray for a water power on upper Bear River, and an excellent one promising a maximum of power with a minimum of preparation, was soon found. Here a block-house was constructed commanding a corral (also solidly built of logs) and access to water which could not be cut off. Here we settled down to the winter's work, cutting, squaring and fitting timbers for dam and mill and preparing the wooden machinery of the latter from oak wood seasoned in the large log chimney, the cogs being boiled in the camp kettle for the same purpose; but this being only deep enough to hold one end

[9] This was John Elliot, Jr., a stepson of Thomas Shipley and half-brother to Samuel R. Shipley, now President of the Provident Life and Trust Company of Philadelphia.

at a time, we took turns in watching and turning them through the night. The cattle being required for work most of the day, had to be driven daily at 2 A.M. to the top of a lofty grassy plateau two or three miles distant for pasture returning to work at breakfast time, and fastened up safely in the corral at evening. Though such relations as we had with the neighboring Indians were professedly friendly, driving the cattle to pasture alone by night was not a job that any one hankered after, and therefore it fell to me. I always got them on the grass before daylight, concealing myself till ready to return, so that the danger lay principally in traveling to and fro, especially as over part of the route but one track was available.

Nearly all wild animals, where undisturbed, seem to be active just before and after the break of day. It is then the deer feeds, plays, and makes love; bears of all kinds are digging for roots or hunting mast; wolves, coyotes, foxes and other small predaceous animals are returning from their nightly prowlings, and if they are bachelors without families at home, seeking safe places of concealment for the coming day. Though afraid to fire a gun so far from camp, I had many interesting hours in watching the various habits, pursuits and gambols of such denizens of the forest, the more so perhaps that I was not covetous of spoil. By means of judicious ambush I often found myself in the very midst of a small family of the polygamous deer, with opportunity of observing unseen their most unstudied frolics and domestic discipline, and the bear's method of hunting his breakfast became almost as familiar as my own.

At last, as the long mountain winter began to draw to a close, our dam and water-wheel were completed, material for the mill was being set up, machinery ready to put in place, a large supply of saw logs cut and hauled, and we were beginning to look for speedy results of our labors, not having seen a white man in the vicinity, when we were surprised by a visit from an American ranchero accompanied by a lot of his Spanish and halfbreed vaqueros, who claimed ownership, by a Mexican twenty-league grant, of the ranch at the debouch of the river into the plains twenty miles below, on the limits of which he pretended we were trespassing. I have since had reason to believe the main facts he alleged were true except as to limits. Such a grant made in an unexplored territory with reference to some one point on a river or a mountain, and without any specified boundaries, had not, and could not have, any limits till these were fixed years afterwards by the Surveyor-General of the United States under the treaty of 1847. Till such adjustment, of course, a claimant could claim any limit he pleased, but there never was any pretense that until judicial ajudication of his title, and official adjustment of his boundary line, he had any right whatever sufficiently definite to maintain ejectment.

But at that time we knew little of the facts, and nothing of the law or treaty, and laughed at the 'cheek' of our visitors, till getting tired of them, we ordered them away, inviting them to come up and put us off whenever they felt ready to begin. It was not many days after, till taking us at our word, some fifteen or twenty vaqueros, led by one or two Americans, suddenly descended from the hills in the rear, shouting and firing, but a timely alarm having been given, we quickly had force enough at the house to hold them, while our men working at a distance slipped in by routes inaccessible for horses. When our force was complete, as the enemy, notwithstanding their noise and wild shooting, did not seem inclined to assault the cabin, we all sallied forth and opened fire from rocks, trees and stumps, and whipped them with ease in a few minutes. We then let them recover their wounded and retire, warning them that if we had lost a single man we would have caught and hung the entire gang.

A considerable time elapsed, during which we heard no more of them and had almost ceased to think of the affair, when another stranger appeared of very different character but on the same errand. This was Captain D. of the U. S. Army, who showed an order from General Riley, Military Governor of California, with headquarters at Monterey, requiring him to remove all squatters—and especially us—from Gillespie's Ranch, in accordance with the treaty of Guadaloupe Hidalgo between Mexico and the United States, and informed us that he had some forty soldiers on the other side of the river with a howitzer, brought up for the purpose. This was, of course, a high-handed and wholly illegal proceeding, neither the grant in question nor any other Mexican grant having yet been adjudicated or surveyed, nor had any machinery or tribunal been yet organized with special jurisdiction for executing the details of the treaty. No civil law or government existed in the territory, nor even a court, other than the old Mexican alcaldes of the most limited and local jurisdiction. There was not even an alcalde existing within several hundred miles, and we had never so much as heard the name of General Riley. Nevertheless, military law is the will of the commanding officer, and there stood his representative with the means of blowing us all to kingdom come, without loss to himself, unless with ten men we could take the gun from a force four times superior in number, in a position of their own choosing. The Captain was sympathetic and kind, and deeply regretted his orders, especially when he learned how we had made good our claim by administering a good licking to his clients, which immensely delighted him and all his party. But he must execute his orders. He would give us any reasonable time for decision, in fact did not like enforcing Mexican claims against Americans, anyhow. But he had no option in the matter; orders must be obeyed. After much discussion, I personally became convinced that law or no law, we were to be put off summarily and were in presence of a force amply sufficient for the purpose, upon which we could inflict little or no injury. Our men were willing to stand by us, but what good would it do us to pick off a few poor devils of soldiers, who, would much rather fight with than against us, and then have our place shelled and destroyed about our ears?

All the money I had was in the enterprise, but it could not be recovered by fighting; even if momentarily successful. It seemed an infamous thing that these wild mountainsides, inhabited only by semi-hostile Indians, with only one house between us and Sutter's Fort, a hundred miles distant, and where we had never seen a white face, should thus be adjudged without a hearing to a hostile claimant, by a distant general who had never seen, and knew nothing about, either the property or the 'squatters.' M. was undecided, and I did not like to seem to desert him, but being myself convinced that nothing—not even satisfaction—was to be got by fighting the soldiers, I offered to sell out to him all my rights in the premises for his American mare—brought from Missouri and now in fine condition—and a pair of blankets. The proposition was accepted, and next morning at daybreak I departed for Sacramento, leaving M. as sole owner, to settle with the Captain as best he could.

Before going on with my personal narrative, I will here state the issue of the saw-mill contest as afterwards learned from other parties, since I never again saw any of those concerned. Though M. was a professed 'fighting man,' he had plenty of cool sense at bottom, and becoming convinced in due time that he could not fight the United States, he gave in and surrendered. Keeping his party together, he conducted it to Grass Valley (Nevada City) where he made quite a fortune by the successful construction and management of a 'ditch' or conduit to supply water at the proper level for miners' use. But he or some other interested person must have kept a watchful eye on the saw-mill property, for during the following summer when it was in successful operation producing lumber with a ready sale at $300 to $400 per thousand, when everything was baked dry with the summer heats, it was set on fire one night and everything about the premises destroyed. By whom the deed was done, was never ascertained with certainty, but I never heard that the public lay awake much at night guessing about it.

For myself, I took leave of my companions in the early morning, poorer than the day I crossed the Sierra, and giving Gillespie's a wide berth, kept on down the valley hugging the river banks closely, as the entire central part of the great valley was at this time a boundless lake. Reaching the Sacramento at the mouth of the Feather I found established a ferry scow operated on a rope suspended across the former river, which it was necessary to cross, a large part of the eastern bank being entirely under water. I therefore rode down into the scow and asked to be set across. The ferryman seemed to make needless delay which I scarcely noticed at first, till a man ran out of the ferryman's cabin, some hundred yards back from the bank, and ordered me to bring up 'that stolen horse.' Then

I understood the game, and drawing my rifle, ordered the boatman to cast off and be quick. The man on the bank seeing I was not going to be a docile prey, ran back to the house from which he soon emerged again with two others all carrying guns. But by this time the current had caught the boat and was rushing it across at a rapid rate, and I faithfully promised the boatman to 'save' him first if any delay or an accident happened to the boat. Seeing the fellows on the bank, though they had made a little miscalculation, meant business, I laid down at the far end of the boat, where I had the boatman securely in front of me, took a good solid elbow rest and fired. The nearest rascal dropped his gun, which went off in the air, clapped both hands to his breast, and staggered back to his friends, one of whom retired with him, while the other took a long shot at me which passed close but missed.

By this time I was reloaded, but refrained from firing, partly because I judged the increasing distance too great, and partly because I desired at the proper time to settle accounts with my friend in the boat. As soon therefore as we touched the landing, I ordered my man forward among some trees growing on the bank and followed close with the mare. He soon showed that he was himself unarmed, and averred that the others were robbers who had taken possession of his house against his will, and that this was their first attempt. Partially accepting his story, I ordered him to get into the boat and cut both slings, which would have sent him and it flying down the river. But he protested his innocence and begged so hard, that on his solemn promise to remain where he was for one full hour, I cut one sling only, and threw it in the river, thinking it would occupy him most of that time to make the necessary repairs.

Though not long afterwards I was again at this place—as presently to be related—all the parties had departed and I never heard anything more of them. One fellow certainly learned a good lesson, but I have ever since been in doubt whether—considering the murderous character of that class of wretches—full justice was done to the boatman. I quickly mounted my mare which had behaved with the most lady-like propriety—interested in but not scared at the shooting—and took my way as rapidly as possible down the river. The high water and far extended inundation in the tule, reaching apparently to near the foot of the Coast Range, confined the passage to a narrow strip of bank mostly but not everywhere free from water, and fairly well marked out by the marginal trees. It was intersected by many deep and some wide sloughs, the wading and swimming of which kept me soaked from head to foot, but I found a dry place to camp. In the evening of the following day I reached Sacramento and was soon ferried across to the new town.

CHAPTER VII

FROM SAN FRANCISCO BY SEA TO PANAMA

Sacramento had already grown almost out of my recollection, and a much more orderly condition of affairs prevailed. The streets had been leveled and the stumps cut out, the dead cattle had been covered up or removed from the big hole which had formerly occupied most of J street, in the center of the place, and even a theatre had been started on the bank near the mouth of the big slough, in a canvas structure composed of the sails of abandoned vessels. Large embankments had been constructed to keep out the water which stood higher than the streets. I even found a safe corral with plenty of hay, in which I deposited my mare in place of picketing her out in a back street, and had the privilege of sheltering myself in the stableman's tent. In the evening I visited the theatre, being the first similar place of amusement I ever attended so far as I remember. The stage, curtains and seats were rude affairs, with candles for light, and for floor the muddy ground.

Next morning, American horses being in demand for harness, and commanding many times the price of the natives, I sold my mare at a high price and promptly converted the proceeds into a half share in a whaleboat, which we lost no time in loading with provisions and started for Nye's Ranch, now known as Marysville, the head of navigation on Feather River.

My new partner was an Irish sailor, a good, honest, hard-working young fellow, as long as the atmosphere was free from whiskey. The mysterious promptness with which his cherished bottles vanished from the places in which they had been carefully stowed, filled him with amazement, as it never for an instant occurred to him that anyone could be so lost to all sense of comfort and pleasure as wilfully to throw them overboard. At the mouth of Feather River I proposed that

142

we should land and clean out the gang of robbers, through whose hands I had slipped a few days previously. This he was willing enough for, but as we were having a tough job working up against the swollen current, proposed we should defer it till our return with an empty boat and favorable stream. At Nye's we quickly sold out to the mule packers engaged in supplying the miners in the mountains, and started down with no work to do but steer. We landed at the ferry, on hostile thoughts intent, approaching the shanty from the rear, but to my disgust found a new ferryman, the old gang who had attacked me having cleared out.

We made several trips from Sacramento to Nyes, doubling our capital on each occasion, but as "Man never is, but always to be blessed," I soon got tired of the monotony, and could not be content without getting back to the mountains. So, finding an opportunity to sell out to good advantage, I purchased pack mules, and loaded them at Nye's for the upper bars of the Yuba. To these I made a number of successful trips, increasing my number of mules, and hiring the necessary labor to help, and had I possessed a more moderate ambition, or been in less 'haste to be rich,' might have avoided much loss and travail of body and mind. All travel above Foster's Bar, having been cut off by heavy snows, numerous exciting rumors prevailed of the starving condition of the successful miners who were shut in above with plenty of gold but no food. Having my mules in good condition, at this time I conceived the idea that by selecting ten of the best and loading them with half the usual weight, the forty miles of deep snow which had for some time past barred all communication between Foster's and Goodyear's, could be traversed. Accordingly my partner, an Indiana man, and I prepared a small train and we both started with it ourselves, leaving our Mexicans in charge of the remaining mules to recruit in the valley. There is—or was then—but one practicable mule trail between the places named. Crossing the river at Foster's it immediately ascends a long and steep spur about ten miles to the top of the dividing ridge, which it keeps for over twenty miles, most of which is along a narrow knife edge and then by a bad and rough descent of six or eight miles comes down to Goodyear's Bar at the Fork of the North Fork of the Yuba.

Swimming the mules across at Foster's the night before and giving them two good feeds of barley, we started up the ridge at daybreak with the intention of getting through in one day if possible. With picked mules and half loads there was little difficulty in getting up the ridge, notwithstanding there was then some snow even down on the bar, which of course augmented in quantity as we increased our altitude. But on the summit, untraversed for some weeks past, the snow lay deep and unbroken and in many places was too soft to bear animals. The narrow ridge was frequently intercepted by fallen trees, which were difficult to get over or around, the adjacent snow being kept soft by radiation of heat from the wood. Hence the labor of filling holes with snow, and of unloading and loading mules was almost continuous, and it was getting dark when we arrived, wet and weary, at the top of the long and rough descent to Goodyear's. Another storm had come on, fresh snow was falling, and a freezing tempest swept across the narrow ridge. The descent, hard for loaded mules at any time, was not to be thought of in a dark and tempestous night, with the rocks and brush covered and concealed by masses of fresh snow. Though doubtful whether ourselves or the mules could endure till morning where we were, there was no admissible alternative but to try it. Unpacking the mules with half-frozen fingers, we secured them by twos and threes in the most sheltered places accessible, fed them with flour, and ate some raw bacon ourselves after vainly trying to make a fire.

There could be little moving about for us, and none for the animals, as the drifting snow rapidly covered the brush, leaving dangerous hollow traps underneath. Finding the mules disposed to lie down as it grew colder, we were obliged to alternate through most of the night between whipping them up, and jumping about ourselves to keep from freezing. When morning dawned at last, three mules were dead and the packs, covered deep with snow, could only be found by prodding for them with sticks. Only eight complete packs and saddles could be found, and packing them on the seven surviving mules, we at last effected the descent by following closely the edge of the ridge, all traces of the trail having been deeply covered.

It is said, and I have no doubt that snow lay full thirty feet deep on the divide during that memorable winter, and probably twice as deep in the hollows. During the ensuing summer dead mules abounded along the trail, hanging in the trees overhead where they had lodged as the snow disappeared. There were several score of starving men at Goodyear's and points above, who having plenty of gold, took our entire lading at four dollars a pound before it was off the mules' backs. Though there was little snow down on the river, there was no food whatever for mules, and as there was no possible way to get them out except by the same route, it was necessary to abandon them or return at once. The trouble was to get them up the mountain, where the trail was obliterated and the rocks and obstacles so concealed as to make it very dangerous for animals and by no means easy for men. The unfortunate mules, after getting a scanty feed of flour, had the aid of a lot of miners in getting up on the ridge where we camped that night, and on the next evening after an exhausting day's journey through snow not yet packed, reached Foster's Bar, and next morning hurried on down to grass.

That trip though successful itself to a certain extent, had a sequel. A number of packers had accumulated below Foster's detained by the snow above, but ready to rush their loads in at the earliest opportunity. I frankly gave the prices I had obtained, with the equally frank opinion that the trail was for the present effectually blocked. Thinking quite naturally, that we were hurrying down to return quickly with another load, many of them hurried in their trains. Some of these were lost on the mountain and never reached Goodyear's at all. But a number of mules variously estimated at from two to three hundred, got through to the bar, where they were effectually blocked in, and all perished except about a dozen which were bought for a trifle by the celebrated 'Cuteye Foster' and brought down through the river cañon with the help of a large tribe of friendly Indians, a passage which probably no four-footed animal ever traversed before or since.

My expedition, though it saved the miners, seemed destined to bring disaster to everyone else including myself. On my next trip into the mountains, I was rather suddenly attacked with what was there called 'mountain fever,' probably one of the protean forms of bilious intermittents. As a fatal issue was inevitable if laid up where I was, I rode down almost without stopping to Nye's, where I arrived nearer dead than alive and in a delirious condition. My partner had the grace to put me in a small canvas lodging-house, where I lay ill and helpless for some time, during which he disappeared with the mules and everything else except the contents of my pockets, and I never saw or heard of him afterwards.

Rest, a milder climate and a strong constitution sufficiently improved my condition to enable me to take passage in a small sternwheel steamboat, which had just found its way to Nye's and was lying at the bank, bound for 'the Bay,' as San Francisco was then known in the interior. I had myself carried on board by some kind-hearted fellow-lodgers, but remember little of what transpired till I was taken ashore at San Francisco by the deck hands and deposited like any other worthless cargo, in a sailors' boarding-house on the beach near North Point. This house was a long narrow canvas structure containing three tiers of bunks on each side, all closely occupied at night, and many during the day, by drunken sailors of all nations, in various stages of rum, fisticuffs and brawling. Drunk or sober, they were all kind and sympathetic with one in my condition, and searched out and brought me an individual who, though he certainly looked more like a pirate, passed for a doctor, and charged me an ounce a visit, which soon swallowed up my modest 'pile.'

Whether owing to him, or in spite of him, my health and strength improved, till my money was gone, when the 'doctor,' suddenly losing his interest, informed me that he could do nothing more for me in so bad a climate, and that my only hope for life lay in a voyage to the Islands (Sandwich) or some other mild climate. As the condition of my funds would have about equally justified tour of Europe, this advice left me a prey to patent medicines, of which every sailor possessed his own infallible variety. At last, finding it necessary to work or starve, some English sailors offered to ship me, and supported me to the beach, where Captain Franklin, of the English barque *Change* was trying to ship a crew and glad to get anyone, as many fine vessels were then every day being abandoned for want of men to navigate them. With him I engaged at fifty dollars a month—about half the current wages —for a voyage in ballast, via Callao, to Iquique and the Chinchas, there to load guano for Liverpool. The ship lay at anchor in the lower bay and was to sail the same evening, her crew possessing the usual tendency to run away as fast as they were shipped and received their advances.

Not much preparation was required by me, for my boarding-master confiscated all my advance money, and every other possession had been lost or stolen except what I wore on my back. So three or four of my British hearties borrowed a ship's boat, wrapped me up in the stern sheets and undertook to beat out six or seven miles to the anchorage against a smart sea breeze which raised a rough choppy head sea in the bay, but finally had to take to the oars. When after a long pull and a good drenching we got alongside, and the mate saw me rolled up in the wet sail, shaking with chills and looking like death, he sung out, "What have you got there?" "O, he's drunk; heave us a bight." This being readily accepted as a very natural explanation, I was soon hauled aboard and sent to the forecastle to 'sober off.' The captain soon came aboard, without having had much success in getting a crew, and as there were not hands enough on board to weigh the anchor and beat the ship out over the bar, the crew of the American ship *Charleston,* which lay at anchor near by, was borrowed for the purpose, returning to their vessel with the pilot.

As there is nothing so well understood and so heartily sympathized with by honest sailors of all ranks and every nation, as a good, plain, helpless 'drunk,' of which I possessed the credit, I was considerately let alone till next morning, when all hands were mustered to count off the two watches. Though frightfully seasick, a marvelous improvement in my general health had already occurred, and though I was put promptly at work, it was but a few days till I was entirely well, with strength and spirits rapidly returning. The *Change* was a good and staunch, but slow-sailing bluff-bowed old collier of 400 tons, then deemed a good-sized vessel. Besides officers, she had but three men before the mast, including myself, instead of at least twelve, which would have been a fair crew for her. But beside the captain and mates, who had grown up from apprenticeship in employ of the same owners, she carried two stout apprentice boys and a carpenter—half officer, half man—who was the best seaman forward of the quarter-deck. Everyone on board, except the three newly shipped foremast Jacks, were of well-tested fidelity, having declined to desert the ship at San Francisco and run away to the mines, a temptation to which even men-of-war's crews then usually succumbed when they got the opportunity. The captain was a worthy man, and a safe, slow, conscientious navigator, who never 'carried on,' and who in view of the short-handed crew, spent almost every night on deck, where wrapped in a rubber coat he got his naps with one eye open, close by the wheel. The second mate was a stupid ass, never conspicuous for anything, but the mate was a smart, driving young fellow not very much older than myself and perpetually oppressed with an unquenchable desire to take all the change he could get out of me, as the only Yankee and 'Johnny Raw' on board. We were therefore not long in getting into collision, and our perpetual rows and shindies furnished the principal topic of daily interest during the long and monotonous voyage.

Since with the mate's hospitable intentions and my inflammable temper, we never agreed about anything, it was not difficult to find subjects of contention, which would possess little interest for anyone, except for the serious events to which they led. Though less exacting with the other hands, he was afflicted with an absolute moral inability to see me on deck, watch or no watch, without setting me at work of some kind, whether useful or not. The most prominent of these occasions, all occurring during my proper watch below (for of course I could not object to work in my watch on deck) were as follows: First, he put me to work, in an insulting manner, at coal-tarring the chains, anchor and hawse-holes, when I promptly took occasion to capsize—accidentally—the coal-tar bucket, whose contents ran up and down in great black streams over the newly painted forecastle deck, with the rolling of the vessel.

When this was investigated, although I received a good public 'wooling' from the skipper, I am convinced the mate got as good in private, the subject being suddenly dropped. His next haze was to send me to the foremast truck to slush down spars, the slush bucket being suspended in the usual manner alongside of me by a single whip purchase under my control. As this was in effect requiring one man to work in both watches —for a trifling job not in the least necessary, and which might have waited for a month without injury to anything—I was justly exasperated, and maneuvered, by watching the ship's roll and letting go at the right moment, to drop the bucket, which weighed at least fifty pounds, on his head. It just cleared his nose, and smashed to atoms at his feet! My continued succession of 'accidents' and this narrow escape, seemed to quiet him for a time, but one day, seeing me smoking my pipe in peace and tranquility on the combings of the main hatch, while the deck watch was painting ship, he could not resist the opportunity and ordered me over the side to paint, which I flatly refused. On reference to the captain, my contention was practically supported, though he reprimanded me severely for my words, in order I suppose, to let the mate down easy.

The mate having now exhausted his official dodges, while I had become quite sailor enough to do my duty and know my rights, a final settlement became a necessity for the mate, who was bound as chief officer, to maintain his authority. The occasion was not long in coming. Some short answer of mine having excited his ire, he came for me with an iron belaying-pin snatched from the rail, and though I warned him I would kill him if he struck me, he being possessed with the idea that all Yankees were braggarts and cowards, disregarded the notice, whereupon I cut him across the body with my belt knife, which was not sharp, or my promise would have been made good, then and there. Nevertheless, as I put my strength in the blow, he was badly hurt and disabled for the time. After the skipper had swabbed him off and tied him up, he sent for me and gave me the pleasing information that he was about to put me in irons and hand me over to the admiral at Callao to be taken to England for trial. I asked him if he thought I could get away from the ship, or if he thought he could navigate her any better without me, or if he had ever had any fault to find with me, or had ever known me to have a bad word with anyone but the mate? To all of which he freely answered in the negative, like an honest man as he was, and even admitted that personally he had no fault to find with me. He had, I believe, rather a private fondness for me, especially since an occasion not long before, when I had succeeded in taking the weather earing from the carpenter in reefing topsails; he finally agreed to dispense with the irons, and as the mate recovered, in course of time everything quieted down, with the understanding that the matters between the mate and me were to be settled at some future convenient opportunity on shore. The *Change* was a slow, old-fashioned sailor, about five or six knots being all that could be got out of her with a fair wind and lee studding sails. Owing to this and our scanty crew, with the captain's consequent prudence about 'carrying on,' the voyage was long and tedious. Provisions got scarce in quantity and variety and the skipper determined to touch for wild hogs at the Isle de Cocas, a solitary, uninhabited island lying in about five degrees north latitude, a few hundred miles off the coast of Central America.

This island is about nine miles long, with half as much width or less, and almost entirely mountainous. On the weather side the land slopes by apparently accessible declivities toward the sea, but on the lee side it presents a lofty precipitous face, over which at that season a number of lovely cascades, 'half concealed, half disclosed' by the dense tropical vegetation, fall many hundred feet into the sea. On the same side, the mouth of a creek, quite large for so small an island, became visible, apparently affording opportunity for landing through the moderate surf. As we dare not let go the anchor, in consequence of the inability of all hands to weigh it, sail was shortened, and my friend the mate and myself were left to work the ship on and off, while the captain landed with all the rest of the crew. They were absent all day, finding plenty of pig tracks but no pigs. They however shot plenty of large fowl, and made a good haul of fish in the mouth of the creek. During their absence the ship was absolutely covered with hundreds of sea fowl—mostly boobies—who covered the spars, rail, booms, and every rope on which they could find footing, while other myriads hovered round the ship. They had no fear of us, biting viciously when handled, and roughly fighting each other for standing-room. A turtle several feet long, floated by just awash with the surface, which we watched with greedy eyes, but had no means of capturing, being just out of reach with the harpoon.

The island lies far out of the track of vessels and has been rarely visited. It was discovered by Anson or some other of the early navigators of these seas, who according to our skipper's chart, left on it pigs, goats and fowls. It seems from the sea a lovely spot, and from its heavy mantle of vegetation must possess a fertile soil, notwithstanding the picturesque inequality of its surface. Somewhat after the time of this visit, its name became well known in San Francisco from the following tale told by a Dr. M. of Illinois. That gentleman in trying to make his way to California by way of Central America lodged one night at a native's cabin in Costa Rica, the owner of which lay dying. The doctor, moved by the distress of the family, remained caring for him during several days, when he died, but not before presenting his benefactor with a rude chart of the weather side of the Isle de Cocas and the following statement:

One of the ancestors of the dying man had been an English seaman who was captured in the Pacific by pirates, whom he was induced or compelled to join. Off Acapulco they lay in wait for and seized a Spanish treasure galleon bound for the Philippines, in which a vast quantity of government, church, and private valuables had been shipped in consequence of a panic caused either by the destruction of Panama or some other depredations of the buccaneers. That treasure which was contained in some twenty casks and boxes, had been deposited by the pirates on the weather side of the Isle de Cocas, in the bed of a torrent temporarily diverted from its course for the purpose. Before they had any opportunity to reclaim it, their vessel was destroyed by an English cruiser after a desparate contest, in which the pirate was sunk with most of her crew, the few survivors being taken.

These were ultimately carried to England, tried, convicted, and hung in London, partly on the evidence of the sailor in question, who was pardoned to serve as 'King's evidence.' Falling into poverty, he afterwards endeavored to make his way back to the island by the way of Central America, but being without friends or money, stuck fast in that country, where he at length married, settled, and in due course died, leaving a written statement and such a rude chart as he was capable of making, which thus now came through his descendant into Dr. M.'s possession. The latter finally made his way to San Francisco after a two or three years' journey from Illinois. There he soon interested some acquaintances in the story, whose romantic character was not ill adapted to find converts among that adventurous population. These caused application to be made to the proper English records from which it was ascertained that such a piratical craft was really captured about that time and place, four of whose crew were actually tried, convicted and executed in London.

This confirmation of the exile's tale reached San Francisco about the year 1855 or '56, and came near setting the bay on fire with excitement. As I was the only person there, or probably for that matter, in the whole United States, who had ever seen the island, that fact soon got out, and I was able at least to inform the numerous anxious inquirers that such a place existed and the beds of its picturesque and tumbling torrents were well fitted for such a place of deposit. A corporation was organized with beautifully printed certificates of stock, the schooner *Julius Pringle* chartered, and a numerous and hopeful body of explorers went down in her to find the treasure and make their fortunes. As always seems to be the case in such enterprises, they found everything just as described—except the treasure—which they were obliged to come back without, after all their stores and provisions were exhausted. I have heard that the search has since been several times renewed by other parties, but without success.

On board the *Change,* the mate and myself were not sorry to see the return of the captain and crew, for as the round-bodied and bluff-bowed old barque would not look within seven points of the wind, any sudden freshening of the latter might have sent us off to the leeward much faster than the boat could follow. It was indeed not very long after the island visit that two events occurred showing that even in the steady monotony of the 'trades,' and with the most sober and well-behaved old craft, the ocean is nowhere and never without its occasions of excitement and adventure. The first was the advent, with barely a few minutes' notice, of a severe white squall which, preceded by an ominous lull in the regular trade wind, came up from the leeward about eight bells in the evening, with tremendous violence, very nearly taking the ship aback with studding sails set. The squall brought with it a dense pall of almost inconceivable darkness, rent by nearly continuous lightning, and discharged torrents of rain that seemed to fall in sheets rather than drops. Notwithstanding there had been time to haul down most of the kites, let go halliards and haul up clews, the ship was instantly knocked down, and must certainly have filled and foundered, but for the seamanlike prudence of Captain Franklin, who in consequence of the short crew, habitually kept all deck-openings closed and battened, except the forecastle scuttle and companion-way, the slides of which were nearly water tight. Fortunately, the sea was smooth and had no time to get up, and the lee foretopmast studding-sail with one of the head sails having got adrift, floated off to leeward and towed the ship's head in that direction, so that after a time she was got before the wind and righted, affording a chance to stow sails and repair damages. During the height of the scrimmage, as I and one of the boys were trying to haul down a studding-sail by the tack, the latter suddenly parted on the bowsprit cleat, and the free end struck the captain—who was rushing to help us—in the face, knocking him down to leeward, where he would certainly have gone overboard but for striking against a man secured to the fiferail, who was engaged in slacking off the sheet of the same sail, and pinned him just in time. He carried about a fine pair of black eyes for a while, but in view of such a lucky accident, scarcely had reason to complain.

The other event was the occasion of a splendid act of heroism on the part of my enemy, the mate, who, whatever his other faults, was no coward. The ship was at the time hove to in a moderate gale and long heavy sea-way, under close reefed main topsail and fore staysail, riding with great ease, though pitching head under to the heavy seas, when the jib gasket was washed loose or parted and the sail went adrift. As some of its tackle still held, the effect was that the loose sail would ride up to the boom at every pitch, and as each sea struck and filled it, would drift off to leeward bringing up with a tremendous jerk that must soon carry away the jib stay and boom, which in turn would probably wreck the fore topmast or worse. The seas were long, and the ship's pitches deep, easy and regular, but notwithstanding she was only in ballast, there was so much water on deck it was scarcely safe to go forward of the mainmast. Nevertheless, someone must go out on the boom and cut loose or secure the sail. Several of the watch were hanging to the weather-rail as near the scene as it was safe to go, shouting their views into each other's ears through the deafening noise of wind and water, and all eyes turned on the carpenter, by common consent the best and bravest sailor on board. That seaman, recognizing the cogency of 'noblesse oblige' was already stripping for the job, when the mate came runnning forward, ordered the carpenter to the bowsprit cleat, to handle the running rigging if required, and taking one of the men's knives in his teeth, rushed out on the boom. There he worked a considerable time, hampered by the inky darkness and carried under water at every pitch of the ship, but in spite of all obstacles stuck to it, and not only removed the immediate danger, but with the carpenter's help, saved the sail. He came in at last much exhausted and half-drowned, and was assisted by the men aft to the captain, who threw his arms around his neck, as every one of the crew would have liked to do. This act of fine seamanship and splendid gallantry, well illustrates the value of the English system of maritime apprenticeship, as then and perhaps still prevailing, and the fine seamen that it breeds. The captain, mate and carpenter had all been apprentices to the large ship-owning firm to which the *Change* belonged, and they with the two boys had stuck by and saved the ship for its owners, even in the confusion of San Francisco, where the remainder of the crew had run away. When the present round voyage should be completed, the skipper would probably get a larger or better ship, and the others a step in promotion, or an increase of wages; all fully looking forward to spending their lives in the same service, with certain advancement, according to the records they might make.

It was somewhere near the Galipagos, off the coast of Ecuador, and during a dead calm, that we drifted down on the first sail seen since sinking the lofty heads of San Francisco, which proved to be the ship *Sea Queen,* of Dundee. Her captain came aboard of us, and we forecastle men learned from the boat's crew that the *Queen* was last from Panama—where she had landed a cargo of English coal—which place was thronged by thousands of Americans willing to pay any price for passage to San Francisco. This information was too much for the equanimity of our skipper, who, doubtless having plenty of discretion from his owners, forthwith determined to break the articles we had all signed and run for the golden shower.

Accordingly our helm was put down for Panama, and after getting clear of the trades, we had a long and weary beat against light and baffling breezes to that place, which we reached after a seventy-three days' passage from San Francisco, anchoring several miles from the town. Panama at that time remained very much in the condition it had maintained for centuries. All land is beautiful to the seaman who sees it from the deck of his vessel after a long voyage, where nothing had been visible but sea and sky, but pristine Panama had a beauty and loveliness of its own. The grey medieval masonry of the fort and town, embowered in tropical foliage, and backed by the picturesque mountains of the Isthmus—the whole seen across the fine bay with its islands, vessels and native craft—was irresistibly attractive to eyes which for months had wandered idly over the weary expanse of an almost untraversed ocean.

There was no man-of-war in the harbor, of the English or any other nation, which fact gave me a certain sense of security against the entertainment the skipper had threatened me with, notwithstanding I had always expected his good nature to prevail in the end. Nevertheless, as he went ashore at daybreak every morning for several days, during which time we were all kept on board, and as pride, policy and etiquette alike forbade me to ask questions, conscience compelled me to feel some uneasiness about what fate he might be preparing for me. The skipper's habit—as is usual in that climate—was to go ashore early and return before noon, but one day he remained absent till late, when he came off with several new men just shipped, and at once sent for me to his cabin. I had a genuine respect and affection for the 'old man,' and never did really believe he was going to be very hard with me, and his first words removed all doubt. He had made a fine charter of the ship to carry some hundreds of American passengers to San Francisco at either $200, or $300, per head—I cannot now remember which—but the aggregate several times exceeded the entire value of the barque. A gang of carpenters were coming off in the morning to fit bunks and other necessaries, after which the vessel would haul in to the watering-place at Tobago to load water and provisions. Though seamen were plenty in Panama, I could have plenty of shore 'leave' and then go back to San Francisco with him at the same wages, or if I preferred, I should be discharged and paid off the next day.

Now as an English man-of-war might heave in sight any day, and there might be others to complain of me besides the captain, I preferred anything which would set me on shore, and out of their reach in the shortest time, so the skipper, not overmuch pleased as I thought, at the rejection of his offer, told me to be ready to go ashore with him to the consignees at eight bells (four o'clock) next morning to be paid off. Promptly at that hour I was waiting for him at the gangway, the mate engaged with the new hands washing down decks, when the captain appeared in his patent leathers and white flannels, and ordered me into the boat. But it was not in unregenerate human nature to miss the last opportunity of giving the mate a piece of my mind in the presence of the new hands, which I proceeded to do, daring him to come on shore while the ship lay in port. Immediate collision was prevented by the captain, who hurried me over the gangway and down the ladder, the mate promising to pay me all the visits I wanted on shore.

After a three-mile pull to the postern, I accompanied my skipper to the office of Zachrisson Nelson and Company, the ship's agents, who had the account and pay prepared for my actual time on board. That I refused to receive, and the captain with several merchantile aristocrats, was called from the sacred retreat of the inner counting-room to settle the row between me and the clerks. Knowing nothing at that time of my actual legal rights in the premises, I thought the sure thing would be to ask enough, so my modest request included additional wages for the estimated length of voyage from Panama to Iquique, passage money to the latter place, and my board in Panama till a vessel should be ready for Iquique. Such cheek from a foremast Jack, I suppose had never before been heard in the British marine and nearly took the skipper's breath away, while his aristocratic friends were so shocked they nearly fainted from sympathy.

In the presence of the commercial great men, his friends, he was at first disposed for some British bluff, loud and strong, but on being reminded that that settled nothing, wanted to know if he had not let me off from a prison offence and always stood my friend? I replied I had nothing to complain of against him, but when I had to lick the mate for abusing me as the only American on board, he threatened to send me to England in irons. "Now," proceeded I, warming up as I went on, "you can't do that, for there is no man-of-war here, and if there were, the place is full of Americans. I saw 500 of them in coming along the street. If my claim is not legal, I don't want it, but if it is, I need it worse than you do. There is no use in wrangling over it. I will just take a little walk and inquire of some lawyer whether I am entitled to it or not."

Now, I suppose there is nothing afloat or ashore—not even a pirate—which a shipmaster hates and fears as much as a lawyer. Any controversy with them, especially with the rascally sailors' pettifoggers who infest ports and ships, involves a libel, bonds, detention, loss and expenses without end, in which all the pecuniary responsibility is confined to one side, and even success brings almost equal loss. So after giving my commander time to cool, with a few innocent hints at such blessings in reserve for him, he compromised by paying about three-fourths of my demand and I bade him a respectful good-bye. I have never seen or heard of him since. He was a brave, skillful and prudent seaman, a fairly good shipmaster, and no owners ever had a more faithful representative.

Having got clear of the ship and of British justice, which though it has the reputation of being a good article, one may get too much of, the next thing in order was to have a settlement with the mate. Since his gallant conduct at sea, I cannot say I hated him, notwithstanding the numerous wrongs I had suffered at his hands, but at that foolish period of life, I had, as is not unusual, a natural tendency toward unprofitable controversy, and rankling with a sense of unjust treatment, would have cheerfully paid down the whole of my hard-earned wages, if necessary, rather than miss a chance to meet my enemy face to face in fair and honest battle. Having no acquaintances in the place, I adopted poor Jack's only resource in a strange port, and made my way to the sailors' boarding-houses, where I soon fell upon a choice lot of sea-faring men, embracing half the deserters, beach-combers, and sea lawyers on the Pacific, both English and American, all unanimous for a row with a mate or any other lawful authority.

At that time, the new commercial town since grown up around the steamer landings and railroad terminus had no existence. The old town was surrounded by its ancient wall with a long and high sea face, at one end of which was the castle or fort, and at the other, an open paved square used as a marketplace with a postern or water-gate known as the 'sally-port,' from which a short flight of steps led to the water. Here the pongys or market boats landed their cargoes long before daylight, and later the place was used by the various ships' boats to land their skippers, stewards and other officials. It was guarded by a sentinel and a few others were posted about the market square, there being no other soldiers nearer than the guardhouse, or the fort, still more distant. A scheme was soon arranged, to await my mate's arrival every morning from daybreak, at the sally-port, with details which will presently appear. My enthusiastic friends were for jumping on him promiscuously, but that I positively vetoed, not so much,

I fear, for fairness' sake, as for its inadequacy to settle the personal issue. I sent off a daily message to the mate by the *Change's* boat and have no doubt that he would have been prompt enough unless restrained by the skipper. At all events, it was not till after several mornings that he at last appeared in charge of the ship's boat. The moment he entered the sally-port in advance of his boat's crew, the gate was slammed to and fastened behind him, a sailor knocked down the negro sentinel with one blow, while another broke his musket and hove it over the wall. The mate understood perfectly these little preliminaries, and immediately began to strip, I being already in shirt and trousers. As far as I remember, not a word passed between us, the heavy business commencing without delay. The sailors quickly made and held a ring, outside of which soon gathered a big crowd of market negroes highly excited and delighted at the white men's shindy.

After a good deal of sparring, with more or less superficial damage given and received, finding that my antagonist could take any amount of pounding and wait, I concluded it was best for my interests to get him down; so, watching my opportunity as he was recovering from an overreach, I gave him a head butt and went down with him, taking care to fall on top. Here we inflicted considerable mutual damage, he still endeavoring to disable me with his fists, and I trying to get hold of his head to beat it on the ground, both having a fair amount of success. The result was yet uncertain, when I felt myself suddenly dragged off and was told to run, and caught sight, amid a general flight of the negro spectators, of a platoon of black soldiers charging down with fixed bayonets.

I soon concealed myself by dodging among the market people, who helped me wash off and repair damages, so that about the only man arrested, was my late antagonist who certainly was not much to blame, and was soon allowed to go. He might have set his consul and consignees on me, but did not, and I have never seen or heard of him since. He was a brave man and a gallant seaman, and I do not believe he likes the Yankees any less after fighting them a little. Doubtless he has since sailed his own ship on many seas, and if still living is enjoying a well-earned competence in some one of those remote British seaports where the retired British skipper loves to seek a quiet anchorage in his latter days.

The width neither of the streets nor of the adjacent mule tracks in the old town admitting of wheeled vehicles, there was not then one in Panama. Everything was transported on the backs of mules or men, and as the former were scarce and in great demand for the transisthmian traffic, the latter were the approved intra-mural beasts of burden. As I could speak a little Spanish and rapidly increased my knowledge, I got together a gang of cargodores and did the principal transporting business within the walls for merchants and others, till everything was thrown into confusion by the celebrated American riots. Though bad feeling and personal collisions had previously occurred, the immediate occasion of the riots was the lighting of his cigar by some dare-devil, on a bet, from a candle on the high altar of the Cathedral Church of San Juan de Dios, during the most solemn moment of the mass, when fifty priests were officiating before a congregation of 3000 people devoutly on their knees. I saw that outrageous act, and I regret to say did nothing to discourage it, for which I have no excuse to give but the reckless and stupid folly of youth. There were but few Americans present, who were collected at one of the principal doors, and who fled when, after a moment of horror at the sacrilege, the whole congregation, priests and all, went savagely for them. After considerable desultory fighting, the Americans gradually got themselves concentrated on two streets of massive stone houses, whence they sallied to sack and destroy the cabildo or guard house, and to which they returned when hard pressed, keeping the street clear by pistol fire. After a week or more of this disorder and some loss of life to both parties, in which of course the negroes were the principal sufferers, a large body of troops was assembled near to but outside of the town, and the authorities, not relishing the job of getting the Americans out of their stone houses, were induced by the foreign merchants, consuls and others to make peace with amnesty.

I suppose most sensible persons will agree with my present view; i.e., that while the mass may be a puerile and trifling baby play, with a tendency to sacrilege, yet unpardonable is the ass who, because he thinks he knows better, dares deliberately to insult the solemn and harmless convictions of others possessing equal rights with himself.

My transporting business being destroyed by this bloody episode, I took to speculating in steamer tickets with profitable results. The condition of affairs which made this sort of gambling possible was as follows: The new steamer lines from the east to San Francisco being able to load any number of vessels for cash freights and passage to Chagres, dispatched round the Cape to Panama a wholly inadequate number of vessels for service on the Pacific side. The sea voyage from New York round the Cape to Panama is several times longer than from the same place to Chagres, besides which the distance from Panama to San Francisco is nearly double that from New York to Chagres so that on any reasonable calculation the steamers intended to ply from Panama should have been dispatched a month before those destined to Chagres, and twice as many steamers were required for the Pacific as for the Atlantic service. But no such honest precautions were pursued. All were received at New York who could pay the cash, and the natural result was that a great number of cheated and deceived passengers congregated at Panama, among whom poverty, pestilence and death ran fatal riot. Hundreds of these deluded victims idled their days on the ramparts looking anxiously for arriving steamers whose smoky banners were discernible at many hours' distance. If on such appearance the old salts—of whom there were plenty—pronounced her to be, for instance, the steamer A, the tickets held for that vessel rose in market price to $1000 and upwards while those for steamers B, C and D correspondingly fell to a fifth of that price or less, notwithstanding these might arrive next day. This was gambling, of course, of much less respectable character than if the subject had been stocks or bonds, which latter, as we all know, are permitted to the most pious and exemplary moralists, but the circumstances of my debut in Panama were not such as to entangle me in fine distinctions, and I became much interested in it and was quite lucky, having at one time got ahead about

$5000 in gold sovereigns. While this comparative wealth lasted, I was a popular character with my seafaring acquaintances, whom I treated liberally, and might have had the command of any of the several desperate enterprises then projected. One of these, I remember, was the purchase or seizure—the parties were not particular which—of a schooner, getting a lot of negroes on board at Tobago (the neighboring island where all the vessels then took aboard their water) shutting the hatches on them, and landing them to plant coffee at some such out-of-the-way place as the Isle de Cocas. But all such schemes were fortunately cut short by the loss of my entire capital one unlucky night at the well-known Monte tables of G. & F., at the corner of the Calle de San Juan de Dios and the Grand Plaza.[10]

[10] To illustrate the ups and downs then and there common to all, it may be added that G. who had been a well-known Mississippi steamboat captain, afterward become, successively, a banker, steamboat agent and capitalist in San Francisco; then went into railroads in New York and died but a few years since, leaving an estate commonly rated at over twenty millions. F. also became a prosperous San Francisco banker and money-lender, but I believe has been dead for many years.

CHAPTER VIII

LAND AND SEA JOURNEYINGS

The morning after such injudicious bucking on an inferior 'layout,' I found myself absolutely penniless, and when I and my beach-combing followers got sufficiently hungry, there was nothing left for us but to ship at $40 a month on a Spanish schooner called *La Favorita,* bound and all 'ataunto' for the coast of Central America for mules, then in active demand for travel on the Isthmus. This I proceeded to do. *La Favorita,* notwithstanding her name, was a played-out, rotten old tub, ill-fitted and ill-found, commanded by a drunken Spaniard who, when he was not asleep, divided his time with impartiality between swilling rum and praying to an old, painted, wooden saint, nailed up in his cabin. He had an English mate who was a fine seaman when sober, which was never, when he could get access to the skipper's rum. The crew was ample in number, mostly of English and American deserters and 'beach-combers,' including several first-class English man-of-war's men, and had they been under any adequate discipline or command, would have made such a crew of A. B.'s as a trading schooner does not often get in any part of the world.

Keeping inshore of the 'trades' after getting clear of the gulf (the wind was almost always light and generally ahead), by making long tacks to sea and short ones on shore, the skipper managed to see the coast pretty often and pick up a few mules at nearly all accessible points along shore from San Jose to Realejo.[11] But as most of the towns and haciendas were in the interior, and nearly all their ports were exposed and bad, while our ground tackle was extremely worthless, we often had to cut and run before we could get either mules or water.

[11] Now, I believe, called 'Corintos.'

The method of loading mules was primitive. A small lot would be swum off, frequently a mile or more, by natives in pongys and canoes. Arrived alongside, frequently accompanied by a school of the small ground shark which infests those waters, our men with poles and boat hooks would slip the slings around the mules and hook on, when they were quickly run up by the men on deck, with a double whip purchase. Until the mules' legs were clear of the water, the fight with the sharks was incessant, mules, sailors and natives making common cause against the enemy, who, nevertheless occasionally got in some sharp nips.

Owing to our few and leaky water casks, we were nearly always short of water for the mules, though as it rained nearly every day, a great deal was caught in old sails. How the wretched old tub ever succeeded in making her round voyage back to Panama, is certainly hard to explain or account for. There was absolutely nothing sound and whole on board, from the old hull itself, down to her fished booms, rotten rigging, patched sails, and spliced hempen cable. As for the running rigging, it was as much as a man's life was worth to trust his weight when aloft to a stay, halyard or tack, so that the light sails were rarely set in wind from any quarter. Nevertheless, she brought a fair cargo of thirsty and starving mules into Panama, the profit on which must have exceeded many times the entire value of the vessel.

Safely back in Panama, after an opportunity for some sound reflection on recent events, I found myself somewhat ashamed of my indifferent surroundings, and cut the whole concern in an effectual manner by shipping immediately, while I still had money in my pocket, on the American *S. S. Columbus*—Captain Peck—as a foremast hand, for San Francisco, claiming and receiving the wages of an A. B. The steamer had been built at Philadelphia to carry perhaps a hundred passengers of both classes between that city and Charleston, South Carolina. By filling her entire between-decks and building four rows of standees, three bunks high, on her spar deck, 1100 passengers were crowded into her, with whom she sailed on her voyage of 3500 miles.

I believe I have never seen such a jam before or since. The spar deck having for the most part no covering except an awning for fine weather, most of the passengers were entirely exposed to the open sky, and dependent for health and comfort on whatever weather Providence might see fit to send. It is true they were all young men in search of adventure, covered with knives and pistols and thinking themselves hardy and dangerous desperados, till a few knock-downs from the cross and crowded sailors, taught them better manners. The ship's officers and crew were first-class, but in such a crowd it was almost impossible to hear or obey orders, and it is terrible to conjecture what a catastrophe any really heavy weather must have produced.

But though we enjoyed fine weather throughout the voyage, with little wind and less rain, the thoughtless crowd was, nevertheless, destined to pay dearly for the avarice of the agents or charter party who had so abused and exceeded the capacity of the vessel. We had scarcely dropped the headlands of the deep gulf of Panama and got clear of the land, when the 'coast fever' —which is, I believe, pretty much the same as 'yellow Jack'— broke out, venomous and deadly from the beginning, and the scenes on deck soon beggared description. Within two or three days the crowded spar deck was full of cases, nearly all delirious and necessarily lashed down in their bunks by the crew, who otherwise might as well have abandoned the ship. The vessel was soon a howling bedlam constantly increased by fresh victims, who usually became delirious and tried to jump overboard at an early stage. On the third or fourth day, Captain Peck, a fine old Philadelphia seaman, got the ship's hands on the forecastle—it being impracticable to call them aft—and talked to us like a father. He said he had learned from much experience that the disease attacked those who were most afraid of it. That though the passengers had lost their heads from panic, he felt he had a good crew with no cowards, and could save every one of us if we would trust him and obey all orders implicity and intelligently, notwithstanding the difficulty of getting about the ship, and the impossibility of a proper superintendence of the watches by the officers. But for humanity's sake, we must all, officers and men alike, do many things we did not ship for, such as looking after the sick, separating and disposing of the dead, restoring the spirits of passengers, etc. He would have no more formal funerals with tolling of the ship's bell, etc. Each watch coming on deck was to sew up the dead in their bedding and heave them quietly overboard under supervision of the officer of the watch.

This conference had an immediate and excellent effect on the crew, who were not in the least scared, or if they were, did not admit it, but who had felt ugly and disposed to rebel at their unusual difficulties and hardships, and especially at the difficulty of the usual communication with the officers and each other. About this time the captain mustered both watches and under his personal supervision, had all the delirious and noisy patients carried forward to the ship's head, where such cases were thenceforth promptly brought, secured in their bunks, and kept till they were dead or quiet. This was probably the best single measure adopted to allay the panic and consequent spread of the disease among the mass of passengers. Those worst cases were constantly attended by Mrs. Hagler, a cabin passenger from Texas, and the ship's chambermaid, who belonged in Philadelphia, but whose name I am very sorry I cannot remember. These were, I think, the only females on board, and not a sailor seeing their voluntary and devoted labors, hesitated to respond to their calls and render them every aid in his power. Mrs. H., who was the widow of a Texas ranger, had learned in Texas to deal with yellow fever by what she called the 'Raspail method,' and no doubt saved many lives, though, of course, the most engrossing labor of two middle-aged women could not go very far in such a crowd of frightened, sick and dying men.

I never knew and I do not believe that after formal funerals were dispensed with any account was kept of the number of deaths, but they must have amounted to a hundred and probably more. Fortunately the weather was almost uniformly good, and off the Gulf of California we began to encounter a sensibly cooler temperature, under the influence of which the disease rapidly diminished both in the number and violence of attacks. The voyage occupied, as I remember, about thirty-four days, and scarcely half a dozen had to be carried ashore on stretchers at San Francisco. To the best of my recollection, both officers and crew were exempt from first to last, showing the effective prophylactic influence of hard work and fearless minds.

An astonishing transformation had already taken place in San Francisco. The gigantic mudholes in Montgomery and other streets had been filled up and planked, and even the unwonted luxury of sidewalks of the same material had begun to make their appearance, though as no two premises had adopted the same level, and there were no street lights, traveling by night was still attended with difficulties, especially as a principal evening amusement consisted in shooting from the doorways at the multitudes of rats which lived in security under the planking, and depredated in and out of the wooden store-houses at pleasure. Wharves, constructed on piling, were pushing out into the bay, by means of which passengers and freight could be landed at many places directly from vessels instead of from small boats and lighters. A crowd of vessels of all nations lay at anchor in front of the city, many of them abandoned or used as storage hulks. Some comparatively substantial frame houses of two and even three stories had been built, and in many other respects the city began to give indications of its speedy growth and royal future.

As I was illy versed in city ways, I had now to consider whether I should again repair to the mines or adopt the sea as a profession. I had not passed several months at sea without learning something, and felt quite competent for a position abaft the mast even in a square rigger, and might have had a mate's berth in a small trading-schooner then fitting for a voyage to the Marquesas for hogs and poultry. But notwithstanding the hundreds of square rigged vessels from all quarters of the world which filled the harbor, very few were able to get away or were worth the expense of moving, and on such the few vacancies for officers were filled by virtue of eastern influence or acquaintance. As idleness did not suit my temperament or pocket, I concluded to try my luck in the mines again, and repairing to Stockton, invested my savings and credit in mules and started out with a small pack train to the Mokelumne mines. My first trips were fairly successful.

But as the competition in the southern mines of Mexican packers, and of the wagon routes constantly being opened, must evidently soon reduce prices of transportation to wagon rates, I turned my thoughts to other and newer portions of the country.

As much excitement then prevailed respecting the mines in the extreme north of California, I conveyed my mules to San Francisco, and shipped them, with a lot of staple merchandise, for which I obtained a partial credit, on board the Scotch *S. S. Eudora,* Barkman master, bound with a large freight and passenger list to Trinidad Head, a landing point below the mouth of the Klamath, from which it was believed the coast mountains could be successfully crossed to the then little known mines situated on the upper Klamath, Trinity, Salmon and Shasta and their several tributaries. The *Eudora* was a barque rigged screw, and a large vessel for those days, with a tonnage of probably 1500 or thereabout. Her hull was sound, but her engines, standing and running rigging, and all her furniture and fittings were in bad condition, few repairs being then possible at San Francisco. She carried about thirty cabin passengers, with 600, including myself and Mexicans, in the steerage, to whom was assigned the entire between-decks fore and aft. Her hold was well-filled with provisions, water in casks and cargo, and her entire spar deck forward of the cabin houses was occupied by hay in bales, and a large number of mules, for whose safety at sea little preparation had been made beyond scantlings lashed fore and aft over each rail to tie them up by. There were no stalls, deck cleats or any other of the ordinary safeguards usually adopted for transporting live-stock by sea. Between the long ranks of mules, almost the entire deck space outside the hatch combings, was occupied by water casks, bales of hay, and barrels of provisions, with little or no precaution as to storage, lashing and security in case of bad weather.

I by no means liked the bad order and general unseaworthy appearance of ship and cargo; but as the voyage was short and there appeared no other present way of reaching my destination, I was induced to take the risk of good weather. We had scarcely cleared the harbor, however, before it came on to blow fresh from the N. and N. W. and in a day or two the wind had increased to a heavy gale from the same quarter with a head sea, against which the ship could make no progress. Of course this worked havoc on the deckload of mules, who lost their footing and trampled each other, while the unsecured and miscellaneous trash on deck, rolling backward and forward athwart ship, pounded them to death. The decks were cleared by heavy boarding seas which carried away the rails and swept off all loose material. On the fourth day out, the ship laboring heavily in a rough head sea, the long steerage table just set for dinner broke away in a heavy lurch, and no attempt being made either by the steward's crew or the sick passengers to clear away the wreck, the between-decks was thenceforth adorned with broken crockery, smashed tableware and miscellaneous cutlery, which soon became churned up with mule dung and sea water to a general depth of about a foot. The hatches could not be battened on such a crowd without suffocating them, so a quarter-section of each was left open, down which poured occasional cascades, well-charged with all sorts of unspeakable rubbish from the upper deck, until that was at last swept clean by the breaching seas. As wind and sea increased, while every thing below was sickening and disgusting, the scene on deck, where none but a sailor could venture, was soon appalling.

The captain being drunk or incompetent, few or no attempts had been made to repair damages. Remnants of sails and broken running-rigging were flying out to leeward, the deck forward of the quarter-deck was a wreck, and the main topsail chain halyard having parted, together with its port lift, the heavy yard hung for a while by the other lift with a hundred feet or more of the broken chain, the whole sweeping the deck from side to side, smashing something at every roll of the ship. Finding steerage-way mostly lost and the vessel falling off more and more frequently into the trough of the sea, the captain still invisible on deck, I sought the mate E.[12] (a good seaman from Philadelphia, who afterwards commanded one of the most celebrated clipper ships in the New York, California and China trade). Finding I was a sea-faring man he informed

[12] Nicholas Essling.

me confidentially that one engine was broken down, and the other geared to a pump of large capacity which barely held the water at a stand. The quantity of water in the hold and the rate it was making, indicated considerable leakage beside the quantity coming on deck and through the hatches. Should it reach the fires, or the engine break down, the ship must founder directly. I asked E. what was the matter with the captain, and why, with so many lives at stake, they did not repair or cut away the wreck aloft, and make sail enough to get the ship about, and run off the wind for Monterey or any other leeward port she could make? He intimated the captain was drunk and cross as the result of a row with me a day or two before, and insulted him every time he made any proposals respecting the condition of the vessel.

My difficulty with the skipper had been about as follows: Exasperated at the wretched management and my own loss of property, I had driven away the barkeeper and cleared out a small deckhouse used as a barroom, throwing the contents overboard, nailing cleats on the deck, and packing the place full with four of my best mules—spiking up the door and cutting a hole on the lee side to admit food and water. About the time I had finished the job, the captain appeared, pistol in hand, demanding loudly to know 'who had done that.' I stood by and said nothing, though quite resolved to stand by my work. As no one replied, he called the mate and watch, and ordered them to clear the place. My time having now arrived, I warned the mate I would kill the first man that touched my property, and told the captain that as it was going to be a dangerous job, he had better try to be man enough to undertake it himself. I drew no weapons, though I had them convenient, but watched B.'s movements closely, fully resolved to kill him if he raised his weapon or meddled with the mules, which were the last ones surviving on the ship. As the mate and watch sympathized with me and did not care to risk their lives in the captain's quarrel they stood quietly by, when he commenced storming at the mate for a Yankee coward, telling him, with plenty of coarse and obscene language, that I dared not shoot. At last I lost my temper, a dangerous thing to do when weapons are out, and walking up to the captain, ordered him to pocket his pistols and clear out 'before I counted three,' fairly running him off his own deck.

As the passengers took no trouble to conceal their approval of that episode, and the Scotchman suspected his officers and crew of the same feeling, I don't wonder he was cross, though that was a poor excuse for keeping full of rum and letting the vessel with seven hundred lives go to destruction, without one effort to get her before the wind. The gale continued with severity—though I have seen worse—and the condition of the ship and people constantly became less and less endurable, till after about six days of it the mate and chief engineer told me they were satisfied the engine would not last through the next night, in which case the ship must go down. The only boat left on board was a surf boat belonging to some passengers, which was capsized and lashed solidly to ring bolts on deck, and in case of sudden disaster must be swamped and lost in the rush of so many hundreds. They therefore proposed, as soon as it should fall dark, with certain good men of the crew to cut it loose and try to launch it overboard and make for the nearest land, supposed to be not very distant, and invited me to join them. Apart from moral objections, there were other difficulties about this project. No preparation of the boat or its most necessary implements and stores could be made without exciting a general alarm. If she could be launched from the deck without damage, which was very doubtful, she would almost certainly be swamped or stove before getting clear of the ship, and even if the land could be reached, it was inhabited only by hostile Indians whose reception would probably be worse than shipwreck. Thus, even if we should bring ourselves to seize upon the only chance of escape for all these hundreds, it remained very uncertain whether our position and chances would really be improved. Hence I proposed the alternative of taking the ship from the captain, and getting her before the wind for any leeward port she might be able to make under canvas.

The two officers declined to take any active part in the scheme, but if the passengers could be worked up to it, would offer no resistance, and fully agreed with me there was no other chance in sight for saving ship and passengers. Upon going among the seasick and frightened people in the steerage, and stating the real condition of affairs, it was soon apparent they would agree to anything that offered a change from the wretched present, provided someone else would take the responsibility and do the work. A short penciled petition was therefore prepared and signed by a number, asking the captain to put the ship about and run to some port to leeward or even beach the ship if necessary, while still possible to save so many lives. Meanwhile I was called to a cabin stateroom, where lay three incensed Texans, savage, disheveled and seasick. These were David E. Terry, who became, in after years, Chief Justice of the State, his brother William, and Doctor Ashe, formerly of North Carolina. Like myself, having lost all the property they had brought on board, they were in a burning rage amusingly mixed up with seasickness. "Now," said T., "we don't know anything about ships and are awful sick, but not a bit frightened, and if you want to kill that d—d captain, and all his crew, we are going to come in and take some chances with you. We may look pretty sick, and can't get up till the shooting begins, but when you are ready just call us, that's all."

The captain roughly declined to accede, on account of his insurance policies, and warming up as he proceeded, declared with oaths, that the ship was going to stay under his sole command; she had started, and was insured for Trinidad, and "by G—, was going to Trinidad or the bottom." Negotiation having failed, I so informed the crowd of steerage people and immediately put the question—"As many as are in favor of, and will help take the ship from the captain, say Aye." A shout of ayes came from the least seasick, and without putting the alternative, I called on as many as would or could, to follow, and rushing to T.'s stateroom, informed my Texan recruits that if they would promise not to shoot before I did, the fighting was ready to begin. Feeling a burning anxiety to sacrifice some one to the shades of their departed mules, even that onerous condition was accepted, and all three came rushing after me, pistols in hand, though not overladen with other apparel.

Promptly kicking open the captain's outer door, I turned by a lucky chance to the left of the two staterooms he inhabited, and clapped a pistol to his head as he was in the act of picking up his own. These I at once secured, and notwithstanding the difficulty, even with the aid of the narrow passageway, of keeping my too ardent supporters behind me, which was the only way of saving the rascal's life from their instant vengeance, I proceeded to lay down the law to the vanquished. Canvas was to be got on the ship to get her about and headed for the most northerly California port the wind might permit, San Francisco if possible, but if not, Monterey, or even San Luis Obispo. If the prisoner remained in his room he would not be maltreated, but if he came on deck or meddled with ship or crew he would be thrown overboard.

The active revolutionists were then mustered, and E., the mate, was ordered to take command, with the above instructions respecting the ship. If he accepted, his authority would be supported, if he refused, he was to be thrown overboard and the command offered to every officer successively, according to rank, with similar penalty. The matter was adjusted by E.'s acceptance, after protest that it was under 'fear of his life.'

Sail being made upon the foremast, the ship paid off handsomely and was safely, though after much risk, got before the wind, lee braces hauled taut, and all hands set at repairing rigging, and clearing the wreck. As luck would have it, the wind soon moderated, and hauling more to the westward, it was not more than two or three days till the ship was run into San Francisco with a fair wind, and safely beached on the flats off Rincon Point. When inside the heads, with the pilot in charge, Barkman emerged from his prison and marched up and down the quarter-deck, rifle in hand, to keep off the numerous shore boats which in those days thronged around arriving vessels to land passengers and baggage. His signals soon brought off two boatloads of marines from as many men-of-war lying in the harbor, one of which, if I remember rightly, was the *Cyane*. At this significant and unlooked-for apparition, the four principal malefactors, knowing the importance of getting ashore to have the first telling of the story, surreptitiously coaxed a bold boatman under the head, and sliding down a rope's end, got away in the fast-gathering darkness, just as the man-of-war's boats hauled in to the after gangway. When the ringleaders were found missing, the aggrieved skipper lost his interest in the less guilty crowd, and after some hasty investigation by the officer of marines, they were allowed to go.

By a judicious division of labor, and the help of enthusiastic friends, we four interviewed the newspaper offices and got our story started on a correct basis. It is probable the ship's agents when they came to hear the whole story, thought the less fuss made the better. At all events, no attempts that I know of were ever made at arrest or prosecution, notwithstanding I went to the steamer next day with a scow and some friends, to recover my four mules. I had no difficulty about getting them, my friend the captain, being on shore, but on examination found them so terribly wounded and ulcerated by strains and salt water, that it must be a long time, if ever, before they could be fit for use. I therefore drove them up to the Plaza, where I auctioned them off for a trifling sum, the only salvage from the wreck of my humble fortunes on the ill-fated *Eudora*.

It was not till some years later that I resumed acquaintance with my three fellow 'pirates,' which was afterwards agreeably maintained for many years. David E. Terry became, as already stated, the first judicial officer of the State, resigning that position to fight a duel with the notorious Senator Broderick in 1859, and was at last murdered in a cowardly manner by a United States official. William was killed at the head of a confederate cavalry regiment in the Civil War, and Ashe, as I have heard, died later in California. They all became honorable, upright and distinguished citizens, eminent and trustworthy in every relation of life, notwithstanding the animosities excited by the first named, near the close of his life, through some unfortunate errors of judgement in certain of his domestic affairs.

The supposed favorable position of Trinidad Head for communication with the interior—thus avoiding the long and rough land route from Sacramento, then dangerously infested by the Pitt River and other Indians—was at this time more than ever favorably regarded in San Francisco. No one there had ever seen it, or knew anything of its merits as a harbor, and

still less the practicability of its routes across the obstacles
of the Coast Range.   Nevertheless, the short distances represented on the worthless maps of that day, as separating it
from the headwaters of the northern rivers, supposed to
possess a numerous and prosperous mining population, so
stirred the adventurous, that several sailing vessels of all
dimensions were already up, or were quickly put up, for the
place.

The condition of my finances no longer permitting me
to aspire to a pack-train of mules, I effected a small loan from
one of my recent Panama shipmates, and became the happy,
but not proud, possessor of ten Mexican 'burros,' which I
shipped, together with myself as sole man-of-all-work, on a
small center-board schooner (name not remembered) of about
eighty tons, bound again for Trinidad.   How this small craft
had got round either cape to the Pacific, I do not know, as I
could learn nothing of her history.   Almost anything, however,
was considered fit for a California voyage in 1849, and though
many such craft were never more heard of and left their
bones on the bottom of far-off seas, some almost incredible
voyages were successfully made.   I remember seeing at Nye's
on Feather River, a Central American pongy or 'dug-out,' with
raised sides, canvas half-deck, and two masts with small lug
sails, which had safely brought six men from Panama, a
voyage of 3500 miles, involving constant landings on a surf-
bound shore for water and provisions.

The schooner on which I now embarked, had in the course of
her adventures settled down to the essentials of what sailors
call 'plain sail,' aspiring to no topsails, kites, or light follies of
sail or rigging.   Her hull was worn, battered and paintless, but
tight, and her modest hold was crowded with provisions, water,
baggage, and over thirty passengers, while her low deck found
room for more water and provision casks, my ten asses and a
few mules.   Trinidad ought, by all accepted rules, to have
proved an El Dorado, for it was certainly a very difficult place
to reach.   Hardly out of sight of port we sailed into another—
or the same—gale from the N. W. and our small hold soon
contained more seasickness to the square foot than ought
safely to be stowed in a modern Atlantic liner.

But we had a smart Yankee skipper who well understood the handling of a 'fore and after,' and notwithstanding the anguish below, she made beautiful weather, looking up handsomely to the wind under close-reefed mainsail and jib, shipping surprisingly little water for such a low-decked craft, of less length and tonnage than many a New York pilot boat. But as a quarter-section of the main hatch had necessarily to be left open for air, a good deal of what water there was could not be kept out of the hold, and during most of the voyage there was hardly a dry spot aboard the vessel and the pump was constantly kept going by night and day, even the seasick passengers joining in the relays. In spite of the skipper's watchfulness and skill, during the long beat up to Trinidad in the teeth of wind and sea, most of the deckload went overboard, including all the mules and several of my donkeys. One of the latter fell through the hatch and behaved himself with such gentlemanly tact and propriety, that I brought the remainder down and crowded them in between the center-board and the port bilge forward, where they lived with the passengers on the same grub, making themselves quite interesting and amusing, to the satisfaction of all, not the least amusing feature being the equanimity with which they accepted their sudden and extreme changes of position, at the frequent changes of tack.

At Trinidad, notwithstanding the protection afforded by its far-projecting promontory, such a mountainous sea was rolling into the harbor—if such an open roadway deserves that title— that our skipper was afraid to take the schooner in, although affairs transpiring inside were much too exciting to run away from. Four vessels had been caught by the gale at anchor inside, which delayed heaving up so long they found it impossible to beat out when they wished to, and were driven to the desperate expedient of trying to 'ride it out.' The brig *Wakulla* and two schooners were already piled up on the rocks, while the fine barque *Josephine* was as yet safely riding through the tremendous rollers which were making a clean breach over her, their spray sometimes almost hiding her from sight, and affording a stirring view for spectators, however poor fun for those on board. The barque had veered her chains to full scope, and sent down royal and topgallant masts, and was evidently in charge of a seaman, but the rollers were so large and long that she rode nearly up to her anchors after the passage of one, and the next surged her astern till brought up on her chains with a shock and jerk distinguishable above all the roar of wind and waves. Lying just outside but not quite clear of the first break of the rollers, each one deluged her fore and aft, the clouds of spray flying over her topsail yards. The sight was so interesting to our skipper, who expected to see her windlass torn out from moment to moment, that he could not tear himself away, and kept our little craft standing off and on in a way that showed well her weatherly qualities and his seamanship.

Just before dark, the sea getting a cant upon the barque, her bowsprit went at the ship's head, carrying with it the fore top-mast and a lot of rigging. During the night her main and mizzenmasts went over, her rail and deck houses were carried away, and when first made out the next morning, as we ran in from our offing, though still riding gallantly at her anchors, she was practically a wreck. With hatches battened down and all hands below, one could but think of the terrible night her crew had passed, their lives hanging on the endurance of each link of the chain cables, conscious that each thundering blow might be the last. Our schooner, shabby as she looked, proved weatherly and reliable, able to do almost anything but talk. With the bonnet off her jib, and a small storm-lug on the mainmast, she was well and fearlessly handled by the skipper, who for several days, kept close into the heads by day, and taking a good safe offing at night, only ventured in when the gale had blown itself out, and the rollers ceased to break inside. The battered wreck of the *Josephine* still swung at her anchors, but the fine brig *Wakulla,* and two large schooners were on the beach totally wrecked, with the loss of most of their crews.

The town was a small and shabby assemblage of tents and canvas shanties, then, like many other western towns, living mostly on its brilliant expectations. As I first entered it in the wild fury of the elements, I ultimately—as will be seen—left it amid the still wilder passions of men, and I cannot say I have since felt any unconquerable yearnings to see it again, though its famous Head was then the best place to shoot wild geese that I almost ever saw. One could sit in the short chaparral which covered it and bring them down from the flocks continually flying over, about as fast as it was convenient to load, fire and recover the game.

As there were plenty of traders, and no great number of purchasers, since ten times as much merchandise was brought by vessels as could be carried away on mules, I had no great difficulty in obtaining on credit a load for my surviving jacks, and lost little time in setting out for the mines, the nearest of which were on Salmon River, about 150 miles distant over a mountainous country infested, down to within a few miles of the town, by much the worst Indians in California. As jacks cannot with their short legs keep up with mule trains, I had to resign myself to starting alone, and trusting to chance and watchfulness for evading these dangerous marauders. To this day I recollect the forlornness of that solitary departure, which seemed to be shared by my four-footed companions, and which even the good accounts I heard of the mines ahead and the profitable results I hoped for from my carefully selected cargo, did not serve at first to dispel.

But my persistent ill luck had not yet done with me. The very first night out produced an adventure which, however ridiculous it may seem in the retrospect, was not in the least amusing while it was in progress. It was already afternoon when I started from the village, crossed the stupendous ravines known as the 'one-mile' and 'four-mile' gulches, and it was getting dusk on the hills and pitch dark in the ravines, when I arrived at the deep gloomy bottom of another of the great hollows running down into the seat. Here was, as usual, a deep and ugly quagmire, across which I got most of the heavy-laden and tired jacks safely, but the last one tripped over a root on the nearly vertical descent, and from quite a considerable height pitched headlong into the mud. I quickly cut a lot of brush to stand on, got the pack off, and vainly tried till long after dark to pry and lift him out. Entirely failing in this, and the unlucky patient ceasing to make efforts for himself, I at last gave him up, and lugging his pack up the hill on my back, laid myself down, covered with mud, depressed in mind, and too tired and exhausted even to cook any supper.

Now, all these ravines were swarming with grizzlies, and I would by no means have chosen my camp in such a likely place for them, if I had had any choice about it. Constrained, however, by the circumstances, and too tired to think much about anything, I rolled up in my blanket and soon fell sound asleep, till at some early hour in the coldest and darkest part of the morning, I was suddenly awakened by a slight but unaccustomed and suspicious sound. Possessing all my life the habit of waking instantly to full possession of all faculties, I was immediately aroused, and alert to listen without budging a muscle, the darkness being so intense one could scarcely distinguish the tree tops from the open sky. The object, whatever it might be, was evidently approaching but with so much hesitation and such extreme caution as to suggest the wariness of a human enemy. I had cautiously rolled over on my face and taken a good elbow rest, resolved not to fire prematurely, and to make my one shot tell for all it was worth. In this posture, with rifle cocked and finger pressing the trigger, I gradually made out through the gloom a large dark body but a few feet distant, and was only waiting till I could recognize some vital spot, when through the solemn silence of that crucial moment suddenly resounded a mournful and sonorous bray.

The dimly-seen monster, for whose heart my muzzle was searching at ten feet distance, was the unfortunate and abandoned jack, who, finding he was to get no more help, had concluded to help himself, and in his search for companionship had found me, I suppose by his smelling faculties. My joy at the unexpected recovery of so large a fraction of my modest capital amply compensated for the very bad ten minutes I had suffered. Since that time I have had to face many situations that might be considered startling, and have been correspondingly alarmed, but never more than by that investigating but friendly *burro*. To be gobbled ignominiously in solitude and darkness without a fair fighting chance, or a single sympathetic comrade to bury one's bones and report one's fate, simply on account of one's unavoidable poverty and loneliness;

these were some of the not very cheering reflections that rushed tumultuously through my mind during what I was quite persuaded were my last moments, as I gazed along the rifle barrel with a desperate hope that same miraculous Providence or friendly chance might yet interpose to direct the momentous bullet on which I supposed so much depended.

At earliest dawn I was off without further adventure, and after a long day's work reached the crossing of the Redwood, in the heart of what has since become well-known as a body of the largest timber in the world, just as a train of light mules was crossing on its way down. Here at last my abominable luck took a favorable turn. As jacks are too small to ford rapid and deep streams, I had been anxiously cogitating the respective merits of rafts and other expedients, when here was the question solved at once without an effort. The river being in flood, that circumstance which I had most dreaded, was the very one which smoothed my path, for the people of the mule train, finding the ford impracticable even for mules, had spent the day in felling an immense redwood tree across the river, which constituted a perfect bridge ten or twelve feet wide, and free to all comers, till some greater flood should carry it away. The method used to fell these immense trees was to cut a 'curf' all round as deep as practicable with the ordinary ax handle, then deepen it with ax handles of four feet length, and finally build a fire in it.

These people informed me that after getting clear of the redwoods some miles ahead, at a block-house called Elk Camp, the trail led for several days over high rolling grassy mountains, known as the Bald Hills, where grass and water were abundant but Indians numerous and hostile. In due time I reached Elk Camp, which was attractive not merely by contrast with the muddy and gloomy depths of the redwood forest where no sun's ray could penetrate, but as the threshold and entrance to one of the finest tracts of country in California. The region known as the Bald Hills, stretches along on both sides the Klamath from the inland margin of the great seacoast belt of redwoods for perhaps 100 miles by the river's course to the base of the higher snow-covered range of the Cascades, or as they are called in California, the Coast Range. Elk then roamed over them in bands of hundreds, or perhaps thousands, finding the ideal conditions preferred by them. Deer abounded in all the brushy ravines, while bear and bighorn were plenty in the surrounding mountains. Water was found in every hollow, luxuriant grass grew everywhere, and timber was nowhere more distant than a few hours' ride. There can be few places in the world that furnish such a combination of circumstances favorable to the hunter or the cattle-owner, as there exist in respect of soil, climate, water, wood, pasture and scenery.

CHAPTER IX

TRADING IN A HOSTILE INDIAN COUNTRY

But that lovely and enchanting country, long since no doubt occupied and settled, had then one terrible drawback that rendered few miners willing to traverse it a second time, and kept even hunters and packers on a stretch of caution and anxiety. It was infested from end to end along all the streams with numerous small Indian tribes, of deadly hostility to the whites, and fortunately for us with strong proclivities for fighting with each other. Had they been united their numbers and courage would have kept their country inaccessible for a long time; but their tribes, habits, dress, ornaments and even language, changed every few miles along the main streams, rendering concerted action against the whites impossible.

It had become a custom for the packers to delay their trains at either end of this open country till a sufficient number had accumulated to make a safe passage and maintain the necessary night guards for mules and camp. With this view Elk Camp was being secured by a block house then in course of construction by some men who expected to find their compensation from the liberal expenditure of the packers for meals and whiskey during their detention. The mule packers, by whom such a large part of the transportation was done in early days, were a liberal and adventurous class, closely following, and in fact often leading, the first prospectors into every mountain defile, fond of hunting and adventure, making money easily and spending it freely, always ready for a hunt or an Indian fight, or any other excitement.

While the mule train was collecting, I remained several days at this delightful spot, some of us guarding the stock while others hunted elk on the hills, or deer and grizzlies in the

182

ravines, or, I regret to say, gambled with each other at the camp which was made at the margin of the great redwood forest. Always ready to try any new hunting scheme myself, I improved the enforced leisure by the construction, with the aid of one of the post men and a friendly Indian, of a heavy crib bear trap of as large logs as we could handle, which yielded more fun than profit. On the first night we caught a fine panther, or, as the miners erroneously call it, 'mountain lion,' this last being a different and very rare animal with a partially striped hide and other distinguishing characteristics peculiar to himself. The panther being inexperienced in the wiles of men, had fallen a prompt and easy victim and when we cautiously crept up on the lee side of him at daybreak he was busily engaged in making an exhaustive examination of the curious invention so easy to get into, so hard to get out of. We worked a long time in the effort to take him out alive with the aid of a couple of raw-hide lariats, but he became so savage and excited we were obliged to shoot him. The next night was altogether wasted by a worthless wolf getting himself into the crib and keeping better company away. On the third and last night a well grown grizzly cub had pulled the trap down, but his mamma in order to extricate her baby had torn it to pieces and left only a ruin.

On that and subsequent occasions we shot numerous grizzlies at this camp. At the present time long range breechloaders and prepared cartridges render that sport easy enough. But with the muzzle loaders of those days having an extreme safe range of less than a hundred yards, one must kill at first fire at the peril of his life, because if the bear showed fight, as is not uncommon, it was rarely possible for a single hunter to reload in time for a second shot. Hence few hunters cared when alone to molest the animal except under peculiarly favorable circumstances. When a bear has his nose to the ground drinking, digging or feeling for acorns, as is often the case, a square right-angled shot at the top of his head will reach the brain and is the surest of all shots. Even when he is coming for the hunter, unless excited by wounds and rage, he is given to rearing on his hindquarters for better view or smell, and in that act often shows a whitey brown spot at or below the base of the throat, which is a fair mark for a heart shot. There are men reckless enough to risk a side shot at the point of the shoulder, but for a solitary hunter with a short range muzzle loader all these shots are uncertain and dangerous except the first. With a companion of course the case is different, as the bear nearly always loses some valuable time whenever his attention is freshly attracted.

I once knew a hunter who killed many grizzlies in the Sonoma and Russian River valleys, and rarely declined to attack one with the sole assistance of a small noisy terrier dog. That wary but irrepressible animal had been taught to remain at heel till his master fired, and then make straight for the enemy's rear where he kept up such an insulting and alarming snarling and snapping as to tempt the bear to waste precious time by attending to his case first, giving the hunter time to reload and get in a second shot. But with muzzle loaders the best way to hunt this formidable animal in a safe and comfortable manner is for two or three reliable persons to hunt together on opposite sides of the small streams and swampy little valleys which they love to frequent at early hours for the berries, acorns, and kamas root with which such places abound. This magnificent, and on the whole, fearless animal, though equaling most others in activity, and exceeding all in strength and power, is very rarely aggressive unless wounded or followed up closely to his lair, and in my opinion he retreats to such places less from fear, than from a habit of attending strictly to his own business and a modest disinclination for a fuss. There is nevertheless one notorious case, that of a she-bear with cubs, when the mother will attack without any provocation whatever except mere vicinity.

I was once hunting grizzlies in the Russian River country with two settlers from Missouri, one of whom, named Boggs, separated from us to hunt down the opposite side of a narrow bottom closely fringed with large timber, having a close undergrowth. Before long, hearing an excited shout from the other side, we ran quickly in that direction, and scarcely three minutes could have elapsed before we reached the body of Boggs, dead and terribly mangled, his entire left side having been torn off by a blow of the bear's paw. His gun, broken but undischarged, lay near. From an examination of the sign it appeared that B. had approached within twelve feet of a well-used, but now empty lair, from which the bear had sprung upon him without warning, and struck him down before he had time to fire. After making this summary disposal of B. the bear had made off so quickly with her cubs, that we did not get a glimpse of her. As in such a dense jungle she had probably not gone very far, we hastily removed the body without interference from her, and lashing it on a couple of poles, carried it sixteen miles to the nearest settlement.

On another occasion at a far distant locality in the Rocky Mountains some distance north of the *Tete Jaune* pass of the Athabasca, where the grizzly bear is a smaller and less formidable animal than his California relation, and not near so abundant, I was witness of another incident which illustrates the sudden and savage onslaughts which the female will make in defence of her young. Two of us were following the top of a long, high, thinly timbered ridge, about the last place to look for a grizzly, driving before us a few unladen pack horses, when a large bear sprang suddenly from a small thicket, killed the leading horse by a single blow, and frightened the rest over the side of the ridge. Being fully prepared for Indians, she received both our bullets at once, and so instantaneous was the whole affair, that a single minute had scarcely elapsed from her first rush, before the scrimmage was over and the bear lay dead in the trail. The attack seemed unprovoked and contrary to the usual peaceful habits of the animal. But here also there was a bed close by, still warm, and the tracks of two small cubs who had taken themselves away but were probably concealed not far off.

At various times and places I have seen a great number of grizzlies of both kinds, in divers sorts of interviews, both active and passive, some of which may perhaps crop out in subsequent parts of this narrative, but as far as I now remember, the above are the only instances in my own knowledge where the bear was aggressive and vicious from the start without intended provocation, and in view of the domestic circumstances the excuse for these may be regarded as reasonable if not satisfactory. I have heard stories of hunters treed and detained by watching and revengeful grizzlies, but never myself knew of any well authenticated case. Nevertheless, in order to illustrate another of his traits, I am tempted, notwithstanding the length of this digression, to relate another incident tending to show that when, from his point of view, he is wantonly attacked, he is not without a passion strongly resembling a deliberate desire for vengeance.

It was at a place on Eel River near Humboldt Bay, not far below Trinidad, where in a dense redwood forest had been constructed a small log storehouse with roof, door, and a single window shutter of heavy 'puncheons' or plank split several inches thick. It was at some distance from any other house, and among other goods contained a store of barley in bags, for the mules of packers who sometimes fitted out there for the interior. A few days before our arrival a grizzly had torn off the shutter at night, reached in and carried off a bag, and liked it so well that he repeated his theft almost every night, on each occasion appropriating the moderate toll of one bag and no more. Happening to camp there one night in company with an experienced 'mountain man,' the storekeeper told us his trouble and begged us to kill this persistent depredator, there being no other resident ambitious to distinguish himself in that manner. Having heard plenty of such panicky yarns before, and not much expecting the bear to come when he was really wanted, we nevertheless carried our blankets down and slept on the roof, which was nearly flat and about six feet high at the eaves.

In the course of the night the shutter, though firmly spiked on, was torn off with a crash, and through the dense gloom which prevailed under the tall redwoods, we could dimly and doubtfully make out the bear's huge bulk moving off with his plunder. Since the view, indistinct as it was, could be but momentary, I rashly fired at what I took for the small of his back, hoping that if the shot missed the spine it might in ranging forward reach the heart. The bear at once dropped his booty and came for the broken shutter, which he minutely examined, walking once or twice around the small cabin and returning again to the window, all the time growling a vicious soliloquy to himself. Suddenly detecting us, probably by the smell, he stood up, placing both paws on the roof. Whatever his intention, the movement gave Francois the shot he had waited for, and he planted his bullet at the base of the throat at arm's length. The bear dropped back on all fours and made off. Now the forest was not very dark, but the ground between the vast trunks was covered with a dense and tangled growth of 'brake' or fern higher than one's head and offering an uncommonly poor place for a rencontre at close quarters, so we prudently remained where we were till daybreak. The morning light disclosed a bloody trail which we warily followed for quite a hundred yards, when we almost stumbled over the bear lying in an upright position on all fours, his head resting on his paws as if asleep, which is not an unusual position of the grizzly when getting ready to 'pass in his checks.' Approaching through the dense undergrowth on opposite sides we found him nearly cold, having been dead for hours. The last shot had done the business, the first having been merely exasperating.

The grizzly bear is really such a formidable animal and was at first so astonishingly numerous in the fertile berry, root, and nut bearing valleys of California, that every old hunter who has ranged the superb hunting grounds which once bordered the Pacific Coast from San Diego to the Columbia, must remember him with regret, and I cannot take my leave of the monarch of the mountains, without relating another reminiscence which is of the amusing kind and which I know to be true.

When I was at Redding's Springs—now known as Shasta—at the head of the Sacramento and in sight of the glorious peak of the same name, a certain Dutchman had found some good diggings some miles from town, which he kept very secret and worked alone, coming in only on Sundays for the week's provisions. One night, having suffered some delay by the necessity of evading the boys, he reached home late with a good back load, including some fresh beef, which he hung up, and in order to keep off the thieving coyotes, made his bed underneath. During the night he was waked by a tremendous pressure on his body which seemed as though he must be squeezed flat. He was not long in finding that a huge grizzly, attracted by the savory smell (for though mostly frugivorous, they will not refuse meat when it comes in their way) was standing astride of him making little jumps after the meat which he could just reach but not lay hold of. After each failure he would take a seat on the Dutchman and grunt a little to himself on the tantalizing nature of the situation. At last by getting a good footing on Dutchy he made a successful grab and went off with the plunder, paying no attention whatever to the lawful proprietor. The latter lost no time in getting back to town, where with eyes as big as saucers he told his moving tale to all who would listen, whereby his carefully concealed bonanza at once became public to all the world.

A sufficient number of packers had collected at Elk Camp and the time had come to make a start. Notwithstanding the slower gait of my animals, I hoped by starting earlier and arriving later, I might be able to keep up with the main party in a general way. At all events there was nothing better to be done, so on the appointed morning I took the trail at daybreak in advance of the mules, with numerous misgivings. The train came up in due time and being large and long was a good while in passing, but when the rear guard, who lingered a little to talk with me, had gone by, I felt decidedly sorry for myself, especially as it was naturally to be expected the Indians might be following them to pick up stragglers. But nothing molested me, and I came up with the train at its night camp before dark and turned the jacks into their guard, from which I was magnanimously excused. Substantially this course was repeated daily, till the Bald Hills and the worst of the Indian country was passed, during all which time I saw nothing to be afraid of, though usually received at night with cheers and congratulations which indicated plainly enough what was expected for me.

The trail, then new and rough, struck the first mining settlement at Orleans bar on the main Klamath, which however had been abandoned by the miners in favor of the better diggings above. It then, if I recollect right, ascended the Klamath to within fifteen or twenty miles of the mouth of the Salmon, where in order to avoid the nearly impassable precipices which line both rivers in that vicinity, it crossed the Klamath, climbed up twelve or more miles to the top of a rough mountain ridge, and came down on the other side to the Salmon not far below its forks. At the latter place, it again ascended and traversed the long mountain ridge between the North and South forks and came down on the former by a vile precipitous route at a place called Best's tent, where the 'human face divine' was once more to be seen. Scattered along the creek over a space some twenty miles long above and below this point were several hundred miners, mostly prosperous, but cut off from the rest of the world by snow during nearly half the year, and in those days illy supplied with even the necessities of life.

My loads were soon well disposed of, and still better, I found even my despised jacks in good demand, and worth even more than mules for prospecting purposes. No other domestic animal can so well find food and exist among the wild mountain solitudes habitually traversed by prospectors. A jack on any fair ground can carry the outfit of two or three men, and on bad ground the man can carry him. He can live where a mule would starve, can be got into a canoe or on a raft, in short anywhere, and is so docile and sensible that he rarely leaves the camp and gives hardly any trouble. As mine were the first ever seen in that sequestered spot, I had no difficulty in selling them at almost my own prices, and without waiting for a train, started down the trail on foot at the rate of forty or fifty miles a day, mostly lying in concealment by day and pushing on by night.

It was, I think, at the fork or mouth of the Trinity where one Durkee kept a small block house, that I rested one night in anticipation of having to make next day the entire distance of sixty miles to Blackburn's post at the lower crossing of the Klamath. At Durkee's one Wooley, a mountain man well known in those parts agreed to accompany me next day, but four miners who had been waiting there some days for a traveling party of safe numbers wished to go with us. In vain, backed by Durkee, we represented to them that the route lay through the worst Indian territory in the whole country, and must be covered in one day, without admitting of stoppages for any purpose; that a couple of mountain men alone, could fight, hide or run, according to circumstances, but six men were too few to fight, and too many to hide, and that anyone who should give out or break down was lost. They insisted on going with us, but on the clear understanding that happen what would, we were not to stop for them on the road.

The morning start was made from the river so as to get on the mountain by daybreak, the ascent being through heavy timber to the ridge where the trail emerged on the Bald Hills. Just before reaching the summit, in the dim light of early dawn, a couple of bucks painted for war (breast bones and ribs white like skeletons), who had evidently been ambushed for a smaller party, jumped from behind a log and took silently to the woods. The incident was not encouraging, as our presence could no longer be kept secret. Two of the miners here thought better of their enterprise and started back to Durkee's, which as was afterwards learned they never reached, and were heard of no more. The other two insisted on keeping along with us though it was now certain we should be watched and probably followed, and our only safety lay in keeping ahead of the alarm and halting for nothing. We therefore swung along at our best gait, keenly watching all the distant swells and ridges, and for a time detecting no enemy. But towards sundown, first one and then the other miner began to lag and fall behind. Wooley and I waited for them several times at great risk to ourselves, and finally after warning them that the enemy were probably gathering and waiting somewhere between us and Blackburn's—left them, and saw or heard no more of them. Arriving toward dark within a few miles of Blackburn's which was on the opposite side of the river, here running at the bottom of a deep hollow, smoke columns began to appear successively in front, rear and to the right. Seeing we were cut off on three sides, we moved along more leisurely till it became quite dark, and then plunged down a little hollow on the left which soon became a great ravine well filled with brush, sheltered by which, we reached and swam the river, and cautiously worked our way down among the rocks and willows on the water's edge, frequently obliged to enter the latter but without splash or sound, reaching B.'s late at night. The unfortunate miners were never heard of again.

At Trinidad I bought mules which were now arriving in considerable numbers, many owners being deterred from going to the interior by the Indian troubles above. Hiring a couple of Mexican muleteers, and loading up the mules, I quickly started again for the mountains. At Blackburn's a party of about twenty men, mostly belonging to the train I had formerly gone up with, were getting ready to go out after Indians and insisted on electing me captain, a position I was reluctant to accept with the brilliant personal prospects I thought I then saw ahead. However, as nothing else would content them, I could not well avoid it, and assuming command, pushed out towards the north, into a country then quite unknown, whence had appeared the flank smoke signals which alarmed W. and myself on the last trip down. Finding a good-sized stream we followed it into the mountains, finding two recent nests warm but empty. I had no scouts fitted to send ahead prospecting, and my party was much too insubordinate to permit my leaving them behind and undertaking the job myself. So, after burning the empty villages, we returned and raided up and down the main river valley. This almost bloodless enterprise failed to shed glory on any one, but undoubtedly rendered the hostiles more cautious and kept them farther removed from the trail.

After this episode I proceeded to work my mules for all they were worth, making several round trips to the mines, usually doubling my capital, or more, on each occasion, notwithstanding a few days off to rest the stock, which I generally devoted to Indian or elk hunting. The former, though attended at times with some disgusting cruelty from the miners who deeply resented the shocking mutilations practiced by the Indians on the bodies of their victims, and who could scarcely be restrained from any excesses when on rare occasions they could surprise a village, nevertheless tended to make the lower Klamath much safer and more peaceful. Elk hunting, whether mounted or by still hunting on foot, was then in its best condition, and supplied unsurpassed sport. Thousands roamed over the Bald Hills, and could be found in almost any of the great ravines, from which when started below, they would rush out above in large bands with a sounding tread like the rush of a cavalry regiment. I cannot forbear relating here an odd adventure with them which involved more work and excitement than usual, though reflecting little credit on the hunter.

In company with a mountain man and good hunter who was traveling to the mines with my pack train, I was one day hunting some strayed mules, with little thought of elk, when rising over a small elevation near the upper end of a deep and grassy ravine, we came plump upon nine elk which did not notice us at first, we having the wind of them. We did not need any meat, and had no mules with us to carry it, but finding such a tempting opportunity thrusting itself upon us, resolved to test a certain favorite tenet of all old hunters, namely, that if one can distinguish and kill the leader of a small band without sentinels, keeping to leeward and reasonably out of sight, one can, without much trouble bag all the others. We soon settled on a splendid antlered bull, and waiting a favorable shot, laid him low. The others at first startled by the shot, after a little galloping about huddled together round the fallen leader, without giving much attention to the mysterious cause of his disaster. Two more were soon bagged, and so on with the same result till the six bullets which we had between us were exhausted, leaving three fine young cows still lost in wonder at the strange events occurring around them, but showing no disposition to leave the scene. One of these investigating about, walked up in front of and close to us, lying quiet on the grass, and after taking a good look at us, tossed her head saucily and trotted off. My weapon was an old army yager with an iron ramrod, borrowed hastily before leaving camp, my own rifle being out of order. As the ground was open, being covered only with short grass, and the shot was close and certain, when a good side shot presented itself, I could not resist firing the rod at her, but not allowing enough for its weight, it dropped considerably even at the short distance, and instead of striking behind the shoulder, the light end struck her knee which it shattered, and the heavy end coming on hard behind, twisting the rod around both knees, like hobbling a mule. No sooner did we try to approach, however, than we found the animal could get about pretty lively, and it began to be a nice question how to recover the rod. Without it the gun was useless, and the country contained no suitable timber to make a wooden one. Therefore it must be had, and after lashing our knives on poles, lance fashion, we spent half a day or more following that confounded elk over several miles of country—practically unarmed and liable to run plump upon Indians at every step—before we finally recovered it. It was a foolish and useless piece of folly, which might easily enough have cost both of us our lives.

Two other notable events occurred that summer, one of a tragical, the other of an amusing character. The first was at Blackburn's post, before mentioned, which having exerted such an important influence in opening up the lower Klamath, deserves some description. The place included a scow ferry across the river and was held by B. with eight hired men. The latter occupied a small canvas house in the rear of which was a small shanty of clapboards scarcely eight feet square, in which B. slept with the amunition and some extra firearms. These structures stood on a low bar near the water's edge, and near them rose a vertical bluff perhaps forty feet high, from which stretched a small prairie of a few hundred acres, shut in on all sides but the river by the forest. On the prairie close by the edge of the bluff and overlooking and commanding the ferry, the men had commenced the construction of a block house not yet sufficiently completed for occupation. Beyond the river rose the mighty buttresses of the Bald Hills, sweeping up and away for several miles to the distant summit, along whose flank ran the pack trail gradually ascending the mountain side, till it disappeared up the river.

Camping one night in the timber a few miles below Blackburn's, with a large pack train of twenty men (besides Mexicans, who don't count much in an argument with firearms) we made a daylight start next morning, and as we approached the prairie back of B.'s, began to hear firing at his place. Quickly getting the white men in front we cautiously opened the prairie and charged down to the ferry, seeing no Indians, although the firing ceased. When we arrived and opened communication with B. who was shut up alone in the small house, a horrid scene was disclosed on the bar. The canvas shanty had been surprised and all its occupants simultaneously massacred. Their dying groans had aroused B. who opened fire and had successfully defended himself in the clapboard house. The eight bodies were scattered about the bar mutilated in every shocking manner that the ingenuity of the savage had been able to devise.

Sometime during the night a body of Indians had surrounded the place quietly, cut their way into the canvas house and at a signal had killed without noise, every man. B., awakened only by the groans of the victims, had knocked off some of the upper clapboards of his shanty and opened fire. Being an old mountain man he wasted no shots, but the Indians knowing the small house could contain but one man, were ashamed to run away and leave him. After rushing several times on the house with disastrous results to themselves, they retired and tried to crush the roof by stones thrown down on it from the bluff. But as they had to carry the stones up from the beach, and the stones they were able to heave so far were not heavy enough for the purpose, they returned to the beach and after considerable discussion among themselves, commenced a series of single rushes on the door, one at a time, trying to chop it down. They might have kicked in the slight clapboards anywhere, but thinking, naturally enough, that the place to get in at was the door, they gave their whole attention to it, each volunteer shouting his death song, as like the Homeric heroes, they successively devoted themselves to death. But as the door was much the strongest part of the house, being made of split puncheons several inches thick, and B. did not give them much time for chopping, their devotion went for nothing and all their efforts failed. B. thought he had 'saved' at least six, though their bodies had been successfully carried off. We buried on the prairie the horribly mangled remains of the eight men as far as they could be found and gathered up and took B. along with us, but not before he had buried a box of powder under one end of the ferry scow then being built on the beach. In the box he placed a flint lock cocked, and the trigger made fast to the scow. It was afterwards learned through friendlies, that when the Indians returned after our departure and tried to push off the scow, an explosion occurred, which perhaps gave them a new idea of the ubiquity of the white man's vengeance.

The other incident referred to, though it entailed damage to some of the individuals concerned, was ludicrous enough to the spectators. One Young with a few others had built a canvas house near the sight selected for a block house on the main pack trail, which here led along the bench of a side hill several hundred feet above the river, behind which the bald, treeless hills rose steeply for several miles to the summit of the ridge. Two trains, of which mine was one, camped here one night, carrying up a crowd of miners sufficient in number to occupy for sleeping quarters the entire floor of the house. These men were scared and nervous about Indians, and being extremely tired were soon asleep, the canvas roll which closed the front of the house being let down on a closely piled barricade of tables, benches and boxes. Late at night, or rather early in the morning, when everything was snug and quiet and the stillness of night was only broken by the nasal music of the tired foot travelers, some scared mules came running down the hill, the cry of 'Indians' was started by some fool, and a panic, sudden and unaccountable, as such things always are, at once prevailed. Such as were not tangled up and struggling with their blankets, rushed to get out and tumbled over the barricade. A furious miscellaneous struggle commenced inside, everyone hitting out in the dark at pretty much every moving object. When order was at last restored almost everyone inside had been hurt by blows from shovels, pick handles and other extemporized weapons, one man having been killed by a blow from a hand-saw.

Personally I had slept outside with the packs to keep an eye on them and the mules. Young, who was an old hunter, with myself and the other packers, who all lay outside, were in position to know the folly of the affair from the beginning, but as the terrified miners stoutly defended the entrance, it was as much as one's life was worth to venture into the pandemonium raging inside. Fortunately the miners had few firearms, or it was too dark and confused to permit of their use. At all events grievous as were the bruises, wounds and broken heads, no shots were fired. The skinned carcass of a deer killed the day before and hanging outside near one end of the house suffered severely during the row. One bold fighting Irishman was caught furiously belaboring it with a pick handle, the venison persistently swinging back and hitting him after each vicious and well aimed blow.

Before taking leave with reluctance of the Bald Hills, I must not forget to mention the extraordinary skill of those Indians in snaring elk and other large animals in nooses of stout rope made by themselves from bark, which sometimes got them into trouble with the whites, as in the following case. At Durkee's some of his friendlies once confided to me, with much secrecy, a mysterious accident they had met with which they feared would peril their friendly relations with Durkee, who while protecting them from others was sometimes disposed to be rather violent with them himself. Accompanying them therefore at their urgent request, some miles to the top of the ridge, they pointed out an unlucky ox belonging to D., which must have been dead for a fortnight and still lay just as he perished in a running noose set for elk on a well-marked runway. The noose had been skillfully arranged by placing a log for the game to step over and a branch necessary to stoop under, the two together well calculated to divert attention from the snare itself. Two long brush fences extended from the spot on either hand obtuse-angled toward each other, so that any animal traversing the runway would surely be led directly to the noose, and get entangled while avoiding the obstacles placed to distract his attention. Unfortunately D.'s ox, unaccustomed to such fiendish contrivances in the far-off Missouri prairies of his youth, had in this case fallen an easy victim, and perished by a lingering and solitary death. As D. had already missed the animal and had repeatedly sent them to look for it, I advised them to make a voluntary confession before he should discover the fact for himself. That they were afraid to do, but recognizing the sound nature of the advice, insisted that I should tell the tale for them so that in case of too violent an ebullition of wrath they might take to the woods for a time.

To account for such excessive apprehension it should be explained that stock stealing, natural and tempting as it is to the Indian, is deemed about the worst sin he can commit, and if strongly suspected he would have about as much chance for his life as a sheep dog caught red-handed. On this occasion it was smoothed over for them with D., who was amused with their fear of him, and went up with them himself to see how the mischief had been done. Though D. was liable to be so violent and exacting with his friendlies, he was a safe and good friend to them, and like most of the mountain men who have passed their lives in fighting Indians, would have defended them against rascally white marouders with his life if necessary.

After a summer's hard but not unprofitable nor unpleasant work, I went down to Trinidad, as it proved to be, for the last time. In order to rest and improve my hard worked stock, I camped some ten miles below the town on a large and lovely prairie not far from the beach of the Pacific though surrounded by forest, known as Dow's prairie. The place was well grassed and watered, full of strawberries even at that season, and teeming with game, especially elk, in great numbers. At daybreak almost any morning, one might find immense droves of that noble deer feeding and sporting in the numerous deep bays of the prairie projected in all directions into the surrounding forest. In this attractive spot were a number of mountain or company men, resting themselves and stock till it should be time to start on their winter's hunt in the mountains. One of these whom I met here casually and for the first time, I was destined to know long and intimately during a future not yet revealed, and to share with him many wild adventures of the wildnerness such as I little contemplated at the time.

Francois Bisell was like many of his class, a half-breed of Canadian and Huron stock, the Indian blood predominating, since his father had been a half-breed before him. In my partial eyes, he retained most of the best traits of both races, possessing, with the tenacity and coolness of the whites, the Indian's taciturnity and silent endurance, with the courage and intelligence of both. He was exactly of my age, having been born on the same day, six feet high, handsome and well proportioned, fearless in character though extremely amiable, and was by far the best hunter I have ever met. Our intimacy commenced with a circumstance which I am sure neither of us had cause to be ashamed of or regret, although it led to subsequent acts not perhaps so easily defensible. We had been up the coast some miles above Trinidad to an Indian village where we occasionally got a sea otter skin or two, and were returning to camp by way of Trinidad, the only available mule trail lying through the town. On emerging from the 'one mile gulch' just above the town, we came upon several of the boiled-shirt gentry (gamblers) who had three Indians bound to trees and were discussing in what manner to put them to death. The Indians, who knew us, called on us to save them, and we recognized them as inhabitants of the village we had just come from. Some cattle had been killed near the town, and the gamblers, who knew nothing of Indians and could neither find nor catch any wild ones, had seized these poor friendlies who were in frequent and amicable communication with packers and fur men, and living in permanent quarters near-by at the whites' mercy, would have as soon thought of suicide, as of hostile acts against such dangerous neighbors.

The gamblers however were determined to have the fun of murdering someone, and the only effect of our remonstrance was to draw their cheap wrath upon ourselves. They cursed us for d—d 'fur men' and 'mountain men,' who were no better than Indians ourselves, and in fact were in league with them and should by right be hung also. Like the rest of their kind they flourished bright shiney six-shooters and bowie knives, but had no rifles, thinking no doubt their numbers gave them a sure thing on us; but not of that opinion was Francois. F. possessed that dangerous sort of temperament that becomes cooler in exact proportion as danger comes nearer, and at the very crisis, he was sure to be almost painfully deliberate. Without taking his eyes an instant from the enemy, he remarked to me in a drawling tone in Chinook "Will you fight?" "Yes." "Then I will be captain; watch me." It must be explained that the first step of mountain men on getting into a tight place with Indians or others, is to select a captain whose actions and words are to be closely regarded. Thus no talking is required, and the captain, knowing the others will do what he does, neither too soon or too late, need not remove his eye an instant from the enemy. Suddenly drawing his rifle F. ordered "Throw down your pistols. Hands up!"

Now the gentry before us were professed desperados and fighting men, killing each other or some unlucky miner nearly every night; but not expecting hostilities from the smaller party, were fairly taken by surprise, and possibly somewhat impressed by the reputation for quick and sure shooting, usually attributed to mountain men. They were well huddled up together, and may have had time to reflect that at their first hostile motion two or more would be dead for certain, with a smart chance for some more. At any rate, the order was obeyed and their pistols secured. The Indians were cut loose and directed to back off slowly into the gulch and then run, which they obeyed to the letter, and in the course of about one minute after they disappeared over the edge of the gulch, they would have been about as easy to find as a weasel in a stone pile. The most risky thing remained, to get away ourselves. We feared to take the pistols, as that would have really put us in the same category with Indians, and these gambling rascals controlled the opinion and action of the town. They were therefore discharged and handed over, and their owners ordered to move on toward town, while we, getting our horses with much more rapidity of movement than F. had been recently displaying in face of the enemy, disappeared in the timber and by a wide detour around the town got down to camp the same night.

There we found sympathetic hearers, and ascertained that by sending for three men camped near Humboldt Bay, we could at once muster eleven reliable mountain men, who might be counted on to stand together. It was certain none of us dare go to the town again separately, and extremely probable we should be attacked where we were. It was therefore determined to send some of my neutral Mexicans up to reconnoiter, while making hasty preparations to anticipate hostilities by raiding, or in the frontier vernacular, 'bully ragging' the town. We might have done it the same night but for my pack train which was loaded, and could neither be driven on the main trail through the town, nor immediately concealed. The ponies of the fur men were driven off and cached in the timber, and with plenty of help, I got my train through the red woods and avoiding the town by a long and rough detour crossed the Redwood River well up towards its source and camped in a grassy ravine which penetrated the forest from the Bald Hills above Elk Camp. There the train was safe from anything except the prowling Klamaths and not difficult for me to join later by a short cut through the timber.

These matters being disposed of and our party reassembled, the following plan was agreed on. It was lawless, unjustifiable and even criminal, yet two considerations may be urged in palliation. First. Though planned by an illiterate Scotch half-breed who had never seen so much as a platoon of soldiers, it was both in conception and execution, relative numbers and obstacles considered, a splendid piece of military strategy which any soldier might study with advantage. Second. We had been badly treated, could not venture into the town without being set upon and killed *seriatim*, and with our inferior numbers there was no other way of getting even with the twenty or thirty gambling rascals who controlled the place, except to surprise them by a vigorous initiative. The following brief topographical description is required to render intelligible the events that followed.

The road from Dow's prairie leads up about ten miles on a beach of hard sand, crossing over several precipitous rocky points of timber running out into the sea, each of which affords a good defensive position either to retard pursuit, or to escape to the mountains if hard pressed. The town is situated on a bluff rising vertically from the beach several hundred feet high at the lower or southern end, but diminishing to nothing at the other end where the landing is situated. From the landing a single road turns from the beach and ascends the bluff parallel with the coast to the top, a distance of a quarter of a mile or more. This road or street is, or was, the only one in the place, and was lined on both sides with tents or canvas shanties, the only frame being a good-sized two-story house at the lower end by the landing. This house was occupied by the gamblers who both preyed upon and controlled the town, and in the evenings by a crowd of their dupes. The rear part of the lower floor displayed a large and gaily furnished liquor bar, while the front part was filled with gambling tables renting at twenty dollars a night each. Some of the gamblers slept on these tables, the others on the second floor. Though fights and rows were of nightly occurrence, in which the gamblers usually came off first best, there was no doubt that in any attack from outsiders, the town, as far as its prowess went, would make common cause to defend the place. Just south of the town where the bluff was highest, there was a narrow bench somewhat more than half-way up the height, but a few feet wide containing a small *rancheria* or Indian village of three or four houses and a spring of water, through which a steep and rough Indian path never used by, but not absolutely impracticable for, horses mounted the bluff.

The following was McLeod's plan exactly as adopted and carried out. All effects having been removed from Dow's prairie, our eleven men with advance and rear guards ready told off, left that point timed to reach the foot of the Indian path just before daybreak. Everything being quiet and a guard quickly set over the Indian houses, the whole party succeeded in getting their horses up the bluff and withdrawing the guard, concentrated at the top of the street. The advance guard then giving the Crow war-whoop, galloped down to secure the gambling house, the others riding leisurely after them in single file reserving rifles, but firing pistols at every head seen and at every opening door. The shopkeepers were thus kept from assembling and furnished with useful reflections to occupy their minds. The advance guard closely supported, entered the gambling house through every downstair door and window, seized and smashed about twenty rifles stacked behind the bar, pinned a lot of gamblers who were sleeping on the tables into a corner, and notified their friends above that we didn't want any of their money, but if a single shot was fired, we would fire the building and let no one come out. Then the barkeepers having been hunted out, all hands rode their horses up to the bar by detachments and obliged the dishevelled officials to treat each astonished nag, as well as his rider, to a bowl of their best beverage. The visit having been well rubbed in by the above and more objectionable methods, and some of our men showing a dangerous inclination to drink too much, old Mac called us off. All the arms, boots and clothing in sight, being a considerable pile, were carried out and tossed into the sea, and the enemy being thus disabled from immediate pursuit, no time was lost in traveling down the beach to Dow's and thence scattering into the mountains.

Though the vicinity of Trinidad is by no means uninteresting, and the 'Head' which gives it such harbor facilities as it enjoys, was the best place to shoot wild geese I ever saw, I have never seen it since. Rejoining my train by devious routes through the forest, I pushed on up the river, by no means sorry to see the distance lengthen out behind me. At this time I had accumulated a train of fine mules, owed nothing, and had six Mexican *Arrieros* to perform most of the daily drudgery. These were a murderous but cowardly lot, worthless for Indian fighting but very dangerous to their padrone, especially on the down trip when his pockets were well filled with gold dust. On such occasions when there was no white passenger along, I frequently slept apart in the woods, not being much afraid of them by day, but much objecting to having their rascally knives feeling among my ribs when asleep. It was not uncommon to hear of packers being murdered by them, and I never considered my life very safe among them, which accounts partly for not losing it, but my next catastrophe was to come from a different source.

CHAPTER X

CAMPING AND TRAPPING IN MIDWINTER

It was on an evening late in the summer, and quite frosty among the mountains, that I camped on a high bar of the upper Klamath, some fifty miles or more above the debouch of the Salmon, hunting out a practicable passage to the new mines then thought to exist about Klamath Lake. The mules were turned out as usual and the packs and *aparejos* piled in a row to make a windbreak for our blankets on the lee side, which was toward the river. Lofty mountains hemmed us in on all sides, the calm silence of a quiet evening prevailed, and night closed gradually down on us and all the property I possessed, but was destined never to see again.

During the calm moments of that deceitful evening, in the hidden recesses of the mountain solitudes, a catastrophe was even then preparing which, before another sun should shine, was to sweep upon us with resistless fury, destroy the lives of most of us, bring ruin to many homes in far tropical Mexican valleys, reduce me to poverty, and change all my prospects, hopes and plans. A few eventful seconds sufficed to work all that ruin and it is difficult to convey to those who have not witnessed the shock of a midnight Indian onset, the horror of the moment when an unprepared and sleeping camp is instantaneously converted to a scene of carnage and blood. There are some sober moments during the first deliberate advance of a determined infantry charge, and a wild intoxicating excitement in a tumultuous rush of cavalry, but such enterprises have been well considered, and one is quite prepared for what is to be done, and, stirring as they are, they have little to remind one of the unexpected lightning-like shock of a successful Indian surprise by night.

It was at some late hour of the night that a mounted band of up-country Indians, who had doubtless watched us long and marked our camp well, deployed quietly on the high bar we lay upon, between us and the river and in an instant covered us with a thick flight of arrows and charged home. At their first yell of battle, quickly followed by the rush of horses, I kicked off the blankets and partly rose, but seeing they must go over us, threw myself down flat on the ground till they had passed, and while the horses were stumbling and jumping over the row of *aparejos,* I sprang up and ran for the river, rifle in hand, jumping in the darkness from the high vertical bank as far as possible to clear the rocks. Fortunately I struck deep water, and though the current was strong, succeeded in swimming back and finding concealment in shallow water among some rocks and small willow brush. Here I drew my load, wiped out, and reloaded, soon discovering for the first time a broken arrow sticking painfully in the front or upper part of my thigh. It was too dark to see anything, and owing to the noise of the water I could hear nothing from above, so I proceeded to examine the injury as well as I could by feeling. The arrow had entered on one side, passed an inch below the skin and the point projected slightly on the other side. There was considerable laceration and bleeding, and in consequence of the barb, it was impossible to draw it back, so after getting rid with some trouble of the broken end, I finally pushed it through in the original direction with much pain, and tied up the wound as well as I could.

After an hour or two in the water, during which I nearly perished with cold, there being some signs of daylight, I succeeded in climbing up the bank and carefully reconnoitered. Not a sound disturbed the silence, and gradually and with caution I approached our late camp. Here lay four dead Mexicans fulls of arrows and some of them showing considerable cuts about the head from the long heavy knives carried by those Indians. By cautious signals I at length found one of the Mexicans hiding in the timber, and with his aid discovered another lying near, still living, but shot squarely through the body. Daylight gradually appeared, enabling us to make sure that the Indians had definitely cleared out, apparently satisfied for the present to get safely away with the stock. While occupied in making a better dressing of my own wound and doing what was possible for the wounded Mexican, I sent the other man to follow the retreating trail in hopes he might find a mule or two escaped from the main lot, as is not at all uncommon, mules thus suddenly startled and run off to the mountains, often showing surprising ingenuity in concealing themselves so as to get left behind and return to company or pasture that has proved agreeable. The trail which was of course broad and easily followed, led at first up the small creek which came in at the upper end of the bar, and in no great time the man returned with two good mules which had escaped in the darkness, confusion and thick undergrowth, and were leisurely returning down the ravine.

Having arranged to take turns in holding the wounded and apparently dying man, fire was set to the packs and *aparejos,* and the mules quickly saddled and mounted, I undertaking the first charge of the wounded man, which proved not only painful to the feelings but extremely fatiguing. At the first suitable place we swam the river and plunged into a ravine leading up the opposite mountain, intending if possible to strike the miners' settlements either on the lower Shasta, or Scott's River, estimated at about sixty miles distant, by as straight a cut as practicable through the mountains. We rode all day through a rough and extremely difficult country, taking frequent turns with the wounded man, who suffered extreme agony and rapidly sank. Having become mostly unconscious the same afternoon, it became necessary to seat him in the saddle and ride behind him, and not long before dark while changing seats it was discovered he was dead. Quickly covering the body with rocks, we pushed on more rapidly till dark, when we turned loose the mules, and walking back on our trail about half a mile in the bed of a small creek, lay down where we were certain to be disturbed by, and get timely notice of anyone following on our track. Nothing appeared during the night, and we resumed the road as soon as we could see, making much better progress now that we were relieved of the incumbrance of the previous day. It was late one evening on the second or third day of this difficult and painful ride that we came down on the lower Shasta and soon struck a miner's camp.

It was while pottering around this vicinity nursing my wounded leg, that I was overjoyed to meet my dear Francois, that pearl of mountain men and staunch comrade whom I had parted from on the retreat from Trinidad with little expectation of ever meeting again. It was a timely and joyful meeting. We were now both 'broke,' both piously hated the regular humdrum labor of mining, and both had a dangerous secret to keep; so after living awhile on the proceeds of the deer which F. shot for the mining camps, we concluded with the three mules remaining to our joint estates, to push out for the mountains north of the big river (Columbia), where F. knew the country, and pass the winter in trapping sable, or martens, as the Americans call them.

It was late in the season for so long a journey. Since our animals would have the whole winter to rest in, we did not spare them but pushed on rapidly, passing the Rogue River and upper Umpqua districts without trouble from those Indians, who had not yet been driven to the long and bloody war they were forced into some years later by the depredations of settlers and politicians. Crossing the Calapooyas we hurried on down the great Oregon valley, crossed the Columbia, where we traded our mules for a larger number of Kayutz horses, and coming out near the head of the Okanagan, crossed the divide to the Thompson, getting across that fine river with much difficulty below, and not far from the Shuswap lakes. We had expected to get into the Rockies somewhere in this vicinity, but finding the Wapta, Tete Jaune and other passes of the Saskatchewan and Athabasca, all infested by Blackfeet, we kept on up the North Thompson crossed the upper Frazer near its head and got into the Rocky Mountains by the Smoky Fork of the Peace.

Though on this long route we had met with a number of Company men returning from the American mines, and likely to be belated like ourselves, yet we were quite a month too late to find a good place and make suitable preparation for a northern winter. Under the experienced guidance of F. we were not long in choosing a good district for trapping, nor even in getting horses through the mountains though snow had commenced to fall and already lay in large quantity on high elevations. But after getting down to the eastern foothills and out on the plains, we found the great buffalo herds had disappeared, leaving no recent sign, and it was necessary to rely on moose, caribou and an occasional wood buffalo to provide material for the winter pemmican. Selecting a fine valley in the foothills to serve as winter quarters for the horses when we should be done with their services, we had a good deal of hard and laborious hunting in the vicinity, which only produced a moose or two, a few caribou and mule, or jumping deer, and perhaps a couple of wood buffalo, a variety rather larger and more solitary than the buffalo of the plains and rarely found out of the mountains. Not having the good fortune to secure many fat animals, we were obliged to smoke-dry most of the meat, contenting ourselves with but little pemmican, which requires fat in considerable quantity to make it good. Much difficulty was encountered in packing these provisions up into the higher region selected for the winter's trapping ground. The snow by this time covered most of the country, and the ground was everywhere hard frozen; in fact, we owed the hard and uncomfortable winter which followed, to the lateness of our arrival and preparations. It was extremely difficult to get worked-out horses through the snow, in consequence of which we hurriedly chose for winter quarters a place which proved to have indifferent advantages, and it was even more difficult and dangerous to get the wretched animals back to the valley destined for their quarters. Though we lost none on this occasion, they had many bad falls and for at least a fortnight got little to eat but willow brush. Hard travelling, poor rations, and stumbling over snow-covered rocks and logs, left them little better than bags of bones when at last after *caching* the saddles in a dense fir tree, we let them loose and turned our backs on them for the winter.

In that wintry valley it is probable that grain-fed horses would have starved to death in a week, but it is surprising how these hardy Indian ponies will live and get fat under such unpromising circumstances. They know how to get a good living from the old grass still standing on wind-swept places comparatively free from snow, and on vertical rocky banks where it cannot lie, and with plenty of time and no work to do, when all else fails can live for weeks at a time on alder, poplar and willow brush, and can probably come safely through the winter anywhere that the summer produces such growth at all.

For myself I knew but little of the kind of work laid out for the winter, but my companion had been in the H. B. Company all his life, and was as experienced a trapper, hunter and traveler, as was to be found throughout all its vast territory. There was no fish, bird or animal whose habits and resorts he did not know. If there was a deer anywhere within ten miles he was sure to find it, and I doubt whether he had a superior anywhere as a mountain man and hunter. I never knew him to lose his bearings in the most intricate and perplexing mountain ranges, except on a few occasions in consequence of my bad advice, and then, when I gave it up, he was always able to rectify it quickly, and I never heard a reproach from his lips. It is no very difficult thing to get about through the mountains on foot, provided one knows the various resources for procuring food, and is not pressed for time. But to get horses along, especially when loaded, one can afford to make few mistakes, because the animals fail or die while one is trying to rectify blunders. I suppose persons whose mountain travels have been confined to well marked trails with good guides, can hardly realize that the two surest traits of a good experienced mountain man, are first, the faculty of knowing at the beginning whether a bench, pass, or stream which has a promising entrance will do to trust to; and second, the certain and unfailing knowledge whether one has actually crossed a high divide, and is really coming down on other waters, or whether in the endless intricacies of the mountain ranges, he has only got from one long ridge on to another, and is really descending on the same waters. The last mistake is extremely common, and has cost many a man his life, some instances of which will appear later on.

Before settling down to our winter's work it may be well to describe what a sable trapper's work is like. It is totally different from beaver trapping, which requires an outfit of steel traps, and must be pursued along streams and rivers which are also frequented during the winter by Indians, whose hostility is often extremely dangerous. The marten, or sable is a small animal of the weasel tribe that lives well up in the middle district of the mountains, where the Indians unless travelling, rarely come in winter. The trapper having deposited his livestock in a safe place, and laid up either pemmican or smoked dried meat for provisions, sits down on some remote, difficult and well concealed stream, well up, though not too high among the mountains, and makes a small brush shelter, open in front, and if possible with plenty of dry, wind-felled timber close by. Here he can have as much fire as he chooses at night, when the smoke cannot be seen, but if he is prudent and regards his scalp, he will not risk much of it during the day. Nor will he ever discharge a gun either by night or day, except in circumstances of stringent necessity.

Here he is soon snowed in, and shut off from all the world, provided he has been sufficiently careful of his trail, and the marks and signs he has left behind him. His horses turned out in some distant valley, may be and often are discovered and stolen, in which event he must, when spring comes, replace them in the same way, or abandon all the proceeds of his winter's labor. Having made his quarters comfortable, safely disposed of his provisions, and prepared snow-shoes and trap sticks, one of the pair starts off taking a long leading ridge for forty miles or more, setting traps in favorable places as he goes, crossing over and returning by some similar ridge as far as practicable. Each of such trips may occupy a week or more; sometimes if fresh snow falls, considerably more, and on his return his partner does the same, of course avoiding the same ridges. Thus they alternate all winter, setting and resetting traps, skinning, and packing in the skins. While in camp there is plenty of work, *fleshing*, drying, stretching and packing the skins and trapping small game for fresh provisions when it can be had.

But if a *carcajou*, or as the Americans call them, wolverine, gets on the line of traps, or if quarters have to be moved in midwinter in consequence of scarcity of martens, or, worst of all, should the sign of some prowling Indian be detected, it may become necessary to move the camp and the entire theatre of operations far away to another district, in which case the skins already collected must be *cached* and protected from the weather, and from hungry prowlers, and every other asset backed on snowshoes through the wildest and roughest intricacies of inhospitable mountains covered deep with snow.

Supposing, however, that such accidents and removals can be avoided, the mere routine of trap-setting and attendance gives but little trouble except after fresh falls of snow, especially when caught by storms far away from camp. Notwithstanding that in the low temperature of those regions, snow frequently falls dry and hard-frozen like sand, it has a constant tendency to settle and pack, and can often be traversed without snow-shoes, though when these are not worn they must always be carried ready for use, usually over the shoulder with the bag of firesticks.[13]

Indians in reasonably safe localities, are not apt to be troublesome in winter, they also preferring to stay near their camps, the large game they seek also mostly retiring to the lower elevations. Perhaps the worst enemy of the trapper on the whole at that season, is the *carcajou,* or wolverine, which is active and ubiquitous at all seasons, and when it discovers a single trap or trail, seems to possess an extra-ordinary and devilish ingenuity for tracing out and infesting the entire line. He is a solitary and mysterious animal, often felt but rarely seen, and most trappers credit him with a malignant and superhuman intelligence always applied to evil purposes. In fact, his habit of remaining all winter in

[13] The fire sticks, which are the sole means of producing fire, used by trappers and Indians, are two in number. The first is of hard wood, rectangular in section, about two feet long, half an inch thick and perhaps an inch and a half wide at the center, tapering to nothing at both ends. On the top surface are one or more depressions to engage the end of the other stick, each depression having a small deep notch leading from it to and through the edge of the stick. The second stick is of soft wood eighteen inches long, half an inch thick, round in section, blunt at the lower end and tapering at the other. A little tinder made from the dried and pounded inside bark of certain trees, is carried with the fire sticks. To make a fire, the first stick is laid flat on the ground with some tinder under the outlet of the notch before mentioned. The operator kneels with one knee on each end of the stick, the notched edge being directed away from him. The blunt end of the soft wood stick held upright, is inserted in one of the depressions and a rapid twirling motion given it by rolling between the hands. The friction immediately produces a fine brown powder at the point of contact which as it rapidly increases in volume fills the notch and flows out into a minute heap upon the tinder. This at once begins to smoke and soon ignites, when the tinder is folded around it and either exposed to the wind or waved once or twice through the air when it bursts into a blaze and being properly inserted in a small pile of suitable material laid ready for the purpose, the fire is secured. The whole operation rarely exceeds two or three minutes and if the weather be very bad is facilitated by gathering a robe around the operator and his implements.

the most inhospitable regions, from which most of the small animals on which he preys have departed for lower levels, and the unerring manner in which he follows out for long distances a line of traps carefully concealed and separated by ingeniously contrived breaks and intervals, may well puzzle wiser heads than those of the poor trapper.

Marten traps in themselves are simple enough; it is in the locality, lines, directions and modes of concealment from uninvited guests, that the trapper's skill consists. They are made by arranging a small enclosure of driven stakes with a single opening. Across that is laid as threshold, a log, stone or even a flat chunk of ice, upon which at one end rests the moveable deadfall, the other end of the latter supported by some of the various kinds of trap sticks, the common 'figure four' being usually preferred. A small bait of fresh or dried meat, the former preferable when it can be had, is carried by the triggerstick inside the enclosure where the marten can only reach it by introducing his long neck through the entrance. As soon as he seizes it, conscious of the suspicious character of the arrangement, he quickly backs out, bringing down the fall which breaks his neck or his back on the lower log without marking the skin, which in that climate, even when covered by snow, will keep fresh a long time if not found by the carcajou, or other carnivorous prowlers.

After the trapper has laid in his provisions, disposed of his horses and settled down in his solitary winter-quarters, incidents are few, and as none of a pleasant character are likely to occur, the fewer they are the better for him.

The Indians, if wild, are living down in the valleys of the foothills along the streams, where the climate is less severe and food more abundant. If friendly, they are scattered about in lonely places like the trappers, engaged in the same occupation of catching furs for the Company. Few large animals continue to frequent the high mountains through the winter. A solitary moose or caribou may be found occasionally, even along the highest streams, but the elk, the wood buffalo, and most of the deer are down among the foothills. Panthers, cats, wolves, and foxes follow the animals they prey upon. Bears of all kinds are rarely seen, perhaps because they are hibernating, though I never myself caught one in that act. Considering the marten as the principal object and study of the trapper, it is surprising how much less is known of his habits than those of other animals of much less consequence to him. Though considered entirely carnivorous, he remains all winter far up in the mountains whence the small animals and birds on which he preys have to a certain extent departed, and where scarcely any animal or track is to be seen but his own and those of his enemy, the carcajou, or perhaps an occasional mink, or belated squirrel. Another mystery, by no means well understood, is where he keeps himself, and how he is occupied all winter. Even where most abundant he is rarely seen at that season except dead in traps, while during the summers months he is lively, playful and almost sociable, and though nocturnal in habit, shows himself frequently by day. On summer mornings and evenings he loves to examine the trapper's camp, dodging around a pine trunk like a squirrel, climbing about overhead, stealing a little from the fresh game when there is any, and even chasing about and running over the trapper's bed before he is up. All these sociable habits he abandons during the winter, when he is rarely seen, and if seen is sure to be engaged in paying close attention to business. Many of the credulous trappers believe the marten is quite aware that his skin is commercially too worthless to bring him into danger during the mild season, and bends all his sagacity to the work of preserving it through the winter. But credulity is a principal characteristic of all the race of trappers, and like the Indians they attribute superhuman qualities of intelligence to most animals against whom their sagacity is pitted.

In ordinary circumstances there is little in the trapper's winter life to vary the unexciting monotony of work, privation and exposure, unless scarcity of fur or food, or the signs of too inquisitive Indians require the removal of quarters, in which case he is apt to meet with plenty of incident, none of which is likely to be agreeable. Such dangers principally arise from the severity and sudden changes of weather, and especially from high winds during very low temperature, which away from shelter cannot be faced with impunity. Indian hunters, or runners, indolent as they are disposed to be at that season, are sometimes seized with an inconvenient spirit of enterprise, and wandering far from their camps below, may come upon some neglected evidence of the trapper's presence which may cost him dear. Of course if trap, trail or sign be once found, the entire village is sure to turn out in cautious search, and it is only a question of time when his camp will be hunted down and surrounded at such time, and in such manner as may give him poor opportunity for escape or defence. Hence the importance of leaving little sign and making few trails, and where these cannot be entirely avoided, of making them only on side hills and rough places not likely to be frequented by a hostile traveler or hunter. When a strange sign is discovered it must be cautiously traced out and the locality of the Indian village ascertained and avoided, and if notwithstanding all such prudence the neighborhood is found too dangerous, new quarters must be found. In looking for a new camp in severe weather, but little food can be carried, and if the search is prolonged or carried to a distance, it sometimes becomes very difficult for the most expert mountain man to supply his necessities.

In our case about this time, martens being scarce and the camp in consequence of the lateness of our arrival having been badly chosen, it was found necessary to shift it in the dead of winter, for which purpose taking but little provision from our scanty store, and *caching* the rest of our effects, we pushed out in a northerly direction, hoping to find a better location on some of the other tributaries of the Peace. But with ground covered by heavy snow, streams hard bound with ice, and frequent wind storms which at the low prevailing temperatures none can face and live, our progress was slow and no place looked very attractive. Hence no great time had elpased before we found our provisions exhausted, in a difficult country with game not to be had. Making a temporary shelter in a bad place and under unfavorable circumstances, we therefore proceeded to devote our whole attention to hunting, till after some days we became awake to the fact that the district was absolutely without game. Every day the weather permitted, we covered long distances in opposite directions, without finding so much as a recent sign or track. Then we set traps for fish in such rapids as remained open, and for birds and small animals, but without success. Travel over the rocky side hills concealed by snow, was exhausting and dangerous, both of us getting some bad falls. Moreover, as one dare not stir from camp in the uncertain weather without carrying a considerable weight and bulk of articles like furs, snow-shoes and so forth, which might at any moment become essential to life, we soon became weak and exhausted. After trying in vain all the resources practised by trappers in such straits, all of which were well known to Francois, we ate the grease in our rifle stocks, all the fringes and unnecessary parts of our buck leather clothes, gun and ammunition bags, and every scrap of eatable material, boiling it down in an Assinaboine basket with hot stones, and were finally reduced to buds and twigs. After many days of this extreme privation, no longer possessing strength to travel or hunt, I became discouraged and as we lay down one night I determined to abandon the struggle, and remain there, enduring with such fortitude as I might the final pangs which could not be long deferred. At this last stage in the struggle, an event occurred of the most extraordinary character, which cannot seem more strange and incredible to anyone than it has always appeared to me on the innumerable occasions when I have since reflected on it. Notwithstanding our exhaustion and desperate conclusion of the night before, F. rose at daylight, made up the fire as well as his strength permitted, blazed a tree near by on which he marked with charcoal a large cross, and carefully reloading and standing his gun against that emblem, proceeded to repeat in such feeble whispers as he was yet capable of, all the scraps of French and Latin prayers he could remember, to all of which I was in no condition to give much attention. When he got through he remarked with much cheerfulness that he was now sure of killing something, and urged me to make one more effort with him, which I rather angrily refused, and bade him lie down and take what had to come, like a man. With cheerful assurance he replied that he was not afraid to die, but our time had not come. He knew he would find and kill, and we would escape all right. Then desisting from his useless effort to get me up, F., leaving his heavy snowshoes behind, directed himself with weak and uneven steps down the little stream in the deep gorge of which our camp was made, and never expecting to see him again, my mind relapsed into an idle vacuous condition, in which external circumstances were forgotten or disregarded. But scarcely a few minutes had elapsed, and as it afterwards appeared he had hardly traversed a couple of hundred yards, when I heard his gun, which I knew never cracked in vain.

I had thought myself unable to rise, but at that joyful sound promptly discovered my mistake. I found F. in the spot from which he had fired, leaning against a tree in such deep excitement that he could speak with difficulty. On that rugged side hill apparently destitute of all life, in that most improbable of all places, within sound and smell of our camp, he had seen, not a squirrel or a rabbit, but a deer. Attempting to climb for a better shot, the deer jumped, and with terrible misgivings he had fired at it running. He had heard it running after his shot, but was sure he had made a killing hit. Scrambling with difficulty up the hill we found a large clot of blood and a morsal of 'lights,' which we divided and ate on the spot. After taking up the trail we soon found the animal.

I do not undertake to explain that astonishing circumstance. I suppose it must be regarded as an accidental coincidence, but it is of the kind that staggers one in the acceptance of that easy and common explanation. Its extraordinary character is most of all apparent to such as may from similar experience be able to realize the desperate nature of the situation. Two good hunters had ransacked the vicinity for miles without finding a living thing, and had tried in vain all the numerous resources known to the trapper, when a caribou, the wildest and most timid of all deer, walks right into camp, as one may say, at the last moment when further delay was death. How came he there? Where did he come from, and whither was he going? Where were his companions, and what attraction of company or food brought him into that wild and snowpacked gorge at that critical moment? No one can guess any plausible answers to such questions, though Francois believed, and till his latest breath will continue to believe, that after all human efforts had been put forth in vain, the holy Saint Francis, his patron saint, moved by his suffering and prayer, had himself bared an arm for our relief.

Francois, of course, had many tales to tell to justify his faith. A lifetime of adventure and association with superstitious Indians and pious and credulous half-breeds, had not failed to include many perilous dangers and escapes, and to establish an unswerving reliance on the sympathetic and simple priests, who in the humble frontier villages of Canada are the depositaries of all the mysteries of Nature and religion. Of the many such relations with which his memory was stored, the following, of which I have not the slightest doubt that all the facts were true, had firmly fixed in his mind the conclusion that dogs understand human speech.

Somewhere in the Big Horn Mountains, probably south of, and not far from the site of the present Yellowstone National Park, while travelling late in the fall with two other trappers, one of whom possessed a dog, an early snow-fall caused the loss of their horses, and not long afterwards they too found themselves in a country without game, and with most of the other usual resources for food covered up or cut off by snow. After some days of terrible extremity it was one night agreed to take another hunt next morning and if still unsuccessful, to kill the dog. But when morning dawned on the wretched camp the dog was gone, and was seen no more. Terrible sufferings and privations ensued, from which they only extricated themselves by living for a time on the 'jerked' flesh of one of their number. At last the survivors managed to effect a journey of several hundred miles on foot to Fort St. Vrain on the upper Arkansas, where almost the first thing they saw was the missing dog coming cheerfully to meet them! How he had travelled that distance alone through the hosts of canine enemies, with every old bone and buffalo head covered deep with snow, is hard enough of explanation, but the cause of his disappearance offered no mystery to F., who fully believed the dog understood the conversation. While receiving contrary views and arguments with tolerance and politeness, it was plain enough that nothing would ever shake that settled conviction.

After passing safely through that period of starvation we were glad enough to get back to the old camp and make the best of it during the remainder of the season, which furnished little more of incident to vary the monotony of our solitary occupation. One or the other occasionally got caught in a storm of snow, or still worse, of wind, but though sometimes thus long delayed on extremely curtailed diet, we always made shift to find or make some shelter and get back in safety at last. The cold was mostly intense, but being steadier and drier than on the plains, gave no great trouble till the diurnal thaws set in toward spring. As when these arrive it is already too late to catch marketable furs, we might have lain quiet but for our insufficient stock of pemmican and even of jerked meat, both of which became so reduced that we were obliged to hunt almost constantly without much regard to weather. Surface thawing by day, and freezing by night renders travelling equally difficult and laborious with or without snowshoes, since the crust becomes very slippery, when they are used, and constantly fails and breaks through when dispensed with. The spring thaws also keep wet the 'duffeling,' or fur wraps worn inside the trousers and moccasins, causing chafes and sores, and sometimes dangerous frost bites.

By March, except in extreme northern latitudes, the marten's fur begins to deteriorate, and those taken after April the Company will not receive at all, so that in medium latitudes the trapper's work is over long before he can safely bring up the horses and get away with his pelts. Much of that interval we passed below in the foothills, where we reclaimed our horses safe, healthy and fat, and amused ourselves with trapping fish and hunting, enjoying our liberation from the gloomy mountain fastnesses, and the comparative abundance and variety of the fare. Falling in with friendly Assinaboines, who are the ancient friends of the trappers and mostly engaged in the same pursuit, we also enjoyed the pleasures of society, which are best appreciated by those who have been totally secluded during a long and dreary winter. It was perhaps not before the end of May, that the little patches of new grass in sheltered places along the streams were sufficiently forward to permit of commencing the long and somewhat risky journey required to dispose of our peltrys. The Saskatchewan country, which enjoys the earliest spring and contains the best posts, bore at that time such a bad name for Blackfeet, that our Assinaboine friends insisted on travelling down Athabasca waters,

even should we have to go out on the plains as far as the big
Forts Saskatchewan or Assinaboine, and we actually started
with such intentions. The grass was short, the plains bleak,
streams swollen, and the buffalo not yet arrived; and knowing
nothing of the actual whereabouts of the hostile tribes, the long
journey before us was by no means inviting. The Assinaboines
were so demoralized, that we had even begun to doubt how far
they could be depended on in case of a rush from some fleet
mounted band of Surcees, Bloods, or Blackfeet, when we were
overjoyed to learn of a temporary post established for just
such emergencies, at no great distance.

CHAPTER XI

Several of the five tribes of the great Blackfeet nation, and especially the Surcees, frequently pushed their war parties as far north as the Athabasca and even the Peace, being often particularly alert in the spring of the year in order to pick up small parties of white or Assinaboine trappers coming out of the mountains with fur, and when they are more than usually enterprising, or when there is special reason to apprehend them, the Company's factors in charge of the large forts, sometimes establish temporary posts near the heads of the rivers for the safety of their trappers and their valuable furs. The parties sent out for such purpose, build block houses, and send out Indian runners with the information, often trading with both sides, though of course with many precautions to prevent hostile meetings. The Blackfeet, the boldest and most aggressive of all the tribes, are required to give several days' notice of their coming, and to make a solemn engagement to attack no one near the post. The time being fixed upon, runners are then sent out to keep away friendly, trading, or family parties; stock and other outside property is placed in security, and the Blackfeet received into the fort during the daytime only, a few at a time, and under such conditions that however treacherously disposed, they can only injure the individual who is trading with them. The trading is done through a small aperture connecting the store room with the Indian room, a small apartment holding but three or four at a time, with a single door operated from the inside, the whole top, bottom and sides being strongly built of logs. During the trading, a few men are stationed in the loft over the Indian room to shoot down between the logs of the ceiling if necessary. Of course a flank fire is arranged for on all external faces, and though rows and shindys often occur, and the temptation is well nigh irresistible to the Indian, such posts have rarely been captured. After the trappers and friendlies have all come in and finished their trading, the post is emptied and abandoned, for the time, and the furs escorted down by a sufficiently large party, reinforced for the purpose.

At this small post we disposed of our furs which were good but not numerous, partly for reasons already given, and partly because the seat of our operations had been too near the Assinaboine country which has long been industriously trapped by those friendly people, and by the less enterprising white trappers who are content with fewer furs in consideration of greater security. They were sufficient however to satisfy our necessities and permit us to bear a modest part in the festivities which occur on the occasion of these annual reunions, which often afford quite romantic meetings and incidents. Men meet here who may have last seen each other years before at some far distant post, and have strange and stirring tales to tell of their own adventures, and perchance of the fate of mutual friends. On this occasion nothing very remarkable occurred, the talk being mostly of the whereabouts of the Blackfeet and their expected war party, respecting which there were innumerable rumors, but little definite information. F. and myself, having heard so much and seen so little of the threatened danger, felt very brave and inclined to think disrespectfully of the hostiles, as is not uncommon with those who have not themselves felt the fire, but the poor Assinaboines who better knew the risks, and were moreover embarrassed by the presence and care of their families, showed quite a different mood. Our intention was to try another winter in the mountains, selecting some less known and frequented territory to the north of last winter's trapping ground. But as there was yet plenty of time to attend to that, and the Assinaboines were very desirous to have our additional strength on their return journey, for which purpose they gave the most seductive accounts of the attractions of their safe mountain valleys, we concluded to begin the summer's holiday by travelling back with them, and without more definite designs, set out some time in July, the party consisting of only some half a dozen lodges besides ourselves. During this trip,

notwithstanding the general apprehensions, we saw no worse
enemy than buffalo bulls, and after a pleasant and uneventful
journey, camped with our friends in a lovely valley well up in
the foothills, where we enjoyed a delightful summer, reveling
in all manner of abundance, and forming sincere attachment
for our Indian neighbors, especially the children, who were
never tired of being with us. We constantly made excursions
to several lovely spring valleys in the high mountains, where
the grass growing up to the edge of the snow was fresh and
tender, and the deer and bighorn were as fat as prize cattle. As
a great favor to them, we usually took some of the boys with
us, who were useful about the camp, and as good as hounds
in tracking down wounded game.

In this vicinity there were all sorts of game, fish, berries,
and roots, and a considerable friendly rivalry occurred between us and the native hunters, all whose methods we had
good opportunities for becoming familiar with. If I were to
attempt a comparison, I should say that, while as a rule the
Indian is the better hunter, the white man shoots better, and
on the whole prevails best with large game, a distinction however which is traceable ultimately to the difference in weapons.
When the Indian possesses firearms at all, which is the case
with all the Assinaboines, who are among the best of hunters,
they are only the wretched 'Hudson Bay guns,' so-called, being
the inferior and only firearm supplied by the Company, so
cheap and bad that nearly all the barrels have been over and
over again bent and straightened by the owners. A sure shot
cannot be made with them even when new, at any reasonable
distance, in consequence of which the old habits of bow and
arrow hunting have been but little changed. Hunting, or finding game, and shooting it, are very different things. Anyone
who has a good gun can soon learn to shoot, but to find the
game, see it first, and make the best approach under circumstances never the same twice in succession, is an art taxing both
physical and intellectual powers. It cannot be said to be
ever completely learned even by the most expert hunter, who
constantly acquires new experience; and men differ in success,
just in proportion as they differ in intelligence, patience,
temperament, judgment and many other qualities. From an
habitual want of confidence in his weapon, the Indian has

learned any amount of caution, wariness and patience. He
knows how to select the right places, decides quickly and with
intuitive correctness how to make the best approach, and rarely
fails to see the game first, but he will hunt it patiently for half
a day, and refuse many chances that a white man would
accept without hesitation, before he will peril all by a shot.
But when at length his judgment is satisfied to risk it, he is
sure to be within a few yards, where even with his weapons
he can hardly miss. Outside the buffalo range, deer, moose
and elk are the Indian's favorite game because by skill and
patience he can get close and sure shots at them; but bighorn
and mountain goats, which must generally be shot at long
distances, they rarely get except by watching favorite passes or
watering places.

With the modern long range breech-loaders now in use, it
seems to me little hunting skill can be required, and but a
minimum of the pleasure of conquest enjoyed, since it must
be a greenhorn who cannot get within such distances of almost
any game. But on the other hand, the fascinating charm and
delight of measuring one's judgment and skill against the
instincts of these wild creatures, and quickly seizing the
advantages of wind, hills, ravines, timber and other fortuitous
circumstances to get close upon the wary game, and above all,
the interesting knowledge of his most private and domestic
habits, thus and thus only, to be gained; all these must remain
unknown to the hunter who pulls his trigger at telescopic
range. There can be few hunters who do not derive a keen
delight from observations of the manners and habits of animals
rarely seen at leisure, and fewer still who in coming close and
unsuspected on a herd of large game, have not held back their
shots in the intense interest of noting those natural and un-
trammeled movements of feeding, playing and fighting. But
all that must be lost to the man who fires from several hundred
yards' distance, thus substituting for the finer and more intellectual qualities of the hunter the mere mechanical skill of
aiming at a mark.

Be that as it may, there were few kinds of hunting, snaring,
trapping or fishing that we failed to have a hand in during that
idle summer, and when the time came to start northward,

notwithstanding our former experience of the disadvantage of
a late arrival, we had no little difficulty in breaking away from
surroundings so comfortable and attractive.   Nevertheless,
getting at last upon the line of march, we plodded on along the
base of the mountains, keeping close to and sometimes within
that great storehouse of supplies and place of refuge in case of
necessity.   Unlike the west-bound streams issuing from the
Cascades and the Sierra Nevadas, which flow in nearly straight
courses with few tributaries to the sea, the great continental
rivers of the Rocky Mountains linger long in the vicinity of
their solitary sources, returning often on their courses, finding
their rapid but sinuous way among and parallel to the ranges,
and gathering a vast number of tributaries before they at
last leave the snowy ranges for good, and flow forth into the
far-stretching yellow plains.

The Missouri, Saskatchewan, Athabasca, Peace and Liard
on the east, and the Columbia, Thompson and Frazer on the
west of the mountains, each drains many hundred lineal miles
of the great range, flowing in turn toward every point of the
compass, and receiving almost innumerable tributaries, many
of which are themselves large, long and numerously branching
rivers.   So countless are the streams coming down to swell
the Athabasca, Peace and Liard, on their long courses to the
Polar Sea, and so various are their initial directions, that it
is often difficult to know when one has definitely exchanged
the waters of one of them for another.   Passing all the tributaries of the Little and Big Smokies of the Peace, we got
through the main range by a rough and difficult pass for
horses, made by a principal northern branch of the last named,
and soon found a good valley for horses on the western side,
where though the climate is supposed to be milder than on
the eastern side, the furs are in no respect inferior, and the
Indians as a rule less aggressively formidable.   Nevertheless,
in the course of this long journey we were not without various
Indian encounters, some of which seemed destined at first to
involve dangerous and unequal combats, which were in the
end, for the most part, happily avoided.   One of these, which
may be worth relating, seems ludicrous in looking back, though
it was regarded as extremely embarrassing and serious at the
time.

In riding over the extensive plateau of a flat-topped mountain one afternoon, with the unladen pack horses following behind, we came suddenly upon two women endeavoring to conceal themselves in the thin undergrowth, and as they were encumbered with large conical baskets strapped on in the usual way, we had them both lassoed and secured in an instant. They could not or would not understand any word or sign, and doubtless expecting a speedy and certain death, assumed an air of stolid and hostile indifference, absolutely refusing to have any participation in our efforts for intelligible communication. It was impossible to guess what they were doing with baskets, as neither roots, nuts nor berries were to be looked for in such a locality; but they were evidently at no great distance from their people, who might be brought about our ears in a few minutes should the prisoners be allowed to escape. We therefore took them along for the present, but as we might at any moment be taken *flagrante delictu,* we exerted our best fascinations to atone for the rudeness of leading them with rawhide riatas on their lovely necks. In the course of two or three hours we came down to the banks of a fine stream with some grass, and turning out the animals, sat down to consider how to get safely rid of our embarrassing captives. Of course the readiest solution that would have occurred to many in our situation was to kill them and conceal the bodies, but we could by no means make up our minds to that. To leave them gagged and bound was only another and crueller way of reaching the same result, and was equally set aside. They must be already missed, and the earliest dawn would surely set the entire hive buzzing in pursuit. Amusing as the conundrum now seems, its solution was fraught with such momentous consequences to us, that we sat up the whole night in the vain effort to devise some means of getting safely out of the scrape. Finally, the best plan we could think of was the simple one of getting our horses saddled up before daybreak, and after seeing the ladies fairly started up the hill they had come from, to follow down the river a mile or two, cross it, and take up a practicable looking hollow on the opposite side. It is unnecessary to add that the next few days we did not spare the horses, and allowed many lengthening miles to grow out behind us, before we deemed ourselves clear of their tribe, and safe from pursuit. In such rencontres the principal safety of the trapper consists in the fact that with the exception of a few considerable nations of allied tribes, nearly all the remote tribes infesting the trapping grounds, are small in numbers and at war with most of their neighbors, who thus mutually confine each other to a limited territory, beyond which they trespass at their peril. Thus if a trapper has difficulty with one of these small tribes and can get safely clear of its jurisdiction, it may be a long time before the news can follow him into a hostile tribe only a few miles distant. As has before been intimated, there is a certain skill in keeping clear of Indians, even in their own haunts, by avoiding routes and lines of country they are likely to follow. To do this successfully requires a knowledge of Indian peculiarities as well as of the intricacies of mountain travel, and notwithstanding all such wary precautions, one may sometimes come plump on a hunting or travelling party, as occurred to us somewhere during this same journey.

It was near the close of the day, and we were following down a big ravine by a well marked deer or Indian trail high up along its precipitous side hill, expecting from the appearance of the country to debouch on some large stream with grass, when we were startled by finding an Indian horse standing alone on the trail, saddled and tied to a bush. This, like Robinson Crusoe's strange footstep, was embarrassing. Events ultimately showed that we were even then watched, and if like honest travelers we had let that horse alone and passed on, we should have been followed to camp, surrounded and attacked at night, with an uncommon poor chance for escape. But though we did not then know we were watched we did know that our fresh trail would be at once detected by whoever should come for the horse, so as it was as well to be 'hung for a sheep as a lamb,' we took the horse along with us. At this, a fellow who had been concealed in the ravine below, appeared from the brush and commenced bawling for his friends. We might easily have disposed of him, but as it was plain we were near a hornet's nest of unknown dimensions, we simply dropped the innocent cause of the trouble and passed on, looking for a good defensive position. We had scarcely gone a hundred yards before a dozen or more came tearing down from the mountain above, and as it was impossible to get away we prepared to negotiate, or sell our lives dearly. There is little doubt that our lives were saved at this juncture by reaching at the nick of time a large flat rock over which the trail passed, which showed a vertical scarp of four or five feet toward the ravine. Hastily tying our horses in threes, we jumped down and took position behind this natural breastwork and got ready for business, determined not to begin hostilities but to meet them promptly.

The enemy were a hunting party and not a war party, but all the same they came rushing and bawling through the brush, and were within a few feet when the strength of our position was suddenly revealed to them and they halted all in a heap. White men in their position would have obeyed some leader, who would have amused us till a flanking party could have been sent out to cross the ravine, get up the opposite side and pot us from there safely and at leisure. But our friends had neither the leader nor the weapons to permit of so rational a plan. Their arms were bows and arrows, with two or three 'Hudson Bay guns,' which at long range were little better. The descent from our position to the bottom of the ravine may have been eight or nine hundred feet, and was extremely precipitous. To take us out of our stronghold with their short range weapons, a front attack must be made, which was feasible enough with their numerical superiority, but would certainly cost dear, so notwithstanding their noise and insults we succeeded before long by the aid of a few Indian words and some Chinook, but principally by signs, at which all male Indians are intelligent, in getting into communication, peaceful at least in form. The horse act was explained as well as that rather bald depredation admitted, friendship professed, and the intention alleged of camping at the mouth of the ravine to make peace with them at leisure.

They were no whit behind us in professions of friendship and affection, but insisted on our coming up from behind our rock for a talk, which we agreed to on condition they would fall back and leave six feet of clear space between us. This was done, but they soon took advantage of the noise and con-

fusion to crowd in on the neutral ground, and began to pass in
their few guns to the front-rank men. F. was captain, and had
already notified me to be ready to jump down again behind our
rock, when I noticed a stout fellow opposite and within arm's
length of me, holding a gun which he had not possessed an
instant ago, at 'present arms' with hand on the lock, with which
he might blow my head off by a single motion if so disposed.
As F. had his own hands full, and I dared not remove my
eyes a second from my *vis a vis,* I quietly cocked my pistol
without raising it or moving my rifle, which latter I could not
depend on for instant use since too many were ready to grab it.
My big friend opposite was never in all his life nearer to losing
it than at that instant, for I was watching his face and at the
slightest change of his glance or swelling of a muscle he would
most surely have started for the happy hunting grounds. He
was not unaware of the state of the case, for hearing the click,
he immediately turned round and ostentatiously handed his
gun to the man behind him, making signs to me to uncock the
pistol, which I did after again getting a few feet of space
cleared in front. Such incidents occurred several times during
this excited colloquy. The front-rank men, who would have
been the first to suffer, we could get along with by themselves,
but they were pushed and urged on by the fellows behind,
everyone of whom was constantly bawling at the top of his
voice and held his bow ready bent, with arrows drawn to the
head.

This agreeable conference must have lasted half an hour
during which we held our lives from second to second, and only
by the most constant watchfulness. We dare not even glance
behind, whence I expected momentarily to get an arrow in
the back from such enterprising individuals as might be
climbing up the precipice in our rear. Finally, as it would
not be possible to stand the strain much longer, and we were
nervous respecting the vulnerability of our rear and the approaching darkness, we resolved to bring things to a point,
and put the question directly whether they wanted to fight
where they were, or make peace and come to our proposed
camp next morning to trade. We were their good friends but
were ready for either, and our "little guns (pistols) could
talk without stopping." Nothing is more certain that the

ardent desire of our noisy friends to cut our throats and get possession of our horses, arms and scalps, and if they could have screwed themselves up to the certainty of a broad gap of destruction among their front-rank men, they must have succeeded at some price. But like most Indians, though brave enough in their own way, they were not game for it at the cost, preferring negotiation and postponement for a better or less expensive opportunity. An exceedingly unsubstantial truce was therefore effected, they agreeing to retire a few yards, and allow us to proceed without being followed by any of their young men, and to come down with their head chief to trade next morning after sunrise. Neither party had the slightest intention of keeping the agreement, and both were well aware of it. Nevertheless, after an immense amount of shouting, talking and threatening, each of us alternately facing about every few yards to cover the retreat of the other with the horses, we at last got clear of them, reached the mouth of the cañon, and as soon as it was dark, probably just about the time they were getting ready to surround us in the brush, we swum the river, got into the mountains beyond, and halted for no trifle till we had put a few days' journey between us.

It was not without many similar adventures, mostly however of less exciting character, that we made our way over such an extensive region and prosecuted the search for a winter location which should offer better promise than that of the previous year. Many a weary day passed before we found what we wanted with its concomitant advantages of horse-quarters, hunting-grounds, and so forth, but this time we took ample time for preparation, and when we had once settled down in winter quarters, encountered scarcely an incident worth mentioning during the solitary months that we had to spend in the gloomy seclusion of the snow-covered mountains.

We had plenty to eat, no Indian alarms, but little persecution from the carcajou, and bouncing luck with our traps. With the exception of the ordinary vicissitudes of that severe climate, and getting caught and detained away from the camp by an occasional storm we had little to complain of, and the long cold winter was over and signs of breaking up apparent almost before we knew it.

At my present declining period of life, after a long succession of efforts and associations of such totally different character, I sometimes try vainly to remember how I ever managed forty years ago to endure and even enjoy the privation, cold and solitude of winter in those gloomy northern forests, for objects that now seem so trivial. But the continuity of occupation and purpose has been so broken and destroyed, that I can now scarcely realize even the problem, much less any reasonable solution. In recalling such forgotten incidents as recur to me from time to time, it requires a distinct intellectual exertion to remind me that it is really my own and not some other person's life that is ever rising up with long forgotten incidents from the dim and receding vista of the past.

In the region where we found ourselves, the winters break up late, though the process itself is short, vegetation pressing close upon the receding snow. We supposed ourselves nearly equidistant between Fort Liard on the river of that name, and St. John and Hudson's Hope on the Peace, but all those posts were only to be reached over mountain trails which it was scarcely probable could be traversed by laden horses before July. There were other posts in the Cascades and on the streams discharging from them into the sea, but they lay beyond a wide stretch of country unknown to us, and far from any course we wished to take. Besides, I was beginning seriously to reflect that I had had fun enough, and as for business, surely it was time to use my youth and such education as I possessed to better advantage than in rivaling Indians and half-breeds in the occupation of savages. Hence I determined to return to California, and F., always amiable and agreeable, readily consented. For this purpose it was necessary to carry our skins to some place within or adjacent to the American frontier, where only they could be converted into horses or money, the Company only receiving them in trade. Our horses being in excellent condition it was therefore determined to get the furs out of the mountains on hand-sleds as far as some point to which the animals could be brought, and then head for the far south and a cash market, even if the quest should carry us to the lower Columbia, a distance by any practicable route of many hundred miles.

This plan being resolved on, no time was lost in putting it in execution. The skins were got out in fine condition, the horses taken up, the gear put in good order, and long before the mountain defiles were passable for horses, we were clear of them, and away *en route* for the lower Columbia, where there was little doubt we could find a practicable market, and push on for the Oregon and California mines. The scheme, although in breach of the laws of the Company, which require their free trappers and *coureurs des bois* to trade with it alone, did not seem unfair to anyone, and we had no doubts of its feasibility. We could readily avoid all Company posts, and it was improbable we should meet its travelling parties so early in the season, or be interfered with by them if we kept our own counsel. To observe the law strictly would condemn us to the trapper's life forever, since the Company's trade articles had little value outside of its own territory, and even there, only to trappers and Indian traders. As long as we were anywhere north of the Columbia, our trade might well be designed for some of the lower posts of that river, and once across it, the Company possessed little authority, and we should soon be among American settlements. Our journey was at first rapid and successful, notwithstanding the high streams and swampy bottoms, and some severe spring snowstorms, which caused trouble and anxiety for the horses. Avoiding all Company posts, and evading the Indian marauders we most feared, we had covered more than two-thirds the distance to the lower Columbia, and left far behind all the dangers and obstacles we had expected to encounter, when we suddenly came to grief when it was least looked for, at a place and in a manner there was scarcely any just reason to anticipate.

We had got clear of the upper Frazer and Thompson; had crossed the divide south of the latter, and were travelling down a stream of considerable size which we took for a headwater of the Okanagan, or its lakes. The Indians in that country, though professing friendship with strong parties, were considered unreliable and dangerous to small ones, but as we were getting well down toward Fort Okanagan, and within the sphere of its probable influence, we thought no more of such difficulties, and took the shortest and easiest route for the main stream, taking little heed of any trouble ahead except the necessity of evading the fort itself at the proper time. But we reckoned without our host. Hostile signs appeared and soon became abundant, showing suspiciously large parties close at hand. Examination showed that these were either war parties or hunting parties of greater magnitude than usual, disclosing no sign of women, children, dogs, lodges or other evidence of ordinary domestic life. Finally further study proved that we had been actually seen and avoided by small parties on at least two occasions. Mischief was then evidently intended, and our every move was watched. Even then we might perhaps have cached our packs, killed or abandoned the horses and escaped, since an expert mountain man unencumbered with horses and packs can go where a wolf can and is about as easy to catch. But we had no notion of sacrificing our property so easily, nor of making a long and tedious return journey to recover it at some future time, and in short stuck to it so pertinaciously that we not only lost everything, but had an uncommon close call for our lives.

Supposing ourselves on Okanagan water and every hour getting nearer to that river and the fort which must have a more or less wide circle of friendly influence; and knowing that since we had been seen it was too late to take to the mountains with loaded horses, we pushed on all the faster, when smoke columns began to be visible in the rear, on both flanks, and at last in front. We were surrounded, and the attack itself was only a question of time, reserved till place and time should suit the ideas of Indian strategy. There could no longer be any thought even of concealing the packs, as of course keen-eyed scouts were by this time watching every motion. When the hostile signals at last appeared in front, it was well toward evening, and we were pushing down a fair trail along a good-sized river with high mountains on both sides, but with signs of a break in the latter not far ahead and between the signals and ourselves. In pushing for this break, we observed a fresh tree-mark so carelessly made as to indicate almost indifference whether it should meet our eyes or not. It was made with charcoal on a fresh blaze, and consisted of two arrow-heads point to point, with a small vacant space between, on which a short vertical line was interposed considerably nearer to the arrow pointing against us. This indicated that the intercepting party was in satisfactory position close in front and wished the pursuing party to drive us forward upon them and close in on us from the rear.

Anyone but an experienced mountain man reading this sign, the meaning of which was plain enough, and knowing his pursuers were intended to see it within a few minutes, would probably have abandoned the animals at once and attempted one of two desperate expedients, neither of which had any chance of success at this stage, viz., either to attack and cut away to the rear through the pursuing party as presumably the weakest, or to seek a passage over the mountain between the flankers. But F. reasoned differently. True, there was now little hope of saving anything but our lives. But night was coming on, and therefore time gained was important. The break ahead where the attack was probably to be made was not far off. It could be no worse for us to be attacked there than to precipitate a fight now, while night if it came first, offered a hundred chances which could not exist by daylight. Obliterating the mark, therefore, we kept on at a moderate gait, and about dusk came out at the break in the mountains we had been so anxiously looking for. This proved to be the entrance of a small side-stream coming in from the right, with a long and wide bottom which at some former time had been dammed near the mouth by beavers, converting the whole valley into a swampy pond half a mile wide, and extending back a considerable distance among the mountains. It was pretty certain the destined place of attack was at the opposite bank, where we were to be stopped and closed upon from all sides when emerging in more or less confusion from the water. Though not a soul was yet to be seen, there was little doubt that the opposite bank was well held and the party in the rear would not long delay falling on us from that direction.

The large level bottom before us, though in some places merely marshy, was mostly covered by shoal water with a large number of small brush-covered knolls or islands extending along its center and considerably interrupting the view across. It was now rapidly falling dark, and there being little time for examination or reflection, we plunged in without delay, deciding to make our stand on and among the islands, at least for the present. The depth varied from one to three or four feet and though embarrassed by holes and inequalities of bottom we reached the islands by the time it became quite dark. These, though but a few yards each in extent, were numerous and well covered with brush growing ten or twelve feet high. The position was a strong one for the present, since we could not be surprised, the splashing in the water in case of attack being sure to give us ample notice, and the thick brush forming a covert from which we could not be routed without giving a pretty good account of ourselves. We therefore unpacked the animals, and were left in peace through the night, the horses munching bushes in the absence of grass.

The light of morning dawned on a scene as peaceful and solitary in appearance as any painter's ideal landscape. Not an enemy was to be seen, nor the faintest sign of morning camp fires, or any other human presence. It was a lovely morning of spring, the buds of all colors everywhere bursting into life, and already large enough to give practical value to our brushy screen. We were beyond doubt, surrounded in strong force, yet the distant banks on either hand were, to all appearance, as lonely and silent as if no living thing existed within a hundred miles. The day passed without disclosing much, but there was an ominous avoidance of both shores by ducks and other large birds and glimpses had been obtained, at different times, of two hostiles on the bank we had quitted, and a flash or two had been caught from some bright object on the other shore. From the attention and inclination to neigh, of our horses, it was inferred that strange ones were not far off, but not one was seen or heard. At this distance of time— forty years—I cannot be sure of details, but several days, probably four, passed by with little incident except the occasional disclosure of some incautious Indian on one bank or other. The horses were failing for want of proper food, and though for ourselves we had dried meat to last some time, and might have existed indefinitely on the horses and furs, we felt that something must soon be done. It was plain the Indians' original little plan was upset and they would not attack us where we were; but unless occupied in devising some other scheme, they could afford to wait forever, as all the resources of the country were open to them, while we must come out some time. Whenever and however our attempt should be made, we must abandon horses and packs. The former were now too exhausted to be of immediate use, even if extricated, but the furs were in perfect order, and not only represented a winter's hard labor among the northern snows, but had been since transported with infinite labor, across plains, rivers, mountains and deserts, nearly or quite a thousand miles.

Nevertheless, they must be sacrificed, so they were sunk with stones in the adjacent water—where I presume what is left of them still remains—while the horses were quietly killed one by one with knives so as to conceal all intention of movement from the watchful foe. A rendevous was fixed upon, as usual in such cases, and about midnight, after the young moon had set on a cloudy night, we abandoned the refuge which had served so well, and struck out separately by different routes, arranging to strike the opposite shore at points far removed from each other, and if we should get safely out, to keep along down the river on the side hill as less likely to be closely watched. There was probably a principal channel to be crossed somewhere, but in the absence of any knowledge of its locality or depth, we drew our rifle-loads before starting, and arranged to protect and make quick use of the ammunition if required.

It was with very doubtful forebodings, in fact with not much hope of escape, that when all was ready and F.'s last prayer was said, we turned from each other, as we could not but fear for the last time, to attempt the almost desperate enterprise before us. No doubt a hundred keen eyes and ears were on the watch for any indication of our movements, and it seemed a forlorn and almost hopeless effort to move slowly and noiselessly through the telltale water, ignorant of all before us, and nearly certain of detection either in the water or on shore by so many eager watchers. I lost sight of F. almost at once and after a cold, tedious and muddy wade, the difficulties of which were much enhanced by the necessity of absolute silence of movement, I landed nearly a mile above our recent abode, F. having taken his course still further up the stream. There was no evidence as yet of any alarm, and we were no doubt

much aided by the Indians' expectation of hearing the movement and splash of horses. I soon got on the mountain side,
took off and wrung the water from my clothes, loaded my gun,
and moved cautiously on. Not a sound could be heard from
any quarter, a silence that augered well for F., and I slowly
made my way along the rugged side hill, aware from the
absence of any alarm that Francois was doing the same at no
great distance. After an hour or two, deeming myself clear
of the worst of the crowd, I put on more speed, and by daybreak,
notwithstanding the bad ground and cautious movements
necessary, had put some twenty miles behind me, and considered it safe to get up on the high ridge where I could travel
twice as fast. All now depended on when the Indians would
discover our absence from the islands. If they should give us
another day we should have a long start of them. Before noon
I discovered a mark [14] made by F. which showed he was
before me on the same ridge, and it was needless for me to
leave more marks for him. I pushed forward to overtake him
all day and most of the following night, but toward morning,
fearing I might overrun the rendevous, I halted and got some
much needed rest. At daylight I ventured down on the main
stream and followed it, as agreed, to the mouth of what I
considered the 'first large branch,' where I was delighted to
find another mark by F. and turned up it about five miles,
according to arrangement, where I found him and we were
again together.

In the absence of any knowledge respecting the tribes and
boundaries of this district we could not yet consider ourselves
safe from pursuit, and with as little delay as possible got
back on the high ridges, and pushed on for some days longer.
We did not go to the fort as it was no longer necessary, and we
should have had some trouble in explaining our presence in
that vicinity with furs taken in the far-off districts of the Liard
and Peace, without exposing our intention of taking them out
of the Company's territory. It was south of the Thompson,
and somewhere in the high rolling region between the lower or
main Frazer and the sources of the Okanagan, that we gradu-

[14] The marks agreed on as being readable by us but by no one else, were: a
wind-fallen branch leaned against a tree in the direction being followed by the
marker.

ally assembled a party of trappers, who like ourselves had been despoiled of their outfits in the same disturbed territory, where the unexpected outbreak had caught numerous parties travelling in with their winter's spoil from much nearer points than ours, and in fancied security. As usual, the suddenly assumed hostility of those Indians was due to the influx and depredations of the American settlers below, a circumstance which did not tend to mollify the hatred usually entertained for those gentry by the mountain men, upon whom in such cases the penalty falls first. Nevertheless, the first efforts of these impoverished men must be devoted to placing themselves again in a position to travel. Wherever their new plans might lead, whether back to the northern regions to try it again, or to the now far-famed and constantly extending mines beyond the Columbia, it was useless to try to get anywhere without horses, and the only way to procure any was to take them from the Indians of the plains. The extensive region lying between the Frazer, the Thompson and the upper Columbia, abounding in lakes and streams, and everywhere intersected by small mountain ranges and protective hills fairly supplied with grass, was then occupied by numerous small tribes of equestrian Indians, at this time hostile to all whites, even including the Company men, who were known to possess large bands of horses. Our force had increased to eleven, all expert mountain men smarting under their undeserved losses, and these destitute and desperate men were not long in devising a raid upon the horses in the hope of running off a band of them toward the growing settlements on the Cowlitz, the Chehallis or the lower Columbia.

Most of us soon picked up horses enough for mounts, but to make good our losses, not to mention injured feelings, it was necessary to discover and run off a large band, and it was to that effort we now devoted ourselves with all the skill, tenacious purpose and patient perseverance which characterizes mountain men when those well known qualities are brought to bear upon a single purpose. The Indian habit is to keep a few horses about their villages for current use, but the main herd, whether together or divided, is always kept at a distance under sufficient guard relieved at considerable intervals. As the numerous tribes are always stealing each other's horses, much concealment and strong guarding is required, and it is not easy to find a large band without exposure to the numerous active scouts and hunters always on the watch. Should the raiders' presence be discovered directly or by their sign, unless strong enough to fight the whole tribe, they would be promptly hunted down and exterminated. It is therefore difficult for one not experienced in such enterprises to realize the extent to which our movements were fettered and embarrassed by the paramount necessity of exciting no alarm and leaving no trail or sign. In vain we separated and singly and in squads searched wide reaches of country, tracking down without result the numerous broad horse trails which abounded everywhere but led to nothing, and coming together again at some distant rendezvous always with failure and disappointment, every day adding to the danger of discovery and disaster. The innumerable expedients resorted to would only be fatiguing in the narration, though one of them which came near extinguishing me personally, may serve as a sample. Two of us undertook the rather desperate scheme of concealing ourselves by night in an extensive willow swamp or thicket abounding with springs, where the inhabitants of a large neighboring village came throughout the day for water, with the hope of capturing a prisoner and getting information. At early dawn the women began to arrive, but always in squads and often accompanied by children and dogs, from whose sharp noses and prying eyes we were in perpetual peril without the possibility of getting away till night should again interpose its friendly curtain. We were several times discovered by the dogs who raised a frightful clatter, but which we could not catch and dared not shoot. Fortunately for us the place was swarming with rabbits, which saved us by getting credit for the dogs' excitement. No beaten general ever longed more earnestly than we for the screen of night, and when its friendly shades came down, we were glad to retire, baffled in purpose, but satisfied to keep whole skins. In ordinary war the scout or picket may at the last moment surrender without loss of honor and save his life, but in Indian warfare it must be victory, escape or death, without thought of quarter given or received.

CHAPTER XII

The most exciting as well as the most disastrous part of that reckless undertaking was yet to come. We must have wasted some weeks to little purpose, when a scout came in with the exciting news of a large band of several hundred horses, some thirty miles distant, easily accessible, though watched by a strong guard whose numbers he could not ascertain. We had trailed their relief guards destined for this place at least twenty times, but hitherto with no result, as they always took a false direction, scattered, and ran the trail out to nothing, meeting again at some distant rendezvous, before venturing to the right place. The relieved guards were still more baffling as they invariably came in singly or in pairs, and from every point of the compass. Thus the whole country had become covered with horse trails leading in every direction and impossible to unravel, especially as while they could only be followed by daylight, detection was certain death. But our scout had at last been equal to the occasion, and not a second was to be lost in following up the welcome intelligence.

Quickly getting up our own horses, we were not long in making a descent on the long sought herd. Coming down on them a little after midnight with a wild rush, we succeeded in making a general stampede in the direction agreed on, some of our party leading the way, and the others pressing on the rear. What with our yells and gunshots and the thundering rush of horses, the guard, probably exaggerating our number, fled at once, and notwithstanding the skillful disposition of a small rear guard of our own, we saw no more of them. The horses were wild and terror-stricken, and to keep them in that desirable state of mind, they were kept on a full run whenever possible, halting only to change saddles to fresh horses. By midnight of the next day a long stretch of ground had been covered and the horses were tired enough, but we were well used up ourselves, and after a run estimated at over a hundred miles in the twenty-four hours, rest and sleep must be had. Already hard-worked before the start by constant scouting, the riding and driving had been continuous and exhausting, and when I dismounted I could scarcely stand, my legs were excoriated and raw, and my buck-leather trousers glued fast to them with blood. Few others were in better condition, and the immediate and peremptory necessity for all was sleep, which was so pressing that we took barely time to change saddles to fresh horses, go through the form of sending three men to the rear on guard, and appoint a rendezvous in case of disaster, till every man was asleep, holding fast by the bridle of his fresh horse. The halt was made in the densely timbered fork of a large stream, the horses being driven into the angle enclosed by the river on two sides, and the camp on the third. We only proposed to rest a few hours, reasoning that as the Indian guard must go thirty miles to the village for men and horses, and return by way of their late horse camp, we must have had a sixty-mile start; but on the other hand, the pursuers were fresh and our trail was so broad it could be followed at a gallop. Should we get off again safely, it was the intention of our leader, McTavish, to leave a few men to delay the pursuit at the crossing, while the rest should gain time with the horses.

The plan was good, but the men who were to carry it out were already overtaxed. The guard probably yielded to the overpowering pressure of sleep which could not be resisted, and at all events were never heard of more. We could not have been down long when our pursuers overtook us and repeated our tactics of the previous day, dashing in with shots and yells to stampede the horses. In an instant I found myself alone in a tumultous rush of horses, succeeding with the greatest difficulty in gaining the saddle, in fact only saving myself by clasping the horse's neck and being dragged through the rout till I could get a chance to wriggle on his back. Even then it was hard to prevent being crowded off, unhorsed, and trampled, as the crowd of terrified and frantic horses pushing on against those who vainly refused to take the water, piled up on each other, screaming, biting and kicking in a wild frenzy of terror. Judged by their shooting and yells a large body of Indians were pressing on them but could not penetrate the mass, which I verily believe were in places piled two or three deep.

The objection of the horses to take water was partly due to the intense darkness, partly to the furious current of the stream, and most of all to the dense growth of deciduous trees which, crowding out horizontally over the water in search of light and air, formed an extremely difficult obstacle on either bank. By dint of spur, I forced my horse onward, over and through the tumult to the bank, and out upon the obstructions through which he at last fell headlong into the water, turning over in the fall nearly on top of, and spilling, his rider. By sticking to his mane, I urged him into the current of the river which was by this time full of horses, and quartering down stream, reached the opposite bank, and after infinite trouble and delay, scrambled through the *chevaux de frise* of timber, and gained the bank, still holding on desperately to horse and rifle. Here were already assembled many horses, while others were drifting down the stream, some no doubt drowned, and the main gang still crowding each other over and through the obstacles on both banks. Up to this time I had not seen a man of either party, but feeling tolerably sure of being joined by some of ours, my first care after getting my horse quiet, was to draw and reload my rifle which, of course, had got thoroughly wet. Before long, several of us had got together, and concluding the Indians had work enough for the moment, in securing the main body of horses which would soon be scattered by the current for miles down the river, we resolved to push for the rendezvous with as many horses as could be kept together. Nothing but useless danger to the survivors could be gained by fighting or remaining, and as nothing had occurred to make known our small number to the Indians, we hoped they would be content to recover so large a proportion of horses and abandon further pursuit, which turned out as anticipated.

Some of us riding in front as leaders, and others driving on the horses from the rear, we carried on quite a number, and after a couple of days of hard riding reached the rendezvous agreed on, where in the course of a few days we mustered six men of the original eleven, and about seventy horses. We remained here in a fair hunting and grazing country during about ten days, scouting backward for many miles, but no more men came in, and the missing were not heard of again. Though McTavish himself was among the lost, yet to my intense joy and thankfulness, Francois was among the survivors of that disastrous night. After dividing the horses and somewhat increasing my share by means of the simple but insidious pastime of 'Monte,' the party broke up, as I wished to return to the States, and the others, including F., preferred to return to the territory and service of their beloved Company, which to the half-breeds is family, home, friends and country, all in one. I have never laid eyes upon or heard a word of any of them, from that day to this.

In the American settlements on the Willamette, I traded horses for young cattle to good advantage, and obtaining the aid of a village of friendlies from the upper Coquille, started to drive the cattle across the Calapooyas, and down to the northern California mines, a distance of several hundred miles through tribes of doubtful amity, most of whom, as the Coquilles, Umpquas, and Rogue Rivers, when sufficiently robbed, teased, persecuted and murdered by white settlers and U. S. Indian agents, afterwards became famous as hostiles, and inflicted severe losses even on Government troops, before they were subdued, or rather exterminated. Of course those Indians, being then little acquainted with cattle and settlers, were disposed to treat the former like any other game, and caused some anxiety to the owner of the herd, but otherwise this journey was one of the most delightful and entertaining I have ever made in any country. Game was abundant through most of the route, and kamas roots, berries and fruit were procured in large quantities by the women and children. The party including the last was quite numerous, ensuring easy work for all, and my friendlies, soon understanding the advantage of good pasture and easy stages for keeping the cattle content and in good order, developed into herdsmen as skillful and reliable in some respects as if they had been bred to the business all their lives. In places where Indian relations were doubtful or bad, my people entirely relieved me of the laborious and sometimes perilous duty of selecting eligible routes, pastures and camps in advance, invariably smelling out the hostiles in time to evade them, and keeping me well informed of the surrounding country, though most of it was as new to them as to me. Though white man's cattle were quite new acquaintance they soon became fond of them, supplying endearing and poetic names to most, and watching over them with interest and solicitude not less than the proprietor's. The women did all the camp work and collected large quantities of food, filling up the intervals of spare time, in the sewing of trousers and moccasins. The men drove and cared for the cattle, watching them by day and night, and keeping me well informed of the country for many miles ahead. It is hardly necessary to say that I became much attached to these poor people, and would have trusted, and in fact did trust, everything I had to their affection and fidelity without hesitation. They well understood their own danger from white ruffians, and yet I have known one of them in search of lost animals by himself, to stick to them for nights and days, and finally bring them in safely at the risk of his life, for being unable to offer any explanation except with my aid, he would have been certainly shot if caught alone with cattle by some of the cowardly and bloodthirsty rascals who unfortunately are by no means rare among miners and settlers.

As it was impossible to think of taking these faithful friends into the settlements where they would encounter so many risks, and the time approached when I must part from them forever, I revolved in my head every possible and impossible scheme by which our friendly association might be continued. I even thought of procuring some breeding cattle, and searching out some secluded valley far out on the plains, where gradually, trained in the arts and arms but not in the rapacity and vices of the white man, some remote commonwealth might in time arise, far from the selfish and vulgar din of civilized life, to save at least some poor remnant of the persecuted and perishing natives of the soil. The notion might not have been so very chimerical, could I have got hold of two or three reliable aides, like Francois for instance. Alas, poor Francois! The best, bravest and surest friend I ever possessed. Many a sad day and sleepless night have I regretted him, and I do surely hope and believe that far away in the northern wilderness he also may have passed some hours in thinking of the old comrade who trusted him so implicitly and loved him so fondly but can never see him more. Notwithstanding his affection for me, he entertained a theoretical hatred and distrust of 'Bostons,' or Americans, and after surviving the horse episode, could not bring his mind to following me across the hated border, preferring to return to a hard life and constant adventure in the far northern solitudes he had roamed so often.

> Oh Bold and True,
> In bonnet blue,
> That fear or falsehood never knew;
> Whose heart was loyal to his word,
> Whose hand was faithful to his sword.

No, I could not remain always with my Indians, and there was no place where white men might be encountered, to covet their property and corrupt their families, that was safe to leave them at. Hostile tribes may be whipped, driven away, or conciliated, but neither resistance, nor docility, can hold or tame the rascally scum that ever floats first on the advancing wave of the white man's advance. The frontier abounds in cowardly, murderous wretches, who delight in robbing and maltreating the weak, when it is easy and safe, and notwithstanding the invaluable aid I should have had from my native herdsmen in California, I dared not take them any farther. I therefore left them encamped somewhere not far above the crossing of the upper Klamath, under the protection of 'Captain Jack' a famous Rogue River chief, while I rode on to obtain blankets, ammunition and so forth, to pay them off. This was at length effected to mutual satisfaction and after a most sentimental leave-taking, at which the men looked sober and the women wept, I rode sadly away and saw their faithful and loving faces no more. I had already hired some white men, who answered the purpose but gained no such place in my affection as my untutored but faithful friends.

'Captain Jack,' who stood my friend on that occasion, was even then a well known character, but as a gallant leader of his people in the Rogue River War, afterwards filled all American newspaperdom with his fame. His territory lying on the main route between Oregon and California adjacent to the northern mining districts, the miners and prospectors soon came into collision with him, and after enduring numerous outrages and atrocities at their hands, he was forced into a hopeless war in spite of his earnest wishes, and for a considerable time kept the troops at bay and the trail closed. He was an energetic and able leader, measured by any standard, and long made the best use of the force which his small tribe afforded. A large number of regular troops, besides the comparatively worthless but murderous 'volunteers,' were accumulated against him, and after eluding them a long time and inflicting many losses and two severe defeats upon them, his tribe was at last exterminated or dispersed, and himself captured. With one of his principal subordinates, he was carried to Portland and shipped to San Francisco on a steamer, whose name I cannot remember but of which one Dall was master, in charge of a corporal and another soldier.

After the ship got clear of the bar their irons were removed, and when a day or two out of port, Captain Jack and his man determined to capture the ship, notwithstanding its numerous crew and a large crowd of passengers. Inhabitants of their distant mountains, they had never before even seen the sea; nevertheless, watching an opportunity, they one night, by a sudden attack, overpowered the guard and secured their weapons, and raising their war-whoop, commenced a desperate attack on the entire steerage. A wild panic ensued, the passengers making their way headlong on deck and leaving the two lone warriors in full possession below, from whence the entire gang of frightened fugitives were not game to take them. At last Captain Dall with his crew attacked them simultaneously from the fore and main hatchways, killed Jack's assistant and captured him bleeding from a dozen wounds. Then the cowardly herd, who had been driven on deck and nearly frightened to death by two men, made a desperate attempt to kill him, and he was only saved by the determined courage of his captor Dall, who stood by him, pistol in hand, and at last got him into a safe place in his own cabin. Soon after his arrival at the Presidio at San Francisco, and long after my former acquaintance with him in his own country, I being then resident in that city, went out to the fort to see poor Jack and take him some small presents. As soon as he fairly identified me in my 'store clothes,' as the same roughly dressed mountain man he had formerly known, the remembrance of his old friends and lost home overcame him, his stoical demeanor gave way, and he could hardly contain the mixed and various emotions of his soul.

Though kindly treated by the army officers, he was depressed and despondent at his long confinement. He talked freely of his last exploit, and acknowledged that he had no expectation of escaping on that memorable occasion, but wished to die a warrier's death rather than be shut up in the 'strong house' at San Francisco. Nevertheless, from other of his remarks I inferred his idea was that if he could force the whites to jump overboard, the ship would drift ashore somewhere and afford him a chance to escape. What ultimately became of Jack, I do not remember, but have the impression that he died in confinement, which no Indian can endure long. His tribe, and I believe all the other tribes located near the great Oregon and California trail, now occupied by a railroad, have long since been exterminated, the celebrated Modoc war terminating in the expatriation of the few survivors; and the 'enterprising' settlers possess the lands they had enjoyed for centuries till the Great Spirit launched against them the curse of the white man and his Christianity.

Scott's Valley, where I now established my cattle camp, notwithstanding its great altitude, is a rich and lovely valley some thirty miles long and averaging perhaps three or four in width. It is traversed by the river of the same name, a large tributary of the Klamath, and lies at an elevation which ensures more or less frost during every month of the year. Nevertheless, it as well as all its lateral valleys extending deep into the hills, is covered with fine grass, and abounds in two kinds of excellent wild fruit usually called cherries and plums, from

a fancied though distant resemblance to those fruits of cultivation. The river abounded with beaver, otter and fish,
and the surrounding foothills were full of game in great
variety. Across the head of the valley rose the lofty barrier
of the Trinity Mountains, through and over which wound a
rough and difficult pack trail to Redding's Springs (now
Shasta City) at the head of the Sacramento Valley. On the
west, ascending ridge above ridge, glistens the precipitous and
snow-covered range of the Salmon River Mountains, and on the
east is a range of low mountains free from snow at that season
and full of game, separating it from the similar but less
attractive valley of the Shasta, near the lower end of which
is now situated the considerable mining town of Yreka.

Across the inaccessible and untrodden range of the Salmon
River Mountains lay the heads of both branches of the Salmon
River, whose remote and secluded mining region, extending
along both forks for a distance of thirty or forty miles,
sustained a scattered mining population of several hundred
men. Having been well acquainted with the place and its
wants two years previously, it was there I proposed to market
my cattle. Except for the long and difficult trail from the coast,
up the Klamath, which I had formerly so well known, it was
then only accessible by a circuitous pack trail leading up from
a point near the head of Scott's Valley, around the head of
the range, through a high and rough pass—which, however,
was clear of snow at that time of year—then following a long,
deep-curving ridge to a junction with the Klamath trail, and
descending by a steep descent of about ten miles to the ford
near 'Best's tent,' the principal trading post on the river, in all
about seventy miles. After leaving Scott's Valley there was
no grass along the road or at Salmon River, and the packers
were obliged to give their stock a feed or two of flour, or let
them go hungry. To drive well-fed, strong and half-wild
cattle from their accustomed pasture through such a rough
country for that distance would require at least two days, and
as any permanent corral constructed on the road would only
invite Indian ambushes, a sufficient number of herders would
be required to watch the cattle by night and frustrate their
frantic desire to get back to pasture.

As there was no beef and little game on the Salmon, the market was too promising to neglect, so leaving the stock on grass, I started on foot to prospect a shorter route directly across the range even if only practicable for loose cattle. Following up a principal tributary of the Scott, I reached the snow in about twenty miles, passed over it for about six more, and then by a bad and rough descent of fourteen miles came down not very far above the highest camps on the Salmon, making in all about forty miles; which though mostly very rough, seemed practicable for loose animals provided the snow should be crossed early in the day before it became softened by the sun. In order to do this, it was necessary to start early enough to get well up to the bad part of the ascent by break of day, which under ordinary circumstances, barring accidents and soft snow, usually rendered it possible to get the cattle down to the foot of the pass on the other side by or before dark. I had two pretty good men herding the cattle but neither of them could or would undertake to drive half-wild cattle forty miles a day on foot over a mountain pass bedeviled with snow and infested with Indians, so that part of the business fell to myself, and during the course of the summer I drove every one of those cattle, in lots of three or four at a time, across the mountain alone, butchered and sold them, and returned promptly for another lot.

Driving up the gulch was hard work, especially before the ravine became narrow, the cattle being desperately bent on getting away and returning. Taking them through the snow was worse, because when one of them bogged down and required help, I was interrupted by the constant necessity of watching and heading off the others. But after by hook or crook they were got over the summit and on the down grade I had my turn, and though it was the steepest, rockiest and worst of the whole, I had little trouble except from falls or when belated in crossing the snow. After getting down it was about six miles along a level but rocky bottom to the nearest miners' camp, where I built a strong corral. As the miners were prosperous, and gold dust was plenty, I had no difficulty in disposing of the beef at a dollar a pound all around, the first-comers getting the best cuts. After shooting the cattle, the rest of the work was mostly done by the customers themselves, who helped hang, skin, clean and cut up, a crowd being usually on hand by daylight on the days of killing, all willing and anxious to help in consideration of hearing the news from outside, and getting first chance at the beef. I occasionally met Indians on the mountain, or in the gulches on the west side, but succeeded in making friends with them by carrying small trinkets and being always ready for war, though I must say their company was not a pleasure, as they were regarded as unreliable or hostile, and they and the miners would kill each other without quarter whenever they met, rendering it a difficult sort of friendship for me to maintain.

During the whole season I think I lost but two animals, one by falling down a precipice, the other abandoned in soft snow. The work was severe for I wished to 'make hay while the sun shone,' and therefore wasted no time, but as it was extremely profitable and I had no intention of wintering there, I drove it hard, expecting to realize enough to warrant an early return to civilized life at San Francisco. Of course such a rough business could not be carried on without some adventures of my own, and some pretty serious ones to others who chose to charge theirs to me. I will relate some of the former first. One morning when I was absent on some business down the river, I found on my return that some steers which were to be executed next day had broken out of the corral and taken the back track. Knowing they could not very well get over the mountain without better management than their own, I started after them just as I was, wearing only leather trousers and flannel shirt, and armed only with a Colt's heavy revolver.

I followed their trail easily enough to the foot of the mountain, but at that place several gulches came in nearly together, all of which the runaways had explored either for grass or a practicable ascent of the mountain, and had so confused their trail on the rocky surface that darkness was coming on before I could unravel it. Seeing I would have to camp there for an early morning start, I cast about for a supper and soon marked down a pheasant which alighted in the small brushy valley of a creek coming in on the opposite side of the stream, which of course was here quite small. When I reached the little valley which was only a few yards wide, I found it so densely covered with brush that it was difficult to traverse without noise, and as a small rivulet came down it, I took its bed which had been cut into the gravelly soil, the vertical banks being fully ten or twelve feet high. It is necessary to get pretty near a pheasant to kill it with a pistol, and I did not wish to lose my supper, so as I had marked mine down carefully, I resolved to follow the bed of the stream till I got close to the place and then rise cautiously over the bank to get a close and sure shot. The little branch was extremely crooked and sharp-cornered, and its bed full of boulders and rocks. In stepping along carefully on those to keep my moccasins dry, I turned a sharp corner and saw right before me, almost within arm's length, a large grizzly which had been squatting in the water but now rose to its full height, looking to my startled eyes about the size of a house.

My movements having been noiseless, in deference to the pheasant, I saw him first—in fact I do not think he saw me at all. His delicate sense of smell had, however, already sniffed an alarm, and he commenced looking about and sniffing while I held my breath and tried hard to pass for a stump or rock or anything but the guilty intruder that I was. I had my pistol in hand ready cocked for the grouse, and considered hurriedly and anxiously what would be the best use to make of it. Of course under the circumstances I did not feel the least quarrelsome, and was quite willing to 'let bygones be bygones,' if the bear would only be kind enough to take the same view. There was no possible escape without his consent, and to put a pistol bullet into him would have delayed him about as much as firing into a pine tree. So not knowing what else to do, I stood still, humbly waiting his majesty's pleasure, holding my breath and looking as unobtrusive as possible, resolved if he came for me to try and blind his eyes with the pistol and run back down the trap I was in till I could find a place to climb out quickly. Having a good opportunity of watching his small wicked grey eyes, I observed they wandered about and never once fixed themselves on me, and I do not think he distinguished me at all as separate from other inanimate objects. Suddenly, and without the slightest warning that he had finished his reflections, he uttered a vicious growl and sprang up the bank, scattering down cartloads of gravel and crashing off through the brush. Certainly no one ever came, or could come, to closer quarters with a grizzly without actual collision, but except perturbation of mind, the only damage I suffered was the loss of my supper, to which I reconciled myself under the circumstances without much difficulty.

A circumstance occurred during this summer in connection with the new trail I had opened directly across the mountains, which brought some undeserved opprobrium upon me on the part of a few persons. Since my butchering operations had commenced two extremely sharp Yankees, whom I will call F. and S., had come in with a large pack train and established a new trading post near my camp at the head of the little settlement, which F. remained to administer, while the more active or adventurous S. operated the mule train with a lot of Mexican *arrieros*. His method was to make a round trip from Redding's to the head of Scott's Valley, and there leave his mules on grass while he with a couple of men rode over to see whether F. was yet in need of more supplies. If not, he would dispose of his merchandise on the Shasta or Humbug and repeat the trip. Everyone knew that habitually I made the trip to and from Scott's Valley in a single day, and though much questioned, I had refrained from encouraging anyone to attempt my route, especially with animals; and I suppose was generally credited with liking the monopoly of the good thing, which indeed I will not deny, for I certainly did not want any competition in the cattle trade, and in that respect was pretty safe from those who could only bring rival cattle in by the long trail.

I was therefore not much surprised when one day F. invited me to his trading tent to discuss with him and his partner the possibility of their pack train, which was then in Scott's Valley, coming in over my route. I told them it was certainly impracticable for laden animals, and I did not believe they could take even light mules over it, especially as it was not even marked out, since for fear of being ambushed by Indians

I always varied the exact route as much as the ridges and gulches permitted. S. evidently did not believe me, and boasting that he could go anywhere that I could, announced his intention of riding out over it at least, so as to see for himself. Of course, as I was not his guardian, it did not become me to say any more, having simply given my opinion in answer to his questions. F. then asked if I would be willing to describe the route, which I cheerfully did, taking the trouble to sketch it on paper, and warn him against the errors most likely to be committed by a man only acquainted with the mountains on beaten trails. S. accordingly departed and nothing more was heard from him for a week, I having in the meantime been over the mountain without seeing anything of him, when he returned to F.'s on foot, minus his blankets, mule, arms, and most of his clothes, scratched to pieces by brush and nearly starved to death. In this predicament F. sent for me and concealing the animosity which it appears he felt on account of my supposed bad faith in giving a misleading description, told me that S. had *cached* his valuable silver mounted Mexican saddle and bridle in a tree, and turned loose his mule in a certain place described with more or less accuracy, and asked if I could tell what mistake had been made, and especially whether I could find the mule and saddle, which had a value of several hundred dollars. After interviewing S., who was in bed and not in very good condition for talking—having had a narrow escape with his life—I felt pretty sure of the character and locality of his first error, and that if I could once pick up his trail after it diverged from the proper route, I could find the place where he had abandoned the mule, notwithstanding he insisted it was on the other side of the mountain. So, on F.'s solicitation, and more to justify myself than for any other reason I at last offered to find the mule and saddle for a hundred dollars, payable only in case of success, incautiously admitting that if I could find them at all, I could do it in a day. I had no desire to neglect my own affairs for any such job or reward, but there was a little pride mixed up in the matter. S. had come to grief in following my directions—or thought he had and the whole subject, especially my good faith with him, had become a favorite subject of discussion. I felt confident

I could trace out the place and manner of his error, for of course I knew he had never really crossed the range, as he believed and averred, but had gone up some wrong gulch and crossing some high ridge, erroneously taken for the summit, had come down another on the same side of the divide, an error before alluded to, which is common enough with inexperienced, or half experienced persons.

My proposition however was declined, and F. hired a couple of miners whose prospecting adventures had led them to over-rate their accomplishments as mountain men, at ten dollars a day each. As they failed to discover anything, and their report only served to render the mystery still more opaque, another pair was hired with the same result, and at last as a *dernier* resort, my offer was accepted. Of course the job was now much more difficult than at first. The time elapsed had tended to efface such trail as there was, which had probably been additionally obscured by the wanderings of the two unsuccessful search parties, and there was no guessing where the mule might have strayed by this time after grass and water. I was strongly tempted to double my price, but did not, and started early next morning so as to get to the foot of the big range by the first light, and having my own ideas of the nature of S.'s blunder, soon found the gulch that had misled him. Up this he had toiled with the mule for some miles over and through the toughest obstacles, where I had no difficulty in tracing him after once getting on his actual track. He had at last got involved in a crooked narrow cañon full of immense boulders and 'jump-offs,' where he had abandoned the mule and pushed on by himself. Here I found *cached* in a tree, as he had described, his saddle with lariat attached, and making a wide cast, soon discovered the ridge taken by the mule, who like all of his kind had gone straight upward in search of grass, it being much easier to a mule to graze or travel up-wards than downwards.

The animal's trail up the ridge, being on comparatively better ground, was well marked, and I soon found him in a small valley with grass some miles above the cañon where he had been abandoned. But the rogue had already become so saucy and wild I could not approach him near enough to throw the lariat, and after all my trouble, came near giving him up and returning for assistance. But at last getting above him, I succeeded in driving him down the mountain, and having constructed a sort of rude pen or corral among the boulders in the cañon, caught and saddled him and leading him down the gulch to better ground, mounted and rode in to F.'s before dark. It was plain enough to see how and where S. had gone farther and irremediably astray after abandoning his mule, but having got the property I took no further heed of his tracks.

Now this was in reality a long and hard day's work, covering many miles of most difficult travel, but when F. pondered how quickly, and easily as it seemed to him, the mule had been traced and found, he was more than ever convinced that he had been designedly misled, and when I called for the money next morning he refused to pay and offered a less amount. Saying but little at the moment, though fully resolved to have the money from him dead or alive, I went down and consulted W., a very judicious friend of mine from Missouri, who stood high in public estimation and was an excellent judge of public opinion. Calling in a few other advisers, it was at length decided that I should go *alone* and compel payment, and if it came to a fatal collision, I should be sustained. This counsel was at once adopted, and F. in the midst of a number of his adherents and hangers on, paid down the money.

My friends saw me comfortably through with the public, and at their suggestion I offered to take a party up the mountain and demonstrate the precise spot and manner of S.'s blunder, but as no one cared to go, that proposition was allowed to drop, and as even those who chose to doubt my good faith in the first place, agreed that F. having recovered his valuables ought to pay what he promised, I believe I took no harm in public estimation, as I certainly did not in my own, which was of still more importance.

The county of Siskiyou (pronounced Sissikew) being then about to be politically organized, including the Salmon River country, a certain Virginian named Peters found his way in there during the summer, afflicted with an anxious desire to serve the dear public as county judge. As I knew everyone on the creek, and being in the habit of giving plenty of 'tick' to miners out of luck, did not stand badly with a public addicted to fresh beef, he begged me to travel round with him to assist his canvas, to which I consented, and as he was a good-hearted, amiable fellow, soon grew quite intimate with him; and since he soon disappears from my narrative, I will here add that at the ensuing election, which occurred soon after I left the neighborhood, he was duly elected by an appreciative constituency, receiving and wearing the handle to his name that he coveted. But before that event it was necessary for him to visit other districts, for which the old circuitous trail still supplied the only route available for horses. This was at the time infested and watched by a lot of murdering white rascals disguised as Indians, whose facilities for ambushing the narrow mountain path were so good and had been so well used, that it was regarded dangerous for small parties. A number of persons waiting for a good chance had combined to go out with P. and the night before their departure a Dutchman, whom as I have forgotten his name I will call D., having accumulated his small pile, asked leave to join them, and as his camp was below the crossing—the others all coming from above—it was arranged that all parties should start at dawn of day, and get together somewhere on the ten miles of steep and difficult trail, which after fording the river led up to the top of the ridge.

P.'s party started as agreed, and had reached a point not far from the summit, P. himself walking ahead of the animals, without yet seeing D., whose tracks however showed him to be ahead, when high up on a distant horse-shoe-like bend of the ridge he was following, he caught sight of a man and called to him, taking him for the Dutchman. Instead of replying, the stranger instantly dashed down the precipitous side of the ridge, where he was lost to view in a moment, among the rocks and bushes. Not understanding the maneuver, and suspecting mischief, P. concealed himself till his friends came up, when all went forward to the suspicious spot. There they found D.'s horse unhurt and tied to a tree, his boot tracks on the ground being accompanied by numerous moccasin tracks all made by white men. (Indian tracks are so easily distinguishable by their small size and pigeon-toed direction that they cannot be imitated with any great success.) The party having no trail expert among them, could make little of the sign, but as it was plain some mischief had befallen D., they sent back a messenger with the horse and all the facts they knew. About the time that messenger arrived, I was coming in from my new cattle trail, and was at once called on by the general voice to take a party up the mountain, pick up and follow D.'s trail and if possible capture or kill the robbers. I had driven half-wild cattle forty miles over a snowy range on foot that day, and wanted rest just then more than anything else, but as immense excitement prevailed and plenty of men offered to butcher and sell out my animals for me, I agreed to go and asked for five good men. Nevertheless, fifty volunteered and insisted on going, notwithstanding my objections that such a crowd, besides being noisy must necessarily overrun and obscure a trail made by anything short of a troop of cavalry.

The excessive excitement was not unnatural under the circumstances. The infested route was the only one by which miners who did not wish to be snowed in all winter could get away with the proceeds of their summer's work. There was not a house or resident on it, till it came down into Scott's Valley, seventy miles distant. Communications were infrequent, and as everyone robbed was invariably killed, definite intelligence of their fate was rarely received; all that could be certainly known, being the negative fact that news of their arrival at Scott's Valley never came back. Now, therefore, that there seemed a chance of tracking down and catching some of these common enemies, everyone wanted to help, and as all my gallant volunteers insisted on going, we started before break of day next morning and reached the spot by sunrise, the sign sought for being then only one day old. As I had anticipated, it was only possible to get a glance at the sign before it was obscured and confused by the unruly crowd. Nevertheless, the story being simple could not easily be mistaken as far as the sign went.

The horse trail at this spot was split into an old and new path which after separating traversed some 500 yards nearly parallel with each other and perhaps fifty or a hundred yards apart, before coming together again. Three white men shod with moccasins had made an ambush on the old trail on the outside of the arc, the whole place being covered with a thick undergrowth. D. had taken the new or shorter trail, and his route being discovered by the robbers, they had dashed straight at him across the interval separating the two trails, giving D. sufficient time to dismount and rush down the side of the ridge, where he had jumped headlong into a large clump of manzanitas and remained. The moccasins had followed him, passed beyond and all around his place of concealment, fortunately without finding him, and returned to the ridge, where they had, after searching the horse, blankets and saddle, tied the former to keep him from following them, and gone off, following at first the beaten trail to avoid being traced. Their own horses had doubtless been *cached* at some distant place, as only the one horse-track was visible. D. had afterwards come out of the manzanita, presumably after the robbers' departure, as his tracks were the latest, had returned to the trail, and again rushed down the mountain by long leaps and bounds, but this time without being followed, no track but his own showing beyond the manzanita. There was no longer any probability of success in following the robbers, as they might have kept the beaten trail for many miles before leaving it, and their tracks on it were already overrun by P. and his party.

Sending the bulk of my men off on the main trail ostensibly to follow the robbers, but in reality to get rid of them as they were much in the way; with a few picked men I made an effort to track up D. and should have almost certainly succeeded, but for running his trail into a freshly burned region of large extent which could carry no marks, the light dust and ashes borne about by the wind covering all signs in a few minutes. It was ascertained that this fire had started at some point within the burned area, and not at the scene of disturbance nor at any mining camp on the river, and was therefore probably started by D. himself at some of his camps or stopping places. D. could not be traced, and if still living was wandering somewhere on the mountain, although he had but to direct his steps always downward to come with certainty upon some watercourse which whether wet or dry, must by following downward, inevitably lead him to the camps on the main Salmon.

Nearly or quite a week passed and the excitement was coming to be forgotten, when one morning a party of miners

living in a remote and secluded place up a side cañon, came
down to Best's bringing with them on a stretcher what was left
of the unfortunate Dutchy, living, but no longer able to walk
or stand, and almost speechless. He had wandered into their
camp early that morning starved, naked, delirious and nearly
perished. With good care he soon revived sufficiently to tell
his woeful tale. The incidents of the attack on him were
just as has been inferred. After lying quietly in the manzanita
thicket, where he heard them hunting all around for him,
till the coast seemed clear, he had ventured forth and returned
cautiously to the trail, where he found his horse tied, as P. had
found it later. He was preparing to loose him and mount with
the intention of returning to meet the party he knew was
behind him, when he heard P.'s shout, and being confused about
the direction, and supposing his assailants were coming back
for him, again rushed down the mountain, this time to become
irrevocably lost and return no more. This statement, with
the further assertion that he had seen before and could identify
one of the rascals, was first related to a hastily assembled
miners' committee who at once sent for me. Dutchy was too
weak and miserable for further examination at the time, but
the rest of us thought from the description we could recognize
a certain hard character known as 'Oregon Jim.' That individual was by his own account a dangerous ruffian who had
escaped from the Willamette settlements after killing a man,
and had been already suspected, not so much of robbing
himself, as of carrying intelligence to the robbers, under pretence of hunting, respecting persons leaving the creek and
which of them were best worth intercepting.

He camped alone at the extreme end of the settlement, some
miles below on the opposite side of the river, below the debouch of Jackass gulch, a precipitous cañon up which he made
a pretence of mining by himself, though no one else thought
it worth working. The committee forthwith furnished me
with written authority to select such assistance as I desired
and capture Jim alive or dead, the former if possible, and
bring him to Best's, where they would prepare for a general
miners' meeting to be assembled at short notice. As this was
considered a desperate job, I selected W., a good friend of
mine from Missouri, who was a quick and sure shot and with

his partners possessed one of the best claims on the river and were responsible and respected residents. Placing a guard to prevent any intelligence following us down the river, W. and I set out at once, taking with us one of his partners named F., a brave, reliable and resolute man. Leaving F. on guard at the mouth of Jackass gulch to intercept the game if prematurely flushed, W. and I crossed the river and advanced cautiously down the narrow bar which though well covered with brush and large boulders did not exceed twenty feet in width from the river's edge to the base of the nearly vertical cliff. Jim's bivouac had been represented as not over two hundred yards below the crossing, and after warily stalking it about that distance I smelled fire, and looking out from behind a rock saw Jim, seated on the ground before a few embers, with his side presented, resting his back against a log on which his gun leaned within reach of his hand. Making a sign to W. who was following close, we both rose up quickly, covered our man, and ordered him to throw up his hands and come in.

Finding himself completely surprised and at our mercy he obeyed, and finding he had no arms on his person except a knife, which we secured, we called F. and simply told the prisoner there was a miners' meeting above which had directed us to arrest and take him before them. Now Jim although an American, passed for a mountain or fur Company man, which I believe was false. He was a stalwart ruffian of large stature, dressed in buckskin, gaunt, lithe and active as a panther. Give him a start of a couple of jumps into the brush at any of the numerous favorable places along our route of six miles, and he would be hard to get hold of a second time, so I proposed to tie his hands. But on his strenuous objection and promises to go along quietly, I was overruled by the others, so we set out, one in front and two behind, first warning him not to step out of the trail on any pretense and finally brought him safely to the meeting, where perhaps a couple of hundred men were soon assembled. A jury and prosecutor were at once appointed who publicly examined him respecting his peculiar habits of living alone, mining where little profit was to be got, going off on long and frequent hunts where little or no game abounded, and rarely bringing any back with him. Those matters he explained more or less feebly, and admitted, probably because he was unaware how much or how little we actually knew, that he was hunting on the mountain on the day in question, but flatly denied any knowledge of or communication with robbers. He was then confronted with the Dutchman, who being terribly frightened and unnerved, hemmed, hawed and suspected, but failed to identify him. To do the miners justice, they gave us every chance to convict him, for everyone knew that if he got clear he was pretty certain to kill one of us, but with the total defect of actual proof, though all suspected him, a majority voted for his discharge and even voted down the proposition to banish him from the creek.

I have related this long and perhaps tedious story, as a sample of several that I was concerned in at different periods, mainly to illustrate the prompt and rude methods usually adopted in the remote and scattered mining camps of that day, to punish crime and protect the industrious in a primitive and perhaps till then unparalled state of society. If convicted the prisoner would have been hung on the spot, but under the circumstances related he was acquitted, and so far as I know the guilty parties remained undiscovered. As we anticipated, our relations with Jim were not yet over. Although he disclaimed robbery, he was a professed 'fighting man,' and almost an avowed assassin, and as we had no intention of being shot from behind a bush, W. and I thought it expedient to pay a little attention to his movements. On the very next day word came that Jim was principally incensed at me, not so much for accusing or arresting him, as for wishing to tie his hands, and had made known his intention of killing me 'on sight.' Such a declaration in that country, though of course dangerous to make against a resolute enemy, was yet often risked in order to create evidence in advance, for few juries would convict a man willing to accept the probable results of it, for any homicide short of a deliberate cowardly murder from ambush. On the other hand, it was usually held to justify the threatened party in putting himself in the way of getting the 'first drop,' as almost anything except secret assassination is permissible to the man receiving such a notice.

The fact—as I have always believed—was that Jim knew I was collecting my debts and preparing to leave the river, which when once snowed in, is, or was, inaccessible for several months, and thought he might win a cheap credit for 'running me off.' Now in those foolish and reckless days I valued my 'fighting reputation' as well as the next, and would have sacrificed all my plans and property, and camped there a year, before going off under any such stigma, and if such was the ruffian's real intention he made a big mistake in choosing his man. My good friends, W. and F., were staunch and true, and with the aid of their counsels the following plan of settlement was resolved on, based on some of Jim's well known habits. When he was not out 'hunting,' as he called it, or pretending to work at his alleged claim, he was usually to be found gambling in Best's tent. That trading post was a canvas structure about fifteen by thirty feet, with one long side toward the river, and the other on the main river trail. A liquor bar or counter occupied the rear side, the front side rolling up in the daytime. Thus the entire long front toward the public trail was at those hours open. In front of the liquor bar, the only movable furniture was a gambling table and benches all made of split puncheons. W.'s camp was not far above, and mine still higher, all the settlements in that vicinity being on the same, and only habitable side of the river. It was determined that W. should keep a lookout and inform me of Jim's next presence at Best's, where I would endeavor to surprise him, trusting W. to keep his friends off me, and generally to cover my rear.

The desired opportunity arrived next day. Approaching one end of the place quickly, I stepped suddenly round in front, and walking rapidly up to Jim, covered him at arm's length. He was sitting at the table, back to the bar, and face to the front, with gun resting against the counter within reach, but his attention being given to the cards on the table, I was too quick for him and could have killed him by an imperceptible motion of the finger, which after his hostile declaration I had a right to do, and which it required some self-restraint not to make. Withdrawing at my order, under the alternative of instant death, the hand which had begun instinctively to reach for his gun, he said, "Well, you have got the advantage; do you want to kill me?" "I don't want to kill you unless I have to, but I got your notice, and if you feel that way I will give you a chance to come outside with the same weapons and have a fair shot, at the word, but at the first trick I will kill you." "I said so when I was mad because you treated me so rough; you wanted to tie me." Of course when the matter came to that sort of discussion it was soon adjusted with the aid of those present, and we separated professing amity if not friendship.

The popular jurisdiction out of which this 'difficutly' grew, is none the less interesting when we reflect that it is almost peculiar to our own race and has at one time or another prevailed in every State of our Union, except those settled directly from European countries and thence supplied by charter with complete ready-made judicial machinery. In connection with the various unwritten popular civil codes affecting mineral lands and water supplies, the faculty of popular appreciation and enforcement of order is anterior to the advent of statesmen, or legislators, or even of public education. It is embedded deep in Anglo-Teutonic nature, and is traceable far back to those primitive days when our barbarous German ancestors met in the forests in general assembly of all the warriors, and by the clash of sword on shield signified their unconstrained and effective judgment on all propositions, including those of peace and war.

Can it be possible that in the march of luxury and civilization, we have lost, or are in danger of losing, that unique heritage among the corrupt and bungling failures of modern legislative methods, sustained upon the universal suffrage of ignorance and numbers? Must we believe that that early love of the masses for justice and political vigor has been, or is in danger of being, corrupted or impaired by the poverty and struggles which seem more and more incident to the civilized condition?

CHAPTER XIII

BACK TO CIVILIZATION AND THE SEA

As already explained, the miners on the Salmon were so hemmed in on all sides by lofty mountains that during the season of snow they were secluded for long periods from outside communication. I presume if that district be yet productive and inhabited, better roads have been made to obviate that difficulty, but in those early days one was put to his election at the first appearance of snow, either to get away at once or remain all winter. Having determined on the first, and collected all available debts, I started with one companion, who was the first person besides myself that ever traversed the new or direct trail. It did not require long to settle my affairs at the cattle camp in Scott's Valley, and take a leave which proved to be final of that interesting locality, but before it drops out of my narrative I must relate an incident or two connected with that vicinity and its abundant game.

Riding down the valley one evening with a single companion, we discovered a small bunch of wild plums covering something less than an acre, every tree bending under an untouched crop of ripe fruit. As it was getting dark, we hurried on to find a good camp on water, intending to ride back in the morning and fill a sack with the plums. On reaching the place before sunrise next morning, we found only a scene of devastation and ruin, some grizzlies having visited it in the interim and broken and torn down every tree, smashing and destroying such fruit as they could not eat, so that we scarcely got enough for a breakfast. The low divide which separates Scott's from Shasta Valley not only abounded in fruit and edible roots, but with nearly every kind of game existing in that country. Down in the deep, gloomy bottom of one of its darkest and most secluded cañons, I once came upon a curiosity seldom found anywhere, in the shape of a complete and untouched skeleton of a grizzly, unfound even by the wolves and foxes. It was bleached clean and white, with just enough of the cartilaginous attachments remaining to hold all together. The position was one not unfrequently assumed by the animal in death, that is, prone on all fours, the head resting on the forepaws, something like a dog which waits impatiently for his master.

Encamped on the Scott near the lower end of the valley was a small party of half-breed mountain men, enjoying their leisure while waiting for the season for trapping. These men were beaver trappers, and though the skins of those animals are worthless during the summer, they kept a few traps set to supply the demand of the Yreka miners for beaver meat, which except the tail, the trappers never eat themselves when they can help it, as it is red and stringy, much like that of a cat, and by no means equal to a good fat Assinaboine dog. Nevertheless, after the trappers had reserved the tail for themselves, they had no difficulty in getting five times the price of good venison for the rest of the carcass, from the enterprising restaurant keepers in Yreka, who proudly advertised it on extempore signs, just as the city restaurateurs advertise 'Green turtle here today.' Though there were good mines all around, nothing would have induced these easy-going half-breeds to work at anything during their holiday season, but hunting not being considered work, I could always find one or two of them to go hunting with me when I could afford to take a day off, especially as the Shasta-Scott divide was easily hunted on horseback.

There was no end of deer and bear in the foothills and low ranges and any two good hunters working together could kill far more meat than they could take care of and pack in with a reasonable number of animals. Although the salmon running season was over and the fish not then considered very good, a considerable number remained in pools near the heads of the stream, perhaps because they could no longer get out, and once I killed, with no more deadly weapon than a stick, a large heavy fish that was struggling in a little rivulet in Shasta Valley, not near deep enough to float him in an upright position. The miners of Salmon River during the running season caught all they wanted in all sorts of ways, many being killed with shovels.

That reminds me of a circumstance which, as I never knew much of the habits of lamprey eels, always seemed strange to me. I was interested with a lot of men who undertook to, and did, construct a dam and flume on the Salmon with a view of mining the river bed. The evening when the work was completed and the water turned in, an ox hide was placed at the entrance, to guide the flow into the structure and prevent the washing of the dam. Neither I nor anyone else had ever seen or heard of a lamprey in the river, which was a clear, dashing mountain stream rushing between and over rocks and boulders, and looking like anything rather than a *habitat* for eels. Yet at dawn next morning the hide was absolutely covered with them, clinging to it by their suckers as close to each other as they could take hold, their long bodies floating and twirling in the rapid current. Where they came from so suddenly, and how they managed to seize hold in such rapid current were equally inexplicable. I do not know the actual rapidity of the current running into the flume, but it was such that though six feet wide and less than one deep, a man could not stand in it without being instantly swept off his feet. The flume was of the same size throughout, of a single steep gradient and several hundred feet long. I cannot now remember in how many seconds an object was carried through, but it must have been at express railroad speed, at least.

The many incidents connected with that flume which disappointed so many splendid expectations, as the bed of the river contained no considerable quantity of gold, remind me of the queer conduct of a young rattlesnake, to which the transition from lamprey eels is not very violent, as both animals are worthless either for fun or food, and neither have many friends. The considerable quantity of lumber required for the flume and its supports, was sawed with a whip saw, kept running night and day by relays of men. The saw pit was located on a bench of the mountain side several hundred feet above the river, and the lumber slid down a straight and very steep way cut out and prepared for the purpose. One morning about ten o'clock (the lumber having been thundering down the slide since daylight continuously, or as fast as several men could start the boards) wishing to know how much was left of it, I signalled to stop the slide, and proceeded to climb up it to reach the pit. More than half-way up the slide, a small tree less than a foot thick had been cut away leaving a hollow place on the lower or down-hill side of the stump, in which lay a young snake of two or three rattles, so torpid with the cold that, though he saw me, and feebly dragged himself into some effort at a coil, he was unable to strike, even when poked with a stick. Now in that condition he could not have come there that morning, which at no time had been warmer nor so warm as at that minute, and we must therefore suppose he had taken up his quarters the day before, and had lain contentedly or stupidly there while hundreds of boards were thundering continuously over and within a few inches of him!

It is hard to tear myself away from the recollections of that delightful country about the upper Klamath, Shasta, Salmon and Scott Rivers, and I do not wonder the poor *Modocs* made many a desperate fight before they were forced away from a not very distant locality, a quarter of a century later; but the time had come, and after closing out my affairs in Scott's Valley, as I had already done on the Salmon, I made my way to Redding's Springs, a little town near the head of the Sacramento and not far from the base of the magnificent Butte of Shasta. I may state here that at some later period I heard that after my departure from the Salmon, several men with a few pack mules had attempted to get out by the new cattle trail, but becoming lost in the intricacies of the mountain spurs, were overtaken by a snow storm and all perished but one, who finally extricated himself, coming down on the same side of the mountain without crossing it, probably by the identical error previously made by S. The direction of the main range and the confusion of its lateral ridges at that place were well calculated to cause such errors, and probably nine inexperienced men out of ten would have come down on the same side, convinced they had crossed and got clear of the main range.

At Redding's I took stage for Sacramento, about three hundred miles distant, and had a delightful journey. The line was just started, and harness trained horses being scarce, had been arranged with the view of having at least two collar broken horses in each team, the other four being wild or half-broken *bronchos,* just as they were driven in from the plains. The road was level and the team was usually kept on a run to prevent them from getting into mischief and to keep up their enthusiasm. The changes were made about twelve miles apart, and it was a lively process to get a new team started, and still more exciting to cross the deep, dry *arroyos,* which in places intersected the road, and had to be taken on a wild run to prevent the green horses from stalling. Obtaining a seat beside the driver, I do not remember ever seeing livelier riding than during that three hundred mile trip, which, if I remember right, we made in about twenty-four hours. Sacramento City, which I had last seen a squalid collection of tents and cloth shanties, was now a large town with well-kept streets and numerous frame buildings, and had become the capital of the State, itself organized since I was last here. I remained there all day, trying with only partial success to identify old spots and find old friends, and then taking the fine steamer *Senator* in the evening, landed next day in San Francisco, and there also found a great city with long rows of wharves and buildings, and hardly a landmark except Telegraph Hill and the Plaza to remind one of its early days.

Though the city contained few or no other persons known to me, I was fortunate in finding one old friend, P., a passenger on the *Columbus* in 1850, now become a successful and prosperous business man, and what was of more importance to me, the depositary of a pile of accumulated letters, some of them two years old, which he had obtained and kept for me on the faith that I would some day turn up. From him I also learned, greatly to my surprise, of the presence in San Francisco of my brother Caspar, some years younger than myself, whom I had left a little boy at school. He had become subject to epileptic attacks, which failing to yield to any medical treatment at home, my father had been advised might be overcome by a long sea voyage with plenty of work and physical occupation. He had therefore been dispatched with two other lads of similar condition in life, on the fine new ship *Cambridge,* sailing from Philadelphia to make the circuit of the world by way of California and China. These lads had been assigned to a separate deck-house fitted up expressly for their use, and placed in the personal charge of the captain. Deeming themselves hardly used and overworked by him, they all ran away from the ship on her arrival at San Francisco, from which place the ship had, at the time of my arrival, already sailed for China. P. informed me that Caspar had declined giving any address, but called occasionally for news and letters. Of course, not knowing where to look, I found it impossible to trace him, and went every day to P.'s where I remained several hours daily for a long time without success.

At last as I was sitting one day in the counting-room at the rear of the store, conversing with P., a tall, stout, good-looking young fellow of about eighteen years, walked in, and after ignoring me, and saluting P., was formally introduced by the latter as my brother. Both of us required strong assurances from our mutual friend to convince us of the other's identity, so completely had we grown out of each other's recollection. I learned from C. that while at sea he had enjoyed comparative immunity from his attacks, which had nevertheless returned since he had been living on shore, with a decided tendency to increase in frequency and severity. He had at first obtained remunerative employment in the harbor as a rigger, but being afraid of getting a bad, perhaps fatal, fall, during some sudden access of his disease which came absolutely without warning, he was now employed at the semaphore station on Telegraph Hill as vessel reporter, where his employers valued him much but intimated that he underrrated the terrible severity of his attacks. C. absolutely declined either to return home or to receive any assistance, priding himself with becoming spirit on having 'never borrowed a dollar in his life.' He was, however, quite aware that in the condition of his health he ought not to live any longer on shore and at length concluded to ship on a small brig belonging to an Italian friend of mine, who was going in her himself, to the Marquesas for fruit and live stock. I accompanied the brig till the pilot left her outside the bar, where I took my last leave of the poor afflicted boy who was making a solitary and gallant fight for life at an age when other lads of his condition are enjoying the first keen joys of opening life. Years subsequently passed without any further intelligence of him, when in 1857, not long prior to my final departure from San Francisco, I received official notification from London of a letter addressed to me lying there in the general dead letter office, which on being reclaimed, proved to be a letter from him giving a brief statement of the brig's loss and his own arrival at Melbourne in 1853. As this letter, which I still possess, contains his last words, and indeed the last ever heard of him I give it here entire, notwithstanding the poor fellow meant it only for my eyes.

> Melbourne, District of Port Philip,
> Australia, June 23rd, 1853.

Dear Brother,

I have just sat down to let you know by what circumstances I have brought up in this part of the world, as I suppose I shall leave it shortly, either for Callao or some port in the East Indies. In the first place I must inform you that the little brig *Mary Helen* is among the things that were, having been condemned at the island of Upolu in the Navigator group. We had hardly got out of San F. before she commenced leaking like an old basket, notwithstanding which, we made a first-rate run down to the Marquesas Islands where we lay off and on among the various islands for about three weeks, trading with the natives for hogs, sandalwood, cocoanuts, &c. We then sailed for the Society Islands intending to dispose of the cargo and return to San F. with a cargo of oranges and fruit. Arrived within 150 or 200 miles to leeward of them and doing our best to beat up against the trades, the leak, which had been growing worse, suddenly increased to such a degree that both pumps had to be kept going for two hours out of each watch, the water even then gaining, when one night during a smart gale of wind, the vessel laboring hard under close-reefed topsails, she commenced making water in a fresh place and about 10 P.M. the water had so increased that the forecastle was half full, and the water stood within four feet of her decks. It was useless to pump any more and as we expected every minute to see her roll on her beam ends we lowered away the boat, put in compass, instruments, provisions and water, and all hands, ten souls in all, got into her, intending to steer for the Societies. But before we could shove clear, the boat was swamped under the brig's counter, whereby all the provisions and water were lost. We got her righted and got in again without anything to eat or drink, and by constant bailing managed to keep her above water till morning by which time the wind had considerably moderated and the sea much settled, so we concluded to go back aboard the brig, as she was still floating and in sight. Once on board again we concluded to give her another trial and commenced heaving overboard the few hogs that had not been swept away, cut away topmasts, threw over the anchors, chains and indeed everything not absolutely necessary for working the ship. We then tried to work up to the Societies but finding she made water as fast again when close hauled, had to put her before it for the Navigators, which we made in twenty days, during which time the pumps did not cease working for five minutes. All the sail we could make was the courses, and lower stay sails, the rest having been thrown overboard. After lying at Upolu for some time the barque *General Wool*, with passengers from San Francisco to this place, put in for provisions and we all obtained a passage here, where we at last arrived, having lost money, clothes, and in fact everything but what we stood in.

I am making enough here to pay expenses and shall leave as soon as I can find a ship to suit, which is no easy matter as I want an American vessel, of which there are very few now in port. As for the mines that are so much talked of, I would rather take my chance in California, from the reports brought down by thousands who have come down disgusted. Every man in the mining region, whether miner or not, is taxed thirty shillings a month, which, with the high price of provisions, is as much or more than most can make. Freight from here to the mines is 65 to 70 pounds a ton, which is not so very high considering the state of the roads, many teams requiring thirty days to go ninety miles, and the public house charge on the road is a guinea a feed, for each horse. Wages here are from two and a half to three dollars a day and board, about the same as at San Francisco. I suppose before receiving this you will have heard of the loss of the *Monl. City* [Monumental] with thirty-three lives, for which the Captain is now undergoing his trial at Sidney. As I have not much room left, I will now close, requesting when you write home you will let them know where I am, though if I can get a berth aboard a vessel for Callao and the States it is likely I may go home myself or to England.

Your affect. Bro.

CASPAR WISTAR, JR.

Though my father caused extensive inquiries to be made through consuls, merchants and others, in all principal South American, Australian and Indian ports, no further intelligence of Caspar has ever been received. My father of course never ceased to reproach himself for this fatal result of his plans, but I have always thought, with injustice to himself. C. was a worthy, affectionate and promising lad in every other respect than his one sad affliction, and as his life was hardly worth living thus menaced, and every possible curative remedy had been tried at home in vain, it was, in my opinion, a very just conclusion that the most radical and effective measure must be resorted to while youth still rendered it hopeful and practicable. Although this had not a successful result, treatment at home could in all probability, only have prolonged for a brief span a life thus doomed from its beginning, and only at the expense of slow but certain mental and physical failure, than which no end can be more sad and painful. For myself, or anyone dear to me, of the two evils I would unhesitatingly prefer a fall from the yard-arm and quick death in the infinite depths below, to the lingering agony of a hopeless disease, slowly crushing in its relentless grasp all the waning faculties of mind and body.

As no great social niceties prevailed in San Francisco in those days, I soon made plenty of acquaintances, but not being familiar with any kind of city business, and soon tiring of an idle existence, I cast about for some such occupation as I might have become qualified for by my rather erratic and amphibious experience. The point on Contra Costa where Oakland now stands, opposite San Francisco, was then a most attractive place, shaded by groves of ancient liveoaks, watered by numerous tidal inlets from the bay, and backed in the distance by the rolling and grassy mountains of Contra Costa, with the heights of Monte Diablo still further in the background. Notwithstanding my former disastrous experience with Spanish titles and Mexican land grants, I purchased for a moderate sum a squatter's possessory claim in that lovely region, consisting of one hundred and sixty acres lying at the head of a deep tidal inlet, and watered by a small but never-failing rivulet of fresh water. It was unimproved, but the land was rich and sufficiently level, and afforded a fine site for a house on the end of a high point covered with venerable live-oaks, and beautifully situated on the inlet between the mouths of two small streams. Here I built a small frame house, with stable in rear, bought some three-horse teams, and set some hands to ploughing, while with a small hired sloop I transported seedwheat and barley, with lumber, fencing, and other necessary material, which at high tide could be landed on the premises. My intention was first of all to sow a hundred acres in wheat and the remainder in barley, and make the fencing and similar improvements later. This being the infancy of agriculture in those parts, little was known by the American settlers of the best method and time for putting in and cultivating grain, the small wants of the country having been theretofore supplied by importation from Chile, or 'round the Horn.' I therefore followed the plan of the neighbors whose settlements were beginning to fringe the lovely bay of San Francisco, which was to commence ploughing and sowing with the first November rains, and sow after the plough continuously till March. I do not know the methods of the great California grain farmers of the present day, but our system seemed to answer, and if it could have ensured prices equal to the crops, we should have all grown rich incontinently.

Of course at the time of the last March sowings those of November were knee high, but as the dry season followed close, all seemed to mature nearly together, and were in fact harvested together, but long before the last, and even before sowing was finished, my agricultural enthusiasm had begun to evaporate. The dull monotony of ranch life became more and more insupportable, and more and more I realized the conclusion that the life of a hunter, or sailor, or tramp or anything was preferable to the tranquil and bucolic delights which had seemed so attractive from a distant view. There was, indeed, a little tame hunting within reach. Any number of geese frequented the bay shore, including my own place, and a few deer, or even a rare grizzly, might be found in the ravines of the coast range at no great riding distance. In the neighboring ponds, creeks and inlets there was abundance of teal and other ducks, and at early daybreak immense flocks of geese could be seen grazing about the numerous points and headlands, and if gently treated, were quite indisposed to be driven from their long-accustomed haunts. But beyond the requisite amount of pot-hunting, I failed to acquire or could not maintain an interest in that sort of shotgun trifling, and in short the change of life, however, praiseworthy and respectable, had been too sudden to last, and a deep gloom of ennui and disgust settled down on me, from which I felt that I must run away or die. My neighbors were agricultural young men from Western States, unmarried, immersed in the varying fortunes of their 'craps,' and knowing nothing of adventure beyond the one memorable episode of their lives— the journey from Illinois or Missouri across the plains. As for following the plough myself, like them, rather than trudge day after day up and down those monotonous furrows, I would have preferred a midnight watch on the foreyard in a gale of wind, or a still hunt of the wildest Indian village or horse camp in the Rocky Mountains.

I suppose it would be impossible to convey to another mind the growing and well-nigh irresistible longing for the forest trails, the tumbling streams, the snow-fringed valleys, and all the perpetual and varied attractions and adventures of the mountain solitudes so far away. And then the buffalo and moose, the elk and caribou, the bighorn and the grizzly, the cunning marten and the prowling Indian, and all the other denizens that give a never-failing variety and excitement to the wilderness. I hated and despised myself when I reflected that I had voluntarily abandoned all these joys, to grub after wheat and barley and potatoes, and was to be rewarded by an endless succession of future mornings with tiresome views of the same dull fields, and no more exciting adventure than shoeing a horse or mending a strap! In this condition of mind it was not unnatural to frequent the San Francisco wharves, among whose busy scenes, and vessels arriving and departing from and to all parts of the Pacific, was always to be seen and heard something of the adventures of those lucky fellows who, being unshackled by farms or any other possessions, enjoyed all the freedom of movement from which I was for the first time debarred.

Among the numerous enterprises always being planned in San Francisco, one in particular seemed to possess special attractions. The barque *New World,* had been chartered by a sort of association or joint stock party, and was then preparing for a voyage to Puget Sound, at that time little known, but credited with a fine growth of fir timber then in especial demand for wharves and foundations, and with unlimited quantities of whale oil and salmon to be traded from the Indians for a trifle. It was proposed to admit to this party a sufficient number to man the ship, cut and load piles, trade with the natives, and in short, to sail and load the ship, each man putting up a small sum toward the capital required, most of which had been contributed by the original promoters. Sufficient progress had been made to make it certain the barque would sail on or about the day appointed, but there was still room for experts in the several capacities of seamen, axemen, hunters and explorers, and I was earnestly pressed to join. Inducements and persuasions were brought to bear which would have been more than sufficient had I been rid of the uncongenial enterprise in which I was already embarked. But notwithstanding the whispering of prudence, as the sailing day approached I found myself less and less capable of resistance, and as I fortunately had for boss-farmer an honest and capable man who undertook to care for my interests while absent, the result may be easily guessed—I consented.

The barque was a fine vessel well commanded, manned, and found, and made a quick and uneventful voyage to Cape Flattery, where she entered the straits of San Juan de Fuca with the intention of feeling her way up toward Olympia, a small settlement at the head of the sound, and the only one on its waters, with the exception of the H. B. Company's posts at Victoria and Steilacoom, and a settler or two about starting cattle farms on Whidby's Island. Off the latter a whaleboat was supplied and manned from the ship for a side visit to Victoria, and subsequent exploration of the east shore, and Hood's Canal, in which party I was fortunate enough to get included. We accomplished everything that was expected of us and something more, frequently seeing and communicating with the ship, whose progress, guided in those unknown waters only by the lead, was necessarily slow. Timber abounded everywhere on the mainland down to the water's edge, but much of it was too large for the purpose required. A permanent anchorage was at length selected in the mouth of Duwamish River and Bay, opposite a large village belonging to the friendly chief, Seattle, on the site of which the present city of that name now stands. In this vicinity the axemen went to work, while two hundred empty barrels were towed by the whaleboat to the mouth of the Puyallup, where they were left with a small party to trade for and salt down salmon. In the same useful tender I then made an exploration of the upper Sound, visiting Fort Steilacoom and the H. B. cattle farm and the settlement of its superannuated employees adjacent, also the lovely cascade of Skookum Chuck, and the village of Olympia, and thus returning to the ship. The Sound with its several bays, natural canals, passages and islands, is one of the loveliest sheets of salt water in the world, smooth as a river and sheltered from all violent winds, surrounded by bold and lofty fir-clad banks, and swelled by many fine tributaries, then all abounding in game and fish. The Indians being much harried by the Hydahs and other fierce tribes from the vicinity of Queen Charlotte's Island, were very friendly to the whites, and a large quantity of oil was obtained from them in bladders at the rate of one ten-penny nail for a bladder of oil, but the stench caused by the shifting of this half rotten stuff into casks was enough to depopulate a city.

While the ship lay at Seattle I obtained from that kindly old chief a large canoe and a team of six young bucks as paddlers, with whom I ascended Duwamish River to the large and beautiful lake from which it flows, making one small portage at some rapids. The lake which according to the testimony of my crew, had never before been seen by a white man, is an extensive, picturesque and lovely body of water. Much of its shores are open and park-like, interspersed with fine groves of deciduous trees, abounding with deer almost as tame as cattle. Beyond, rises everywhere the forest of firs, tall, dark and stately, with the superb snow-peak of Mount Rainier always in view, crowning and completing one of the finest landscapes in the world, of which it is from all points the chief feature. As a combination of the distant scenery of snow-clad mountains with the pastoral fertility of the fine bottom lands, and the finished park-like beauty of the shores, points and islands of the lake, I recall no place possessing more varied attractions for one who could content himself with the society of Nature, buried in a remote but rich and lovely wilderness, far removed from the uneasy struggles and law-made vices of civilized men.

The deciduous trees which, though everywhere interspersed with small prairies, thickly cover much of the Duwamish bottoms, in competing for their share of air and light grow out horizontally for astonishing distances above the clear water of the river, and during the mornings and evenings were filled with countless multitudes of grouse in search of the buds which are their favorite food. These unamiable birds were so occupied with crowding and quarrelling for place and food, and paid so little attention to our craft as it slowly stemmed

HOW THE INDIANS CATCH SALMON

the current along shore, that we had no difficulty in knocking over with paddles all we wanted, with scarcely any delay to our progress. At some distance before coming to the lake, the Indians had placed an obstruction or weir across the river where they were taking large quantities of salmon with scoop nets, as the fish leaped out of water in their efforts to surmount the obstacle. There must have been a couple of hundred natives camped at this place, and the pile of freshly-caught fish constantly reduced by the women cleaners, and increased by fresh captures, was large enough to fill a good-sized apartment, and in such abundance the single fish we required had no appreciable value. This absorption of a whole tribe in catching, splitting, cleaning, drying and smoking, was very entertaining, illustrating in a practical way the inexhaustible multitudes of fish in these streams, where instead of filling our two hundred barrels, we might in a short time have loaded the ship.

The natives below the anchorage at Seattle's, though not hostile were of much tougher character, and being more addicted to sea-fishing and more enterprising travelers, possessed large store of fish oil which they were keen to trade for nails and any other article of iron. A small vessel properly fitted with tanks or casks could have been loaded in a short time with no greater outlay than a few kegs of nails. Could I have extricated my modest capital from the agricultural enterprise in which it was so well and permanently locked up, I should certainly have returned from San Francisco for that purpose. In fact that unlucky farm, however worthless for all profitable purposes, was such a constant and effectual obstacle to every other design, that before I got finally clear of it I became so thoroughly imbued with certain primary principles of finance that to this day whenever considering any prospective undertaking requiring expenditure of capital, almost the first test that occurs is, what is the chance to get out if necessary to realize? Thus whatever may have become of the accursed acres, I am quite consoled by the indirect and incorporeal but substantial dividend that I continue to draw from them, more secure than stocks, houses or lands, being beyond the reach of the most predaceous legislators and all other plagues and vicissitudes of fortune.

I could linger long in recalling the pleasant days passed on Puget Sound and the endless labyrinths of its many branching waters. Whether in exploring with my Indian crew their hitherto unseen recesses, navigating the broad waters of the lower Sound, hunting about the heads of rivers, or observing the curious customs of those amphibious natives, I enjoyed it all and time never hung heavy for a moment. But the completion of the barque's loading was at last announced, and the day fixed for her sailing, the morning of which found myself and two others encamped on what we called after one of our number, Terry's Point, opposite and about two miles from the ship. The weather, notwithstanding the lateness of the season, had up to this time been almost invariably pleasant for out-door occupation even in the cramped and confined position afforded by a seat in a canoe, where I had passed so much of my time, but during the night before the sailing-day fixed upon, several inches of snow fell, and ice half an inch or more thick had formed entirely across Duwamish Bay. The ice was too thin to travel on, and too thick to get a canoe through, without great labor, delay and risk. Nevertheless, the ship having showed her sailing signal at daybreak, we must reach her somehow, and a high old voyage it was, breaking ice all the way. Any small craft but a dugout canoe must have been cut through and sunk, in which case neither rescue nor swimming would have been possible. But ours, though badly cut, stood the racket nobly, and after several hours of hard work we reached the ship, which weighed and made sail immediately, breaking her way out without difficulty, the ice having already become soft, and the snow almost disappeared from the land.

Our principal difficulty in navigating the Sound arose from its great depth, bold shores, and consequent scarcity of good anchorage. Even a ship's length from the shore the depth of water was usually too great for the full scope of cable, and being therefore obliged to keep under sail nearly every night in narrow waters with slight and variable breezes, the skipper got little rest till the ship at last got clear of Cape Flattery, and standing out to sea for a good offing, bowed again to the long swell of the Pacific, and pointed her jib boom for the Golden Gate.

Everything looked favorable for making a good voyage, and we confidently expected to be bowling through the Farallones within a week, when the ship ran into a southwester only a day or two out from port, which soon put another face on our affairs. Not having enough offing for the shore tack, the barque was hove to with port tacks aboard as though looking for Kamchatka, and sail was shortened as the storm increased, till her usual dress for days at a time was reduced to storm stay-sail and close-reefed main topsail. Among some old papers and letters of that period, I have found a few detached pages of a small pencilled log kept at the time, which I recognize as referring to that voyage, and which may serve to give some account of a great storm which turned out to have been one of the most memorable on the coast.

Dec. 30th, 1852. Passed Cape Flattery and got clear of the land early this A.M. and stood S. S. E. down coast with fair wind of six knots.

Dec. 31st. Same as yesterday.

Jan. 1st, 1853. Same till 8 P.M. when wind hauled to S. and E. and blew heavy all night.

Jan. 2nd. At 8 P.M. wind having freshened to a gale, ship hove to on starboard tack under close-reefed main topsail with fore and main staysails. Slashing gale all day, ship rolling rails under, and making water fast, one pump broken or damaged, the other, though constantly going by relays, unable to keep it down.

Jan. 3rd. Gale continues, ship remains hove to, water increasing in hold, impossible to get the timber out, or to go down among it.

Jan. 4th. Gale increased till dark, at which time it blew a hurricane, water slowly gaining, and ship laboring very heavy.

Jan. 5th. The same.

Jan. 6th. Moderated at noon enough to make sail for a few hours, when the gale increasing, she was put back to double reefed main topsail with fore staysail, and spanker.

Jan. 7th. Gale returned worse than ever. At daylight hove to on port tack, under storm sails, and found ship makes less water on this tack. At 9 A.M. blowing a hurricane, carried away staysail and split main topsail. With much difficulty got a small piece of new canvas made fast around lee main shrouds, to lie to by. Were gaining fast on water, when at 12 M. a sea came on board which wrecked galley, carried away spanker boom, cabin skylight and both quarter boats, and broke both legs of the man at the wheel. Water hip-deep in both cabin and forecastle. All hands passing water in buckets. Trysail gaff came down, smashing rail and badly injuring two good men, who were saved with difficulty. Just before dark carried away main topmast backstay at masthead. Impossible to go aloft to clear wreck and repair chafing-gear in the darkness, and all the upper standing rigging is in dangerous condition.

Jan. 8th.   A terrible night; both watches on all night and no sleep
for any. At daylight orders given and men mustered to try and cut
away deck load, but on closer examination, too risky, and orders
countermanded. The sea now running literally mountains high, the
horizon circumscribed to a few ship's lengths, the air filled with flying
foam, the sea frequently breeching the vessel from whose decks everything breakable or moveable is gone. No galley, no cooking, nothing to
eat but a small allowance of wet hardtack from the cabin lockers and
salt salmon from the 'tween deck's cargo.' All the wounded men lashed
in cabin bunks and well attended, but one is evidently dying. Captain
says he has a bully crew, and crew say they don't want a better skipper.

Here the few pages detached from my little log and accidentally preserved for so many years, come to an abrupt end,
and I must recur to memory. The gale lasted, with slight
intermissions, for three weeks, beating all gales in my experience for duration. Though the spars and rigging were
badly damaged, the hull remained staunch and on the port
tack made comparatively little water. The cargo of piles
having been loaded through the bow ports, now replaced and
caulked tight, could not be got at, and even the deck load could
not be cut away in the tremendous sea running, without danger
of carrying away the standing rigging and bringing down
spars. But the worst privation was the entire failure of provisions and scarcity of water. The former gradually disappeared till nothing was left but the salt salmon of the cargo, and
not even bread, sugar, coffee, mustard or pepper. The rain
which almost constantly fell and kept everyone wet and miserable afforded no drinkable water because the boarding seas and
drenching spray kept everything on board as salt as the sea
itself. Consequently we had to content ourselves during
several weeks with the eternal salmon towed overboard to
freshen, and a scant and diminishing allowance of fresh water
to wash them down.

However all things come to an end at last, and when at length
the wind blew itself out and hauled by the west, the skipper was
not slow to make sail and get the ship on her course. But now
came a new difficulty which not seldom tries the patience of
the sailor, after such long continuance of the wind in one
quarter. After a few days, that unstable element proceeded to
dwindle to nothing, and off Point Reyes failed altogether, leaving the storm-tossed barque drifting about among the Farallones almost in sight of port, but without control or steerage

way, in a dead calm. Though by this time so sick of the taste, sight and smell of salt salmon that most of us preferred to endure a considerable amount of the pangs of hunger, we enjoyed what compensation could be found in the rare opportunity of a close and prolonged inspection of the Farallones. Indeed the ship showed an inclination to become so unpleasantly intimate with those lonely sentinels of the Golden Gate, that on more than one occasion we were obliged to man boats and tow lines to counteract the tendency of the lazily heaving but powerful swell to set her against their dangerous points.

These diminutive islands are but the sharp angular peaks of a number of wave-beaten rocks, varying from a mere needle to many acres in extent, rising from deep water twenty miles outside the bar to a considerable height above the sea. From the prudent distance usually preferred by vessels, they resemble a lot of huge white sea-birds as they are alternately revealed and hidden by the heaving billows of the ocean; but at close quarters they disclose numerous odd shapes, and are swarming with marine life. Large herds of seals and sea-lions are nearly always to be seen and heard, and these islands constitute a favorite resort and breeding-place for myriads of sea-fowl, whose eggs supplied San Francisco in its early days, before the placid and home-loving hens were made aware of the brilliant prospects awaiting their emigration to the land of gold.

But by far the most interesting and unique curiosity of these lonely rocks was the vast shoals of sharks and dog-fish which swarm among them, presumably on the lookout for the prey which their neighborhood affords. For hours at a time one could look down through hundreds of feet of clear transparent water absolutely crowded by a jostling and innumerable multitude of those fierce tigers of the sea. Any white object dropped from the taffrail would be pushed about and tossed aside by countless inquiring noses from its first touch upon the water till it had slowly sunk to such profound depths that only a faint and vanishing gleam reached the eye as it continued to run the gauntlet of ever-thickening multitudes, sinking slowly but ever downward toward the deep abysses of the ocean floor.

CHAPTER XIV

ANOTHER VOYAGE UP THE COAST

On arrival at San Francisco the universal subject of conversation was the great storm we had on the whole so safely weathered. Along the coast it had been severely felt throughout the length of the State, which borders the Pacific for nearly a thousand miles; and for weeks afterwards arriving vessels continued to contribute their numerous stories of loss and disaster at sea.

Owing to various causes our voyage had yielded but moderate financial success. The salmon had not been put down in the expert manner required to command good prices. The fish oil had to be shipped round Cape Horn to a market in the States, and the piles having been cut much longer than was at that time required, had to be shortened to a length that, had we properly understood the matter, would have permitted us to stow a much greater number. Then the repairs of the ship, and the charter money for the lengthened voyage, and other items swelled the expenses, so that the net result was small, and even that would not be forthcoming till after a long and tedious adjustment which the capitalists on shore were doubtless not very keen to expedite.

My farmer was getting along well with his work, the ploughing and sowing being still in progress, and as I saw no particular occasion for my presence there much before harvest, I cast about again for some more congenial employment to fill up the interval. As usual, one might have his pick of many, for whatever other fault might be found with the infant city, it was never dull, nor at any time lacking in inventive spirits with their innumerable plans, schemes and devices. The subject now most in favor was an expedition to discover some harbor which it was thought must exist above Cape Mendocino, somewhere on that long reach of coastline stretching some 800 miles from Point Reyes to the Columbia, where no harbor more worthy of the name than the open roads of Trinidad, had yet been found. Such a one, if it could be discovered, must afford sites for towns and settlements with shorter routes to the interior, and by way of reimbursing immediate expenses, would probably furnish a return cargo of piles, which it was evident would be required in large quantity by a city daily pushing its streets farther and farther out into the bay. The half-rigged brig, *Kate Heath,* had already been chartered to carry out such expedition and bring back piles and spars to be cut and loaded, while inland explorations should be pushed forward by detached parties. The voyage would probably be much shorter than the last, and as the time required seemed to fit in well with my occasions, I became one of the party.

The brig having completed her preparations, sailed with a considerable force in excess of a regular crew, composed like the former expedition, of carefully selected men embracing experts in all the several kinds of skill required. The whole was under command of an experienced and capable old whaling-skipper who took charge of the vessel and her expected lading and would lend his sagacious counsel to the other purposes of the expedition. A quick voyage was made and a good landfall on the Oregon coast, where a large and far reaching break in the mountain range was soon made out, indicating the probable debouch of some considerable river. Though no such place was laid down in the chart, this from its position and extent must be the Umpqua, unknown at its mouth but familiar to me near its source beyond the Oregon and California trail. After much maneuvering with the vessel, the skipper, who like most whalers was an expert surfman, discerned an interval in the long wall of heavy surf breaking on the bar, which seemed to afford a tortuous but sufficient passage. No other semblance of a harbor had been made out, and as the changing views commanded from numerous different positions of the ship, more and more encouraged the idea of an inside bay of large dimensions with probably a large and far-extending tributary, it was at length resolved to try the entrance.

Since most of the Oregon rivers are inaccessible from the sea, and even the great river Columbia is only reached by one

of the most hazardous entrances in the world, where even men-
of-war have been dashed to pieces among the shifting shoals
and breakers of its bar, the effort to take a sailing vessel into
this unknown opening, with no knowledge of its extent or
character was an extremely nervous and risky undertaking.
It was uncertain whether there was any accessible harbor at all,
and if so, what sort of passage existed through the formidable
bar that could be seen intercepting the long, smooth rollers
coming in from the Pacific, and dashing them into a far-
reaching wall of surf that seemed to guard with an impassable
barrier the doubtful passage hitherto sealed against all
mankind.

In order to obtain the best conditions for the attempt, our
wary old skipper waited several days for a leading breeze
from the right direction, so as to handle the vessel promptly
in any of the numerous contingencies that might occur.
Getting at length a wind that suited him, he proceeded to make
the following preparations as early as the eventful morning
afforded sufficient light. A whaleboat with ensign, compass,
spy-glass, hand and deep sea sounding lines, and some water
and provisions, was manned by the mate and eight good oars-
men, and sent in ahead to make and signal observations of the
channel. The brig was then put under fore topsail and all plain
fore and aft sail, two good men at the wheel, hatches battened,
crew at quarters, captain on the fore topgallant yard, with
men stationed intermediately to pass word to the wheel. The
last inshore stretch was arranged to bring the brig to the
proper starting point and on reaching in, the helm instead of
being put down for another tack, was kept steady, and the die
was cast.

As the brig with full sails and a good breeze on her quarter,
holding her steady course over the smooth but gigantic rollers,
began to near the tumultuous line of white water, the small
passage seen from outside opened more clearly, but from my
position at the slings of the foreyard, still more distant lines
could be seen breaking beyond, showing that if a through
passage existed at all, it must be crooked enough to tax all
the readiness of the skipper who, perched alone on the topgallant yard, nervously chewed unlit cigars and uttered not
one unnecessary word. As the brig came up to, and entered

the opening, a mighty wall of roaring surf breaking on either hand as high as her foreyard, it was one of those few exciting moments of life which can never afterwards be forgotten. In the continuous crash and thunder of the breakers scarcely any other sound was audible, and face to face with that mighty tumult, the ship and all the rest of the world seemed inconceivably mean, insignificant, and small.

It was at this crisis that an accident occurred that cost the lives of the unfortunate boat's crew in plain sight and almost within reach. The whaleboat whether fearing to venture among the formidable breakers opening to sight beyond the first line or in the effort to get out of the brig's way, had approached or been carried too near the first line of breakers on the port hand, and yielding to a powerful effort of the mate to prevent broaching, the steering becket suddenly parted, and the boat immediately broaching to, her stern was caught by a high curling crest and the entire outfit hurled end over end into the furious tumult which at once engulfed them. Assistance was impossible, every qualified man being at quarters, and even a misglance of the skipper's eye at that crucial juncture might have caused the speedy loss of the ship and all on board.

The wind was already rising and inclined to be squally with spits of snow, but the captain with quick decision and rare presence of mind conducted the brig safely through the crooked and dangerous passage and let go her anchor in a calm and lovely bay three or four miles inside the bar, and nearly surrounded by fir-covered mountains. Here the ship was quickly visited by numerous friendly natives in canoes, who, though burning with curiosity to examine the strange apparition, when made to understand the loss of the boat's crew, immediately manned their large high-prowed surf canoes and rushed away to the rescue. Some hours later a long procession approached the ship with the single survivor of the catastrophe, who had been found in smooth water inside the bar, unconscious, but alive and clinging with clasped hands to the steering oar. None of the others had yet come in through the breakers and must be therefore by this time beyond hope of rescue. To complete the story of that fatal tragedy I will here add that the man thus recovered was restored and saved, the others being all lost. But during the next few weeks and before we left the place, the Indians had searched out and recovered all the bodies, some of them drifted many miles up the coast, and one so deeply covered under an immense collection of drift-logs that it required the labor of several men for considerable part of a day to chop it out. They also from time to time found and brought in with much ceremony all the numerous pieces of the boat, which had been smashed to atoms, the compass, spy-glass, ensign, oars, hand line and, in short, her entire furniture except the deep sea line which having many pounds of lead attached, was never recovered.

On the following day, the harbor having been superficially explored, the ship was worked round a sandy point to a secure anchorage close in shore, her bow ports knocked out, a small zinc house put together on land. The axemen went to work cutting, rafting and loading piles, while a few of us in the ship's boat with a wondering but jolly lot of Indian guides proceeded up the bay and river. At the head of the bay some miles above the ship's anchorage, we entered the true mouth of the river which was ascended for thirty miles, the entire distance closely bounded on both sides by steep fir-clad mountains, affording in but few places smooth ground enough to land and build fires. The farthest point reached with the boat being considered accessible both for vessels from the sea and wagon roads from above, was pitched on for a settlement, and called Scottsburg, the town being forthwith inaugurated by building a substantial log cabin and corral. At this place the mountains first commence to retire gradually from the river, and the bottom to widen out into narrow but constantly increasing prairies. A few miles above Scottsburg was found a small post of the ubiquitous H. B. C., in charge of a Canadian clerk named Garnier, who had of course come in from above, and had lived for twenty-three years in this solitary spot without seeing a white woman, or as he even more feelingly complained, a priest. He however possessed a Chelowitz wife and some grown up children, and was by no means entirely neglected in more important respects, his spiritual interests being in charge of a priest at Fort Vancouver, on the Columbia and punctually attended to by letter once a year! Within the stockade stood two large ungrafted apple trees raised from seed, and in mature bearing condition. An apple of the last crop generously given us was hard, green and sour, but of course the Indians, far and near, never having seen anything of the kind, regard the fruit as a wonderful phenomenon, and make long journeys to see it.

The arrival at Fort Umpqua settled all question respecting the identity of the river, and the Indians being reputed friendly as far up as the Oregon and California trail, the valley was examined to a considerable distance above the fort, constantly widening out into a broad, rich and level prairie with lovely scenery and admirably adapted for settlement, which it has now no doubt long since received. As a good force was engaged in loading the vessel from very convenient timber, not much time could be afforded here, and returning to Scottsburg we again took boat to regain the vessel. Most of this voyage was made by night, flushing nearly all the way continuous miles of ducks, which though invisible in the darkness, rose with successive roars from myriads of wings that must have astonished the echoes of the lonely river. The surface of the water at night being shrouded not less by darkness than by the shadow of the lofty surrounding mountains, we nearly ran over a small black bear who was crossing the river on some business of his own. Resenting the unwonted intrusion, he took the imprudent step of trying to come on board, and after nearly upsetting the boat and frightening some of the sailors almost to death, was at length held off with a boat hook till ignominiously dispatched with a pistol.

This incident brings to mind another interview with a young black bear which may be worth relating even at the cost of a short digression. At some far northern point of the Rocky Mountains on the distant waters of the Liard or the Peace, I was following an old deer or Indian trail along the side of a picturesque cañon, affording through its upper opening a superb distant view of the great snow range beyond. At the culminating point of this view, where a wide circling sweep of the cañon had brought me directly opposite the opening, I sat down on the upper side with my feet in the trail to rest and enjoy at leisure the scenery of the grand amphitheatre thus magnificently displayed. Hearing a slight noise I cautiously looked round and saw a young cub of perhaps five and twenty pounds weight trotting leisurely toward me down the path. I did not care to risk the noise of a shot and had no use for the cub, so I remained quiet and watched to see what he would do when he should run up against my legs. When he was almost in actual contact with those obstacles, his olfactories, I suppose, gave the alarm of something unusual, and following up the obnoxious legs with his eyes, he fastened them on my face, cocking his head on one side in the ludicrous intensity of his inquiring gaze. During this anxious inspection, if my continuations had been under me in proper position for a spring, I might easily have jumped and caught him by the ears, but before I could gradually withdraw and get them in position, he seemed suddenly to arrive at unfavorable conclusions and with a baby growl of astonishment, sprang aside up the mountain and made off for his mama much faster than I could follow him.

Returning to my narrative: When we reached the ship we found her loading nearly completed and in fact she sailed soon after for San Francisco, but in going out, unfortunately grounded on a long spit running out into the supposed channel from the south shore some distance inside the bar. The tide going down, the brig thumped heavily, and a fresh northwester setting in during the night sent in enough sea to bump and roll her about, sweeping the decks, carrying away rails and forward deck-house, filling the forecastle, knocking both topmasts out of her, and in short wrecking pretty much everything above decks. It was impossible to get out the bow ports to lighten the vessel, or to do any other work, the men generally lashing themselves fast on the high quarter deck to avoid being washed off. We could, therefore, do nothing for the time but wait and hope the hull might continue to hold staunch. After two or three days, the wind and sea going down, she was kedged off at high tide, still sound in hull, but with not much else left of her, and in no condition to go to sea. There was nothing now to be done but unreeve and save the upper standing, and all running rigging, cut green poles on shore, where they were fortunately very convenient, and get such jury rigging on her as might serve for the voyage to San Francisco, which there was no other means of reaching.

Headed by the skipper, all hands went promptly to work, except the second and only surviving mate, a tall and powerfully built Norwegian, whose shoulder had been dislocated while the vessel was thumping on the spit. Nothing could be done for him at the time, as the sea was breaking heavily on board and all hands were either lashed fast or hanging on in the lower rigging. But after the wreck had been safely got off, as there was no doctor accessible, the skipper himself undertook the job. The man was not only large and muscular, but as well as I remember, nearly sixty hours had elapsed since the injury, which was complicated by severe bruises, the man having been dashed violently down from the poop to the main deck, striking his shoulder against the chime of a cask which had got adrift and he was trying to secure. Our skipper was no youngster, and was not to be surprised or nonplussed by any contingency the sea affords. After revolving in his mind for a time the whole science of surgery—as understood by shipmasters—the method he finally hit upon was as follows, upon which as far as I know, there is no patent.

A large cotton pocket handkerchief was made fast to the patient's wrist by a couple of half hitches, the other end being secured to a lanyard of strong stuff manned by several stout fellows. The man, who could scarcely bear his arm touched, was extended on his back on deck, and the captain, removing one boot, took purchase with his foot against the patient's armpit, and getting a rolling hold of the arm with both hands, gave the word to 'sway away.' The patient howled, cursed, kicked and swore in vain; the skipper having started in to win, stuck to him till he clicked the joint in. When remonstrated with afterwards by the sufferer for the excessive pain of the operation, the skipper indignantly remarked: "D—n you, if I had another mate you might carry your arm around unjinted as long as you liked, but I can tell you I ain't agoin to try and take this wreck to Frisky with no one-armed mate."

After this successful surgical operation, it soon became apparent that in consequence of the delay caused by the wreck and time required for repairs, a serious shortage of provisions was likely to occur. As the steep mountain sides and dense forests of the vicinity afforded little large game, it was at last determined that I should take one man, reascend the river, and if necessary, cross the Calapooya range to the Willamette Valley to purchase and bring down cattle. As this involved a long journey on foot over a country much of which was unknown, and probably without available trails, I picked out a stout, long-legged fellow named Fisk, amiable and willing, who said he could walk for a week without getting tired. We took the ship's longboat as far as Scottsburg where it was safely secured and left, and then set off on foot up the valley at the rate of forty miles a day, resolved to make it fifty or more as soon as we could get our walking tacks aboard. Going up without encumbrance offered no difficulties. No Indians troubled us, and my mind and muscles were chiefly interested in giving F. some first lessons in getting over ground. Though a seafaring man unused to so much walking, he held out well and kept me pretty busy till we came down to the upper Willamette settlements, then not extending far above Salem. Here we purchased four of the usual half-wild two year olds, with the important proviso that the farmer's boy on horseback, should help drive them to the head of the valley and well into the Calapooya pass, by which time it was hoped they might be somewhat tired and exhibit less of the usual reluctance to leave their accustomed pastures. But I am constrained to acknowledge that I did those Oregon steers less than justice, as when we got them fairly into the mountain passes, their ingenious and devilish contrariness had only fairly commenced.

It was risking as much as they were worth to take one's eye off them a minute, day or night. The only way to retain their society was to run them at the top of our speed all day, and then hunt out some *cul de sac* where one of us could pen them in and guard them while the other snatched some sleep. To crown the troubles of our lot, the rains commenced with vigor worthy of a better cause, and from the crossing of the Calapooyas to Scottsburg, a distance of at least 100 miles, never let up an hour at a time. The prairie and open country being mostly covered by the all-pervading Oregon 'brake' or bracken fern, growing higher than one's head and holding water like a sponge, every touch brought down such copious showers that we never enjoyed a dry moment. On the last day of this moist and musty trip, rather than risk the cattle another night on the prairie, we made a spurt and ran them all the way into the corral at Scottsburg, arriving near midnight after a continuous tramp of—I am afraid to say how many miles. Next day we promptly killed and cut them up, their quarters loading down the boat to an ominous point that would require good weather for crossing the bay. We ran down the river the same day with a fair wind, but on nearing the head of the bay after dark, found a brisk gale and rising sea coming in from the offing, against which we could make no headway with canvas, and therefore stowed the mast and lug, and took to the oars. The wind soon rose to a humming gale driving before it a sea which every moment became more formidable, and it was not long before we were obliged to lighten the boat by throwing over some of the dearly bought beef to avoid being swamped.

The peculiar geography of the place at which we were now arrived, had much to do with the events that followed. The Umpqua debouches into its bay at such angle that a wind tolerably free down the river becomes dead ahead in the bay, and when blowing fresh, drives in a heavy sea that breaks against the tall cliffs on the starboard hand with appalling violence. Being without light or compass and the land concealed by dense darkness, we made an effort to hold our course at least till day-break, by keeping the increasing seas on our port bow, but under a black sky, with everything obscured by driving snow and rain, nothing could be seen but the roaring white crests fiercely sweeping down upon us, and the necessary pulling was materially interrupted by the necessity for incessant bailing. The wind and sea must have carried us farther to starboard than we supposed, for the night was scarcely half through, when we became conscious of an increasing roar gradually subduing all other sounds, and were soon able dimly to make out the white line of crashing breakers

upon which we were rapidly driving. The sight of fixed objects soon showed the rapid rate of our progress to destruction,
and seeing the impossibility of avoiding it, and remembering
the forbidding character of the rocky cliffs, we gave ourselves
up for lost and let the boat drive stern foremost, keeping her
head to the sea to escape immediate foundering.

Finally when nearly up with the breakers, with apparently
the last dread moment at hand, and nothing remaining to be
done but to consider how and when we should jump clear of
the boat and take a desperate chance among the rocks, a large
object loomed up ahead which proved to be one of the immense
firs growing on this coast, stranded just outside the breakers
and projecting a long arm into the air. Fortunately the boat
possessed a long, stout painter with which, notwithstanding the
rushing seas, we succeeded in getting a turn round a stout
branch. Throwing over the rest of the ill-starred beef, we
succeeded by great and continuous efforts in riding safely to
this lucky mooring, but as the set of the sea on shore was
partly across the wind's direction, we were both obliged to row
on the lee side all night—when not interrupted by bailing—in
order to keep head to sea. Daylight disclosed a mountainous
sea rolling in from the offing with few signs of abatement, and
for the first time gave us full appreciation of our marvelous
luck in keeping afloat through the night. The wind snatched
long ridges bodily from the crests of the foaming seas and
hurled them onward, filling the air with water and making it
impossible to see any distance to windward. On shore the
white horses racing in piled high against the cliffs and seemed
to offer nothing but quick destruction in that direction.

But as the light of morning grew clearer, a short and narrow
strip, having the appearance of a small sand beach at the
base of the cliffs, could be discerned a few hundred yards
farther on, and since we must let go at some time, we resolved
to make a desperate effort to beach the boat at that more
hospitable point. Getting her well bailed out, and ourselves
seated at the oars, we watched for a smooth roller, and
anxiously cast off. Immediately the seas leaped on their
escaping prey, and hove the boat shoreward, but pulling for
life with every muscle strained, we succeeded in getting abreast

of the little beach before the outside breaker caught and rolled us over into the wild surge of waters. Though counted a good swimmer, I was instantly tossed and rolled and buried and half-choked with sand and water, deprived of all power to help myself, or even knowledge of my position, or which end was up, till after what seemed an endless period, I struck heavily and unexpectedly on hands and knees. Recovering a glimpse of the shore and the outside world, I was able to struggle with more intelligent purpose till I got upon a heavy breaker which cast me far up on the sand and within arm's length of a big rock, breathless, choked, bruised and well skinned on all salient points, but whole in all essential respects of wind and limb.

F. had also come safely to shore, but being heavier, and having landed first on stomach and face, was much bruised and covered with blood, which however, on examination, appeared to come chiefly from the nose. We were now on an exposed lee shore with a tempest of wind and water driving in, nothing visible in the stormy offing but long lines of roaring breakers, and at our backs a nearly vertical cliff, white with snow and many hundred feet high. After some hunting about I found a place which looked as if the cliff could be climbed, but F. thinking himself entirely exhausted, refused to make the attempt. Covering him up in a sheltered corner of the rocks with the boat sail, which had come ashore, I at last succeeded after many strenuous efforts in gaining the top. Here was a dense fir forest with much undergrowth and some inches of snow. Creeping under the brush I soon found a wolf track so recent that the falling snow had not yet concealed it, and thinking it must lead to more open ground, as that animal by no means prefers the thickest forests, I followed it, much of the time creeping under the brush on hands and knees in the snow. Half an hour or less brought me clear of the woods to an open sandy expanse across which sand and snow were fiercely driving, but beyond which in less tempestuous intervals could be discerned the breaker-lined coast of the open sea.

Eight miles of as tough a walk as anyone need wish for, in the teeth of the gale and constantly tempted to lie down for sleep and rest at a cost which I well understood, brought me at last to the zinc house which had been set up on the beach, opposite and close by the ship's anchorage. Arriving in a condition of great exhaustion and nearly speechless, I was rubbed with whiskey, fed with hot mussel soup, wrapped in hot blankets, and was soon able to make known the condition in which I had left my comrade. The captain would not risk any craft in the storm then blowing, but the weather having moderated later, he manned the only remaining whaleboat with eight good men, taking the steering oar himself. He found the place as described, made out the wrecked boat on shore with his glasses, beached his own boat safely, and found F., still living. Going in through heavy surf is much easier than coming off, but our gallant and skillful old skipper was equal to both, and got back without losing a man, bringing with him besides the shipwrecked sailor, all the boat furniture worth saving, and all the beef quarters wrecked with the boat, the whole having been washed in by the surf. The boat itself having been pounded to pieces was left as not worth bringing in.

Thus terminated the beef expedition, and surely few that had cost so much effort, suffering and danger ever came to a more inglorious end. Nevertheless, more than half the beef had been saved, and though well soaked, salted and sanded by its sundry shipwrecks and adventures was by no means without important use on the voyage which followed. But before taking leave forever of that bay which, lovely as it was, had somehow been fraught with so much disaster, I must take the opportunity of relating a tale of a most unromantic fishing adventure which came within an ace of a fatal termination, although as it turned out, it was only ridiculous. I must premise by explaining that the adjacent country was so extremely rough, as well as densely wooded, that land game in the vicinity of the ship was scarce and hard to hunt, and enterprises in search of food were mostly confined to the water. Ducks were obtained in considerable quantity by the shotgun brigade, and all the steep rocky points running down beneath the water were covered with crabs by thousands. In fact, at certain stages of tide these were so numerous that a canoe could be filled in a short time. But of all the sports offering in that till then virgin solitude, the most amusing consisted of spearing

flounders on the sand flats. Not far from the middle of the
bay lay an extensive sand-bar of which a considerable portion
—perhaps fifty or a hundred acres—was exposed at low water,
though covered again with surprising suddenness on the reflow
of the very high tides there prevailing. In the shoal water
around the edge of the bank this amusing fish abounded in
immense numbers, and as they lie very close and are exactly the
color of the sand as seen through water, they are almost impossible to get sight of till disturbed by the wader, when they
scuttle off with a startling dash, showing in the movement a
momentary white flash of belly which serves as an excellent
but very brief mark.

One day a couple of us repaired to this place as soon as it
commenced to show above the falling tide, and leaving the
canoe hauled up on the sand, began wading about in search of
fish. Now the fun of this sport arises less from the actual
booty than from the numerous misses made in darting the
spear, and especially from the perpetual and sudden dashes
made by the capricious fish from unexpected places, between
one's very feet for example. Becoming absorbed in pursuit,
I lost all note of time or tide till attracted by the alarmed
shouts of my comrade, who by this time was nearly a quarter
of a mile off at the upper end of the bar. The quick-rising
young flood had already covered the sandy flat and carried
away the canoe, which with the paddles in her, was gaily
floating up stream. Not a speck of ground was visible, and
there was no land within at least two or three miles, and in that
strong tideway the only land to be reached by swimming must
have been at the head of the bay, several miles distant. As
my companion was already so much nearer the runaway canoe,
I shouted to him to swim for her at once, which he did while
I waded after him, as fast as I could make way through the
fast deeping water, under which the last speck of the bar had
already disappeared. Fortunately for both of us, my comrade
was a stout fellow and an expert swimmer, and after a long and
tough pull he overtook the canoe, managed to climb in over one
end without swamping her, and commenced the equally difficult
job of paddling back against tide to pick me up, which he succeeded in doing, the water having already reached the level

of my breast. The thing was so absolutely ridiculous that we agreed to keep the adventure to ourselves, but it got out, and it was long before we heard the last of the numerous bad jokes made at our expense.

As the time of departure approached, considerable nervousness began to prevail about recrossing the bar, which may not be appreciated by those who do their navigation through well known entrances, sufficiently furnished with charts, beacons, buoys, pilots and steam tugs, and think no more of making a harbor than of crossing a street. But not so with us, who had already seen one tragedy and well knew that any error or disaster must involve much loss of life, yet for whom there was no other mode of getting away. Thus the subject came to furnish the chief topic of conversation before and abaft the mast, and all hands and the cook became immensely learned respecting bars, spits, shoals, channels, breakers and so forth; but the skipper whose brains and courage were to do the deed, kept his own counsel. But when the eventful day of trial came, what with our captain's experience in entering, his many subsequent observations, and the dear-bought knowledge now possessed of the dangerous spit which had already brought us to grief, we successfully avoided all obstacles, and threaded the crooked opening through the surf without check or casualty. As we stood on the quarter deck looking back at the lines of fierce, but to us no longer formidable breakers, showing from that point little sign of accessibility, the captain, who had till now looked as cool as though he had passed all his life in threading out intricate passages over unknown bars, relaxed a little his *sang froid*, and remarked "Do you all know how many cigars it took to get the ship in there? I took a bundle of twenty-five cheroots up into the crosstrees and chewed up every one of them before I came down"—from which we more clearly understood how little his calm exterior indicated the tumult of responsibility and excitement within.

On this occasion, though a gentle land breeze prevailed with a smooth sea, we enjoyed a sight of the most majestic rollers I have ever met with on any coast. Long after passing the breakers and getting clear of the bar into comparatively deep

water, we met and surmounted a series of those watery mountains rolling in with smooth and unbroken crests, which must
have measured at least half a mile from ridge to ridge. The
brig slowly mounting to the summit would descend the declivity
with a gathering speed that set her sails aback and seemed
as if no power could stop her from plunging headlong to the
bottom, but on reaching the long, smooth valley between,
would gracefully reverse her position, without shipping a
drop, and proceed with indescribable smoothness of movement to mount deliberately to the next huge summit to repeat
the process. On that coast the heave of the ocean seems to
take the ground in comparatively deep water several miles
from land, and gathers into these mountainous but perfectly
smooth rollers which on reaching water too shoal to sustain
them longer, break into a surf whose grandeur is equalled, by
all accounts, only on the West African coast.

As the weather continued good, the skipper who had rebuilt
our patched up old wreck and carried her twice safely over
the worst bar on the Pacific, found little difficulty in taking her
to San Francisco without any particular adventure. The
provisions were certainly miscellaneous, and have perhaps
rarely been equalled for variety, embracing fish, crabs, mussels,
with roots and venison, traded from the natives, not forgetting
the much-traveled beef. We had discovered a fine agricultural
country for settlement and an inexhaustible supply of fir
timber, and had located at least half a dozen town sites. What
ultimately became of all those prospectively valuable properties I never knew, as on arrival it soon appeared that the
expenses and disasters of the voyage had as usual exceeded
the cash results and all my interest was ciphered out to nothing
by the most unassailable arithmetic. Besides I found my attention immediately absorbed by the old interests which,
distasteful as they were, could no longer be evaded, so I was
fain to abandon the future possible results of the land specu-
lations which, however brilliant to sanguine temperaments in
some remote era of the future, possessed no value whatever at
the present time.

CHAPTER XV

The rolling hills of the Contra Costa being by this time yellow with the ripening harvest, there could be no more evasion of the bucolic problem from which I had twice weakly run away, but which must now be squarely met and disposed of. Of all the circumstances of that period there is not one that afforded less satisfaction at the time, nor now in the retrospect, than that ill-starred agricultural enterprise. It was not merely that it now showed itself likely to prove pecuniarily unprofitable, but its uncongenial character, and particularly the difficulty of getting free from it at all on any reasonable terms, gave one the sensation of being caught in a spring trap, like a bear that enjoys the pleasing alternative of losing his paw if he escapes, or his life, if he remains. There was no longer any illusion about the profit. Wheat had fallen from three cents a pound, at which rate I had purchased the seed, to seven-eighths of one cent, for which I was glad to get rid of the crop, which with all the usual agricultural irony, averaged forty bushels to the acre by actual weight after delivery on the wharf at San Francisco.

Again, even if after selling off the personal property, I should sacrifice the land with its doubtful title for any price it might bring, or even abandon it outright, I had come to feel quite conscious that the former expedient of immersing myself in some futile adventure by land or sea, could no longer afford any satisfactory solution of even the most ordinary ambition for the future. True, I had been trained to nothing and had learned nothing to qualify one for any stable serious pursuit, by which alone, as I began to perceive, the fortunes of individuals are solidly advanced. Then I must proceed to learn, and next came the serious question whether there was yet time to begin again and build from the bottom, so as to acquire a knowledge and mastery of some kind of effort which should command sufficient usefulness to attract success? While I was pondering such thoughts alone and without any such advisers as young men usually enjoy, a circumstance occurred, trifling in itself, but which served to unlock the doors that seemed shut against me, and to direct my efforts upon a new course, which has beyond doubt given different shape and substance to every subsequent event of my life.

A neighbor of mine owned a few negroes brought from his home in Missouri, one of whom having been sent to San Francisco on an errand, had been claimed by the abolitionists of that place as entitled to freedom under the new State laws. Of course all the row and excitement then incident to such questions incontinently arose, without regard to the interests or wishes of the negro himself who wished for nothing but to be let alone and allowed to remain with his old master and companions. Some sort of proceeding had been commenced in the court of a Justice of the Peace in Oakland, the nature of which I do not now remember. I do not suppose such inferior courts had jurisdiction in *habeas corpus,* but at all events the litigation was of such character that the lawful custody of the negro, as between his old-time owner and the San Francisco mob, was to be decided by the law's representative on a certain day. It appeared that excitement was already running high before I knew much about the matter, and on the day before the afternoon set for the final hearing, the Justice sent for me and expressed his fears of the imminent danger of a serious riot in his court however he might decide the controversy; and begged me to organize a party to maintain order and reënforce the slight means at his disposal for enforcing his decision.

To this I replied that I should decline to take part unless reasonably assured of the master getting his rights. He had brought up and owned the negro from birth and brought him all the way from Missouri, together with all of his other possessions, on the faith of his legal right to emigrate with his property to any territory of the United States, and if a lot of political wind-bags at San José or Sacramento had patched up any State laws or constitution divesting him of such rights, he at least retained a moral claim to the custody of his servant, if only for the purpose of taking him back to Missouri, and recovering the rights and equities of his first position.

Without actually stating what the decision was to be, the Justice gave me such satisfactory impressions that I agreed to undertake what amounted to the job of an assistant constable without pay, and guaranteed to see the decision of the court executed "if agreeable to justice and satisfactory to me." I therefore spent the evening and part of the night in riding round the country to pick up a dozen or more young fellows whom I knew, and in giving them a little preliminary drill and instruction. Long before the hour set for the hearing, a large and excited mob was on hand from San Francisco, to which place there was already in operation a steam ferry, but when the assistant myrmidons of the law rode in, all mounted on good American horses and suitably equipped for business, those enthusiastic gentry began to realize that the game was not to be won by bawling, and if they wanted the nigger they must fight for him. Leaving a proper horse guard, I placed my men in and about the entrance of the room where, come what might, they could hold the door, and handing my rifle to them, took my seat by the *corpus delicti* among the lawyers in front of the judge, who forthwith opened proceedings.

After emitting sufficient moral and windy platitudes for conciliatory purposes, the decision was much on the lines previously gone over with his Honor, and ended by the unqualified remittance of the darkey to his lawful owner, a decision which, whether expected or not, was received with howls of rage from the mob inside and outside of the room. But the law having spoken, it was now the turn of its extemporized executive, and after a humane and explicit warning to the rabble, the posse received its orders aloud (carefully explained beforehand) in such plain and business-like terms, that the crowd submitted to be hustled out of the way and remained quiescent—if not content—while the champion of law and order marched out with cocked revolver in each hand, closely followed by the owner and a fighting friend of his with the negro between them. Reinforced by all our men at the door, we traversed the outside crowd without actual fighting, and

Isaac Mister
San Francisco. Cal.
1853
Age 25.

started the negro and his white friends on their way home, remaining in line across the street long enough to prevent pursuit. The mob having been overawed and beaten without a fight, which was probably quite lucky for them, there was afterwards little trouble in driving them away from the spot and clearing the court room and vicinity to get fair play for the judge and lawyers.

The principal attorney for the owner was the Hon. Gwyn Page, formerly Speaker of the Kentucky House of Representatives, but at this time junior in the prominent law firm of Crockett & Page, and a leading lawyer of San Francisco. Having been much impressed, no less by his stately old-fashioned manner than by his fearless and able conduct of the cause, I invited him to spend the night at my house as a pleasanter alternative than crossing the ferry in company with the disappointed mob, promising to mount him both ways and see him on the ferry-boat at any hour he liked next morning. Being a bachelor without domestic entanglements, he frankly accepted the invitation, and in my rural retreat we passed a large part of the night in conversation, during which he so entirely won my affections, that he learned all my history and present embarrassments and gave his opinion that it was by no means too late for me to embark in the study of the law. After making an effort to place me with some desirable preceptor without success, he some time later proposed to employ me at copying in his own office—with opportunity for reading and quizzing—at the salary of forty dollars a month. The sum was less than the plainest boarding could then be obtained for, but as I was to be a supernumerary, their real needs being already supplied by more competent men already members of the bar, I cared nothing for salary, and accepted it gratefully, with the privilege of sleeping in the office.

The firm occupied a leading position in the State, possessing as much practice as they could attend to, chiefly of the most important character. Mr. Joseph B. Crockett, the senior member, and afterward Chief Justice of the State, came from Hopkinsville, Ky., and as man and lawyer ranked second to none, but my relations were chiefly with Mr. Page, whom I came to love with almost filial affection, and by whom I hope and believe the feeling was to a great extent reciprocated. As he came to appreciate that my elementary education had been neither neglected nor entirely forgotten, and contrasted it with the rough crowd with whom he first found me, and the still rougher adventures which were skillfully elicited by his questions, he was at increasing pains to smooth down the rudeness of speech and manner which of course I had acquired, and as San Francisco then offered few social distractions, he rarely failed to spend an hour or more of each evening in discussing with me what I had read during the day. As I slept in the office and the preparation of my simple fare occupied but little time, my habit was to rise as I had been long accustomed to, at daybreak and devote every hour to study that could be spared from the writing that was set me to do. Thus I not only covered the ground fast, but was solidly grounded in what I read by Page's questions and explanations of the evening. In this way it was not long before I had mastered Blackstone and Kent, and was put to the best text-books on special branches of the law, and required to hunt up and familiarize myself with the leading cases there referred to. Within a few months I was entrusted with the framing—subject of course to revision—of pleadings and original contracts, and I remember that one of the first of the latter documents that I sketched was a mortgage from the celebrated Cornelius K. Garrison (whom I had good reason to remember in Panama, and who was not more astonished to meet me in a San Francisco lawyer's office, than I was to find him a prosperous real estate operator) to the equally well-known Montgomery P. Blair, to secure notes for a hundred thousand dollars, bearing interest payable monthly, at the rate of several per cent a month, compounding monthly if not paid. Garrison was a remarkable character in more ways than one. After getting his start at the notorius 'bank' on the Grand Plaza corner Calle San Juan de Dios, in Panama, he accumulated a large fortune in San Francisco and New York, and died at the latter place a few years since leaving an estate of twenty millions.

In Panama he fought a duel with the celebrated Vicissimus Turner, which, well known as it was at the time, there can be few now living to remember. It was after midnight when they quarreled, both having drunk quite as much as they could conveniently carry, and being both counted desperate men, agreed to settle the affair at once. The hour not being a convenient one to find seconds and other frills, they concluded to dispense with formalities and repair to the promenade on top of the wall of the old fort, and having tossed for the word, each to lay hold of the lapel of the other's coat and fire together at the word. Turner won the word, and the position being taken, both fired, but having knocked their arms together, in bringing up the pistols, neither was hurt. It was then agreed to load up and try it again, but Turner having a single-barreled Derringer required another percussion cap which he did not possess, and was reduced to borrowing from Garrison, who took one from an unused chamber of his revolver, for the purpose. This did not fit the Derringer's large nipple, and in trying to force it on was dropped and lost. As G. was grumblingly removing another for the same purpose, T. burst out laughing, and on the reason being indignantly demanded replied that he could not help laughing when he considered what a d—d fool G. was for taking so much trouble to lend him a percussion cap when he, G., had him at his mercy. This view also struck G.'s sense of humor, and the dispute was soon amicably adjusted, the principals finding their way home by mutual assistance, and not without considerable difficulty. Turner afterwards became judge of the District Court in Humboldt County, California, where I last saw him about a year later, and where I presume he was ultimately gathered to his fathers in the odor of judicial sanctity and respectability.

About this time Mr. Page began to entrust me with the trials of small cases in courts not of record, and even to aid him in other trials of more importance. One of the first of the former, though of no great consequence in point of parties or amount, was of great moment to me, and of some importance to the public. It was an action of *replevin* to recover certain personal baggage detained from the owner by the proprietor of a boarding-house, or alleged inn, for non-payment of a bill for entertainment. The action was brought by me, with Page's approval, on the ground that the alleged inn was in fact a boarding-house, the proprietor of which, unlike an inn-keeper, possessed no lien on his guest's baggage, either at common law or under any then existing statute. The case having been decided for the defendant, and the decision affirmed in the County Court, went to the Supreme Court which reversed both decisions and gave judgment for the plaintiff, thus definitely fixing the law of the question, in that State, in the absence of direct statutory enactment. As the action had been brought in the magistrate's court in my own name as attorney, though not yet admitted to practice, a doubt rose whether I would be permitted to appear in the Appellate Courts, and as my employers generously insisted on my going on with it in order to vindicate the opinion given in the first instance, I was driven to inquire of defendant's counsel whether or not he would take advantage of my not having been yet admitted, and received a hearty and emphatic reply in the negative.

The attorney who behaved thus generously after learning from me the facts involved, was no less a person than Col. Edward D. Baker of Illinois, formerly Colonel of the 4th Regiment Illinois Volunteers in the Mexican War, afterwards Senator of the United States, from the newly admitted State of Oregon, and subsequently Brigadier General of Volunteers in the Army of the United States; a lawyer distinguished on both sides of the continent, with whom I was soon afterwards admitted to a professional partnership, and with whom I continued to maintain the closest relations of business and friendship till his death by my side on the battlefield of Ball's Bluff, October 21st, 1861.

After remaining nearly a year with Crockett & Page, I naturally began to look about for some opportunity of commencing practice on my own account. My examination was successfully passed, I think sometime in the year 1854. The Chief Examiner for the Supreme Court (whose license admitted to practice in all State Courts) was Mr. E. B. Crocker, an experienced and distinguished lawyer, who subsequently admitted to me that a California-made lawyer was such a novelty to him that he made the examination, at least on elementary subjects, as searching as he knew how, from curiosity to know if it were possible for such a *lusus naturae* to have really learned any law under such circumstances. I gave a good account of myself in real estate, commercial, criminal and even maritime law, which latter could hardly be considered within his province as examiner for the State Courts, and the only question on which I failed to give a more or less satisfactory reply was in regard to the definition of the antiquated term 'essoign' day, which as it has been obsolete for centuries, really belonged rather in the domain of history than law. I will add, however, that I was not long in burnishing up my memory on the defective point, and though I have quit the bar for more than thirty years I fancy few English-speaking persons entertain today a more praise-worthy knowledge of that old Norman-French term than the student who then stranded on it.

I have since been admitted to the Supreme Court of Pennsylvania, 4th January, 1858, and to the Supreme Court of the United States, 17th December, 1860, as well as to other judicial tribunals of less renown, but the Sacramento event of course holds the chief and foremost place in memory over all similar ordeals.

Although Col. Baker was then about forty-three years of age, and widely known throughout the State, my association with him in the case referred to—though on opposite sides—and the admiration of many traits of his mind and character, particularly captivating to young and ardent temperaments, led to as much intimacy as could readily prevail consistently with such disparity of age and attainment. He was by no means dissipated—in fact, he was absolutely without any of the ordinary masculine vices, except a passion for cards—but with all his rich stores of memory and transcendent talent in statement and speech, there was absolutely no trace of order or system about his character. So far from keeping any pecuniary accounts, he had not even a docket of his cases, relying solely on his memory and a mass of papers carried in his hat and about his person. His office was a bare, half-furnished and desolate apartment, where nothing that was wanted could ever be found, and from whose dreary precincts he himself shrunk as from a prison cell. He cared nothing for money, squandering his large fees as fast as received, and in spite of his great earnings, was most generally penniless. A street beggar was as likely to get from him a twenty-dollar piece as a quarter-dollar, when his pocket was full, and perhaps an hour later he would be unable to satisfy the most deserving creditor. Though devoid of all sorts of affectation or pretense, he was in almost every respect unlike other men. Even his personal history was remarkable. Born in England of humble Quaker parents in 1811, he was brought by them when but nine years of age to Philadelphia, where as a child he labored for a time in a cotton factory. Accompanying his parents in a later emigration to Illinois, some accidental circumstance directed his attention to religious subjects as professed by the sect of Campbellites, and long before his legal maturity he had acquired wide reputation as one of the most eloquent preachers in the State. At twenty he married a lady with some property, which was soon squandered or lost, though the happiness of the domestic relation remained unimpaired through all the vicissitudes of fortune till his death. Of course in a young and growing state like Illinois, with its ambitious and able bar, ebullient politics and chaotic law, it was inevitable that such a genius should ultimately find his way into the law, and having studied its elements while still in the pulpit, he was admitted to practice soon after he was of age, elected to the legislature as a Whig in 1837, to the State Senate in 1840, and to Congress in 1844. He abandoned his seat in Congress to raise and command the 4th Regiment Illinois Volunteers in the war with Mexico. At Cerro Gordo, after the wounding of Shields, he took command by seniority of his brigade, whose final charge swept the enemy from their partially entrenched position on the heights. After enduring an attack of fever in Panama which brought him very near death, he reached California in 1851, where he was not long in placing himself far in advance of all the gallant lances of that able and distinguished bar.

The more I came to love and admire that strong and generous, but ill-regulated and erratic character, the more forcibly it appeared even to my juvenile perceptions, that to acquire the solid place and power at the bar which he deserved, something more was requisite than grand bursts of eloquence on special and irregular occasions. It was not enough to confuse judges and bend juries to his will by sporadic and uncertain flights, however grand and noble. The solid and substantial reputation which alone can successfully carry the superstructure of success, must be based, in this profession as in all others, on order and system; and the client must possess the assured conviction, not merely that his interests will be brilliantly handled at the last moment, but that they will have been judiciously advised, directed and kept in ready array, and above all that the advocate be always posted, on guard and ready for the fray.

Baker with all his general reading, abounding talent, and tremendous energy in the shock of actual contest, was never to be found, never ready, and always wanting in those sober but essential qualities. In short he required to have his splendid powers supplemented by those of some less brilliant but more orderly and laborious associate, and after pressing such views on him with more or less conviction, I modestly suggested myself as the *Camena Egeria* for this splendid but erratic and uncertain *Numa*. The unequal partnership was accepted by Baker after a single night's reflection, and in a far more complete and generous manner than I expected or intended, for notwithstanding that he, at least in the first instance, possessed all the elements of success, and I none, yet when some months afterwards having some joint funds in my hands, I inquired his idea of the proper proportion of their distribution, he promptly replied that he never had been and never would be associated with any partner except on the single basis of equality. My remonstrance was of no avail, and the only modification I could prevail on him to consent to was, that while I would continue to aid him in the criminal part of the business, the fees thence accruing should go to him alone.

The association was immediately, and I think I may say remarkably, successful. Baker being hitherto difficult to find and by no means dependable at the critical moment, had derived most of his business from other lawyers throughout the City and State, who desired his transcendently successful influence with juries. We now took and furnished a fine suite of apartments, supplied them with a well-selected professional library (on credit), and at once acquired a clientage which, though attracted by his great reputation, was retained and increased by the close and careful preparation and attention given to their business. One of the first, or perhaps I should say the first, case of importance that I personally tried made a lasting impression on me, and may serve to show that although the junior partner had certainly enjoyed a wonderful piece of good fortune, his lot was nevertheless not entirely one of 'sweetness and light.'

Baker had already brought an action, or rather several actions, in behalf of an Illinois man named L., against a number of so-called bankers, or in plain and proper language, money-lenders, to replevin a large quantity—$40,000 worth in all—of lard, purchased on speculation by L. for cash and stored for a rise with one G., a warehouseman and commission mechant. G. having drifted into failing circumstances, proceeded during L.'s absence and without his knowledge, to pledge this property to the pawnbroking 'bankers' aforesaid to secure his own notes, until after some weeks the whole of it had been so disposed of, when his announced failure brought L. back from the mines to the city. Baker had commenced the actions on general principles only, and more from his strong sympathy with L. than with any great expectation of maintaining them, unless by some chance of formal irregularity in the transactions which might possibly crop out on investigation.

There was little probability of such error or neglect to be expected from several of the shrewdest and most experienced private bankers in the place, but on further study of the cases it seemed to me they might be maintained on the old principle that though a factor necessarily clothed as such with possession and other *indiciae* of ownership, may sell his principal's goods as a usual function of a known and advertised agent or factor, he cannot validly pledge them; the latter act being outside the scope of his ordinary duty and authority, and therefore sufficiently unusual to put the pledgee on inquiry, as to the real extent of his rights as factor.

This view, with sustaining cases from other states being submitted to my friend Page, was approved by him as matter of law, and warmly adopted by Baker, and the cases prepared accordingly. The defendants were severally represented by some of the ablest members of the San Francisco bar, among them being Doyle, McAllister, Whitcomb, Pringle, Felton, and others, who had arranged to combine on the first as a test case, the facts in all being similar. While I had carefully prepared and briefed the case both as respected law and facts, I had no expectation whatever of pitting myself against those renowned champions of the bar, except as a humble and comparatively irresponsible assistant, but on the day of trial, Baker could not be found. In vain the terrified L. mustered all his friends and ransacked all the faro tables and every other possible and impossible place in town; the fateful hour arrived and I stood alone. As L. was even more frightened than myself, I considered whether I should face the music or let the combined enemy take judgment by default on the chance of getting the case subsequently reopened on a more promising occasion. On reflection I considered such pusillanimous course would be less than justice to the Court, the plaintiff or myself, and determined to go on with the trial, though with more abject, pale-faced fear than I have since sometimes felt when moving on a hostile battery. It was, I fear, a pitiful and cowardly appeal I made for continuance to the mild, and as I thought, sympathizing Judge, who I think was Shattuck of the Superior Court of San Francisco, but all the hostile giants jumped on me at once, indignantly asserting that I was counsel on the record, had myself notified them for trial, and was thus without the slightest legal or moral pretext for continuance. The Judge felt obliged to take the same view, and bade me proceed. In the course of putting in my testimony, I was obliged to place the defaulting factor himself on the stand to establish some formal fact lying only within his knowledge, and when McAllister took him for cross-examination, there ensued an excoriation such as a malfeasant witness has rarely received in court. On some pretext, the lawyer successfully maintained his right to go beyond the brief subject of the direct examination, and dragged the wretched witness through all the miserable facts, subjecting him alternately, as such a master well knew how, to the scorn, indignation, ridicule and contempt of judge, jury and spectators.

While this spectacle was in progress, the Court adjourned for dinner, and in the crowd jostling each other down the staircase, finding myself next to G., I foolishly allowed myself to say a few encouraging words of no special significance, but which of course had much better been omitted under the circumstances.

The words were hardly spoken, when I perceived the bad taste, if not impropriety, of any private communication with a witness still practically on the stand, and realized the foolish figure I should cut if at the resumption of the examination, McAllister should ask the usual question, whether the witness had been spoken to about the case since adjournment? Seeing no other honest way out of the scrape I had so thoughtlessly walked into, and believing that McAllister would not be insensible to a personal appeal, I went directly to his office, told him the entire story, that the present was the first considerable case I had ever tried, and that unless he should extend a generous forbearance he would oblige me to forestall his thunder, by volunteering an acknowledgment of my folly in open court. Looking me straight in the eye, he said, "Do you give me your word of honor that you have related in good faith, everything that passed?" "Yes, unqualifiedly." "Then, my dear fellow, you shall never hear any more of it from me."

Just before the summing up to the jury, Baker walked into court as cooly and composedly as though he had spent the day in performing every conceivable duty to his client, myself and the rest of the world and added, as it were, insult to injury, by declining to give me any aid whatever, on the plea that he had not heard the testimony. Being unable to move him either by denunciation or appeal, I therefore proceeded with many misgivings, to address the jury. Now I knew well enough, theoretically (for Baker, one of the most effective orators in America, had constantly insisted on it) that a jury speech to be effective, must come hot from the emotions; that while one may consider well the order, arrangement and arguments, the words and sentences must never be prepared except at the peril of grandiloquence, stiltedness and weakness. Nevertheless, having myself taken a pathetic view of the manner of our client's spoliation by a trusted friend, during his absence, I was anxious to communicate some of my feeling to the jury, and had thought out a few—only two or three—very fetching sentences. These were duly fired off at the jury, but under the legal instuctions and charge of the Court, the verdict was against me; though the cases having been subsequently argued in the Supreme Court were reversed, and the principle contended for, firmly established in California.

In delivering my slyly prepared slices of eloquence, I felt a little guilty, as everyone must who simulates a red-hot passion in phrases coolly prepared beforehand, and cast a surreptitious glance or two at Baker, but as he was leaning his head on his hands, over a table, apparently half-asleep, I flattered myself I had escaped detection by the critic I most valued and feared. But after all was over and we had got back to the quiet of the office, he remarked, "You made a very fair speech which would have been good, but for the blemish of those prepared sentences which you, no doubt, considered very fine."

"What possesses you with the idea that any sentences were prepared? Can you specify them?" Whereupon he repeated them, word for word, with a cold-blooded and merciless fidelity that made me shudder. The lesson sank so deep that ever since if some phrase that seems particularly fine, forces itself on my attention in advance, I make a point of avoiding it. The fact is that though great speakers of set orations, like Webster or Everett, may deliver a literary essay from memory, with studied gesture and carefully regulated emotion, the off-hand orators of the people cannot venture to smuggle in false notes or simulated passion, without subjecting to dangerous contrast, the setting and the frame.

The San Francisco bar at that time abounded with able men culled from every state in the Union, embracing in addition to those already mentioned, such celebrated lawyers as Hoge, Shafter, Williams, Randolph, McDongal, Inge, Thornton, Crittendon, Peachy, and many others distinguished in every branch of the civil and common law, and embracing all the numerous varieties of professional talent that contribute to make up a brilliant whole. The community with its pursuits and interests was new, the late Mexican jurisprudence had been abandoned so far as it could be disentangled from land titles; all sorts of questions long set at rest in older states, were pressing for solution, and from simple, sheer necessity, the judiciary, spurred on by the bar, was running a race of law-making with the legislature. Lawyers were daily obliged to commit themselves to opinions affecting great interests at home and abroad, with little adjudicated law to go upon, and based rather on their notions of what views the courts might be induced to take, than on existing statutes or recorded cases. Thus a majority of cases brought to bar afforded, in the hands of young, able, and ambitious men, opportunity not merely for pyrotechnic jury speeches, but for arguments to the bench which attacked and discussed everything, effectually sifting the real value of principles and maxims elsewhere accepted as elemental or taken for granted; so that perhaps no other great forum just then afforded equal facilities either for studying diversity of mental character or acquiring broad views of the principles, scope and philosophy of the law.

So also, the complicated facts and relations requiring the application of such principles, were of still more infinite variety. The almost instantaneous planting of an energetic and speculative community entirely composed, like the bar, of young and active men, so remote from all others, both as respects time and distance, prevented the ordinary commercial and financial coöperation with neighboring cities, and led to emergencies and events that could scarcely occur at all under any ordinary circumstances of communication. One of the most striking illustrations of such peculiarity of condition, occurred in the first months of 1855, when, following the embarrassment of the great private banking firm of Page, Bacon & Co., a local panic ensued that caused the immediate suspension of every bank, saving's bank, express, and other concern transacting a deposit business, in the State. With insignificant exceptions, these were obliged to close their doors with large quantities of bullion—impossible to convert suddenly into coin—lying in their vaults, the bullion asset in possession of Adams Express Company alone at the time of its suspension exceeding a million and a half dollars. Corporate banks were then prohibited by law and the only lawful currency was coin, and the only difficulty was a sudden appreciation of the insufficiency of all the coin existing in the country to make actual necessary exchanges, and the impossibility of augmenting it in reasonable time from any other quarter. The only mail communication with the Eastern States and Europe was by steamer *via* the Isthmus, and as it required sixty days to send a message to New York and receive a reply, a ruinous havoc was wrought among wealthy firms and institutions, simply for want of adequate communications with the rest of the business world.

But notwithstanding such novel, or abnormal obstacles and disasters, an immense shipping and commercial business grew up in San Francisco, during those years, with Europe, Asia and the Eastern States of the Union, and under the comparative freedom of trade then enjoyed, with the consequent easy exchanges and moderate cost of production, the country's shipping tonnage, enormously stimulated by the new markets of California and the Pacific, reached and actually passed that of Great Britain, theretofore and now again, the largest ship owner of the world. The new business of the round voyage from and back to New York, *via* San Francisco, China and Liverpool, by furnishing continuous freights in both directions, even contributed to originate and build up such intermediate foreign ports as Shanghai, Hong Kong and Singapore, and produced a new class of American clipper ships of large capacity like the *Norma,* the *Palmer, Flying Cloud, White Squall* and others, which placed American shipbuilders and seamen at the head of their professions. It was not till greedy schemers and incapable statesmen at last succeeded in crushing the enterprise of our merchants, by pushing to absurd lengths the plausible fallacy of 'protection,' that that pre-eminence was at length destroyed and American shipping gradually driven from the ocean. At the present time the mischief seems fast extending to the mass of population, and under pretext of securing to a handful of manufacturing capitalists a monopoly of the 'home market,' we have managed to exclude our manufactured products from all other markets, increased the expense of living in every household, and seriously impaired the prosperity of the millions engaged in commerce, agriculture and shipping.

Among the financial wrecks of the California bank panic of 1855, was the private savings bank of R. & S. at the corner of

Clay and Montgomery Streets, which failed for a large sum principally due to a great number of comparatively small depositors, largely belonging to the working classes. This institution having after the crash employed our firm as counsel, it fell to me to conduct a laborious examination of its assets and accounts, and I may say I owe to that single case a fairly good understanding of the system of double entry bookkeeping, hitherto as inscrutable to my untrained apprehension as the procession of the equinoxes. Unlike most of the suspended banks, this firm had exhausted both coin and bullion before giving up the fight; nevertheless it was solvent in the usual sense of that abused word, i.e., provided the large excess of speculative assets standing on its books could be made to realize anything near cost. Those assets consisted of suspended paper, loans to, or interests in, all sorts of enterprises not yet arrived at fruition, inchoate gold mines, litigated land claims, and so forth, which in the temporary destruction of credit, the rush by the country upon the city, and the wild storm of writs and attachments, mostly perished as assets; being either destroyed or frittered away in the innumerable proceedings of individual creditors then unrestrainable by equitable proceedings, and invariably commenced, as the law then permitted, by the actual seizure in attachment, of every real or supposed item of property. S., the junior partner, being by temperament averse to excited controversy, gave up the contest early and retired to his home in the Eastern States, but R. though older, was of tougher fiber, and notwithstanding he would inevitably have been murdered if seen in the streets, and therefore labored under extraordinary disadvantages, he made a long and brave fight against the inevitable. He even induced me, against Baker's advice, to preside at and generally take charge of a public meeting of his creditors called at Maguire's Opera House, to enable him—under police protection—to offer his explanation of the affair. The house—which was not the large structure of the same name subsequently built, but nevertheless of generous dimensions—was densely packed by a silent but sullen crowd with a body of police in front of the footlights, myself and a small party of fighting friends seated on the stage, when R. appeared from the stage entrance in rear to offer his promised explanation. The exasperation of the crowd at the actual sight of their *bête noir*, almost immediately burst all bounds. The benches were torn up for weapons, and a rush made for the stage which overwhelmed the police contingent, and left myself and friends just time to close round R. and his books, and get them safely away by a rear door. The litigation went on *ad infinitum*, but even R.'s desire for a *vis à vis* explanation with his creditors was heard of no more.

The clientage of Baker & Wistar, which owing to the former's wide reputation as an advocate had been large from the first, had after awhile increased to dimensions which during the remainder of my residence in San Francisco absorbed my entire time during seven days of each week. Aided by a competent translator and a sufficient number of assistants, organized to the best of my ability, I found no more time for relaxation than was afforded by an hour's gallop every evening at dusk, and a long walk over the surrounding sand hills at daybreak every Sunday morning. The records of professional practice in civil cases usually supply few items of general interest, but in some celebrated criminal prosecutions, in which I was concerned with my chief, the case was different. Two of these in fact, although directly concerning the fortunes of individual malefactors, rise to almost historical dignity, in view of their connection with the celebrated Vigilance Committee of 1856; and a third ended in a dramatic climax which had sufficient interest of its own.

The first was the prosecution of one Cora, a well-known professional gambler, for the murder of Richardson, U. S. Marshal of the District. The latter was a man addicted to drinking and extremely dangerous when so excited, being reputed to have killed a number of men both in Texas and California in private combat, and indeed sometimes without much combat at all. One evening about midnight, having had a verbal difference with Cora at the 'Blue Wing,' a celebrated Montgomery Street saloon, both being under the influence of previous festivity, they repaired to the street to discuss the matter alone. The bystanders induced them to return and make it up just as relations were becoming dangerous, but the difficulty recurring, they again repaired to the street, both men concurring in the desire for a private discussion, and insisting on the others remaining behind. A few minutes later, the report of a pistol being heard, the others ran out to find Richardson lying dead, opposite a closed doorway round the adjacent corner, with Cora standing over him. The remaining facts rested mainly on the assertions of the latter, who stated that they had walked round to, and taken position in, the doorway, when the discussion becoming hot, he had caught a glimpse of a flash of steel in R.'s hands, and though himself what is known as a 'fighting man,' being afraid of the still more desperate character of the other ruffian, he had instantly drawn, cocked and shot Richardson through the heart. Two facts gave a certain confirmation to this statement. R.'s sheath was empty and his bowie-knife was found—but unfortunately not till the following morning—lying in the cellar area under the iron grating upon which both parties were standing. A woman of bad character in passing along Montgomery Street, had heard an angry voice which she could not identify, exclaim, 'You are drawing on me,' or some similar words.

This homicide was the occasion of much public excitement, and under its pressure and the clamor of the newspapers, the sheriff made unusual efforts to summon a respectable jury who should command the confidence of the public, several of them being well-known merchants of high standing as citizens. At the trial which was conducted by four counsel on a side—including Byrne, the District Attorney—before a judge of conceded integrity, and a jury selected with unusual care, the verdict failed; the jury being about equally divided between murder, manslaughter and acquittal. Before a second trial could be had, Cora was taken from the jail by the Vigilance Committee and hung the next day, after an alleged but secret midnight trial without counsel or witnesses for the prisoner, or the safeguard of lawful oaths and general rules administered by a qualified and impartial judge. At that secret trial by the Committee's celebrated council of twenty-one whose unanimous vote was required for conviction, it strangely happened that no less than three members had also sat upon the jury by which the prisoner had been lawfully tried, on which occasion two of them had voted for 'manslaughter' and the other for acquittal! Whether Cora was guilty of willful premeditated murder, or acted in lawful self-defense, was, in consequence of the paucity of evidence and his own bad character, enveloped in much doubt, yet three respectable merchants, all inclined to the liberal view when subjected to the oaths and aided by the wise precautions with which the law seeks to solve such capital questions, cast all doubt and hesitation to the winds when such precautions were omitted and the voting done in secret, behind closed doors, without any orderly public responsibility, and under the pressure of the passions which swept unchecked around them.

Another case of ours that was cut short at an earlier stage by the murder of the prisoner by the same lawless gang, was that of Casey, held for the murder of the notorious 'James King, of William'—as he called himself. King was a broken down banker or money dealer, who had recently commenced editing a small scurrilous evening paper, which he succeeded in bringing into notice by devoting his leading column to the daily abuse, without much regard to facts, of some public or well-known person. Having fallen out with Casey, who was the editor of a Sunday paper of not much more fragrant character, he denounced him—*inter alia*—as a former convict in a New York prison, and declined to receive or publish what negative proof could be offered to the contrary. Finding the charge cut deep, as intended, he continued to ring all the changes on it for a week or more, refusing the victim's challenge to fight, and offensively daring him to a street attack, for which he avowed himself in print, as always ready and prepared.

As none but a violent remedy was to be had, Casey entered King's office one afternoon, a short time prior to his usual hour for departure, and personally notified him to arm, as he, Casey, intended to kill him publicly on sight. The same afternoon, as King, having come from his office in Merchant Street, turned into Montgomery, the principal street of the city, walking in the middle of the roadway, Casey stepped from the sidewalk, threw off a large cloak he was wearing, and with the warning, distinctly heard by the bystanders, 'Draw and defend yourself,' drew his pistol. King stopped, faced him, and partially drew from his overcoat pocket a cocked pistol, whereupon Casey fired, inflicting a wound of which King died about a week later.

It may be conceded that Casey fired an instant prematurely, since 'fighting men' do not ordinarily maintain the courage of one who, being himself prepared, fires before his adversary's weapon is leveled, or at the least fully displayed; but he was acting under excessive and willful provocation, and down to that point all his acts were in accord with the everyday customs and standard ideas of the country; and, public excitement apart, no California jury would have convicted him of anything more heinous than manslaughter. The Governor of the State—Johnson—offered to become officially and personally responsible for the safe custody and speedy trial of the prisoner before Norton, a judge of the highest public and private character, but on the day after King's death, Casey, having been forcibly taken from the county jail, was hung by the Committee on a beam projected from an upstairs window of their fortified stronghold, in the presence of at least 10,000 of their adherents marshaled in arms, of whom more than half were foreigners. His trial, if he had any, was in secret, without counsel or witnesses of his own, and without the allowance of any communication with his family or friends.

Still another capital case of ours was that of R. B., a young man respectably connected in Philadelphia, who without cause and in mere drunken frenzy, killed an inoffensive and unarmed man in a brutal and cowardly manner that excited the numerous German population to a white heat. This wretch's habits had become so degraded, that his uncle, the manager of one of the principal express companies, could find no better employment for him than driving one of their city delivery wagons. Arriving at his home one night, drunk, a low woman with whom he lived in an alley of unsavory reputation, running north from Washington above Dupont Street, pointed out to him a small man of half his size, whom she declared had attempted to rob her. B., without asking a question, drew his pistol and rushed for the man indicated, who turned out to be a German of good character, only three days arrived in the country, and unable to speak a word of English. Though ignorant of any cause of offense, yet being unarmed, and seeing himself chased by an infuriated man with a pistol, he ran out of the alley and down the middle of Washington Street, closely followed by B. who, when he found himself unable to overtake the German, fired from a short distance, the bullet striking the flying man in the back of the head and making its exit near the centre of the forehead.

Col. James, and James A. McDougal (afterwards U. S. Senator from California) having been retained for defense by the uncle, thought proper to secure for their side our professional aid, while the German population held excited meetings, subscribed a large fund and retained several distinguished gentlemen, at the head of whom was Mr. S. W. Inge of Alabama, to assist the District Attorney. The ground of defense at first agreed on by counsel, was the familiar one of insanity from long-continued dissipation, and the uncle, P., was instructed to procure all available information and testimony tending to sustain that view. Such testimony not proving very strong, Baker declared it insufficient, and insisted on the substitution of what is popularly called 'self-defense.' At a meeting of counsel, this radical change of plan found no other advocate, but was reluctantly agreed to in deference to Baker's deliberate judgment and unsurpassed experience, but P. was so opposed to it he had to be plainly told he must accept our view or procure other counsel. As the case seemed desperate he acceded, under this stress, and before long produced an extremely ill-looking and hard-featured individual named Collins, who would swear that he was present and saw the homicide, and at the time of, or an instant prior to the fatal shot, the deceased had placed his right hand under his coat simultaneously with a halting or hesitating movement toward his right. On cross examination, first privately by myself, and again in presence of all the counsel for the defense, he admitted that he kept a low groggery much visited by the prisoner, whom he had long known, and with whom he was in fact intimate; and could assign no explanation but mere accident for the extraordinary fact of his presence so far from his accustomed haunts at a moment so critical for his friend. But on the other hand, he was so well informed of the event, and endured so well a searching cross examination respecting the persons and objects in the vicinity, the vehicles in the street, and other minor facts of the *res gestae,* that notwithstanding his vulnerable character, vicious associations, and unprepossessing appearance, it was not deemed proper to suppress him on mere suspicion, against the wishes of the prisoner and his friends, and it was decided to risk him on the stand.

The excitement of the trial was such that a number of special deputies had to be sworn in to protect the Court and counsel, after which the prosecution briefly proved the homicide, and it fell to me as junior to open for the defense and commence with the witnesses. Almost the only affirmative testimony on our side, besides that of Collins, was proof of the finding by the police, soon after the occurrence, of an old rusty bowie-knife, under the wooden steps of a house a short distance *above* the debouch of the alley, i.e., in a direction contrary to that taken by the deceased and his pursuer. Collins' direct testimony was given with a readiness and precision not calculated to allay my suspicions, after which he was turned over to the prosecution, and Inge, the lion of that side, for the first time addressed himself actively to the case, and proceeded to cross-examine. But instead of the ordinary expedients of tearing all concealment from the character, occupation and associations of the witness, or requiring him to explain what curious coincidence procured his timely presence on the scene, or confusing his statements of the persons and vehicles in the vicinity, Inge ominously contented himself by committing the witness irrevocably to his original statement in a manner to exclude any subsequent modification, concluding somewhat as follows:

"Your testimony is of course important, and tallies with your statement on direct examination, but by way of testing the accuracy of your observation and memory, I will ask you a few questions respecting the killing itself, which I desire you to answer with deliberation. You say that at, or previous to the moment when the prisoner fired, the deceased made a halt, or half halt, inclining to the right?" "Yes, sir." "Well are you sure it was to the right; might it not, for instance, have been toward the other side, the left?" "No sir, it could not have been; I saw something serious would happen and was noticing particularly." "Then you are equally certain it was his right, and not his left hand that the deceased placed under his coat as though to draw a weapon?" "Yes sir, I am sure

of that." "You swear positively, then, to the right side and
the right hand?" "Yes, sir." "And do not wish in any case
or in any manner to qualify that part of your testimony?"
"No, sir."

The witness was then allowed to stand down, and the prosecution called several prominent citizens who were present at,
or immediately after the event, who severally corroborated the
statement of the first one, which was substantially as follows:
He saw the shooting, but noticed no hesitation nor sign of
halting by the deceased, who from first to last was using all his
efforts to escape. When shot, he fell instantly dead, and lay
as he fell without a motion. Witness was the first to reach the
body which was lying on its face with arms extended, holding
in the right hand a cigar still burning!

At this moment, so terrible for the defense, the responsibility
of closing for the prisoner belonged to Baker, who was not the
man to quail before that or any emergency. The single frail
raft to which, for want of a better, the prisoner's life had been
trusted, seemed to have sunk under us, and left us confusedly
floundering without a plan. Contemptuous laughter burst from
the German mob, the hostile lawyers illy concealed their com-
placent smiles, and judge and jury looked with serious faces
to see whether the catastrophe was fatal, or might even yet
in any way be met. But the dauntless Baker—veteran in
countless forensic battles—rose cool and undismayed to the
occasion. Without a visible tremor or change of countenance he
addressed his superb talents to the task, and his plausible arguments and matchless eloquence snatched even that blood-dyed
wretch from the gallows by dividing the jury, four of whom
were constrained to vote for the lower grade of manslaughter.
On a second trial for his life, the prisoner was convicted of
the last-named offense, and sentenced to a term of three years
and eight months in the San Quentin penitentiary, but the
judgment having been reversed on a technicality reserved, the
case was again remanded. On a third trial the accused was
convicted of murder, but the Supreme Court again reversed the
judgment, on the ground that the second trial having been
complete by sentence, the prisoner had been unlawfully placed

in a second and new jeopardy of his life for the same offense, and with some sharp comments, directed the Court below to arraign and try him for manslaughter only. The Vigilance Committee attacked and captured the county jail while he was awaiting the new trial ordered, but P. having sagaciously joined them and contributed his important influence to their aid, on condition that his nephew should withdraw all the later proceedings in his behalf, and serve out the term of imprisonment awarded on the second trial, the contract was faithfully executed; the prisoner's term expiring in time to permit him to serve in the approaching Civil War, where I subsequently saw him wearing the uniform of a staff captain in the quartermaster department.

Here were three notorious homicides all of which received from a mob, claiming to be respectable and well intentioned, the best adjudication it was capable of bestowing. The first man, guilty of defending himself from instant death by the only effectual means, was hung without a scruple. The second, goaded to frenzy by a wrong which could scarcely be rectified without violence, after vainly trying to obtain an equal fight, killed his adversary after fair personal notice, his principal or only error, according to the accepted standards of the place and time, being that he fired a second too soon. For him the punishment was the same. But the third, who committed what scarcely anyone can now doubt, was an unprovoked and wanton murder, was allotted the trifling penalty frequently inflicted for larceny and embezzlement, with the mob's full approval and consent. Perhaps no comment could much improve the illustration which these cases afford of the danger and injustice of mob rule where a full and fair judicial organization of the public's own choosing already prevails; and it would seem impossible for any intelligent person to confuse this view with those expressed on a former page respecting the administration of off-hand justice in an unorganized community.

CHAPTER XVI

One of the unexpected and startling events that seemed always happening in San Francisco in its early days, was the gigantic failure, and flight of Henry Meiggs, who in the desperate effort to control the entire trade in lumber, had uttered and used as collateral security for his own notes, an enormous quantity of fraudulent and forged city scrip or warrants. These having been habitually issued by the city in even amounts of a hundred, five hundred and a thousand or several thousand dollars, were very convenient for such use, and were in high credit. Meiggs having obtained a position for a near relation in the City Controller's Office, was enabled to get possession of entire printed books of blank warrants, which after having the requisite signatures forged upon them, were issued in enormous amounts. The game was worked a long time, pieces about to mature being taken up with new ones, and notes falling due paid with the proceeds of new ones, secured by new collateral of the same valuable kind. Meiggs was a member of the City Council, and reputed wealthy, but when his affairs became so complicated that exposure was at any time possible, he obtained a fast-sailing schooner, which was kept fully manned and ready for sea, off Rincon Point. One night, having ascertained that detection was certain to occur next day, he removed his family and portable effects from the fine mansion in which he lived on Telegraph Hill, to the yacht and at once made sail on her. Next day one fact brought out another, till almost every person of substance in the city found himself in some way interested, and pretty much all businsess was suspended; excited mobs surged about the principal streets in search of the offender.

At last the time and manner of his flight becoming definitely known, it occurred to someone that the day was without the usual sea-breeze; in fact, that rare condition in San Francisco, a dead calm prevailed. About the same time, a pilot reported the yacht as tossing helplessly about in the neighborhood of the bar, and a rush was made to the wharves where, in the absence of steam tugs (not yet introduced) a small steamer was chartered and filled with mad and excited creditors, armed with rifles and shotguns. It required some time to get steam up and the craft under way, and it was late in the afternoon before the schooner hove in sight with all her sails vainly wooing the breeze which came not, and yet was of such vital importance to the fugitive. But when the steamer was nearly within gunshot and the prey almost grasped, the long deferred airs of evening began to mark the glassy surface with gentle ripples, and the large sails of the yacht slowly filled and swung out her idle booms. Gradually but surely she gathered way, and as the shades of night slowly shut her out from the eager eyes on board the steamer, she was last seen lying over to a swelling breeze, which could not have arrived more timely to save the life of a pious missionary or self-sacrificing saint. Meiggs disappeared from human sight, as many supposed forever, but some years later he became known to all the world as a railroad contractor and proprietor in Peru, and finally as the financial backbone of that free and enlightened Republic. While the native patriots proved their intense and uncontrollable love for the dear people by gaily cutting each other's throats, and in desperate rivalry fought—as is the custom of patriots—to get their hands into the Treasury, this wiser son of the Pilgrim Fathers devoted his talents strictly to financial industry till he became virtually the Treasury himself, and came to own pretty much everything in the Republic, always excepting those inestimable boons of liberty, equality, fraternity, and suffrage, inalienably vested in each intelligent, though bare-legged and somewhat parti-colored citizen. This Puritan successor of Pizarro, the second conquistador of Peru, after relieving his adopted country, by strictly legal and constitutional methods, of most of its portable property, turned his attention to devising some safe scheme for revisiting his native land. For years he made ineffectual efforts to buy in his notes and forged collateral, and was said to have invested large sums in an effort to obtain certain California legislation better adapted to his particular necessities than to the public welfare. But that process being carried on at arm's length through agents, was complicated, difficult and expensive, since American statesmen are not to be had for nothing; and death at last found and mastered him before his object was accomplished, so that the 'land of the free' saw his enterprising face no more.

In the year 1855, our offices were on the second floor of a fine structure of Chinese granite, erected and partially occupied by the bankers, Wright & Co., and H. Hentz & Co., on the N. W. corner of Montgomery and Jackson Streets. Few of the present generation of San Franciscans can realize that that was then a choice location, the notion being then generally entertained that in consequence of the deep water front on both sides of Telegraph Hill, the commercial and financial business of the city must gain ground toward the north. Notwithstanding exactly the contrary has since occurred, at that time this was one of the choicest corners in the city, the three other corners being occupied respectively by the bank of Lucas, Turner & Co. in charge of Captain William T. Sherman, who was destined to so much future distinction of another kind; the Metropolitan Theatre, and the great financial and commercial firm of Pioche Bayerque & Co. Beyond the corner, the extensive pile known as Helleck's Building, sheltered half the lawyers of the city, prolonging southward a line of buildings equal or superior to any others then existing in the city. General Sherman's recollections as published by himself, give a flattering account of his able and successful administration of the bank of Lucas, Turner & Co. which was probably not appreciated at the time by his principals, and will scarcely be recalled with equal admiration by old residents of that date. Though several banks of equal reputation were close at hand, I had opened an account there in consequence of its convenient location across the street from our office. Baker and I were then operating with success a quartz mine in Amador County, which being under a competent superintendent, only required my personal presence occasionally. The money for Saturday wages requiring to be shipped on Thursday, while the remitted bullion only arrived on Wednesday, the certificate being usually detained by the branch mint some time later, a considerable amount for working capital was generally on deposit, while we had never needed or asked for pecuniary accommodation of any kind. After the account had been with them for some months, we being well known to them and the public as quite responsible, independently of the mining enterprise, I thought I might need some extra funds on one occasion, and told Sherman I might have occasion to overdraw about $5000 that afternoon, handing him at the same time, as collateral, a mint certificate of similar amount, which documents were invariably worth within about five per cent of their face. I had no idea he would have required any collateral at all, and simply handed it over to avoid being asked for it, having no idea that a similar discount at satisfactory rates would have been refused me by any bank or money-lender in town. I was therefore quite surprised when S., scanning the document cautiously, remarked, "This certificate is hardly security for the amount." I looked at him for a moment to make sure whether or not he was joking, but observing no sign of facetiousness, began to feel warm myself, and taking back the certificate started for the door, resolved to end all transactions there as soon as our funds could be checked out and deposited elsewhere. As I was going out the door he called after me, "Come back, Wistar; I did not mean to refuse. You can have the money, of course." But having become provoked at his hesitation and overcautiousness, I declined it on any terms, and at once terminated my relations with Sherman and his bank. In the same connection it is not inappropriate to add that the bank—though it could not fail with the millions of Mr. Lucas and Major Turner behind it—closed its business a few months later on account of its large losses and unsatisfactory condition, with numerous assets of much worse character than U. S. mint certificates; one of them being a book account to the amount of $60,000—for the overdrawn account of a single firm of bankrupt Jew grocers.

This trifling incident merely illustrates a peculiarity of judgment on a delicate—though to a banker by no means unimportant—subject; but when one notes General Sherman's recollections of his connection with the State authorities in their efforts to suppress the Vigilance Committee mob in 1856, as published by himself some years since in a magazine article, and to a certain extent reiterated in his memoirs, one is tempted to agree with a certain New England writer on California topics, who has expressed the opinion that the particular kind of memory with which General Sherman was endowed, "was hardly meant by the Creator for purely historical purposes, genial and amusing as its productions may be." [15] Sherman had at that time accepted obligations to his adopted State much exceeding those of a mere private citizen. As Major General of the San Francisco division of militia, he had presumably qualified himself by taking the oath pertaining to that office; and it was the judgment of many who were personally familiar with all the events of that celebrated insurrection, including the extreme difficulties and perplexities of the State authorities, that his indecision, vacillation, and apparent dread of personal unpopularity, by embarrassing and delaying till too late the action of the latter, defeated their purpose altogether.

Without entering here upon the ultimate provocations and causes of the Vigilance Committee, all parties have agreed that its immediate occasion was the shooting of the disreputable editor, King, already referred to. During the week first succeeding that event and while the result of the wound was yet uncertain, popular excitement rose high under the industrious stimulation of many influential persons who must have known the dangerous character of their experiment but were flattered by their new born notoriety and seduced by the noxious hope of political preferment. Such persons contributed both money and organizing ability to the movement, so that when King's death at length occurred, after a week or more of minutely published and dramatic illness, the mob had been already organized and drilled in a number of strong battalions and had possessed themselves of all the suitable arms in the State, except such as were the property of the United States in custody of General Wool, the Federal commander of the Pacific Department in the U. S. Arsenal at

[15] American Commonwealths, California, Josiah Royce, Assistant Professor of Philosophy, Harvard College, 1888, page 444.

Benicia. They had also perfected a civil or executive organization by which the ultimate power was lodged in an executive committee of twenty-one, and had fortified or surrounded with sand-bag *epaulements,* a large building in the lower part of Sacramento Street, which served as a secure prison and place of arms.

On the other side, the county officials being mostly of the low grade common with such persons under our elective system, feared either from personal or political motives to take any effective steps in defense of order, and the Sheriff, one Scannell, a low Irish, or half-Irish ruffian from New York, being without personal character or standing, was so badly frightened by the suddenness and power of the demonstration, that he was induced with difficulty to summon the *posse comitatis,* the only possible hope for defending the jail or making any face at all to the mob. That measure met with but little obedience, being responded to only by the judges and lawyers, with a half-dozen rogues and gamblers who must have been astonished at finding themselves for the first time in their lives on the side of order, and whose new-born love of law was perhaps stimulated by a shrewd suspicion of the probable action of the Committee toward persons of their own description.

The entire posse, about 100 strong, assembled as directed at the jail where, as their first act, they did me the honor of unanimously electing me their Captain. The county jail stood upon an unexcavated bank of rock on the north side of Broadway above Montgomery, and consisted of two parallel rows of stone cells at right angles to the street with a passage between them, the whole, together with offices and accommodations for the Sheriff's deputies in charge, being enclosed in a large barn-like frame structure. As it was impossible to defend this building successfully by direct musketry fire with the force and means available, I at once began mining the bank which supported it, by drilling vertical holes outside to the level of the street, loading them with gunpowder and leading the separate fuses inside the building, so they could be fired separately and successively as circumstances might require. Loop holes were cut in the wall (of one inch pine boards) over the cells, the arched stone roofs of which served as infantry platforms, on two sides of the building.

The Sheriff, by this time thoroughly cowed, and whose whole study seemed to be how to prevent the posse he had himself summoned, from making a real defense, soon ordered me to cease the preparation of the mines. As it was plain there could be no efficient defense without them, his position disgusted the individuals of the posse, who, though mostly willing and ready to sell their lives if necessary, in defense of the selected stronghold of law and order, were quite unwilling to be brought to ridicule as personal adherents of a cowardly rogue who, as all now believed, was simply posing to cover an intended backdown and surrender. They accordingly left by twos and threes, until on the morning after King's death when the jail was actually invested by an imposing force and about to be summoned, I was the only individual of the posse remaining. The Sheriff having determined—no doubt from the first—to make no real defense, was quick to avail himself of this defection, and directed me also to withdraw, which as a law-abiding man deriving his only authority in the premises from the official himself, I proceeded to do, after requiring a written order to that effect endorsed on the back of my summons. But the jail being then already invested by a large force of infantry and artillery, the high-spirited representative of the law had the impudence to invite me to sneak out by a back exit, which of course I refused to do, and walked out through the large front gate of the place which I insisted should be opened for the purpose.

Broadway itself was then clear, except that a number of guns were already in battery on the opposite sidewalk, the gunners standing by with linstocks lighted, but every adjacent alley and street was occupied by strong infantry columns already in position for assault, when the order should be given and the doors blown in. I was at once arrested by a patrol, and taken to their commander, Doane, who rejoiced in the title of 'Marshal.' I alarmed this doughty individual by telling him with rather strained military license, in reply to his anxious questions, that I had left the jail on business the nature of which I declined to disclose, that it was well held and would be desperately defended by the Sheriff with regular and special deputies. As I was well known, I was then dismissed and conducted through the lines, proceeding to take up a position on Telegraph Hill, from which I could look down into the streets full of troops, and see the entire panorama unroll itself beneath.

Everything being prepared, the jailer was almost immediately summoned, and surrendered ignominiously without a shot, the prisoners who were wanted being forthwith removed to the Committee's stronghold at the other end of town. Outraged as were the friends of order by this successful issue of the revolt, it was supposed the worse was over when Casey and Cora were hung the next morning, and that affairs would gradually become quieted and resume their usual course. Such I had reason to believe was the prevalent expectation with the mob themselves, but their leaders liked the taste of power and began now to play the game for political rewards. The organization was kept up, their strong places retained, arrests and sentences proceeded, obnoxious persons were put to death, banished or immured, the writ of *habeas corpus* was defied, and there seemed a strong probability that the political anarchy reigning unchecked in the City would extend throughout the State. After the dispersion of the posse and capture of the jail, I had become a subaltern in a volunteer company authorized by the Governor, and then being raised by Calhoun Benham, a distinguished lawyer and former officer in the Mexican war. While thus engaged I received a message from the Governor—William Neely Johnson, of Kentucky—desiring me to call on him in Sacramento at the earliest practicable moment, and took the steamer the same evening, reaching the Governor's office the next morning. He stated that excitement and passion were extending through the State, and he deemed the time had come to exert all the force at his disposal to suppress it at the fountain head in San Francisco. That the entire militia force of that city having actually or practically gone over to the enemy with their arms, he considered it imprudent to call out the weak semblance of such organizations from the country, and had no reliable force in view except one company which might be made up in each of the towns of Sacramento and Stockton, and whatever force we might be able to raise in the very presence of the mob at San Francisco. The latter I placed at two full companies at the outside, making the entire available force about 400 men, all first class fighting men, but almost entirely without any weapons but their private small arms.

He stated that negotiations were in progress with the U. S. army and navy authorities who were indisposed to meddle with the difficulty without orders from Washington, which could not be obtained under sixty days, but that he hoped to get arms from Gen. Wool, and sufficient coöperation from the sloop-of-war *John Adams,* Boutwell, commander, then lying in the harbor, to destroy or at least hold in check the Committee's fort at the foot of Sacramento Street. Capt. Sherman although he had recently received and accepted the appointment of Major General of militia of the second, or San Francisco Division, was indisposed to commit himself by positive action in the raising of troops where his name, example and influence could be so useful, and seemed inclined to wait till a sufficient force could be actually raised, armed and put in his hands ready for service. The Governor considered the thing of most immediate importance was to give confidence both to Sherman and the men it was hoped to enlist, by getting actual possession of the arms promised by Gen. Wool. For this purpose he commissioned me his A. D. C. and dismissed me with the following orders:

To return immediately to San Francisco, obtain a small sloop, man her with a few picked men, and conduct her quietly to Wool's headquarters at Benicia, and obtaining there the arms Wool had promised to deliver on the requisitions furnished me, to carry them to the State Penitentiary at San Quentin, whose employees remained faithful, and whence they could be distributed as occasion should permit, or where such men as should be enlisted, might be collected for organization and instruction. The plan was as good a one as the adverse facts permitted, and might have succeeded had Capt. Sherman been at Benicia as the Governor had arranged and expected, to back my demand, and preserve the stiffening in Gen. Wool's fast weakening backbone. I obtained a suitable sloop, with a well-selected and reliable crew of ten men, of whom three were detailed for navigation, while the others were reserved for general purposes. Among the last was John C. Heenan, a fighting blacksmith, the fame of whose subsequent pugilistic struggle with Tom Sayers, as the 'Benicia boy,' afterwards filled the English-speaking world.

Placing the sloop at anchor near the wharf at Benicia, with spring, or shore lines at head and stern, I repaired alone to Wool's office, which I think was in the hotel, where instead of Sherman, weak and irresolute, but friendly, I found active enemies in the persons of Bailie Peyton, and ex-Governor Henry S. Foote, two politicians who belonged to neither side, but being both 'Know Nothing' candidates for U. S. Senator, were desirous of suppressing all side issues, especially the pending one, and ending an excitement which in no case was likely to bring any good to the old school of politicians. But alike all selfish temporizers, their scheme for ending it was by submitting the State and its officers in all essentials to the Committee, with the hope that as a reward for such good behavior by the lawful State authorities, the mob would then be pleased to abdicate, leaving to the intriguants, individually, the real credit of the adjustment, and the dignified position of impartial arbiters friendly to all sides, and elevated above the passions of both. Their present business was therefore to prevent a collision by inducing Wool to withhold the arms he had promised. I succeeded in obtaining a private interview with the General and handed him the Governor's two requisitions, No. 1 for some 120 stand of muskets which were the admitted property of the State, known as her 'quota' of some former distribution by the Federal Government, and No. 2, calling for the loan of 300 additional stand "to suppress an existing armed insurrection." In spite of my request for privacy, Wool could not make up his mind without consulting his mentors, who of course warmly opposed the grant. After much discussion the matter finally took the shape of an open argument before him, between myself, without the promised Sherman to back me, and the two politicians; in which the above theory of motives was alluded to, and considerable warm language occurred all round. Wool was a long time for refusing altogether, but finally, under determined pressure, agreed to grant No. 1, and refuse No. 2. A hostile crowd was already collecting in the streets (Peyton and Foote having made the matter public) and I demanded that the boxes should be placed in the large warehouse at the end of the wharf subject to my order, which was done.

When assured they were actually in the warehouse, I walked out on the wharf, making my way through the crowd without actual molestation, and ordered the sloop hauled in alongside. Then out sprang my seven general utility men prepared for war, great or small, without counting numbers. The wharf was a long structure (several hundred, perhaps a thousand, feet long) with an offset at the end, the whole standing over the water on piles, the warehouse, a very large frame building of one story, being located in the angle facing the offset. The crowd being without plan or leaders, was soon pushed back to, and held upon the main wharf, when I presented my order to the warehouseman and demanded the boxes, which were refused by the person in charge, who had locked up the warehouse with his employees inside. As the crowd was rapidly increasing and fast approaching the fighting point, I backed the functionary against the door, and producing my watch, gave him two minutes for compliance, promising at the end of that grace to set fire to the warehouse, open fire on the mob, and remove the arms in the confusion, making sure of him as the first victim whatever the issue. The *argumentum ad hominem* prevailed, the doors were opened, and his own employees compelled to truck the boxes to the sloop where they were quickly secured by the crew, the other men being ordered to fall slowly back with face to the foe. When I jumped aboard, the last man, the jib was already hoisted and the vessel several feet from the wharf.

The wharf was by this time crowded to the edge, but as the little craft paid off, and her crew bent on to the main halyard, I informed the mob that if a single shot was fired, I would let go the anchor, and from that inaccessible position sweep the wharf as long as a man remained on it. The language received in reply was not complimentary, the mob no doubt feeling like the boy at school, who, when well whipped by his comrade, remarked that if he could not lick him he could, at all events, 'make mouths at his sister;' but we had secured what we came for, and after getting myself landed at a point below from which I could catch the steamer, the sloop proceeded on her way to San Quentin. It was not till the following morning that I learned in San Francisco, that the Committee, doubtless kept well informed by Peyton and Foote, had sent four well-manned steamers to cruise for the little craft, by one of which she was overhauled and captured during the night with all her crew and cargo.

Thus ended the only earnest attempt by the State authorities to suppress the San Francisco mob by force of arms. On account of the great disparity of numbers concerned, the total want of arms, the sympathy for the mob extensively prevalent all over the State, and the weakness displayed by prominent men in the Federal, State and City service, its chance of success was always desperate, but might have succeeded if all the men in office had displayed fidelity and vigor equal to that exerted by many persons upon whom the State possessed no more claim than on any simple citizen. Even Sherman, though free in his criticism and ridicule of many prominent persons anxious for action, admits the deception and perfidy of Wool; but it was the opinion of many that his strictures upon the Governor, the Chief Justice and other officials and private persons who were ready to risk all in the cause of order, offer a very indifferent explanation of the supineness, inaction, and excessive caution of the Major General of State Militia in the menaced Division.

The Vigilance Committee continued to be run as a political machine, rapidly degenerating into a scramble of the noisiest and greediest for public office; but its subsequent career belongs rather to the history of the State than to these personal recollections. My professional partnership was soon after dissolved, Baker acquiring a residence in Oregon prior to his canvass of that newly admitted State for the U. S. Senate, while I removed to another office in Halleck's Building, and continued to practice, in connection, though not in partnership, with Judge R. A. Thompson and Henry P. Irving, both formerly of Virginia. Though many of my clients were officials of, or active sympathizers with the Committee, I do not know that I was materially injured in business by my active participation with the losing side, and at all events, have never regretted my course. Few will deny that, whether ever justifiable or not, it is an extremely serious thing for any organized community to throw over the orderly methods slowly and painfully developed through a thousand years of civilization, in the effort to rectify by violence the inefficiency or corruption of officials of its own choice, who can in our country always be changed with but little delay by safe and legal methods devised expressly for the purpose; and I know of nothing in the history or achievements of the celebrated San Francisco mob of 1856 to weaken the force of this reflection, or make me regret, in any respect, the course I deemed it right to take.

It is a trite saying that adversity is easier borne by many than prosperity, and it is certain that in my case the desire to visit again the friends and scenes of early life, which had not particularly oppressed me during the first years of absence, grew strong with returning prosperity, and in the comfortable circumstances in which I found myself in 1857 could no longer be resisted. I now possessed a personal clientage including several foreign bankers and merchants which insured a large and growing practice, and had not only paid off my debts incurred in the cause of agriculture, but already derived a substantial income from investments successfully made. The voice of prudence therefore whispered the homely maxim to 'let well enough alone,' yet those who have been tried in the same way will readily understand the strength and persistency of the wish to spend at least one holiday season at home, before definitely abandoning it forever. Yielding at length to that irresistible longing, as well as the urgency of friends at home, I began early in 1857 to set my house in order for a six months' absence. My valued and faithful friends, H. P. Irving and B. T. Pate, both from Virginia, agreed to keep my practice together as well as practicable, and were duly made acquainted with my clients, while another friend, A. C. Whitcomb, of New Hampshire, an able and successful lawyer, eminent as well for practical business qualities, undertook charge of my property, converted as far as possible into short-term mortgages or short interest-bearing bills with collateral.

I purchased a ticket by the steamer to sail on September 1st, but being unexpectedly detained, sold it at a small loss, and took another for the 5th, a disappointment which though impatiently anathematized at the time, undoubtedly saved my life, as the steamer of the 1st connected at the Isthmus with the ill-fated *Central America,* for New York, which foundered suddenly in the Atlantic off Hatteras, and sunk with a million and a half of treasure, and over six hundred passengers. Of some seven hundred of the crew and passengers only twenty or thirty individuals, after clinging to doors, skylights, chairs and hatchcovers all night, were picked up by a Norwegian bark next day and carried safely into some southern port.

There existed in San Francisco at that time an evil practice of blackmailing departing passengers in the following rascally manner: An action would be brought and process served late in the evening before steamer day, followed by arrest on the steamer just before sailing next morning, on a judge's order based on affidavits of the defendant's approaching departure from the jurisdiction. No matter how baseless the claim, anything was enough to support the initial proceeding and hold the defendant until the steamer had sailed, unless he proved squeezable. The plaintiff of course was always irresponsible for any damages that might subsequently be recovered, and most persons of substance who had spent many months in preparing for an absence calculated to terminate at a certain time, would rather pay cash for any reasonable compromise than break up all their plans, and sacrifice the long-expected visit home. This was the game tried on me. Late on the evening of the 4th, I was duly served with a writ of the 12th District Court, at suit of a former clerk of the Superior Court, claiming a considerable amount for old court fees charged against my former partner before I was connected with him or had even been admitted to practice. Of course I knew there would be an order of arrest to be executed on the steamer just before sailing, when I would be surrounded by friends taking leave, and I was sitting in the office considering whether I should abandon my project and lose another ticket, or make the best terms I could get, when Judge Norton of the 12th District Court called to take his leave and wish me a pleasant voyage. Norton was a man of conceded ability and spotless character. Though an elderly bachelor with many of the peculiarities popularly attributed to that excellent class of men, he was clear-headed, vigorous and fearless, and knew me well, having served with me in the posse summoned in 1856 to defend the jail. His manner both on and off the bench was full of dignity, his professional attainments commanded the highest respect of both bar and public, and I would no more have entertained the idea of myself inviting his attention to the scrape I was in by virtue of a writ from his own court, than I would have ventured to propose setting fire to the Court House. His speech in conversation was as peculiar as his manner, consisting of slowly ejaculated sentences with all superfluous words omitted, usually leaving the beginning and end of his crisp sentences to be supplied by the interlocutor.

At the time of his visit I was alone, and his first act after a mutual greeting, was to seat himself in the most remote chair in the room, and conceal the real and kindly interest which had prompted the visit by the cold and indifferent manner which no one believed in, but which it was his custom to assume. The first part of the conversation was something like this: "Going away tomorrow, eh?" "Yes, Judge, I have got all ready to go and fully expected it, till within a few minutes." "H—m, what's the matter?" "Well, that rascal McM. has been using your court to play the usual game on me." "Game, eh, what sort of game?" "Well he has sued me as Baker's partner for some old claims against Baker before I was connected with him, and I suppose of course he will get an order of arrest and blackmail me on the steamer, tomorrow." "H—m, in my court eh?" "Yes." "H—m, order of arrest, eh? Order of arrest—very serious thing. Must be based on sufficient affidavits. Must be full enough to justify such extreme rigor. Such affidavits if sufficient should take a long time to read and consider. H—m, what time does steamer sail?" "At 9 A.M." "H—m, I get up at 8, and am a slow reader—never act hastily. If my opinion is worth anything, I think you will get off."

What happened at his Honor's chambers next morning I do not know, but I heard no more of the claim. I wrote to Whitcomb to defend the suit for me, but it was never pressed after the blackmailing scheme failed, and was ultimately struck from the docket on motion of my attorney. Before proceeding on my voyage I cannot help relating an Irishman's expedient for disposing of the same difficulty. Prior to Norton's visit, my friend Reilly, a rollicking and joyous young Irishman who was a deputy clerk in Norton's Court and a great admirer and friend of mine, had called on the same melancholy errand of bidding goodbye. To him I had imparted my difficulty without reserve, and of course received his warmest sympathy. He studied over it a moment and shouted—"No he won't arrest you; bejavers I'll go right off now and stale the sale of the Coort, and carry it in me pocket till the stamer's gone and you wid it." "Thank you kindly R., for your good intentions, but unfortunately the order of arrest is a judge's order, and does not require the seal." That non-plussed poor R. whose remedies were now exhausted, but who would have needed little encouragement to 'stale' the judge himself, if required to make good his ideas of friendship to those he loved.

As I write these last words of San Francisco, memory seems to renew with life and feeling the painful wrench with which I severed myself from it so many years ago, and which would have been little short of agonizing, had I then known I was to see it and its warm hearts no more. I am thankful to Heaven that throughout life I have at every place and period found friends to admire and to love; but alas, one must admit how rare and hard it is to replace those first early friendships of hot and enthusiastic youth, far away among different scenes and in later life. Memory still goes back to them as the first and best, and persists in according to them all ideal, as well as actual qualities. Many a face I have not beheld for forty years and can never see again, comes back to my recollection as it dwells on those days of long ago. Feasts and frays, friendship and duels, professional struggles and political broils, with every kind of incident peculiar to that delightful life where we slept in our offices, devoting our days to work, and our evenings to study and discussion—rise to mind even at this remote day when, in the nature of things, there can remain such a limited number of survivors. There were then few families in the place, and little of that element of social life that in normal communities constitutes so large a part of our daily interests and affections. Our one daily social event was an elaborate dinner at a certain French restaurant where a few of us always met at six in the evening, rarely separating before eight. In what then existed of domestic as well as men's society there was a decided southern preponderance, and nearly all my intimates were young lawyers from Virginia and other southern States, most of whom in due time came home at the summons of war, and almost to a man met a soldier's fate in the Confederate Army. Nearly every great battle of the war claimed some of them. Many rose to positions of military responsibility and distinction before finding their fatal day, and as far as I have been able to learn, none were parsimonious of their blood, or ever failed in a soldier's duty.

> There's many a lad I knew that's dead
> And many a lass grown old,
> And as the lesson strikes my head
> My weary heart grows cold.

It was early on Sept. 5th, 1857, that I took what turned out to be my last look at San Francisco, as I rattled down Broadway in a cab and stepped on board the steamer, which, unless memory deceives me, was the old *California*, the first put on the line. Every berth was occupied, and the lively party that had assembled to see us off crowded the vessel and all neighboring standing ground. But the decks were at last cleared, the lines let go, and the steamer after slowly traversing the city front, doubled the noble promontory of Telegraph Hill, and pointing her head past Fort Point to the open sea, fairly started on her long voyage of 3500 miles to Panama. Senators, M. Cs., and other dignitaries were plenty on board, and certainly a livelier or more cheerful party was never assembled than that rollicking crowd, mostly young, generally successful, and all stirred with joyous excitement at the prospect of soon seeing the homes from which most of us had been separated for years. We carried a brilliant full moon down the Mexican and Central American coasts, keeping in full view of the land, its bold shores and volcanic peaks, touched briefly at Acapulco, and reached Panama in nineteen days. We landed this time at the new town some distance below the scene of my former adventures, and found the railroad now in operation 47 miles, to Chagres. Debarking, railroading and re-embarking, occupied another day, and ten days more, including a touch at old Providence and another at Havana, brought us into New York harbor at 4 A.M., October 5th, which unfortunately for my impatience, was Sunday when no cars then ran. Having lost my only hat at sea, my astonishment was great when I learned that unlike the customs of San Francisco, every New York shop was closed, and it was with great difficulty and the special guardianship of a hotel waiter, that I was at last able to penetrate a hatter's shop by a back way. At that time while there were some church-goers in San Francisco who gave themselves a holiday on Sunday, most of us knew little or nothing of them and their ways, and steady unchanging work was the habit of most, nearly everyone being found at all times in their respective places of business. I fancy a mutual influence has been exerted since then, and both cities have moved toward a certain uniformity on a middle ground.

Of course before we were fairly in the harbor we were shocked by hearing from the pilot the loss of the *Central America,* whose San Francisco cabin passengers must be well known to us though their names were not yet published. As it was then impossible to get off for Philadelphia till some time after the magic hour of twelve on Sunday night, I bethought myself of the residence on Staten Island of my mother's oldest brother, Samuel T. Jones, a merchant of New York, and set out to find him. Walking up a long hill on the Island I noticed two elderly gentlemen conversing outside the door of a small church which they were apparently about to enter, and took the opportunity to inquire further respecting my route. One of them asked if the California steamer was in, to which of course I replied in the affirmative. "Oh no," said the other, "I think there must be a mistake; I have been watching the narrows all the morning from my house and have seen no signs of her." "That," said I, "is perhaps because you did not get up early enough. She came in at 4 this morning, to my certain knowledge, for I was on board of her." "Heavens!" said number one, "You were on board? Do you know my son, Samuel Ward, of San Francisco?" "Very well." "Was he on board?" "No, sir." "Ah," said he tossing up his arms, "it is then as I feared it; he was on the *Central America!*" "No he was not, for I distinctly recollect seeing him in San Francisco after her passengers sailed on September 1st.'' Thus I was enabled at a chance roadside rencontre to carry consolation to a father's heart, pending the weeks which must elapse before he could obtain more direct information.

It is hardly necessary to state that I arrived in Philadelphia by the earliest Monday train and found my father's family still living at 'Hilton,' their country seat, from which it was not the custom to remove into town till about the middle of November. Sisters grown up and married since my absence, and other relatives congregated there made it a gay autumn for one who had seen nothing of domestic life for so many years. My eyes so long accustomed to the bare yellow hills of California, or the pine clad ridges of its Sierras capped with white, revelled in the lovely undulating hills and valleys of the Colonial States, robed in the gorgeous coloring of the declining year. The green fields, the comfortable and finished homes, the domestic-looking farm houses, the abundance of the fairer sex, the enclosed pastures and well-made roads, the comparatively old and substantial appearance of everything— all these things recalled early memories till now forgotten or obscured, and, backed by the solicitations of all I met, began to shake the allegiance to my adopted land. I had brought with me from California two of the great land cases arising from the yet unsettled Mexican grants, which had been entrusted to me for argument in the Supreme Court of the United States, and naturally sought acquaintance with the professional men of my native city. These, on the whole, encouraged me to think that a legal practice might be slowly obtained, while on the other hand expenses seemed almost trifling, measured by California standards. I could get offices for less annual rent than I paid per month in San Francisco. Books, clothes, board, amusements, everything was at least one-half. Gradually shaken, but not yet fully persuaded, I hired desk room from a lawyer in good practice who possessed a fine library, put up my shingle, and went to work preparing my cases. After a few months I possessed half a dozen local cases of my own, of no great magnitude, to be sure, but full of encouragement, and in short, found myself earning a living before I expected it. Another circumstance influencing me toward a new settlement at home arose from the condition of the commercial panic prevailing on my arrival, and the advantage I was able to draw from it. Gold having mounted to a premium of about twenty per cent, I instructed my San Francisco agent to realize as rapidly as possible and ship the proceeds in gold coin by steamer, with insurance. In anticipation of its arrival I sold for gold in California exchange on New York, payable of course in funds bankable at the place of payment, and as the gold premium disappeared, purchased at somewhere between seventy and eighty per cent, the California State 7 per cent bonds of which the $4,000,000 issued and pronounced illegal, null and void by the Supreme Court, had just been validated by a statute submitted to and ratified by the popular vote. As the facts became known and the credit of the State restored, I resold these bonds in New York at par, and thus in one way and another had transferred to the east a considerable part of my modest and materially augmented effects.

I finally took an office of my own in 1858 at No. 233 South 5th Street, a locality then much affected by lawyers, but long since given up to other purposes. I received two other California land cases from lawyers of my acquaintance who could not themselves conveniently travel sixty days to watch and argue them at Washington, and was also much employed by California lawyers in hunting up and examining testimony from long-lost Alcaldes and other witnesses in similar cases, now residing at various places in the Atlantic States. I was admitted to practice in the Supreme Court of Pennsylvania on January 4, 1858, and took the opportunity of attending the lectures of the Law Department of the University, then delivered by Professors Sharswood, McCall and Miller. What is called in fashionable jargon, 'society,' of course possessed lively attractions for one who knew as little of it as I did, and as I was fortunate in finding relations and friends who kindly communicated as much of their higher social civilization as I was able to absorb, began to hope that I might not have passed entirely beyond the age of improvement.

With all the new distractions and amusements to which I had hitherto been a stranger, I cannot say I worked very hard, but then I found myself in a country where no one worked very hard, according to California standards. I met some California friends by arrangement at the Virginia Springs, where I spent most of the summer of 1858, and worked at the law the following winter, but toward spring when the entire country became excited over the discoveries of gold at Pike's Peak in the present state of Colorado, it is hardly to be wondered at that I was not one of the last to become infected with the prevailing spirit of enterprise and adventure.

CHAPTER XVII

A WESTERN TRIP. OUTBREAK OF THE WAR

As a trip to the new El Dorado seemed easily within the compass of a summer's journey, for the exigencies of which I felt at no loss to prepare, I resolved to go, and bearing in mind the early wants in the mining region of the Pacific Coast, I could think of nothing better to take with me than such simple machinery as is the first needed under such circumstances. I therefore repaired to Salem, Ohio, where I contracted for some simple-planned direct action portable steam engines, and a sawmill or two, adapted either for steam or water power.

When these were completed I shipped them to Chicago, and thence to St. Joseph, Mo., via the Hannibal & St. Joseph R. R., just opened for traffic. At St. Joe and vicinity I purchased wagons and ox teams, and after some delay and difficulty in getting the freight delivered, inventoried and loaded, at last got away and after crossing the river by ferry and doubling teams through the wide and muddy Missouri bottoms, launched forth upon the familiar plains. The prairie roads, though of course better marked and more traveled, were very much as we had found them ten years before, the wagon trail leading over a succession of undulations very slippery and difficult when it rained, as it usually did at that season, and nearly always separated by small runlets, degenerated at the crossings into such unspeakable mud-holes as must be seen to be appreciated. This time I had undertaken to haul heavy freight, instead of mere food and traveler's baggage, but on the other hand had known pretty well from former experience how to equip for it. Though 3000 to 4000 pounds was the usual weight in the wagons, we had six to eight yoke of good cattle in each team, well-selected teamsters and a portable forge, and mechanics always at hand to repair damages. There was now no trouble from Indians, and besides the large emigrant trains, hundreds of single wagons with 'Pike's Peak or bust,' or some similar legend displayed on the covers, lined pretty much the entire 600 miles of road. From some point on the South Platte I rode ahead alone in perfect security, turning in with some emigrant train every night, and made my solitary bivouac on the flats of Cherry Creek not far from where the fine cut stone Union Depot of Denver now stands.

The more vigorous of the emigrants were scattering out into the mountains with their teams; and the present site of the city, or at least the lower part of it down on the flats, contained a residuum of the unfortunate, the sick, idle and lazy, many of whom were anxious to sell their cattle at any price to get money enough for a return passage by the stage-line, recently established. I soon saw that I had brought machinery to that population about a year too soon. No doubt there would be demand enough in time, but affairs absolutely required my presence in Philadelphia, the coming winter and I concluded to sell for what I could get, no matter at what loss, and use the proceeds as well as some bank drafts which I had brought with me, to purchase emigrant cattle. This happy thought repaid all my losses and ultimately yielded large profit. I bought the cattle for from $10 to $15 a yoke, choosing those least run down, as far as practicable, and retaining one wagon, hired returning adventurers at low wages, and started back driving very slowly and carefully, selecting each camping-ground, frequently several days in advance. On this trip we saw no buffalo, though passing over ground which ten years previously had been darkened as far as the eye could reach, with their far-spreading masses. Now, not even a single one came in sight of the road. The deer and elk hunting in the Platte bluffs, was however about as good as in 1849, and these animals with antelope, and nearer the settlements, turkey and grouse, kept the camp pretty well supplied with meat. On many days the cattle were not moved more than a mile or two, and as much time was afforded for hunting and fishing as though it was merely a sporting trip.

At the crossing of one of the Blues, we met a drove of brood mares and well-bred cows on their long road to California, and our mutual surprise may be imagined when I recognized in the owner one Graves, a client of mine in California, whose unfinished affairs I had, with his consent, left in the hands of my friends Irving and Pate. Leaving our several droves to go on their respective ways, he and I at once bivouacked, and had a long and interesting discussion respecting his law interests in California as well as on the new state of affairs in which each had found the other.

Striking the river where the town of Atchison had not long since been started, we turned up the Missouri, which was crossed at St. Joe, and passing leisurely through the northern tier of Missouri counties, entered Iowa not far from the middle of its southern boundary-line and laid our course due east to strike the settlements which then had their western limit at and near the village of Bloomfield. In crossing one of the branches of Grand River, in Missouri, coming in from a hunting-trip a day or two in rear of the drove, I noticed a singular phenomenon. The stream was about twenty yards wide, flowing through a finely timbered bottom, the water very low and muddy, and large numbers of some predaceous fish— probably some kind of pike—were darting in every direction, showing their large black dorsal fins above the surface. Unfortunately I had no means with me of catching any, but the question did not fail to occur, if pike existed in such great numbers, how much vaster must be the multitudes on which they fed? I have never been able to get any solution of the mystery.

In Iowa, some miles before arriving at the settlements, I was witness of a curious and entertaining horse-fight. Among our herding horses was a small but fiery and spirited stallion from the Lipan Indians, much affected for my own riding. He was not over 14 hands, but was fat and saucy and had spirit enough for a herd. Having turned him out late one evening, he failed to find our mañada, which was driven in without him in the morning, and I started out to hunt him. I had walked several miles, having got on numerous wrong trails, through a fine undulating country, when I heard some peculiar noises over the top of the next hill. Creeping carefully up, I looked over the summit and saw perhaps fifteen or twenty mares and geldings evidently belonging to the

settlements now not very distant, standing in a circle facing
outwards. Within the circle, ranged about my Lipan pony in a
terrible rage, attacking first at one and then at another point,
and occasionally getting in his heels with a resounding thwack
that might be heard for a mile. Bites, kicks and squeals flew
around at large, but though surrounded by such superior
force, the Lipan was too quick for them, and made his heels
count every time, scarcely getting a scratch in return. As
my side was not suffering any damage, I watched this unfair
combat for a long time, enjoying the little fellow's game and
prowess but finally put in an appearance, at which the strangers
galloped off, while the pony, though usually wild and hard to
catch, came trotting up with triumphant neighs, showing
plainly enough notwithstanding his gallant and successful defence, how glad he was to find an admiring and sympathizing
friend.

I spent the remainder of the summer and fall in the vicinity
of Bloomfield, east of which place the country was considerably
obstructed by settlers and fences. I had there a terrible
attack of ague from which I recovered in due time by the aid
of such quack medicines as could be obtained, there being no
doctor nor quinine to be had. When not enjoying a fever or
a shake, I occupied myself in selling fat cattle to the Chicago
drovers who heard of me at Burlington, and in scouring the
settled districts to purchase small bunches of cattle and single
steers from the farmers. This business required the handling
of considerable sums of money, which, as there were no banks,
I was obliged to carry on my person. I soon became known
about the country, as well as this habit of possessing cash, and
this notoriety led to what I have always thought a deliberate
and well planned but badly executed attempt at robbery. It
was already dark one evening when, after a forty-mile ride,
I reached a cross-roads rejoicing in the name of Pulaski, in the
middle of a boundless prairie. It boasted of only one house,
a small log cabin with a loft over and a small kitchen annexed,
and a log stable adjacent, with door and padlock. I locked
up my horse, offered the key to the landlord, but on his invitation retained it, and carrying with me a valuable silver-
mounted Mexican saddle, entered the house, where I found

two foot-travelers of not very prepossessing appearance, who were apparently acquainted with the landlord and pretended to be traveling in search of land, to locate. The cabin consisted of one low room about twelve by eighteen feet, with a ladder in one corner, by which the loft was entered through a small square hole in one corner of the planked ceiling. In the other three corners of the loft, which was about three feet high at the eaves and not over seven at the ridge, were as many beds, made by nailing barrel staves on poles suitably arranged. I placed my saddle and blankets on the one nearest the trap-door, and proceeded to eat supper and smoke a pipe, after which I went up the ladder to bed, the other two corners being already occupied by the strangers, while the landlord and his wife slept down stairs. My money which was in large rolls of wildcat bank-bills of the country, being mostly stored about my coat and trousers, I rolled up those garments and placed them under my head after spreading my blankets and blowing out the light, carefully adjusting my belt with knife and large Colt's revolver, ready at hand.

As the only opening in the loft besides the trap in the floor was a small hole cut in the gable, not over sixteen inches square, the place was so dark that literally one could not see one's hand or any other object. Knowing there was no other house within many miles, and not liking the looks of the strangers, nor knowing how they were armed, I felt somewhat nervous respecting the unusually large quantity of money which happened to be then in my possession, and slept with one eye open. It was not very long till I was waked from a light doze by hearing one of the strangers rise and fumble surreptitiously about his bed, as though cautiously putting on some clothes. Cocking my pistol quietly under the blanket I crowded silently as possible against the wall under the eaves, so as to avoid being disabled by a single blow, and waited. Presently I could hear but not see, my friend walk cautiously over the floor to my vicinity, whence after standing a few minutes, he silently retired again to his own corner, perhaps discouraged by my absolute silence while listening so intently. Wishing to bring the adventure to an end of some sort, I therefore used all my ingenuity to counterfeit heavy breathing, in fact almost a snore, and this, as I expected, soon encouraged my *vis a vis* to another effort. After some low whispering, I again heard him approach with great caution, and redoubled my efforts at plausible snoring, for I had so arranged myself that his first blow would fall upon the empty bed, when I intended to rush on him, and the instant I could feel him with one hand, kill him with the other. Either my counterfeit snoring was so bad, or his caution was so great, that he remained for some minutes standing close to me in perfect silence, and as I found it difficult to snore and listen simultaneously, I resolved to have an end of the affair. Keeping him covered therefore, as nearly as I could judge in the darkness, I said, ''I have got you covered and if you budge you are a dead man. What do you want?'' ''I want to go downstairs.'' ''Well then, go, right off. Don't stop a minute or I'll fire.'' When he had gone I drove the other one out, piled both their beds over the trap, and listened at the outside opening for any signs of an attack on my horse. As none came, and both fellows had left the house, I placed my bed also over the trap, fixed a tell-tale in the window opening, and being very tired, proceeded to sleep the sleep of the just.

About daybreak the landlord called me, and complained he had been robbed. Fully supposing he was in league with the others, I gave him a short answer, and told him I was getting ready to settle with him and wanted my breakfast right away. However with the aid of his wife, he soon satisfied me that the two men were entire strangers to him, though they had described and spoken about me before my arrival, and he supposed we belonged together. It seemed that after failing in their attempt, they had stolen the poor woman's watch and a small sum that was on the shelf down stairs, and cleared out. They had—as appeared by their tracks—examined the stable and concluded not to break it, which was well for them, as it was commanded from my window. A few yards farther they had sat down and put on their boots and then turned into the prairie, where they had very probably concealed their horses, and where as soon as the sun rose high enough to dry the dew, their track was lost among the hundreds of cattle-trails parting the high grass in every direction. As after that it was impossible to follow their trail I was obliged to abandon my late landlord to his own devices, promising, however, to make the facts known, as I should reach other settlements in the course of my travels, which I faithfully did, but never heard any more of the affair.

As soon as the first severe frost of autumn struck and killed the prairie grass, having got the cattle gathered well in hand, they were rushed down about a hundred miles to Burlington, in four parcels, fording the Des Moines River which was low, without difficulty. At Burlington I was obliged to hire pasture on the meadows of cultivated grasses which there abounded, and which are not injured immediately by frost, like the natural grass of the prairie. The cattle had to be railed from Burlington to Chicago in lots, as cattle-cars could be procured and made up into trains, the first lots being consigned to persons in Chicago whom I only knew by name. As I dared not leave Burlington till they were all at or fairly on the road to Chicago, the process of shipping, or rather of getting cars, involved delay and exasperation which had almost reached the limit of endurance, when at last I got away with the last lot about midnight, one rainy and stormy night. At Chicago I found all the cattle safe at the old stock-yards of that period, which I have in more recent years vainly tried to locate, even with the aid of some of the oldest residents. To the best of my belief, they were not far from West Madison Street, but a short distance west of the river, a place which is now the heart of the city, and I today possess both stores and populous flats of my own, at least two miles farther west, these localities being at that time open prairie. As the lot of cattle was large and important for that day, all the brokers, dealers, packers and loafers of the place had been busying themselves over it, the result of which was, I had immediate offers with healthy competition, and though general prices were low, and the cattle only grass fed, including a number that had resisted all attempts to ameliorate their condition and would require stall feeding, I closed out the last of the lot within three days, at prices which much more than doubled—I am not sure but they trebled—my investment, with all attendant expenses. Had I driven the cattle to the lower part of Illinois, bought standing corn and fed them through the winter, shipping to

New York in the spring, I should have again doubled the profits. The method of doing this at that time, was to purchase a few hundred acres of standing corn—which few in those parts then thought of husking for market—divide it by cross fences into suitable enclosures and admit the cattle to them successively, at the same time purchasing store hogs to fatten on their waste and leavings.

Western money at that time consisted of the torn, disfigured and greasy notes of an infinite number of 'Wildcat' banks, many of them insolvent, and none negotiable at any distance from the place of issue, which often appeared on no map. I therefore considered it prudent to buy exchange on New York, which to the best of my recollection, cost five per cent. And yet the West contains today a new generation of idiots who wish to abolish the existing National Bank system which has, at no appreciable expense to the public, supplied a perfectly safe currency that has invariably stood at par from one ocean to the other! Of what is not ignorance and folly capable in public affairs, of which according to our political institutions and theories one man is as good a judge as another, or as the Irish enthusiast for equality remarked, 'a d—d sight better.'

During the journey from Chicago to Philadelphia which then occupied several days, the newspapers were filled with accounts of the attack by the mischievous lunatic, John Brown, on the State of Virginia to free her negroes forcibly from slavery. That fanatical enthusiast had formed so adequate a conception of the magnitude of his enterprise, that he undertook it with a force of about twenty men, of whom a third were negroes; his military stores consisting of a lot of Connecticut-made pikes to arm the expected negro recruits, of whom, however, not one came to his aid. This futile attempt to inaugurate, with the instigation and backing of many persons in New England otherwise intelligent, a servile insurrection with its attendant horrors, while it may have served to demonstrate the absurd ideas of southern social affairs entertained in remote northern communities, ended in nothing except the execution of Brown, and as many of his followers as could be caught by due process of Virginia law. Except so far as it tended to impair the fraternal relations of the States, it did not perhaps even hasten the impending civil war, though it has made Brown—like Herostratus—notorious in biographical dictionaries, a punishment by no means undeserved.

After a long and hotly contested canvass in Oregon, my old friend and partner, Colonel Baker, was elected U. S. Senator from that State, and took his seat in March, 1861. Notwithstanding the divergence of our political views, I had gratified my personal feelings by writing of him extensively in eastern journals, and he came by no means as a stranger to the people of the Atlantic States. He was not long in the Senate before one or two great political orations placed him at the head of the speakers of that body, and established throughout the country his fame as the leading orator of the new party, now successful for the first time in the elections of 1860, and just entering on a long career of power. He had been intimately acquainted in Illinois for many years with Lincoln, the new President, both at the bar and in political life, a circumstance not without its influence in his approach to the high public position he was about to take in the councils of the dominant party. But before he took his seat in the Senate, at his request I spent some days with him in Washington, and mixing but little with politicians myself, was not a little dismayed to learn the very serious views he entertained of the situation. It was an ominous fact that he, coming fresh from a popular canvass, already regarded civil war as certain, and was ready to advise me to abandon the law and study military tactics and campaigns.

Long and intimately as I had known him, I now learned, or at least realized, for the first time that this western lawyer who despised muncipal law as a mere breadwinner's science, but was familiar with the biography and speeches of all the great orators of his own tongue, and held stored in his memory entire volumes of English classical poetry, was none the less versed in the marches, campaigns and battles of the great historic soldiers of ancient and modern times. I have no intention of entering here upon any history of war, politics, or any other topic of public affairs beyond the mere incidents inseparably interwoven with my own personal recollections. The public events of the times have been narrated and discussed in a thousand volumes written on both sides, and from every point of view. But to make intelligible the divergence of our views, some brief explanation of our different standpoints may deserve a place here. Baker believing—or thinking he believed—in all the American theories of the infinite wisdom of ignorant individuals however mercenary and degraded, provided only they are collected in noisy masses to vote, was a politician by instinct and temperament, and on the death of the Whig party had naturally drifted to the Republican, its pretended heir and administrator. On the other hand I, while never much interested in political affairs beyond the local squabbles of California, and believing nothing of the mathematical absurdity of a thousand fools when collected in a mob emitting all wisdom, learning and judgment, had been led from the Whig to the Democratic party, principally by the simplicity and attractiveness of a few leading principles, among which may be briefly mentioned the following:

The original and unimpaired sovereignty of the States in all matters not granted by them to the federal government of their own creation.

The limitation of federal powers to those enumerated in the Constitution, the only law for its own construction.

Freedom of the individual in trade as in all things, as far as consistent with public order and the necessity for public revenue.

A sound currency everywhere convertible at par into the one recognized medium of the world.

These principles comprised most of my political creed then as they do now, and I had given little attention to the noisy excitement of the day, taking for granted the row would get itself peacefully settled in some way, as so many teapot tempests had done before. Baker's acceptance of the certainty of war at or immediately after Lincoln's accession, was therefore not a little startling, especially in view of his familiarity with political topics and his intimacy with the coming Republican leaders. After the new Administration took office on March 4th, being again in Washington about some business in the Supreme Court, I found Baker's views had evidently gained ground, particularly among extremists on both sides who, wide as the poles asunder on other questions, agreed in the expectation of, if not the avowed wish for, war. Baker, though no extremist himself, had many Republican friends who well deserved the title, and made no concealment of their wish, while personal friends of my own on the other side, seemed to my provincial apprehension, equally belligerent. Dining with one of these, I met Gov. Lane, the unsuccessful candidate for Vice President; L. Q. Washington, afterwards Assistant Secretary of State to the Confederacy; Boyce and Bonham, South Carolina M. Cs. and other southern Senators and Representatives, and though looked on as southern, or at least friendly in sympathy, found myself practically alone in my aversion to war and to the speeches and acts of hot-heads on both sides, which, if not repressed, could lead to no other result.

In Philadelphia one naturally heard less of the violence of the political ebulition, and immersed in my own increasing affairs, and unable to realize the imminence of the stupendous reality of civil war, I was still fatuously hoping the politicians might get their differences adjusted, when suddenly upon me and other millions of blind and infatuate optimists, burst like a shaking of the solid earth beneath us, the portentous fact of the bombardment of Fort Sumter. Though the event followed logically enough the declarations and preparations openly made by both northern and southern leaders, the general public were so accustomed to political bluster that they were taken absolutely by surprise, quickly followed by intense indignation, directed naturally enough at the authors of the first overt act. The President, either not himself at once perceiving the magnitude of the impending struggle, or with the keen instincts of a practical politician, willing to let it dawn gradually on popular apprehension, contented himself at first with calling on the States for the insignificant force of 75,000 men, of which the quota of Pennsylvania was forthwith ordered out by the Governor from the State Militia. On Major-General George Cadwalader devolved the duty of reorganizing, mustering and preparing for the field the Philadelphia Division, and I at once received from him an invitation to assist in the capacity of aide-de-camp on his personal staff.

Having till now failed adequately to realize the situation, I was unprepared with a definite course for this sudden emergency, and having but a single night to consider a reply which must probably govern my future acts, I passed the whole of it in close mental struggle in the effort to reach a right conclusion. Of course there are those who never having had any difficult or complicated decision to make, expect all men to be forever cocked, primed and ready for any mental emergency however sudden; and I have been accused by newspaper patriots, blissfully ignorant of all sides but their own, of being at first in doubt which side to espouse. Whether, if true, that be an opprobrium or only a proof of thoughtful and intelligent rectitude of purpose, I have always chosen and still choose to leave for others to decide. My State was about to take one side, and all my personal friends, or most of them, the other. My oldest and best friends were southern men counting me as one of themselves, and sure to be in service on that side. They had so surely counted on their old associate that they had even provided me a place, and offered me rank in their army. The course long pursued by roguish politicians, who to gratify ignorant fanaticism and class jealousies, or to win political capital for themselves, had systematically insulted the South, trampled on its constitutional rights, excluded its property from the common territory, and nullified the constitutional compact respecting fugitive slaves, was not a character to win one's mind from these considerations.

On the other hand, crimination and discussion were over and useless; war was commenced, and my native State had called out her strength for defense. I could not, and ought not to evade the struggle. In the prime of youth and vigor, I surely owed a duty somewhere. To whom? Not to the Federal Government whose partisan usurpations and sectional mismanagement had goaded on resistance. Still less to the South, where my only tie was sympathy and friendship for individuals, which could not justify taking up arms against my native State, in whose allegiance, like my ancestors, I was born and reared. But this process of exclusion left but one alternative. I must range myself on the side of Pennsylvania against all her enemies, wherever her march should lead. Though no opportunity then existed for comparing my conclusion with others, and I knew it not at the time, this conviction of the primary allegiance due one's native State, was on the identical line of thought that after long and painful hesitation unsheathed the spotless sword of Robert E. Lee, and so many other high-minded and patriotic men, who when through no fault of their own, they found natural allegiance pitted against Federal obligations, found themselves obliged to give preference to the first.

Early on the following morning, finding my mind at last clear, I accepted the invitation and went to work with my chief upon his arduous and by no means pleasing task of getting the neglected militia into condition for the field. While engaged in this business, procuring and inspecting equipment, filling up enlistments, sifting the claims and merits of the ambitious, and performing many other details pertaining more to the duties of the incompetent regimental officers than to staff duty, I received a telegram from Col. Baker urging me to come to Washington immediately on important business. Aware of his impulsive methods, I telegraphed that I was much occupied, and begged to know the nature of the business. To this I received a reply, dated from the train *en route* to New York, of such pressing character, that I took a night train and met him in that city next morning. The business proved to be an order from the President, dated May 8th, 1861, authorizing him to raise and equip an infantry regiment of sixteen companies, to be called the California Regiment, to be mustered into the U. S. service at New York, and to be organized and commanded by himself as colonel. "Well," said I, "if you propose to leave your seat in the Senate to be an infantry colonel, what do you want of me?" "Can you raise this regiment?" "Not in New York, I have no acquaintance there." "Can you raise it in Philadelphia?" "I think I can, but I am not sure." "Very well; your private business is sure to be broken up and not worth following for a while at least. Abandon it. Go to work and raise this regiment in Philadelphia, bringing the men over here to be mustered. I cannot at this moment accept military rank without jeopardizing my seat in the Senate, but you know my relations with Lincoln, and if you will do that for me, I can assure you that within six months I shall be a major-general, and you shall have

a brigadier-general's commission and a satisfactory command
under me.'' The chance to plunge in *medias res* without loss of
time was so tempting that my doubts and hesitations were
swept aside, and I agreed to undertake the work if my General
would let me off.

As I possessed no staff commission, and General Cadwalader
could not immediately procure me one, he very kindly accepted
my resignation at once. Early next morning all my legal
business, of which I then had a considerable number of local
cases on my docket, was distributed among willing friends,
books and papers boxed up and stored, and the office front
covered with placards; some hired drums and fifes made life
miserable for my unlucky neighbors, and the California Regiment was well under way. In war as in peace, rum seems connected in some mysterious way with the public affairs of a
free people, and everyone knows that saloons and grog-shops
are the chosen abodes of patriotic fervor. It is impossible to
remember how many of these last I had to visit, or how
many drinks of bad whiskey I was obliged to consume and
bestow in the service of my country; but on the second night
I took 100 men to New York by the midnight emigrant train,
at the fare of a dollar a head, which was part of my pecuniary
tribute to the cause. I took sufficient measures to keep up the
excitement during my absence, and at least as often as two or
three times a week I took over a similar contingent, all being
safely locked up and kept at elementary drill in a large new
building at 4th Street and Broadway, secured for the purpose
by Col. Baker. As the commissariat, music and many other
items had for a time to be supplied by myself, I soon found my
beloved country indebted to me in the amount of several
thousand dollars, most of which it continues to owe me to this
day, since the special appropriation by Congress of $20,000,000,
for raising, arming and equipping volunteers, made subsequently, when I was far away in Virginia, was absorbed by
tardier but more observant patriots who enjoyed a better or
more timely opportunity to approach the public trough.

Space would fail to relate the innumerable funny incidents
of this business, in which I constantly had to interview the
families and friends of the aspirants, after exhausting my
eloquence on themselves. Many repented after signing their

names and taking the extra-legal and *ex tempore* devised oath administered by myself on a borrowed Bible, or an old volume of state reports that bore sufficient external resemblance to that venerable volume. Others after a brief trial found they preferred some rival recruiting office, or to go with some friend who had got himself entangled under another banner; and, in short, for every hundred men, drunk and sober, actually got by hook and crook safely on board the cars, at least a hundred and fifty had to be enlisted, in consequence of the ever-changing views of themselves and their anxious relatives. Since notwithstanding all the assurance that could be assumed, I really possessed no legal authority over them till they should be actually mustered into service at the designated place, nothing was safe till hustled bodily on the cars, and the most promising-looking individuals hastily selected for non-commissioned officers and assistants; and even after the trains were in motion, many jumped off, with courage worthy of a better cause, and were left scattered promiscuously in a wide swath across the State of New Jersey.

At last ten companies of one hundred men each, having been made up, carried to New York, and the perpetually recurring gaps filled with new recruits passed by the doctor, the men were legally mustered in by Capt. W. F. Smith, U. S. Engineers, who later became distinguished as one of the most prominent and useful generals of the war, and the regiment in pursuance of an order obtained by Baker was transported to Fort Schuyler for organization and instruction. There for the first time it was possible to introduce some order, discipline and obedience, to inure officers and men to regimental duty and life in the field, and to communicate such military instruction by day as could be extracted from text books by night. The advantage gained for this raw but excellent body of men by the short occupancy of the fort, was very great, and after three weeks of guard and picket duty with almost constant drilling, the regiment made a much better figure in battalion marching and maneuvres than recruits of three months' standing, whom I have since inspected at the Stirling Castle Depot of the British Army, and infinitely superior to continental recruits whom I have had opportunity to see after several months' instruction.

It was in the early part, or perhaps toward the middle of June, that the regiment was ordered to Fortress Monroe, marching through the cities of New York, Philadelphia and Baltimore with a steadiness and martial appearance that compared favorably with any of the new volunteers. At Philadelphia it was encamped a few days at Suffolk Park, where, pursuant to special authority, it received six more full companies, and was reorganized in two battalions of 800 men each, with myself as Lieut.-Col. Commanding (Baker being usually absent at Washington), and R. A. Parrish and Charles W. Smith as Majors. From Fortress Monroe the command was marched a few miles beyond Hampton, where it took position and picketed an extended front. Here it was visited by Col. Baker, who camped with it for the first time, his duties in the Senate having hitherto engrossed most of his time and attention. Constant drill, with marching, guard and picket duty, and such other instruction of all ranks as is best found in actual field work, occupied the entire time till recalled for the defense of Washington after the rout at Bull Run on the 21st of July. There, the panic having subsided, and the disappointed politicians who had expected to follow McDowell's improvised rabble safely and expeditiously into Richmond, having recovered their breath, the regiment went into camp a short distance from the city on some property belonging to the bankers Corcoran and Riggs, or one of them.

For purposes of discipline and instruction this camp was regulated as though in presence of an enemy, with guards, pickets, escorts and patrols, though hard steady drill was never neglected. The regiment was here temporarily brigaded with some Massachusetts regiments, with whom, however, it never camped or drilled. In September it crossed the Potomac at the Chain Bridge and encamped a short distance beyond, where it was employed in constructing the large earthwork known as Fort Ethan Allen, and received another temporary brigade assignment with the 69th and 72nd Pennsylvania regiments, to which the 106th was soon after added. It had previously been taken from its anomalous condition under the direct control of the War Department, and placed upon the roster of the State of Pennsylvania as the 71st of its line.

The brigade association was satisfactory and remained unchanged till the expiration of its term of service in 1864, but the high number on the State roster, though unavoidable under the circumstances, was submitted to with much regret, since the 71st had been really the first mustered in all the Pennsylvania three-year regiments, and but for the absurd errors in the original presidential order authorizing its formation, would have received, as it was entitled to, the first number following the disbanded three-months' regiments of militia.

From the camp near Chain Bridge a trifling movement as far as Lewinsville first brought the 71st under artillery fire. Griffin's battery being deployed on a high ridge of ground and smartly engaged, the 71st was assigned as its support, and was massed in column close behind the ridge, where though it suffered no loss, the enemy's shot and shell flying over the ridge and striking ground in rear, furnished plenty of music. It was during this affair that a small New York newsboy not over twelve years of age, was brought in by the pickets with his bundle of northern papers, which as he artlessly explained, he had, during many days past, been alternately peddling through both armies without molestation from either. Clearly the picket duty of some regiment needed overhauling. During this artillery action the battery became so crowded with infantry colonels and field officers anxious to get under fire for the first time, that they had to be requested to move away. It is fair to our intelligence to add that most of us soon became able to restrain such curiosity with great success.

On the night of the 28th of September an unfortunate collision occurred with friendly troops of Gen. Fitz-John Porter's Division which though it cost some lives and much indignation among the public, first brought the 71st under the test of a really destructive fire. The enemy having occupied Munson's Hill, at no great distance, their skirmishes and patrols began to exhibit an annoying amount of enterprise, closely searching our picket-line every night, in one of which affairs Capt. Lingenfelter of the 71st was killed. As our Gen. Wm. F. Smith was not the man to stand that sort of thing long, a combined movement on Munson's Hill was arranged for the Divisions of Smith and Porter, to take place on the night of the 28th. Our column marched at midnight, the 71st in advance under my command, Col. Baker being in Washington. On reaching a certain point, beyond which I was informed by a staff officer that all troops found would be hostile, in obedience to orders an advance guard was suitably disposed, and a flank company deployed as skirmishers at right angles with the column on either hand, the road being narrow and bad, and lined with dense woods. Moving forward in this order, being myself in person with the advance guard, presently the route turned squarely to the right at a cross roads. At this point some confusion was naturally caused among the flankers obliged to wheel on such an extensive circle in thick woods, and the officers enjoined to silence. This would soon have been rectified by the energy and capacity of Markoe, the Captain of the left flanking company, but for the unfortunate circumstance of a collision in the woods with a skirmish line of Porter's division, which if our column as directed by the Division Staff was moving correctly, plainly had no business to be there.

Our skirmishers drove these men rapidly before them and the fugitives falling back on their reserves, were formed with inconceivable stupidity in line of battle in the woods, in advance of our column and along the road by which it was coming up. It is hard to imagine the muddled condition of the officer's mind who thus ambushed his command against the head of a heavy column coming from the direction of his own rear. Nevertheless, it was so arranged, and the advance guard having passed by, on the arrival of the head of the main column, a long line of fire burst suddenly upon it from the woods on the left, at the distance of a few yards. With the precautions taken, or with almost any precaution whatever, it would have been impossible for the column to be caught thus by an enemy, but it was not proof against the stupidity of its friends. The company officers generally behaved well, seconding with energy the orders at once given to halt, face to the left, and hold their fire. The woods might have been cleared by a detachment, but that would have led to an interminable fight in the dense darkness of the woods, where explanation and adjustment would have been difficult till daylight. It was therefore determined to stand fast where we were, and endeavor to stop the firing, satisfied there could be no troops there but ours. I galloped up and down the road between the two lines of excited individuals shouting and firing on each other across a narrow road, in earnest efforts to stop the firing, which was at length accomplished, though not till we had lost four killed and fourteen wounded, and I had a valuable horse shot under me. As a panicky condition prevailed among the troops in rear, who of course supposed the leading battalion to be engaged with an enemy whom they could not get at, both battalions were suitably disposed to command the road in front, while with G company deployed as skirmishers, I personally raked the woods, from which however the assailants had departed.

Of course the country was excited over this event, the newspapers as usual denouncing everyone from the General-in-Chief down, except only the real culprit who was never discovered. Though the officer in charge of the strange skirmishers was undoubtedly next to an idiot, the person originally responsible was probably some inexperienced staff officer; but the matter received no public investigation. Melancholy as the affair proved to the 71st, I am by no means certain that it did not gain an equivalent in the sharp lesson it afforded of the value of discipline and obedience; since I do not remember any subsequent difficulty in holding its fire reserved in subjection to orders, and it is for this reason I have given so much space to such an insignificant affair. No doubt for a body of men never yet in general action, persistently fired upon in the darkness across the width of a country road by troops of unknown character and force, it was a supreme test of their brief experience of discipline to refrain as well as they did from using the arms in their hands, for certainly not over one shot was fired for ten that they received, and they were the first to yield to their officers' efforts.

Soon after this inglorious affair the 71st marched to Poolesville, Md., on the upper Potomac, where was soon assembled, under command of Gen. Charles P. Stone, the extreme right wing of the Army of the Potomac, nearly corresponding with the troops soon after organized as Sedgwick's Division of the 2nd A. C. The Philadelphia Brigade, as it became familiarly called, was here definitely organized, consisting of the 69th, 71st, 72nd, and 106th Pennsylvania regiments under Baker, who now regularly assumed command of the brigade; the 71st, falling definitely to me as Lieut.-Col. Commanding. The great armies destined to become inseparably connected with American history, and now preparing to spring upon each other, were at this time separated throughout a distance of over forty miles by the river Potomac, averaging more than a mile in width; and it was here on an extreme wing that in spite of generals and plans, fate had arranged the first serious occasion for testing each other's mettle.

CHAPTER XVIII

THE DISASTROUS BATTLE OF BALL'S BLUFF

It was after midnight on the morning of the 21st of October that I was awakened to receive and read by such light as was afforded by the lantern of the sergeant of the guard, the following order, in its immediate results pregnant with fate to many, but of infinitely more importance as the inauguration of the long and desperate struggle by a useless and bloody prologue.

Hdqrs. Baker's Brigade,
1 A.M. 21st October, 1861.

Special Order.

The right wing Cala. Regt. (less camp guards) under command of Lieut.-Col. Wistar will proceed to Conrad's Ferry, to arrive at sunrise and await orders. The men will take blankets, overcoats and forty rounds in their cartridge boxes, and will be followed by one day's rations in wagons.

By command of Col. Baker, Comdg.,
FRED HARVEY
A. A. G.

The rest may as well be told by the insertion here of my official report made directly to the General of Division in consequence of the death of the Brigade General and all his staff, supplemented by a statement prepared a few years ago for the Regimental Survivors' Association, at their request, and read at one of their annual banquets.

Headquarters California Regiment:
Camp near Poolesville, Md., Nov. 7th, 1861.

BRIG.-GEN. CHARLES P. STONE, Commanding Division.

General:–

Being partially released by my physicians from their injunctions of solitude and silence, I proceed to report to you the operations of a part of my regiment on the 21st ult.

At half-past two A.M. on that day, I received your order through our late lamented Brigade Commander, to march with my first battalion, so as to arrive below Conrad's Ferry by sunrise.

At sunrise I was there with the battalion, numbering five hundred and seventy men, in eight companies, including officers. I immediately sent an officer to report to you at Edward's Ferry, between four and five miles below, who returned about half-past eight with your direction "to wait further orders, unless I should hear heavy firing over the river, in which event to cross at once, and support Colonel Devins." Slight firing had occurred there about an hour before, but after the reception of this order there was no more whatever until afternoon. A short time after this order reached me, General Baker and staff arrived. I communicated it to him, when, after a brief conversation, he continued on down the river in search of you. In an hour, an officer of his staff returned with the order: "General Baker directs you to cross at once." I had scarcely time to commence when General Baker himself returned and directed me to proceed with all haste.

I had two scows, of the capacity of forty men each, on the Maryland side of Harrison's Island, and one on the Virginia side, of the capacity of fifty men. I had got four companies on the Island and one on the Virginia side (having been delayed at the second crossing by other troops) when General Baker arrived on the Island and crossed at once to the Virginia side.

After crossing six companies to the Virginia side, I left the Island and passed over myself, leaving Captain Ritman to hurry on the transportation.

The Virginia side of the river was a bluff, eighty feet high, nearly perpendicular, and covered with rocks and a dense thicket. Stretching away directly from the summit was an open field of oblong shape, extending back from the river two hundred yards, by a width of seventy; this was entirely surrounded by woods, except a triangular opening distant about two-thirds of the length of the field from the river, extending into the woods on the left, say one hundred yards.

When I reached the top of the bluff, General Baker immediately explained his plan of battle stating his whole force to be twelve hundred men, at the same time reading to me your despatch, announcing the approach of four thousand of the enemy from Leesburg, and expressing his own serious doubts of the result. The detachment of the Fifteenth Massachusetts was drawn up in the edge of the woods on the right, facing up the river. The rest of our forces were arranged across the end of the open field, at right angles with the former, their backs towards the river; my battalion having the left, three companies being in reserve, and one deployed as skirmishers to cover the left flank.

From the left of our position, at the edge of the woods, the ground fell rapidly to the left, about thirty yards, to a gully, on the other side of which it rose to a hill higher than the ground on which we stood, at short distance.

The enemy's first fire was scattering, some of it from tree-tops around the field, where they had placed their marksmen—our men lying down for shelter, by command.

After comprehending the general condition, I requested permission to make a change in the disposition of our skirmishers on the left, when General Baker directed me to take command of the left flank, and make any disposition I saw fit. In pursuance of this order I was about to advance the skirmishers to the left when General Baker returned, and after a brief consultation with Colonel Cogswell and myself, directed me to throw out two companies as skirmishers to feel the woods in front for the precise location of the enemy's right, getting as much cover for the movement as possible from the woods on the left, with directions if attacked in force, to contest the ground and fall back, fighting.[16]

In the execution of this order, Captain John Markoe, with his company (A), immediately moved out, company D following in support under Lieutenant Wade—the latter company being short of officers—and the bulk of my command needing no immediate attention, I accompanied the movement myself.

The two companies moved rapidly up under cover of the woods on the left, until reaching the triangular open space before mentioned, when they were met by a galling fire from the enemy's riflemen on their front and left. Company A, left by Markoe and closely followed by D, rushing quickly over the open ground entered the woods, when a whole regiment of the enemy (8th Virginia) rose up from the ground at thirty paces distance and charged with the bayonet. A severe contest ensued, but our skirmishers somewhat checked the enemy's charge by taking trees and throwing an effective fire into their crowded ranks, at close distance. The right wing of our skirmishers was soon destroyed, but the left continued to hold ground for some time until Markoe was wounded and taken prisoner, when the survivors slowly fell back, bringing with them several prisoners, including an officer of the 'Eighth Virginia,' whom I had the honor of sending to you the following morning.

These two companies suffered severely in this gallant effort, company A having lost all three of its officers, and all its sergeants, except two, one of whom is wounded.

The enemy, in force in front, hearing this sharp firing on their right, immediately (half-past two P.M.) opened fire on our main body; and as soon as our skirmishers had fallen back, made repeated and desperate efforts, in constantly increasing force, to turn our left. Five times they charged down the gully, and were as often foiled and driven back by the steady conduct, and heavy fire of our men. Our firing in front was probably not very effective, the enemy being well covered in the woods—but on the left it was very destructive, our men bravely enduring a continuous fire from the front, and repelling with steadiness the enemy's repeated charges from that direction. The twelve-pounder

---

[16] See *Evening Telegraph*, February 1st, 2nd, and 4th, 1893, for comments on General Markoe's record as a soldier.

afforded valuable aid. All its artillerymen having been killed or dispersed, it was worked by Lieutenant Bramall, and two or three field officers of the California and Tammany Regiments, with great effect.

At a quarter-past five the enemy succeeded, by dint of numbers, in gaining a footing on our side of the gully, when our men refusing to give ground, they became mixed up, and a desperate hand-to-hand contest ensued.

Our right and center was at the same time severely pressed and consequently unable to afford assistance. At this moment I was finally disabled by a third wound, and a moment afterwards, almost in the same spot, the brave General Baker fell—gloriously, at the head of his men.

His death was instantly avenged and his body recovered by a few brave men, led by Captain Harvey (Brigade Adjutant General), who, I regret to say, was himself killed soon afterward.

A stern and bloody contest was now taking place; fresh masses of the enemy swarmed in on all sides, when an unauthorized order was given by someone to the men of another regiment, "Retreat to the ferry." This withdrew a portion of our numbers, and caused some confusion among the men of the California and Tammany Regiments, who stood by each other to the last, retiring, inch by inch, slowly and with considerable order until pressed over the bluff by the closing masses of the enemy. Our men maintained a sharp fire from the river bank, and made two or three spirited charges, led by Colonel Cogswell, which held the enemy in check at the top of the bluff, until those of our men who could swim had divested themselves of arms and clothing and taken to the water. Finding further resistance useless for any good purpose and with no means whatever of crossing the river (the only scow on that side the Island having sunk some time previously with all on board, owing to the bottom having fallen out) the remainder surrendered at 11 P.M.

The two howitzers, and most of the small arms, were concealed in the river. The 12-pound gun was thrown over the bluff with the same intention, but lodged among trees and rocks.

Color Sergeant R. C. Woods was shot through both legs early in the action. The colors were taken by Private George Suttie, company G, who bore them bravely through the remainder of the action, but in attempting to swim the river with them, afterwards was obliged from excessive cold and fatigue, to let them go in the middle of the stream.

The other Color Sergeant, Vansant, also displayed conspicuous gallantry, and after dark waded into the river, waistdeep, and buried his colors under a pile of stones. They had been first shot to tatters, and the staff cut in two, by the enemy's bullets.

Subsequent events were witnessed by yourself in person.

The bravery and steadiness of the officers and men throughout the whole affair, under circumstances plainly hopeless from the first, was beyond praise. Many of the men supplied themselves with cartridges from the bodies of the dead, after their own had been expended.

Of the eighteen officers, of all ranks, present in action all are either killed, wounded or missing, except two lieutenants.

Of the five hundred and seventy officers and men taken into action, the total loss, in killed, wounded and missing (many of the latter being necessarily left dead or wounded on the field, or drowned in the river), amounts to three hundred and five, according to a report heretofore submitted.

I have the honor to be, General,

Your obedient servant,

ISAAC J. WISTAR,

Lieut.-Col. Commanding California Regiment.

MR. JOHN W. FRAZER,

Secretary Survivors' Association,

Dear Sir:

In consequence of my inability to be present and respond personally at the proposed banquet of the Survivors' Association of the 71st Regiment Pennsylvania Volunteers to the toast "Colonel E. D. Baker —our first commander, a soldier, a statesman and sympathizing comrade," I am obliged to avail myself of your alternative invitation in addressing by letter these few remarks.

It is well for the survivors of the regiment which first introduced most of us to the profession of arms, to hold fast to the memory of that illustrious man who, under the benign institutions of our country, rose from an obscure place in life to such an important position in political and military history, but who at the zenith of his fame did not forget the interests of the humblest of those under his command.

I first met him in the hotly contested trial of a cause in San Francisco in the year 1853 in which he and myself were opposing counsel. There was scarcely any equality between us, for while his great reputation as an advocate had already extended throughout the Pacific Coast, I had been just admitted to the bar, and was almost without professional experience. Nevertheless that lively encounter proved the beginning of a friendship that accompanied us into far other and different fields of effort, and ceased only with his life.

We became associated in the profession of the law, and so continued from 1853 till his removal to Oregon in 1857, when the Legislature of that State chose him to represent it in the Senate of the United States. During the absorbing work of the large practice which fell to our lot during those years of association there was little time wasted on irrelevant matters, and I have always regretted that I did not then use more effort to overcome his uncommunicativeness respecting his early history. So far as my memory of his conversation now serves, he was born in England about the year 1811, of poor but worthy and respectable parents, belonging to the Society of Friends, who emigrated to Philadelphia when he was about nine years old. He was placed at work in a factory in this city, which he thought was in the southwestern part of the city, but could not precisely locate. His parents soon removed with their family to Illinois, where at any early age he became connected with the religious sect of 'Campbellites,' and before he reached the age of twenty-one was one of their most eloquent and renowned preachers. But that quiet and peaceful profession soon failed to satisfy the restless activity and ambition of his youth. He became a lawyer and politician, was elected to Congress, and in 1847 took command as colonel of the 4th Regiment of Illinois Volunteers in the war with Mexico. He was severely wounded by a shot through the throat while quelling a mutiny in a southern regiment on board a transport at Mobile, but recovered and served in the field till the conclusion of the war, winning great renown at Cerro Gordo, where, when General Shields was wounded, Baker took command of his brigade as senior colonel, and led it successfully against the Mexican position.

He was re-elected to Congress after the war, where he became distinguished in debate, and after the death of the President, General Taylor, delivered his celebrated eulogy of that great soldier, which immediately took rank as one of the most classic and elegant orations ever delivered in the American capital. In 1850 he went to California, but suffered an attack of fever on the Isthmus, from which he narrowly escaped with his life, and by which he was prematurely aged and his constitution permanently impaired. At the California bar, at that time an exceptionally able one, adorned with remarkable men from nearly every state in the Union, he speedily took a leading place, and as a jury advocate, had no superior. While our joint practice was confined to the civil branch, he was sought for and accepted retainers as associate counsel in most of the leading criminal cases of the day, some of which remain landmarks in the jurisprudence of the Pacific Coast. I regret I have not space even to glance at the most famous or remarkable of these, or to dwell upon the close discussion of facts, and the extraordinary bursts of eloquence which rendered his jury arguments so powerful and successful. Your association, the members of which knew and loved him during service with him in the great civil war, will naturally prefer to hear more of him in that connection.

During the winter of 1860–61 he was in the Senate of the United States, and being myself in attendance on the Supreme Court, I saw much of him in Washington, where opinions were naturally excited. Though firm in his views, he was by no means a bitter partisan, many of his warmest personal friends belonging to the defeated party. He gave full credit to the sincerity of southern statesmen, and with his positive and ardent nature scorned the talk of peaceful adjustment. He maintained from the first that the differences were unadjustable except by war and that a great war was certain, upon the inauguration of the new President, and earnestly advised me to drop the law and study tactics. Though he knew I was not without some militia experience, he insisted I should join a military company to acquire practical details, and study some of the principal historical campaigns for theory. He especially delighted in those of the most famous of the ancient Greek captains, as well as the modern ones of Frederick, Marlborough and Napoleon, all of which he had carefully studied, and with whose historic marches and battles he was critically familiar.

When at length the sword was drawn he immediately obtained from the President, with whom he had been for many years on terms of intimacy, a commission to raise and command a three-years' regiment in the service of the United States.

That regiment, as you all know, was promptly raised in Philadelphia and served for several months by virtue of that commission before it was taken upon the roster of Pennsylvania, and it was owing to that circumstance that, although the first of the three-years' regiments to complete its organization and muster, it became the seventy-first (71st) of the Pennsylvania line, having lost numbers of its men in action before many of the prior numbered regiments were in service at all. The reasonable limits of this letter compel me to pass over most of the regimental history prior to the action of Ball's Bluff, and proceed to recall your recollections to that disastrous event which nearly destroyed the first battalion of your regiment and closed at once the career and life of Baker.

At 1 o'clock A.M., October 21st, 1861, a division order reached Baker, then encamped with and commanding the Philadelphia Brigade near Poolesville, Md., to dispatch the first battalion of the 71st, under command of its Lieutenant-Colonel, for Conrad's Ferry on the Potomac so as to arrive there by sunrise. Neither Baker nor myself had any idea then of the reason or object of that order, nor of the crossing at Edward's Ferry effected on the previous day by General Stone, the Division Commander, with other troops of his Division. Your first battalion marched at 3 A.M., arriving at Conrad's Ferry punctually at sunrise and reported by a mounted officer (the chaplain) to General Stone, who was at Edward's Ferry, five miles below, in the meantime resting in ranks on the canal towpath. In due time a verbal order arrived from General Stone, who was an able, generous and loyal officer, to "remain where you are till further orders unless heavy firing takes place on the Virginia side, indicating heavy pressure on the scouting party of the 15th Massachusetts, which had been across all night, in which event cross a sufficient strength to assist and extricate them, but with great caution."

Soon after the reception of this order Colonel Baker arrived in person, having ordered the rest of his brigade to follow him, on his own responsibility. He asked for and heard the orders, and started at a rapid gait down the towpath for Division Headquarters. When he returned he rode up to the head of the regiment, and ordered me to cross my entire command as rapidly as possible, stating that General Stone had given him discretion to that extent.

The crossing was commenced at once with the only three large boats obtainable, two of them conveying the troops to Harrison's Island, and the third, aided by a rowboat, from thence across the narrower channel between the Island and the Virginia shore. Down to this time no firing had occurred, except an occasional shot. Baker crossed on one of the first boats, having ordered me to the Island, and another officer on the Maryland side to expedite the passage. As Baker received the small bodies of arriving troops and hurried them into position, the scouting company was driven in and the lines of battle became engaged.

Near the top of a high and timbered bluff, across the end of a large open field surrounded by forest, the line had been formed, including besides your own battalion parts of the 15th and 20th Massachusetts, and part of one company of the 42nd New York, in all about 1400 men. The left rested on a dry gully leading down to the river, but was otherwise exposed. The right extended into the woods, and an unlimbered howitzer of a Rhode Island battery (Bramhall's), without men, horses or caisson, was posted in the center. As the hostile regiments arrived in position the weight and effect of their fire increased, and the action soon became close and severe. The enemy's superior numbers enabled them to detach constantly against our exposed left without slackening their overpowering fire in front.

While much occupied with the difficult situation of our left, Baker came up with a despatch just received from General Stone to the effect that "four regiments have been seen by our scouts crossing an open place and marching towards you."

As the despatch had travelled five miles and twice crossed the river it was considered that those regiments must already be in our front and we were feeling their maximum effect. With our left enfiladed and in close contact with the enemy and an overpowering front fire, it was dangerous either to manoeuvre or withdraw, even had means existed to recross the river. But the command, though pinned fast, was firm, and it was thought that if the gun could be got into action and the enemy shaken in front, our people might be able to clear away the enemy's flanking force and get forward through the woods to the left. Captain Stewart (Lord Londonderry) of the Division Staff, and Captain Harvey, of Baker's Staff, both English officers of experience, at once volunteered, and with two infantry colonels proceeded to work the gun till the scanty ammunition in the limber was exhausted, by which time the piece was disabled by having the spokes shot out of the wheels. Baker constantly traversed the line, watching for an opportunity of movement. Twice wounded myself, he was about the first at my side on both occasions. He was not touched, himself, though a small bush was cut off between us as we talked. The rest of that disastrous affair you know. The enemy's fire increased as their reinforcements continued to arrive. For us there could be no reinforcements, and it was almost certain death to bring up ammunition. Company A made a gallant charge on the left, pushing back the enemy's flankers upon the main body, but was there enveloped by an entire regiment (8th Virginia) and its men mostly killed or captured. When I was at last personally disabled, it was Baker himself who picked me up and had me conveyed to the boats. It was their last trip. Immediately afterwards, Baker, sword in hand and face to the foe, fell dead, and after a successful counter-charge to bring off his body, our troops were forced over the bluff and though for long afterwards a desperate resistance was made as skirmishers, their cohesion as a manageable line was lost.

Respecting the object and results of that movement I venture neither statement nor opinion, preferring to confine myself to the undisputed facts connected with Baker's untimely death. No superior officer admitted any responsibility for the crossing in force, nor did Baker ever distinctly assert it. Knowing his ardent zeal and impatience of delay, we can only infer that some fatal misunderstanding occurred on the occasion of that one hasty interview between the Division and Brigade Commanders, of which there is now no survivor.

But in looking back to those stirring events, whatever we may think of the plan or object of that enterprise, none ever doubted Baker's signal coolness and gallantry on the field of battle. His courage kindled, as he saw the end approach and knew it must be disastrous. Several incidents during the heat of the action showed that he fully understood the situation. One of his remarks was, "The officer who dies with his men will never be harshly judged."

After it seemed to both of us that ruin was certain, in response to a remark that a quick and easy death was now the best thing left us, he quickly replied: "The bullets are seeking for you, but avoid me." That generous and noble heart, sympathetic with all around him and resolved on duty to the last, had abandoned hope and calmly waited for the stroke which alone should separate him from his men. It was after the hostile fire had enveloped three sides of your position and no manoeuvre was possible. Fresh ammunition could no longer be brought up, and except surrender, of which no one thought, nothing remained but the exaction of all and more than it was worth for the position no longer tenable. But I believe that you who are the survivors of that and many another bloody field will agree that even if Baker had lived till the last man, such was the affection and confidence he had inspired, he would have continued to hold your line firmly while there remained a soldier to mark it and a cartridge to fire.

How his heart would have swelled and his eye kindled could he in his last moments have foreseen the future career of the regiment he loved so well—that it was destined to stand the peer of any in the glorious Second Corps; to cover the retreat of Pope's routed columns from Manassas, charge Jackson's veterans at Antietam; receive on its steady bayonets the shock of Pickett at Gettysburg, and that, after blazoning on its standard the historic names of the Peninsula, Fredericksburg, Chancellorsville, Spottsylvania and innumerable minor fights, it should, after the acknowledged expiration of its term and before reënlistment, volunteer at the call of its corps commander to assault the works at Cold Harbor, where you lost 100 men actually ordered home for discharge; and finally that of the 2200 soldiers who from first to last fought under your flag, 119 was the remnant for the last muster out. That look into the future was denied him. But who shall say that during those after years his memory, precept and example were not mustered under your flag when it led the advance and cheered the last moments of dying comrades who fell out of your ranks forever, in the shock of battle?

In the sacredness of our common memories, I remain your friend and comrade,

I. J. WISTAR.

Philadelphia, April 12th, 1887.

The second battalion, under Parish, being on picket duty at a distance, it was only the first battalion of eight companies and 570 men of all ranks that participated in this affair. Of the 305 returned as killed, wounded and missing—being fifty-four per cent of the number engaged—it is fair to add there was no 'straggling,' the 'missing' being all killed, drowned or captured, many of the last being wounded.

The higher military authorities seemed to regard this small but disastrous affair as merely incidental to the first employment on a large scale of raw troops and inexperienced officers, and have observed respecting it, as far as possible, a discreet silence. But the public heart was deeply stirred, and the newspaper press and minor writers have poured forth volumes of criticism, generally rather political or personal, than military. Baker's gallant death having tended—as he foresaw on the field of battle—to exempt his memory, much industry and ingenuity has been exerted to fasten the responsibility upon Stone, but in my judgment with little success. Much material has been collected and discussed with feeling by Mr. John D. Baltz, a gallant young soldier of the 71st present at the action, in a volume entitled "Col. E. D. Baker's defense in the battle of Ball's Bluff, with biographical sketches of Baker, Wistar and Stone," published at Lancaster, Pa., 1888. Mr. Baltz, sensible like others of a grave and disastrous error somewhere, has displayed much industry in collecting everything to be said on that side. The kind manner in which he has spoken of myself, renders criticism of his earnestly written work so disagreeable to me that I content myself with saying that I cannot agree with his conclusions.

The absence of all co-operation in other quarters, and of any preparation for a general advance at that time, is conclusive evidence that no such purpose was in the mind of any high or controlling authority. There is no occasion for and can be no success in searching for any concealed or other object than that plainly indicated by all the orders received or issued by Stone. It was simply for the purpose of extricating the small scouting party sent across the previous evening—since no other is conceivable—that Stone ordered down a single battalion and a few guns, and the details were naturally left to the Brigadier commanding on the spot. An obvious way to perform the duty would have been to place a small infantry force on the island, which being two miles long, offered positions from whence a moderate musketry fire could easily keep clear the top of the bluff from which alone the enemy's fire could reach our troops retiring across the river; while a few guns placed in position on the Maryland side would not only aid the operation, but effectually protect the return of the covering force from the island. For such a small and simple operation the available boat capacity was sufficient, and no considerable loss could possibly have occurred. But to cross a force of several hundred men with boat capacity inadequate for advance and absurdly insufficient for retreat, upon a permissive and discretionary order wrung with difficulty from a superior, five miles distant, indicates that Baker thought he saw an opportunity to strike a blow of sufficient importance to justify the excessive risk incurred. In that, he was terribly mistaken, as was discovered too late when in presence of a largely superior force already in position. From that moment, though a different disposition of the troops engaged might have prolonged a useless conflict, nothing under existing circumstances could have extricated them but an advance by Stone with a large force from Edward's Ferry. But such advance by Stone on the right bank separated from assistance or retreat by an impassable river a mile wide, was opposed to every sound principle, wholly beyond the tenor of his orders, and even if it should not involve further and more important loss, could at best result only in a series of detached, disorderly and piecemeal fights much more likely to bring disaster than success, and even if successful, must have forced most injuriously the hand of the General-in-Chief, who did not expect, and was unprepared for anything more important than the mere reconnoissance he had authorized.

Baker himself would have been the last man to excuse—by seeking to cast upon another—the original error of crossing in force without proper means provided and an explicit understanding with his superior; nor is any necessity laid upon his friends to do so, since the error—if his—was at least of an heroic character, and as he 'died with his men,' all parties have dealt kindly with his memory.

General Stone was an educated officer of high standing in the army, from which he had formerly resigned, like Sherman, to operate a bank in San Francisco—where I had known him well—but returned to the service at the first outbreak of war. A circumstance of a personal nature which had occurred not long before this affair, may serve to shed a ray of light on the otherwise inexplicable mystery of the persecutions which befell him. The Senator (Charles Sumner) of Massachusetts had denounced and even accused him of treason on the floor of the Senate, for refusing in obedience to the laws and orders then prevailing, to encourage the flight into his lines of fugitive slaves, who in fact tended to demoralize the new troops nearly as much as to disorganize the susceptibilities of the Washington politicians. Contrary to the advice of his friends, Stone felt it necessary to resent the outrage in the only way open to him, by a challenge, and as Sumner was deemed slippery in such matters, have notoriously evaded several, at the expense of a caning or two, the General chose for his second Lord Ernest Vane Tempest, a younger son of the Marquis of Londonderry, and a captain in the British Army, who having obtained leave of absence for the purpose, entered our service in the Adjutant-General's Department, and was then serving on Stone's staff under his family name of Stewart. This wild Irishman cared nothing for his American commission and readily undertook to carry the message and get a definite reply. For this purpose he forced his way into Sumner's apartment, not without some violence to the latter's well-trained servant, and delivered the note personally with an intimation of its purport. The Senator, pleading other occupation, tried to put him off with promises to reply by letter at a more convenient time, but Stewart was not to be deceived or cajoled, and insisted on receiving an immediate reply or taking the difficulty on himself. A wordy squabble ensued in which Stewart obtained a written answer under threats of personal castigation, but the Hon. gentleman thus summarily brought to book, nursed his wrath, and seized upon the occasion offered by the Ball's Bluff catastrophe to direct political and newspaper obloquy upon Stone, who, fully occupied in front of the enemy, possessed no adequate means of influencing opinion in his own favor. As soon after the fight as public indignation had been sufficiently worked up, he was arrested without charges, and thrown into prison, where for months he was refused any communication with counsel, family or friends, and after being released as mysteriously and without explanation as he had been confined, he spent years in vainly endeavoring to obtain the name of his accuser or any definite charge against himself. All explanation or employment was denied him till near the close of the war, when he was at last assigned as bear leader to the military mountebank who for his country's sins conducted its disastrous campaign on Red River. After the war he became chief of staff to the Khedive of Egypt, whom he served with distinction for many years until the English conquest of that country, when he returned to America and soon after died.

Stewart reached the battlefield with despatches from Stone, in the hottest part of the action and foreseeing the inevitable catastrophe, chose to remain there. He rendered much useful aid, and remained till after dark, when he swam the river and escaped without a scratch.

Capt. Frederick Harvey, A. A. G. on Baker's staff, was another British officer who had entered our service under leave of absence from his own. He was an accomplished and gallant officer, and with Stewart and Col. Cogswell of the 42nd New York, who was present as a volunteer with one company of his regiment, gave valuable aid in serving the twelve-pound gun, whose proper crew had been killed or dispersed, till it was disabled by having the spokes shot from the wheels by the enemy's musketry fire. Notwithstanding the concentrated fire drawn upon this gun, not one of us was touched by bullets, though we were all more or less scratched and hurt by splinters shot from its carriage. Harvey, after leading several small but resolute charges after dark to keep possession of the bluff and landing-place, was killed late at night and his body left in possession of the enemy for want of means to bring it off. Only a few days before his death, while riding together on a long and weary night-march, he had repeated with patriotic feeling those fine lines which always recall him to my memory:

> Vain all those ships of iron framed,
> Vain all those shattering guns,
> Unless proud England keep untamed
> The strong hearts of her sons.

Two of the most promising officers of the 71st, killed on this occasion, were Capt. Otter and Lieut. Williams, both energetic and capable young men, whose gallantry attracted my attention and who would almost certainly have risen to distinction.

My personal experience was not fortunate except in so far as I escaped worse. Early in the action I was struck in the jaw by a bullet or a small stone dashed up by one. Though the injury did not eventually amount to much, it caused severe pain and loss of blood which became matted in the beard, and dripping down in front, rendered me a ferocious and unpleasant object to behold, as I have since been assured. Later a bullet passed through my thigh within a short distance of the old arrow wound, suffered years before in the upper Klamath country. This though but a flesh wound, filled my boot with blood so that I was obliged to cut a hole to let it out. Just before dark, while endeavoring to change front with the two left companies to repel a charge on that flank, I was struck in the right elbow by a ball that shattered all three of the bones meeting at that point, causing a momentary mental confusion and even suspension of sight. Though I could not see my sword, I stooped to recover it from the place where I knew it had fallen, and having gathered it up along with a handful of bloody grass, had just regained the perpendicular, when I was seized by Baker with a hand on each shoulder. "What, Wistar, hit again?" "Yes, I am afraid badly this time." Then sheathing for me the sword at my request, he called a soldier: "Here, my man, catch hold of Col. Wistar and get him to the boat somehow, if you have to carry him." The words were his last. I hastily communicated the importance of what I had been engaged in and he sprang forward to complete the work. About the same time, the enemy's charging column, which I had seen leave their main line for the usual circuit through the woods, appeared over the rising ground on the left, fired a volley and rushed in. Baker fell to that volley, being struck by several bullets, one of which pierced his brain. The charge was repelled for a moment, and a counter-charge led by Harvey recovered the body, but the gallant soldier, the generous friend, the matchless orator, was lost to us and his country forever.

Though for such a short time in the great national arena at Washington, his celebrated Union oration in New York, in April, followed by two eloquent speeches in the Senate, had fairly introduced him to the country, and his heroic death on a field lost but not dishonored, thrilled the entire North, not yet accustomed to such spectacles. Not long before, the rest of the world had laughed, and our own people were mortified if not disheartened, by the disorderly rout of Bull Run, and held their breath in dread anticipation of the next encounter. But here had been no disorder, no panic, no flight, no Bull Run affair. Our soldiers' fighting qualities, at least, were now assured. A small body gallantly led had been by someone's error surrounded by superior force, in fact ambushed in an untenable position, and though ultimately cut to pieces and destroyed, had long defended itself with perfect order and unflinching courage, inflicting damage little inferior to its own, till it had suffered a loss of fifty-four per cent of its number, including nearly all the officers, and their gallant leader. While, therefore, the friends of the slain received universal sympathy, to the general public the disaster was tempered with a certain proud repose of feeling hitherto unknown since the intense mortification of July.

The body of the dead hero so gallantly snatched from the enemy by his slain chief of staff, was carried from city to city, lying everywhere in state, and visited by vast crowds at each, as it passed slowly across the continent heralded and accompanied by continuous strains of funeral music to the last resting-place, where it still reposes, by the shores of the far Pacific.

To his friend in peace and right arm in battle
this tribute is presented by his brother,

A. C. BAKER, M.D.
Surgeon 71st Regt. Pa. Vols.

'Twas a calm October morning,
    Long before the East was gray,
That our Chief received the order
    Straight to marshall the array.

Lightly from his narrow war-couch
    Gaily up the Hero sprung,
Cheerful as if called to banquet,
    Or to join the festive throng.

Promptly was each order given,
    And before the morn was light,
His beloved and own battalion
    Proudly marched to find the fight.

As he started, I addressed him,—
    "Brother, brother, mind today
You but do a General's duty,
    Do not seek the thickest fray.

"Think how much the country needs you,
    Think your life is not your own,
Do not seek the hottest battle,
    Do not venture forth alone!"

"If the day goes lightly with us,
    If I deem the field our own,
I'll but do a General's duty,—
    Wistar leads the column on.

"But if overborne by numbers,
    We are like to lose the day,
If my own battalion falters
    In the fury of the fray;

"Should I lose my valiant right arm,
    If by rebel steel or ball
'Mid the smoke and shock of battle
    Gallant Wistar chance to fall;

"Then my own, the Senate's honor,
    Western lands and Keystone State
Tell to me a General's duty
    Is to dare a soldier's fate!

"They are trained to move like veterans
    And like veterans they shall fight,
Never while I live to lead them,
    Shall they turn their backs in flight!

"With the cold and silent bayonet
    I will lead our freemen on;
Others then will tell the story
    How the day is lost or won."

Vaulting on his tall bay charger
    With a smile serene and bright,
Thus my gifted, gallant brother
    Rode to that unequal fight.

My brother, Oh, my brother!
    Brother that I loved so well,—
Other pens must trace the story
    How you fought and how you fell!

National Cemetery at Ball's Bluff, Virginia.
The stake marks the spot where General Baker fell.
Drawn by Frank H. Taylor.

CHAPTER XIX

Since these pages claim no higher purpose than a personal narrative, some further particulars of my individual casualties in the late affair may be allowable. My soldier stuck faithfully to me and with such aid as he could summon, led and carried me down the bluff and did not leave me till he had waded waistdeep into the river and deposited me sore, blood-soaked and fainting on the extreme end of the row-boat, now the only craft plying to Harrison's Island, the scow having already sunk. Here with feet dragging in the water, I was held in place by an Irishman wounded in the legs, who kept me hugged close in both arms exclaiming, "No fear for ye, Kornel; I'll hold ye fast or we'll both go over together, jist." At the island I was deposited in a farm-yard filled with wounded and dying men, ranged around the enclosure with heads to the fence, where our excellent Surgeon Dwinelle soon made my condition easier by administering stimulants and tying up my arm in some skillful way, so as to avoid the unspeakable agony of the grating ends of the fractured bones. While engaged at this work, a rifle bullet flying clear of our men on the bluff and just missing the Surgeon, struck a fence-rail within a foot of my head, filling my eyes with rotton wood. As this was more than the Surgeon had enlisted for, I begged him to leave me and retire to a safer place, to which he gallantly replied, "No, I have always obeyed you before, but you are under my orders now and I am not going to leave you till you are in safe condition to send off to camp." The fact was that this field-hospital had been under similar fire all day, and some of the wounded had actually been killed in the Doctor's hands, but neither Surgeon nor assistant had flinched, remaining hard

380

at work till far into the night, sending off their patients as fast as they could be temporarily recovered enough for the purpose; and most of the supposed wounded remaining, had already departed for a land where no surgeon is needed. In due time I was carried across the Maryland branch of the river, placed on a stretcher and carried two miles by men of our second battalion, who declined assistance from the large force now assembled, and deposited me in a small house near the regimental camp. Here I lay nine weeks, during most of which time it was not practicable even to change the sheets. The flesh wounds soon closed, and even the elbow mostly healed over but afterwards had to be laid open by a severe and painful operation for the purpose of extracting pieces of bone and lead inadvertently missed at the first dressings. It was after this operation, as I understood, that the more serious feature of the case appeared. First my life, and later the arm, was claimed by such medical wisdom as could be assembled in judgment, but they were ultimately induced to relent and leave me in possession of both. Maggots appeared in the wound, and though occasionally removed in considerable quantity, derived more enjoyment than they afforded me, pasturing and disporting themselves up and down the feeding ground so providentially supplied them. Finally, as it became evident that I was to suffer anchylosis of the principal joints, the arm was fixed in the position and at the angle it has ever since retained, and one of my faithful surgeons aided by a small detail, carried me home to Philadelphia, where I was placed in my father's house just in time for the Christmas festivities.

I soon learned to write with the left hand and continued to do so until the left arm was injured and partly paralyzed by a wound received later at Antietam, when I perforce returned to the use of the right hand. Though the fingers are permanently fixed in a position but slightly bent and cannot be closed, this remains on the whole the most useful hand, and by using a thick-handled pen, and keeping extended all the fingers except the index, answers reasonably well for writing. Though the practical loss of the right arm by anchylosis of all joints below the shoulder, including fingers, is, as I can from

long experience aver, an irreparable one, often entailing privations at times and places least looked for, yet apart from
constant petty inconveniences, one of the most regretful to
me has been the deprivation of riding, always before one of
my chiefest pleasures. It is hard for one fond of a high-
spirited horse to come down to a plain animal adapted to the
necessities of an infirm rider, and yet if anyone will try the
experiment of putting the right hand in his pocket, and binding
the left elbow to the body, he will soon be convinced that the
free use of at least one arm is required to ride with pleasure,
comfort, or even safety. I have been twice run away with
while reviewing strange troops, who no doubt attributed the
exhibition to another cause; have repeatedly had to accept
the aid of staff officers and orderlies, and suffered so many
minor accidents and mortifications, that after the war I was
constrained to abandon riding entirely.

While lying ill near Poolesville, before my physical condition
was at the worst, I was reminded of the prisoners sent to the
rear by Markoe's company. These were a Lieut. Berry and
two or three men of his regiment, the 8th Virginia. A day or
two after the action, I therefore sent for the officer, who in
the prevailing gloom and disorganization, had been thus far
detained in the regimental guard quarters, and about dark he
came into my bedroom in a state of just indignation at having
had his arms secured by a slight ligature at the elbows. In
reply to my indignant looks, the young officer of the guard
explained that he could not endure the risk of our only prisoner
getting away while in his charge, and as it was necessary to
bring him a considerable distance through thick and dark
woods with but one assistant, he had ventured to resort to
this precaution though the prisoner had been scrupulously well
treated in other respects—as indeed he admitted. No doubt I
should have ordered the bonds removed unconditionally and
immediately, but since the indignity was an accomplished fact,
I hastily and improperly offered to have the bonds off if he
would give his parole not to attempt escape till delivered at
Division Headquarters. This was done and I thought no more
of the circumstance for some days, when Gen. Stone paid
me a visit and remarked that he had received a flag of truce

from the Confederate Gen. Beauregard, sent partly for the
courteous purpose of conveying some papers found in Gen.
Baker's overcoat left on the field of battle, and partly to
complain of me for the above violation of the rights of a
prisoner of war. It seemed that Berry had been sent to
Washington and confined in the Old Capital prison, from which
he had escaped by letting himself down one stormy night from
an upper story by strips of blanket, successfully evaded the
sentinels, swam the Potomac, and returned to his command.
I was of course properly mortified and self-rebuked at the
just construction thus placed on the condition I had thoughtlessly imposed, but Stone said he had already explained the
circumstances and offered sufficient verbal reparation on my
behalf.

About the end of October, Brig.-Gen. Wm. W. Burns of the
regular army, an agreeable gentleman, and one of the most
able and judicious brigade commanders of the army, was assigned to the command of our brigade, and from that aus-
picious event dated the scientific perfection of discipline, drill
and *esprit* which was soon to render it a model of efficiency,
and give it distinction even among the veterans of the far-
famed Second Corps, which notwithstanding its innumerable
fights, victories and defeats, proudly boasted that it had 'never
lost a color or a gun' till the bloody, and to it, well-nigh fatal
campaign of 1864. In January I rejoined the regiment with
a number of Philadelphia recruits, and soon after, the 71st was
reorganized into an ordinary ten-company regiment, for which
the recent destruction of officers furnished the opportunity.
General John Sedgwick succeeded Stone as Division Commander, and General E. V. Sumner took command of the
Second Corps; both officers whose well-won reputations now
and henceforth belong to the general history of the country.

On the 28th of February, Sedgwick's Division left its canton-
ment near Poolesville and marched in support of Bank's Corps
then moving up the Shenandoah Valley against Jackson. The
route was by Sandy Hook to Harper's Ferry, where the
Potomac was crossed on pontoons, and thence by Bolivar
Heights and Charleston to Berryville. Jackson having declined

battle and retired from Winchester before Bank's advance, the Division returned to Harper's Ferry, where it took cars for Washington and marched thence without delay to Alexandria to take transports for the Peninsula. March 28th, Burns' Brigade embarked for Fortress Monroe, the 71st and part of the 69th being crowded into a steamer which also towed behind it some large barges conveying the men, horses and guns of a battery of artillery. On the second day a heavy gale of wind with thick snow rendered invisible everything outside the vessel, and as the captain could only feel his way slowly by compass and lead, there was much danger of collision with the barges in tow, or with some of the numerous fleet of transports, which must have occasioned a large loss of life. Under the circumstances, I ordered the steamer and her tow into the nearest harbor accessible, where we lay one night at anchor, the whole voyage thus occupying four days.

The 4th and 5th of April were consumed by the march of the army in two columns to Yorktown, where it was confronted by the enemy under Magruder, whose fortified lines extended across the Peninsula, reinforced by a number of closed works of strength and importance. During the famous seige that followed, the rain fell daily, almost without exception, the roads were impassable, and while part of the army was employed in developing the enemy's works and batteries by strong reconnoissances, a still larger part was necessarily occupied in constructing corduroy roadways along our line, to render possible the prompt interchange of guns and troops. The 71st had its share in both kinds of work, and I had the honor to command one of the reconnoisances, which was the first occasion that I found myself entrusted with two regiments. The movement was to escort an engineer officer, and cover his observations of the hostile works and positions. As it rained all day, the engineer sat on his horse so well-enveloped in a large cloak that little was generally to be seen of him but his spectacles. We blundred twice under the enemy's infantry fire and lost a man or two, which I was not allowed to reciprocate, but on the contrary backed out so quickly under the Major's directions, that in my ignorance I formed a private opinion by no means favorable to his enterprise. The ludicrous dimensions of that error will be best understood when it is added that the officer was Major A. A. Humphreys, than whom no soldier ever knew better when to accept and when to decline to fight. When he later assumed command of troops, he at once took and maintained the character of one of the most prompt and daring officers of the whole army, without in the least sacrificing the careful and orderly methods which equally distinguished him when conducting a petty reconnoissance at Yorktown, or directing as chief of staff, the general movements of the Army of the Potomac.

Though difficulties of communications and scarcity of supplies were well known to all the armies in the civil war, no other campaign was attended with more privation, sickness and death than prevailed in the muddy trenches at Yorktown. A thousand pounds or less was a good load for a six-mule team, and the necessary ammunition and other military stores could only be distributed at the front by a corresponding neglect of other pressing necessities of the soldier. It was frequently necessary to march a regiment several miles to the landing to carry back a few days' rations on their own backs. The result of hard work, constant exposure by night as well as by day, with inadequate food was wholesale sickness; which kept the actual strength and mobility of the army reduced to a low figure. Bilious and malarial fevers, with diarrhea and typhoid were the prevailing forms of disease, and during the month of April caused a greater loss to the Army of the Potomac than many a famous and hard-fought battle of later date. The 71st lost several promising young officers and many men, and toward the end of the siege I was myself attacked with the usual typhoidal symptoms, and after vainly trying to resist for a few days, on the day before the troops entered the place, was carried in an unconscious condition to a hospital-steamer lying in York River, a few miles below.

I have never had the least recollection of the journey or arrival, and my first intelligent memory of what transpired on the steamer, is my capture one night by two Sisters of Charity, as, after escaping from my cot, I was wandering aimlessly about the cabin. They conducted me back to bed, and it was owing mainly to their unremitting and charitable care that I at last reached a condition of recovery that permitted my conveyance home in a small detail of convalescents, where I was a second time safely deposited in bed at my father's house. Here a relapse occurred, as is not unusual in such cases; all knowledge of military events was forbidden me, and it was only after a long and severe struggle that youth, temperate habits and an unsurpassed constitution carried me safely through, though with the loss of one-third my weight.

As soon as I could get out of the house, I embraced the opportunity of carrying into effect a certain previous engagement, and was married on the 9th of July, 1862, by the Rev. Henry J. Morton, at the old St. James Church at Seventh and St. James Street, to Sarah Toland, second daughter of Robert and Rebecca Toland, both previously deceased; a union which, I may be permitted to add, has been crowned with every happiness that can be reasonably expected from that happy relation.[17]

It was not till the army had fought its way through the Seven Days' Battles, and encamped at Harrison's Landing on the James, that I was able to report for duty. During that series of battles the 71st, besides minor affairs, had been twice severely engaged, first at Savage Station, where the brigade by a decisive repulse of the enemy in superior force, had successfully covered the crossing at White Oak Swamp, and next at Nelson's farm, or Glendale, on an occasion of historical importance to the army and the country. The two corps of Longstreet and A. P. Hill, debouching by two roads against the flank of our army at that central point, had already struck and demolished McCall's Division, capturing its artillery and many prisoners, including that General himself, when it encountered Burns' Brigade hastily put in place and strengthened by the 19th Massachusetts. Burns himself has publicly declared that with this force of five regiments he checked and held the 30,000 men of those victorious columns for nearly an hour, and until troops freshly brought up rendered that vital point secure. Had the Army of the Potomac—then in motion to a new base and presenting its flank to the enemy on a line

[17] Mrs. Wistar died, without issue, at Philadelphia, January 11, 1895.

twenty miles long, with its rear engaged and held by Jackson at White Oak Swamp—been cut in two at Glendale without connection either with its old or new base, the defeat must have been of such a ruinous character as to destroy it for all aggressive purposes at least.

This was the first of two celebrated occasions when it fell to the lot of this brigade to defend successfully the center of the same army against similar efforts to cut it in two, and defeat it in detail. The other was at Gettysburg where the celebrated charge of Pickett first fell upon, and was repulsed by, two of its regiments—the 69th and 71st. The losses of the 71st in the Seven Days' Battles were necessarily heavy, but owing to the loss of its books and baggage on the abandonment of Savage Station, have never been separately reported. After a short rest at Harrison's Landing, the Army of the Potomac, contrary to the plans and wish of its commander, was hastily recalled to Alexandria by the Government, in consequence of the disasters threatening Gen. Pope on the Rapidan. On the 29th of August, Sedgwick's Division marched twenty miles to Chain Bridge, on false information, and, after two hours' halt, was again put in motion toward the heavy firing then in progress near the old field of Bull Run. At noon on the 31st, after a march of forty miles, only interrupted by two hours' sleep, it reached Centreville, and took position to cover the disastrous defeat and flight of Pope, whose disorganized regiments and frightened rabble, were passed through its lines. September 1st, Burns' Brigade, now commanded by Gen. O. O. Howard, in consequence of Burns' absence from a severe face-wound received at Glendale, made a reconnoissance some miles to the right, where the 71st struck and engaged the flanking regiments of Lee's army, then in march for the Potomac. Here occurred a trifling incident not without interest as showing the value of a facetious word at the right moment. The skirmish line being sharply engaged with the enemy partly sheltered behind a row of hay-stacks, the reserve held ready in line, came under a hot fire which it had to stand and endure without returning; a condition irksome and unsteadying to any troops. Having left my horse in a safe place—I had already lost three, and was getting economical of horse-flesh—I was standing with the reserve, waiting for the proper moment to use it, when a stout young recruit suddenly dropped his musket, and pulled up his foot with both hands as if wounded. A glance showed that a ball had torn open his trousers below the knee without hurting him, and as several men were already laid out, and the reserve was evidently not enjoying its position, it seemed a good time for converting the solemn into the facetious, which was done by a single remark: "Young fellow, a bullet never hits twice in the same place; if you will take off those trousers I will give you ten dollars for them." The row of long and solemn faces relaxed into a giggle, and the reserve recovered its cheerfulness. Its firmness had never been in question.[18]

At night, Sedgwick's Division having been assigned as rearguard to cover the retreat of the routed column retiring by the left-hand road—that next the enemy—moved off after dark in the discharge of what, judging by that night's experience, is the most arduous of all military duty. The 71st, with Sully's 1st Minnesota, had the honor to be detached by Sedgwick as extreme Division rearguard, with instructions to Sully and myself to co-operate, and make the best fight we could in case of pressure, without reference to the General, since communication with him was sure to be difficult or impossible. The road was a narrow cart way through a dense and dark pine, or cedar forest, crowded by thousands of disorganized troops and fragments of commands; disorderly wagon trains; guns without officers; caissons without guns; and in short, a hopeless and irredeemable mob. It was necessary for the Division to be held compact, and ready for action to sustain its own rearguard if necessary, while it fell to the latter to keep order by any means however summary; shove on the trains; push forward the mob;

[18] This thorough and timely reconnoissance by two regiments of the Philadelphia Brigade—the 71st and 72nd—disclosed Lee's solid columns in motion by their left to the rear of the Union Army, and led to the all-important check they received at Chantilly, on the same afternoon. Colonel Allan in his excellent work on the Army of Northern Virginia, states that it was ordered by Pope, but erroneously declares on the authority of Gen. J. E. B. Stuart that "it was not made." (Army of Northern Virginia, by Col. William Allan, p. 314.)

drive up the stragglers; and protect the whole by showing firm face to the pursuit, defeating it if possible, but, at all hazards, holding it in check till aid should be summoned from the mass of the Division in front.

These dispositions proved successful against a pursuit both able and aggressive, partly because of the cheerful courage and ability of Sully, and partly because of the unbounded confidence we both had in Sedgwick, whom, as he had predicted, we had no further opportunity of seeing through the night, but who we well knew, would not abandon us. The plan arranged between Sully and myself was simple enough and of no very difficult execution, provided we could keep ahead and clear of us, the rabble, whom we dare not allow to mingle with or hang about our troops. For this essential purpose, a small provost guard, under carefully picked officers, was extemporized, with such imperative and severe orders respecting teamsters and stragglers, as might not have found favor with theoretical patriots at home. In case of attack from the rear, one regiment would take position and deploy for resistance, while the other would gain distance and repeat the process to cover the retreat of the first through and beyond it. The two Colonels always to remain on or near the road for conference, if required. The two regiments, slowly driving the rout before them, had not advanced far when some light guns opened on them from the rear, the shells passing over us, and bursting among the rabble in front, causing among them a panic, restrained with the greatest difficulty. Since this showed it necessary to keep the enemy at a greater distance, even at the risk of prolonging to a dangerous extent our exposed flanks, the 71st was deployed to the rear, on both sides of the road, in two battalions aligned at an obtuse angle with each other, while the column moved on. After remaining here long enough, as was supposed, to give the column a sufficient advance, the enemy's shot striking ground in our rear without much damage, I was about getting the regiment into the road to resume the march, when I caught sound of the tread of horses, who under cover of the thick woods and impentrable darkness, had approached within a few yards. Not being certain the cavalry was hostile, I challenged in person: "Halt, advance one with the countersign, quick, or you will get the fire of a brigade." "Fire and be d—d," came through the darkness, as the order rang out, and the cavalry of the enemy's advanced guard gallantly made its charge. I had barely time to gallop to the rear of the battalion and give the order: "Fire by battalion; right battalion ready, aim, fire, load." "Left battalion ready, aim, fire, load." The two volleys crossing each other at such short distance, quickly disposed of the small cavalry force, leaving the road full of dead and struggling horses, with not a few of the riders; and, after pushing a slight reconnoissance to the rear where the enemy was found in force, a small regimental rearguard was suitably disposed and the march resumed.

We had not gone far before we met Sully and his Adjutant galloping back to learn the extent of the collision, from whom the satisfactory information was received that the 1st Minnesota was already in line of battle in a fine position half a mile ahead. The 71st marched through it, receiving vociferous cheers for its success, and obtained a similar position in its turn, and this system was continued through the night with sundry variations, but entire success; the enemy's guns pressing close behind, occasionally reaching the column with a few shell thrown over the heads of the rearguard, or from some flank position, but on the whole doing little damage. Of course, as a military operation by rearguard, all this would have been simple enough, but for the immense mass of worthless and panic-stricken stragglers crowded between us and the rest of the Division, which made it practically inaccessible, and rendered quick support from it impossible. Many hundred —perhaps thousands—of Germans from the routed Division of Siegel, had abandoned their colors, thrown away their arms, and deliberately gone to sleep around fires kindled in the woods, a spectacle most exasperating to our men, since these stragglers could have no other design than to be taken prisoners after the passage of the rearguard. The soldiers in ranks begged to be let loose on these 'coffee-boilers,' promising there should be none left for the enemy; but the integrity of the rearguard was of too much importance to permit risking it, even for that just vengeance. Nevertheless, such stragglers did not all go unwhipt of justice. Unfortunately, the Adjutant's horse being killed and no Major present, the only mounted regimental officers were Lieut.-Col. Jones and myself, who, when otherwise unoccupied, busied ourselves with charging into these sleeping squads of loafers, to the intense delight of the gallant fellows of the hard-worked rearguard. Lieut.-Col. Jones was a well-qualified young West Pointer, recently appointed to the regiment at my request. He was not long with the regiment before he received the appointment of Colonel of the 34th Ohio, and was killed at its head as it mounted the earthworks at Chickamauga. An amusing adventure occurred to another young West Pointer, on that night. A small and remarkably worthless regiment of volunteer cavalry had been sent early in the night to co-operate with the rearguard, but was so badly commanded that its only tendency was to disorder the infantry by clinging to its flanks, and dashing suddenly in upon it from time to time. Sully and I soon concluded we could do better without it, and in order to get rid of it ordered it forward to report to Sedgwick, with the request to the General for even a single troop of good cavalry if possible to spare it. In due time a young West Point Lieutenant with about twenty regular cavalry reported from the General, and was promptly set to work.

The Lieutenant, whom I now only remember as 'Johnny,' was a brave and capable young fellow, crossing swords with the enemy's scouting parties on our flanks whenever they gave him the opportunity, and retreating upon the infantry in perfect order, when pressed. But having been with his troops in the saddle for several days, both men and horses were fairly exhausted, and toward morning suddenly disappeared entirely. Nothing was heard of him for some days, when he suddenly rejoined the army on a 'private exchange' (of prisoners) with the following mournful story. Finding himself, near daybreak, on an elevated piece of cleared ground, with the pursuit slackening, and no enemy at hand he thought it a good opportunity to give men and horses a few minutes' rest. The horses were therefore unbitted, and the men lay down without sentinels, Johnny intending to keep awake, or get awake within ten minutes and go on with his business like a giant refreshed. He knew, or thought he knew the position of the column in the road by the irregular and intermittent pounding of the pursuing guns, and thought that for such a very few minutes he might avoid sacrificing the rest of even one sentinel. But the Confederate Cavalry of General Fitz-Hugh Lee, just then carefully exploring our flank to find where he could best strike, came suddenly upon and surrounded the whole squad, capturing it entire. In fact the men were so dead-beat they had to be stirred up with difficulty, one by one, to receive the polite invitation to surrender. Johnny having given his personal parole for the purpose of keeping out of the Confederate Provost Marshal's hands as long as possible, was sent to the rear and invited to make himself at home in Lee's tent. There he devoted himself for a day or two to solid sleep, when his host returned and informed him that this parole must expire next day, when he would be under the disagreeable necessity of 'turning him in.' Nevertheless, he should first meet a lot of his old West Point acquaintances at dinner, for which purpose a number of Confederate West Pointers were assembled and Johnny's misfortune freely discussed over whiskey and roast potatoes, the captive's heart being made sore by the sound, but now superfluous advice, never to do it again without affording himself 'at least one sentinel.' But Johnny continued so low-spirited over this ignominious check to his budding career, that a private exchange was at last procured for him—general ones not being then permitted—and he returned to us with resolutions concerning sentinels as firm and uncompromising as were ever formed in a soldier's breast.

About daylight, the pursuit having ceased, Sedgwick's hard-worked Division halted and went into camp at Langley, near the Potomac, and after a day's rest the whole Second Corps marched to Tenallytown, Md. As it was supposed some time would be devoted here to restoring and refitting the Army of the Potomac, I took the opportunity to telegraph for my wife, who immediately came down in charge of her brother, who returned by the next train. He had not been gone an hour when intelligence was received of the reappointment of McClellan to the command of the Army, together with his orders for an immediate march against Lee, who had crossed the Potomac into Maryland. There was no means of getting an escort to Washington for Mrs. Wistar, and the best I could do was to place her and Mrs. Rizer, wife of the Surgeon of the

72nd, in an ambulance belonging to a hospital train under command of a lieutenant of our brigade.

The Second and Twelfth Corps, both under command of Sumner, marched at noon, September 4th, by way of Rockville and Clarksburg to Hyattstown. Burns being still disabled by his wound, Howard continued in command of our brigade. The quiet Maryland village of Hyattstown lay at the bottom of a wide and deep gorge of the Monocacy, where the main road of our advance was intersected by a cross-road following the line of the river. When the head of the column arrived at the brink of the ravine whence it looked down on the town and cross-roads, it was halted by Sumner, who by way of a delicate compliment to the 71st for its recent service, sent it forward to explore and clear the ravine of the enemy's rearguard before involving the mass of the column. After descending the hill and fording the river, half the regiment was left at the cross-roads with orders to send out a company to right and left to clear and hold the two roads, while the remaining five companies were deployed, covered well with a skirmish-line and pushed on up the hill driving the enemy's few skirmishers before them. Not a citizen was to be seen in the town, the houses being closed and the inhabitants in the cellars, as our batteries had commenced throwing shell over it and us, at the enemy near the top of the hill, not yet visible to us. The enemy's retiring skirmishers of dismounted cavalrymen being reinforced were able to retard our progress somewhat, and, as we approached the hill-top our batteries ceased firing over us, indicating that the enemy not yet visible to us, had either retired beyond their range, or that we were getting close to their position. Sending back an order for the reserve to advance half its force in support, the leading companies pushed on through a field of tall corn, emerging directly upon a cavalry column just arrived and commencing a hasty and disorderly deployment. There were two things that might be done, and not much time to choose between them; viz., to form square and wait their attack, or taking advantage of their condition, go right for them. As all the field-glasses in the Second Corps Staff were no doubt levelled at us from the high ground across the river, the last was adopted, and a headlong charge of infantry on cavalry was executed without wasting a minute.

I do not know of any other such charge against mounted cavalry, and am aware it is nowhere recommended in the text-books, but under the circumstances this one proved eminently successful, the enemy falling at once into a disorder which he found impossible to remedy under pressure, and was forced to make a rapid retreat to restore his line. The reserve companies coming up, a long thin line was formed with wide intervals and refused wings. The wounded prisoners reporting Baker's brigade of Confederate cavalry in front of us, with infantry at no great distance, the information was sent back to Sumner, and as it was now dark, we proceeded to bivouac on the ground gained, feeling extensively in front and on both flanks with patrols. Late in the evening Col. Sully arrived with his regiment and two light guns without caissons, with orders to hold the ground, but make no such aggressive movement as might bring on an engagement too big for us to manage. Now as we knew of a whole cavalry brigade in front, and were aware that the rear of Longstreet's Corps could not be far off, and we were at least three miles from any possible reinforcements, with two roads intersecting our only practicable connection with them, a remarkably fine chance was presented for an enterprising enemy to surround and capture our two isolated regiments. As I did not crave for the honor either of defeat or surrender, I proposed to Sully to take command, on his rank as an officer of the regular army. He however insisted that I possessed the oldest commission, which I could not deny, and after some friendly sparring we agreed to share the command between us, and he undertook to post guards and pickets in the woods on the left, while I attended to the open country on the right. After that was done it came on to rain, and S. and I passed a miserable night sitting on the ground under a dripping tree, holding our wretched horses and kept constantly on the alert by the numerous collisions of pickets. The men had a day's rations in haversacks, but the officers had nothing, and S. and I, with our respective Adjutants, were reduced to sup on a bottle of whiskey which he fortunately had in his holsters.

Just before daylight a negro body-servant of the Confederate Col. Baker, who had got entangled inside our lines in looking for a lost horse, was captured in an effort to get away. Feeling his way along our picket-line he dropped into the road beyond the guard but was picked up by a single sentinel concealed a hundred yards beyond, and brought in. The darkey refused to tell anything, but his captors being hungry and wet, and not in a mood to trifle, he was placed on a horse with a noose round his neck, the other end of which was run over a low limb and fastened. When all was ready, and a single blow from the flat of a sabre would have started the horse and launched the darkey into space, he weakened and promised to tell all he knew. The cheeks and throat of the negro at this critical moment entirely changed color, strange as it may seem, presenting a dirty greenish-white appearance. This surprising physical phenomenon which was noticed by all, is my only reason for noting such a trifling circumstance.

At daybreak we could see the head of Sumner's column in motion winding down the hill beyond the river, and knew that we were no longer in danger of a Confederate prison. Two days later when approaching the town of Frederick—Lee evacuating the country before us—General Howard, the new brigade commander, had the impudence to place me in arrest for refusing to obey his order to consolidate my battered drum corps, with the spick and span new corps of another regiment that had never seen an enemy till after the 71st had lost nearly 400 men in action.

On my refusal, twice repeated to his A. D. C., possibly with more emphasis than was absolutely necessary, General Howard ordered me into arrest but declined to receive my sword; I retired as in duty bound to the rear of the regiment, surrendering command to the senior captain, no field officer being present. Howard preferred charges for Disobedience of Orders, of which he sent me a copy, when the following correspondence occurred. I copy from the old papers now lying before me, nearly illegible from being soaked in my blood in the following battle of Antietam.

Hdqrs. Burns Brigade, Frederick, Sept. 13, 1862.
COLONEL: Gen. Howard directs me to say that the above charges and specifications will not be forwarded until ample time has been given for written explanations. Very Respectfully Your Obed. Servant,
To COL. I. J. WISTAR.   E. WHITTLESEY, A. A. G.

CAPTAIN : I have no explanation to offer, either written or verbal. If I or my regiment deserved censure—which has never been the opinion of more experienced Brigade Commanders—a better mode of administering it might have been selected than the insidious insult of breaking it up into detachments to swell the pageant of another. I have the honor to be, Sir, with respect

ISAAC J. WISTAR,

Sept. 13th, 1862.   Col. Cala. Regiment, (in arrest).

P. S. I have no stationary but this old envelope.

On receipt of the last, General Howard sent for me, and I went late at night to the tent-fly under which he was sitting, surrounded by his staff, assembled I presume to be taught a lesson in the niceties of personal and official dignity. As I entered, H. rose and ordered some of them to get me a cracker-box as a seat, to which I replied that I preferred standing. Then, with swelling dignity: "Sir, I consider your communication insulting, and manifestly intended to be so." No answer. "When you receive an official order, it should be at once obeyed and explanations asked afterwards." No answer. "Will you obey the order now?" "No sir, never." "What is your objection?" "I decline to converse about it. You have preferred charges. I will defend myself only before the Court or your superiors." "Well, I must inform you that Gen. Sedgwick discourages the charges, thinking you must be under some misapprehension." "No misapprehension whatever, sir." "Well, but the order was Gen. Sedgwick's and merely transmitted through me." "Then, sir, why did you not so specify as usual with a transmitted order, and it would have been instantly obeyed." "Do you mean to say that you regard Gen. S.'s orders as more obligatory than mine?" "No sir, not his military orders. But this is not a military order; it refers simply to regimental pageantry. Gen. Sedgwick knows me and my regiment well, and we know him, and would obey without question any order whatever from him, knowing he had some good reason."

This, though it could hardly have soothed the General's ruffled dignity, ended the discussion and he released me from arrest and abandoned the charges. On inquiring about it later from General Sedgwick, he informed me the order was neither his nor Howard's but came from Sumner, the Corps Commander, and was general in terms, being simply intended to consolidate the drum corps of each two regiments for better effect on the doubtful loyalty of the large town of Frederick; Howard having through inadvertence or otherwise, chosen to give it a definite application by effacing the music of his oldest regiment in favor of the youngest, instead of the converse, as decency required. Being ostentatiously and aggressively pious, his dislike of me was I suppose purely theological, since I had stiffly declined to encourage or take part in the public wrestlings in prayer with which he bedeviled his staff, and edified the admiring young newspaper reporters. By outliving his contemporaries, and cultivating an obsequious loyalty to the ruling party and its demagogues, he has, without winning a single professional success in his whole career, attained high parchment rank since the war. The shameful surprise and flight of his Corps at Chancellorsville, which came near wrecking the army; his disastrous failure at Gettysburg, followed by his humiliating excuse to Gen. Meade, and his futile and ludicrous chase across the continent after Joseph, the civilized Nez Perces chief—who though a peaceful husbandman, untrained to war, and burdened with a numerous body of starved and half-naked non-combatants, eluded for months the professed soldier backed by twenty times his force—are prominent and illustrative facts of his military career; while his record in civil life must always remain tarnished by the unexplained evaporation of the 'Freedmen's' earnings by the ruin of their bank at Washington, of which he was President.[19]

[19] Editorial from *The Philadelphia Inquirer*, Friday, March 27, 1896.

THE OLD SOLDIERS SHOULD PROTEST

The *Boston Herald* says that Senator Hale and Congressman Dingley, both of the State of Maine, have in charge a bill to confer upon General Howard, also of the State of Maine, who is on the retired list of the regular army the rank of lieutenant-general. Should General Miles be made lieutenant-general, New England, whose soldiers and military historians regret that she did not produce a capable army commander during the Civil war, will have two lieutenant-generals thirty-one years after the war is over.

Accompanying the Howard bill now before Congress is a statement dated Washington and signed by E. Moody Boynton formulating General Howard's claims to the distinction proposed to be conferred upon that officer. This statement

On the 14th, the Second Corps made a forced march to the sound of the guns at South Mountain, arriving after the pass at Turner's Gap had been forced by our troops, and camped on the field of battle. The troops engaged having made sufficient details for bringing in the wounded and burying the

---

is remarkable for its ignorance of history, for its malicious, audacious and false attacks upon much greater soldiers than General Howard, and it is further remarkable for its silence as to what that officer actually did, its avoidance of all reference to what he failed to do upon the field of battle and the unblusing effrontery with which it attributes to General Howard acts of valor and military skill performed by Generals Buford, Reynolds, Warren, Hancock and Meade at the battle of Gettysburg. Here are some of the false assertions and false claims made in the statement in General Howard's behalf:

"He saved his army and his country and secured the unwilling adoption of his position and line by Major-General Meade with the entire Army of the Potomac. The plan of Meade was to have retreated to Pipe Clay Creek. . . . . The battle (of the first day) was over by 4.30 o'clock, when Hancock arrived. He repeatedly on the second day sent messages to General Meade asking the occupation of Little Round Top."

We are also told that Howard urged Meade to attack after the defeat of Pickett's charge, and again at Williamsport and are assured that either attack would have resulted in the annihiliation of Lee's army. The claim is made that it was Howard's artillery that swept Pickett's division from the face of the earth and enabled the Nineteenth Massachusetts to capture what was left of it.

Such a statement would be unworthy of serious attention if it were not proposed to spread it upon the records of Congress and to issue it in the form of a public document. The representatives in Congress from other States than Maine, especially the Senators and Representatives from Pennsylvania, the soldiers upon the Military Committees of the Senate and House should see to it that the government is not made ridiculous by indorsing assertions so ignorant, false and unjust to great military heroes who, being dead, cannot defend themselves, but some of whom in their life time fully exposed Howard's military pretensions. At one time he struggled to take from General Hancock the credit of restoring order after the rout of Howard's corps on the first day. Now he claims that the danger was over when Hancock arrived and that the responsibility was trivial.

The monuments erected on the line of Howard's corps at Gettysburg are enduring memorials of Howard's incapacity as a general. They show him to posterity in the act of advancing to a range of hills beyond the roads upon which the enemy were coming towards Gettysburg. Had he gained the hills the Confederates would have come in behind him. His incompetency at Gettysburg was but a repetition of his conduct at Chancellorsville. At Pittsburg he was lately warned by veterans of the Army of the Potomac not to repeat some of the insinuations which are expressed in the statement of the man Boynton. The surviving soldiers of that army should send their protests to Congress against making General Howard a paper lieutenant-general upon grounds that have no existence.

dead, Sumner passed through the Gap on the 15th, and marching through Boonsboro, took position before dark, near Keedysville, on the centre of the line now forming on Antietam Creek.

During the march to this place the advance had constantly pressed Lee's rearguard, under Longstreet, and as an engagement of any dimensions might occur from hour to hour, it had been possible for me to leave my command long enough to go to the rear to see my wife only on two occasions. As the ambulance division followed the troops at no great distance, I was naturally filled with solicitude in moving through the bloody scenes of the battlefield of South Mountain, at the reflection of the unwonted spectacles that must there meet the ladies' eyes. But even these were exceeded when, after passing through the contested Gap, we came upon the Confederate field-hospitals in rear of their lost position. The worst of these was a blacksmith-shop directly on the road, in which an operating table had been rudely constructed, and the amputated limbs thrown through the window, where they still lay in a blue festering heap that would have filled two or three army wagons. Piles of bloody and mutilated bodies of those who had arrived too late, or had died under the surgeon's hands, encumbered the ground and roadside in front. All I could do was to send a man to the rear with a note to the ambulance lieutenant, begging him to arrange in some way that the ladies might escape this sight; but I afterwards learned that he had not found that practicable, and their sensibilities had been spared nothing.

The 16th was passed by McClellan in completing his concentration, forming his line, and feeling by single batteries for the enemy's artillery positions. One of our batteries had thoughtlessly opened from a slight ridge, behind which was bivouacked Sedgwick's entire Division closed in mass, forming a compact rectangular body crowded as close as the men could lie behind their stacks. I was sitting with Gen. Sedgwick on a wagon-tongue opposite, and not far from the flank of this mass, when the enemy opened with one of their batteries in reply. The first shots as usual flew high, but as they approximated the range, their shells began to strike in our battery, or missing it and the ridge, to fly low over the infantry division in rear.

Someone remarked on the stupidity of uselessly drawing an artillery fire on a crowded mass of infantry, and Sedgwick sent an aide to the battery to inquire for what reason, or by whose orders they were posted at that particular spot. The officer had scarcely galloped off with the message, when a shell skimming lightly over the ridge, whizzed low over the men, causing thousands of heads to duck, and struck fairly in the middle of my own regiment. From the stacked muskets the men had stretched shelter tents for shade, and were lying in all attitudes of rest, apparently covering every inch of ground. Muskets, blankets, knapsacks and shelter-tents flew into the air, and any spectator must have been shocked at what seemed terrible havoc of a single shot. But on running over to ascertain the damage, it turned out that with the exception of one man struck square in the neck, not another one was even hurt; the shell entering the ground without bursting. By comparing this singular immunity with the effect of another shell which on a subsequent occasion I saw strike and explode a limber chest, killing or wounding thirteen men on the spot, one may form an idea of the uncertain and chance results of this, the most striking and imposing of all ordinary arms of offense.

The night of the 16th was showery, and Howard and I slept under a few rails propped up, and partially covered with cornstalks. It being then known at headquarters that Hooker had been severely checked in getting into position on the right, an order came at 2 A.M. to inspect cartridge boxes; followed an hour later by another to distribute forty additional rounds for the trousers pockets. At four, the men were roused for coffee, and soon after dawned with a brilliant but short-lived and delusive sunshine, what all now knew was to be the day of battle. Knapsacks were piled, and every preparation made for instant movement. Heavy firing of all arms advanced and retired on the right (Hooker and Mansfield) but it was not till eight o'clock that an aide came galloping down to Division Quarters waving in his hand the order that we waited for. Though it would be superfluous to give in this place any more ambitious description of the much-discussed battle of Antietam, than such few items as concern the personal fortunes of the narrator, yet to render even those intelligible, some brief explanation is required.

After the restoration of McClellan to command, the Confederate General, finding himself closely pressed by a hand stronger than Pope's, gave up his plan of invasion and commenced a hasty concentration of his scattered columns preparatory to a withdrawal to his own side of the Potomac. His several detachments had therefore been called in upon Sharpsburg, in front of which a defensive line had been formed, intended, but not quite strong enough, to extend from river to river across a deep westward bend of the upper Potomac, there ordinarily fordable. But, notwithstanding the defense of the South Mountain passes on the 14th to gain time, on the 16th Jackson, delayed by the siege and surrender of Harper's Ferry, was not yet up; and Longstreet and D. H. Hill, having been roughly handled on the 14th, had barely preceded the Federal Army to the position assigned them. It is therefore probable that but for the attack by our right on the evening of the 16th certain to be vigorously prosecuted with the return of daylight, Lee would have crossed the river early on the 17th and retired upon Jackson, some of whose divisions were in march to his support during the entire night of the 16th. But that attack made it necessary for Lee to stand at bay, and at any cost inflict sufficient check on his enemy to get time for crossing the river with his guns and baggage.

McClellan, having thus by rapid marching and severe fighting, forced his antagonist to accept battle, proposed to attack him simultaneously on both flanks, and, having driven either or both back upon their line of retreat, to push forward a powerful center to complete the victory. But the execution of this plan was defeated by the extraordinary supineness of Burnside, who with express orders to attack on the left at daylight, and with 20,000 men already in position for the purpose, delayed his movement till one o'clock, and then required nearly or quite two hours more to get his whole force engaged. But at half-past three A. P. Hill having delayed to receive the surrender at Harper's Ferry, and then marched twenty miles *after* the hour at which Burnside was ordered to attack, arrived on the field and at once attacked and drove Burnside back across the creek, ending that General's tardy activity for the day. It was this disobedience and failure of Burnside that enabled Lee to strengthen his left by detaching continually from his right, till much the larger part of his army was available to meet the attacks on his left made successively by the Corps of Hooker, Mansfield and Sumner.

Hooker, resuming his attack at daybreak, was badly defeated, himself wounded, and his Corps dispersed. Mansfield, in support of Hooker, took up the fighting against troops constantly reinforced by Lee from his unemployed right, and shared the same fate, being himself killed. It was now eight o'clock, and though the roar of battle resounded on the right, all remained silent on our left, where no guns of Burnside announced his expected attack on Lee's weakened right wing. Officer after officer of the staff had been sent off in the vain effort to hurry the tardy commander of the Ninth Corps, and it now became necessary to follow up the defeated attacks of Hooker and Mansfield by troops detached from the center where they had been reserved for quite another purpose. This was the emergency that had brought us the order to move off to the right, and take up the attack in that quarter already twice defeated. The rest of the story may as well be told by the insertion here of a statement prepared by me in 1882, at the request of the Brigade Survivors' Association, to repel certain insinuations of Col. Palfrey, a New England officer, who, with a certain selfish shrewdness not absolutely unknown among his compatriots, attempted to cover up the defeat of his own regiment by falsely attributing the cause to others. This statement was carefully made over my signature and generally reprinted by the Pennsylvania press, and has never been controverted nor attacked; even Palfrey himself preserving a discrete silence since its publication.

A recent Massachusetts writer, belonging to a regiment whose distinguished gallantry required no superfluous misrepresentation of others, has stated that on the failure of the attack by the Second (Sedgwick's) Division of the Second (Sumner's) Corps at Antietam, the Philadelphia Brigade was 'the first to go.' That Brigade—or what is left of it—is of a different opinion, and there must still live some of its survivors who will recognize the substantial accuracy of the following statement of the facts.

During the night of the 16th and 17th of September, 1862, Sedgwick's Division was bivouacked with its Corps in close column, near Keedysville, in the center of the general position of the army. Hooker's Corps, followed by Mansfield's in support had crossed the Antietam Creek on the evening of the 16th to take position for attack on our extreme right. During the night the divisions of the Second Corps were twice aroused for distribution of additional cartridges, and again, before daylight, for coffee. Hooker's second attack, made at or before daylight on the 17th failed. His Corps, after some sharp fighting, was defeated and himself wounded. Mansfield's small corps, following quickly in support, had a severe tussle and shared the same fate, its commander being killed. Then soon after daylight came the orders to Sumner, in obedience to which Sedgwick's Division of that General's corps, with whose movements only we are now concerned, moved out by the right flank by brigades, forded the Antietam, which took the men above the middle and faced to the left. This brought the division into an attacking column of three brigades, following each other, each deployed in line and facing west. Gorman's brigade led; Dana's followed; and Burns' composed the third line. In consequence of General Burns' absence, by reason of wounds suffered in the Peninsula, his brigade was on that day commanded by General Howard. It consisted of the following Pennsylvania regiments, raised in Philadelphia: viz., The Sixty-ninth, Colonel Owens; the seventy-first, Colonel Wistar; the Seventy-second, Colonel Baxter, and the One-dred-and-sixth, Colonel Moorhead; the Seventy-first being that day on the right.

The dripping soldiers shook off the water, the lines were dressed. Sumner, who in person accompanied his favorite division, waved his sword, and the division, under its beloved Sedgwick, moved to the front from which hardly more than half of it was ever to return. Not a voice, and scarcely a shot at first disturbed the silent advance of this veteran body of about five thousand men. The men were veterans and knew their business. The three lines, in perfect order and alignment moved forward at the quick step, with arms at right shoulder shift. Soon a single shell flew over all three lines and exploded harmlessly in the rear. Then another, better elevated, fell with effect in the middle of the column, and the range being found, the enemy's batteries, a mile in front opened thick and fast, and a sharp and sustained fire from about a dozen guns of Stuart and S. D. Lee, mostly taking effect in the rear line, warmed up the column for the work before it. Soon the dead and wounded of the two defeated corps were encountered, and as the column held its steady way forward through the historic cornfield, death and mutilation in shocking forms covered the ground on every side. The dead were awaiting for a soldier's grave, and the fast glazing eyes of the wounded turned silently to the charging column marching over them with steady and determined tread.

The piece of woods and the Hagerstown pike were reached and passed. The leading line (no skirmishers) had entered, passed and were emerging from the second woods just as the third line had reached to about its center. The second and third lines were still parallel, but the first had made a slight change of direction to the left, so that at the moment when it passed the fence at the far side of the woods, its alignment formed a slight angle with that of the following line, the apex of which was on the left flank. The enemy, relieved on his right by the prolonged and unaccountable inactivity of Burnside, had been able to detach heavy reinforcements to his menaced flank, and these hastily coming into position with left refused, now offered a line of battle more nearly conforming to Sedgwick's line of march than to the alignment of his front. This condition though of transcendent importance, was unknown to both sides. The woods concealed each from the other, and both were in effect moving forward on the sides of an acute angle toward the point of the angle, which the Confederates reached first. Thus, under cover of rocks and woods, the hostile Divisions of McLaws and Walker had come—certainly more by accident than design—to occupy a position which at the moment of collision not only gave them both front and flanking fire against the Union column, but was more capable of rapid change to meet the attack, as suddenly developed. Hence it was the left forward corner of the attacking column that first struck the enemy's line, from which it was instantly saluted by a destructive fire, delivered at short range in its flank and front.

The first line became instantly and roughly engaged under tremendous disadvantage. The second halted in line and attempted to change front, and the attention of the present writer becoming absorbed by his own concern with the rear line, these observations will hereafter be confined to it, or rather to a part of it, for the thin woods in which the actual collision occurred was obstructed by protruding strata of limestone rock standing on end nearly vertical, and the right regiment (Seventy-first) had, by these and other inequalities, become separated from the other three of its brigade. At the moment of the shock the colonel of this regiment had ordered it down on its face to avoid unnecessary casualties till its service in action might be required. But by the ardor of the Commanding General the three lines of battle had been hurried up to intervals not exceeding thirty paces, and the engaged and reserve lines were simultaneously and equally under fire. In a very few minutes Gorman's Brigade, in the effort to change front under this enfilading and destroying fire, lost its cohesion, and, in fact, broke. The second line being partly faced by the rear rank for the same purpose, was not in shape to withstand the rush of fugitives, and was almost instantly run over by the first, when both came back with a tumultous rush upon the rear brigade. The latter at the order, delivered by the sword, for no word was audible, came at once to its feet with bayonets at the charge. Upon the integrity of this last line, which the writer aforesaid complains was 'the first to go,' now depended the entire right of the army, and a stern resistance was maintained by it, both to the fugitives and the enemy.

In such an action covering several miles of front, few officers of regimental rank can take personal cognizance of a long line of battle, but it can be positively asserted of at least the right regiment, that it held its position and forced the route around its flanks till its fire was unmasked, when the enemy's advance was sharply checked. But the general Union line had become defective on the left, where Richardson was killed, and his division roughly handled, and the superior force which the Confederates were now able, although from inferior resources, to bring upon this vital point soon enveloped the left and threatened the rear of the right regiment, the enemy's fire on it being now effective on its rear, left and front.

At the same time a few of Stuart's guns had got an advanced position on the right, and though some Union guns were coming into battery on the right rear to attend to them, it was nevertheless evident that for this isolated regiment, capture or retreat had become a question of minutes. It had indeed been important to cover the retreat of the Division to the last possible moment, but that had already been reasonably well done, and could not be promoted by an entire sacrifice of the regiment, so the Seventy-first was reluctantly ordered to retire. Its retreat was not effected without sharp fighting and severe loss. Every field and staff officer, including the Colonel was left upon the ground. But one Captain and three Lieutenants remained for duty, and the loss in men—as nearly as can now be recollected with no official papers at hand—reached something over fifty per cent of its force engaged. Under its surviving Captain (Lewis), what was left of it marched to the rear, served fresh cartridges, called its roll and reported to General Meade ready for any duty, and was put into action by that gallant General within half an hour.

The writer viewing these events from the limited standpoint of a regimental officer, is unable to speak from personal observation of the other regiments of the Philadelphia Brigade after separation from them by the roughness of the ground. But they were substantially of the same quality, and their conduct was reported and is believed to have been equally soldierly. Then and always they received the warm appreciation of corps and division commanders, and it is believed that no unfavorable criticism of them, or any of them, has ever before been publicly made. Neither is there any occasion or desire to underrate the quality or services of the gallant regiments of Gorman's or Dana's Brigades. On the contrary they were good troops, ably officered and required no one's indorsement, for their gallant conduct on numerous fields before and after the misfortune in question abundantly attests their quality. It is to be regretted that they should have possessed a single officer willing to give currency to unfounded statements to the prejudice of other troops of equal merit, who on the same fields and in the same corps and division, loyally and cheerfully shed their blood in the same cause.

CHAPTER XX

EXPERIENCES OF A BRIGADE COMMANDER

Returning from great historical events to the small personal adventures which are the humble subject of this narrative, it may be said that while my own individual fortunes at Antietam were better than those of the thousands who there fell to rise no more, they were by no means so good as those of the other thousands who escaped unhurt. First of all I lost a valuable and favorite horse, struck in the knee by a piece of shell, near the crossing of the Hagerstown pike, after which casuality I was on foot. 'Empire' was a high-spirited, three-quarter-bred horse who had learned to fear none of war's alarms and was only cheerfully stimulated by the heaviest firing and most unexpected events happening around him. He was the pet of the regiment, the men having a way of inducing him to lie down at night in a good place where, on occasion, they piled in around him for warmth, a familiarity with which he was not the party least contented. He would accept any reasonable kind of food and rarely went hungry, for many of his friends were always ready to risk their lives in creeping through the artillery sentinels to steal oats and forage for him when those luxuries were not to be had elsewhere on any terms. When he was first struck, his faithful groom, Dougherty, came running from the ranks and received him from me, but upon seeing D. resume his place shortly afterwards, I learned from him the sad news that he had scarcely got the horse a hundred yards to the rear when he was killed on the spot by another shot through the neck.

When Sedgwick's charging column struck the enemy and received a stunning fire on flank and front, the 71st had become separated from the other regiments of its line by certain vertical strata of limestone projecting in some cases as much as twelve or fifteen feet above the surface. The regiment being crowded close up to the two front lines, and therefore fully exposed to the fire without the opportunity to return a shot, was ordered down on its face to minimize casualties as much as possible till it should be needed. When the front line broke and ran over the second, and both came back on the third with an irrestrainable rush of fugitives, the 71st having with all the rest of the rear line been thus crowded up too close by the impetuosity of Sumner, must certainly have been demolished had its discipline wavered. But at the order it rose in place like one man with muskets at the charge and firmly repelled the tumultuous crowd, till it had passed round its flanks when its fire was delivered with immense effect on the pursuing enemy, themselves disordered by their rapid advance and noisy exultation. But their reserves coming up, the enemy rapidly recovered themselves, and were exchanging with us a steady and destructive fire at short distance, when observing an increasing fire coming from the left rear, I climbed a reef of rock for a more extended view, and at once became conscious of an appalling state of facts. On our left as far away as the eye could reach all our troops had given way, and the enemy's pursuing lines were already many hundred yards in rear of us with nothing in sight to stop them!

Almost at the same time Stuart's guns, their first position having become masked by the advance of their own infantry, had obtained a position on our right front, and now opened at short range with canister, which partly enfiladed our fast-diminishing line. There were no signs elsewhere of a rally or reinforcements, and though the isolated regiment was yet firm, it must soon be destroyed by sheer weight of fire in front and on both flanks, and in any case must be surrounded in a few minutes. It had already given a few priceless minutes of cover to the retreat of the eight regiments of first and second lines, and the time had now come to save its gallant remnant. It was therefore got quickly into column of companies with the intention of forcing a way to the rear till some other solid troops could be found to rally upon. As the head of column was wheeling to the left about myself as pivot, its killed and wounded falling at every step, I was myself knocked over by a bullet through the left shoulder. Rogers, the left flank sergeant of G Company was instantly at my side, and as the blood was spouting from under the sleeve at the wrist, hastily clapped on a tourniquet constructed of my pocket handkerchief and his bayonet. He offered to remain with me, and was inclined to insist, till I appealed to him to save my sword. Recognizing that obligation, he quickly took it from me, and rushed after the retiring column, and was scarcely gone till the enemy's line marched over me.

But about this time General Meade, whose own division had been used up in the two attacks of Hooker, had got together a small force composed of the remnants of various regiments coming out in good order, and was leading it forward when he met and seized on the 71st, compact and in perfect order, though reduced to three officers and scarcely 250 rank and file. This force continuing to increase soon met and drove back the disordered Confederates who again retired over me leaving me lying between two fires. Twice again the enemy advanced over me, and were as often repulsed and driven back, finally making a firm stand at or near their original position. The last of these movements was by a heavy line of battle composed of the fresh troops of 'Stonewall' Jackson—that is, if troops can be called fresh who had marched all night and were now put into action without any rest or intermission. As this splendid line moved over me, a young lieutenant seized the occasion to leave his place to demand my sword. When he learned that it was beyond his reach, he wanted my parole, which I refused to give. The little dispute was suddenly terminated by the arrival of several General Officers whom I took to be McLaws, Walker and Stuart. These with their staffs were following and closely watching their line now heavily engaged with our troops, whose balls were striking all around us. Having lost much blood notwithstanding the tourniquet, suffering intense pain and barely able to whisper, I nevertheless managed to attract the attention of one of their couriers, who dismounted, ascertained and reported the subject of discussion to Stuart, who inquired of the lieutenant his name and regiment. "Hill, of the 12th Georgia." "Join it immediately sir.'' The courier then rearranged the tourniquet, which, though hitherto but partially effective, had become excessively painful, handed me a drink from one of the 71st's wounded near-by, who kindly offered his canteen, and leaving me in a much more comfortable condition rode away after his General.

It was not till several years after the war that a mutual friend [20]—accidentally hearing the celebrated Confederate guerilla, John S. Mosby, relate the same circumstance in connection with my name, which he still remembered—brought us together, when I learned for the first time that the friendly courier had been no other than the renowned Mosby, at that time not even a commisioned officer. During the afternoon the infantry-fighting in our vicinity was mostly suspended, but the thin woods where we lay was severely shelled by the artillery of both sides, tearing to pieces the trees, splintering the rocks and producing terrible results on the helpless wounded of both armies, few of whom in my vicinity survived it. After dark all regular firing ceased, and some gentle showers gratefully refreshed such as were still alive and able to appreciate them. Two soldiers of the 71st less badly hurt than myself, insisted they could get me off, if I was able to stand, which with their aid I managed to do, but as the ground in our rear was obstructed not only by the multitude of dead and wounded of both armies who here lay thick, but by branches of trees and other results of the heavy artillery-fire so long concentrated on the place, the only available route for three cripples must at first be nearly parallel with the enemy's new infantry line, not fifty yards distant, and with no pickets out. In response to our explanation and request not to fire, they called to us to ''go ahead,'' which precautionary process had to be repeated several times as we passed in front of fresh parts of their line. At last we came to a small farm lane absolutely piled with Confederate dead who had been there mowed down in heaps in repeated but vain efforts to take a Federal battery which had been posted at the head of the lane. It was difficult in our condition to crawl over and through the two fences and these tangled corpses lying between them in every attitude of death, but at last it was

[20] Bingham, of Lockhaven, Pa.

by mutual aid accomplished, and we came into a comparatively open field whence the hospital men, fully exposed to the enemy if they chose to fire, were cautiously removing the wounded These men got us upon stretchers, and by an odd coincidence, struck first upon our own regimental field-hospital, set up in a small two-roomed negro cabin. Amputations and operations were proceeding inside and outside, and the floor was slippery with blood, but place was made for me on the only bed, already occupied by three wounded officers of the 71st, where temporary relief was administered. Before long an ambulance was brought up and the surgeons decided to send Lieut. Wilson and myself in to the general hospitals at Keedysville. The vehicle jolted horribly over the rough fields, and poor Wilson soon became delirious and died in the ambulance, but I was deposited at a house where Mrs. Wistar had taken up her quarters, to her great relief, as I had been reported dead, since early morning.

The churches of this unhappy village had first been appropriated for the wounded, then successively the houses, shops, yards, and at last the streets, leaving a single track in the middle for the ever-arriving ambulances. On both sides, over 25,000 men had fallen, equal to about twenty per cent of the whole forces engaged. The loss of the Second Corps was twenty-seven per cent of its force engaged; Sedgwick's Division alone, which numbered about 5000 men, losing 2210 or 44¼ per cent. The 'present for duty' of the Second Corps was reduced from 16,013 on July 31, to 9594 on September 30th, of which loss much the largest proportion had fallen upon our Division. I cannot now lay my hands on the official figures of the 71st, but my recollection is that it lost in this single battle between fifty and sixty per cent of its force engaged, including all its commissioned officers but three.

Early on the day of battle, the Keedysville shopkeeper in whose house I found asylum, had crossed the road and entered the opposite field, where he was killed by a stray cannon-shot in the presence of my wife and his own, while trying to see something of the distant battle whose swelling roar already filled the air for many miles around. The house was filled with wounded officers of the 71st, even to the cellar, where lay the adjutant and a captain. After lying here three weeks, my injured artery was pronounced safe for travel, and I was carried in an ambulance to Hagerstown, from whence in a box-car filled with similar convalescents, Mrs. Wistar and I made our slow way *via* Harrisburg to Philadelphia. Notwithstanding the degrading consciousness of the large space in our lives and memories appropriated by mere physical pleasures, I can never forget the gratification afforded me while lying in the ambulance at Hagerstown, by Lieutenant Kirby, 1st U. S. Art., who had the patient kindness to hold a cigar for me to smoke, being my first returning dissipation of the kind, as I was still unable to raise either hand to my face. Poor fellow, I never saw him afterwards as he was not long after killed at Chancellorsville, his excellent battery subsequently becoming famous at Gettysburg under his successor, Cushing.

After lying ill a long time in Philadelphia, suffering much discouragement from my crippled condition, the right arm being already useless and the left now paralyzed, with a very uncertain sound respecting its future coming from the doctors, I began to despair of my capacity for future active service, and forwarded my resignation, which was in due course accepted by General Sumner, in General Headquarter Orders of the Second Corps. This order was legally final under ordinary circumstances, but was sequestered or annulled by Mr. E. M. Stanton, Secretary of War, who wrote me to that effect as soon as it came to his notice, advising me to devote my whole attention to recovery and do nothing till I should hear further from him. As this unusual course had given me fair reason to expect, I received notice in due time that my appointment had been sent by the President to the Senate for confirmation as Brigadier-General, to rank from November 29th, 1862, for services prior to and at Antietam. But objection to confirmation having been made by Senator Sumner of Massachusetts, an extreme partisan, who held sound political opinions—i.e., his own—to be the most important military or any other qualification, the case went over to the extra session called for the 4th of March, where by some adroit management of my faithful friend, Senator McDougal of California, I was at length confirmed, but with eight dissenting votes in a Senate that contained but nine Democrats.

The nervous power and sensation, both of which had at first been destroyed in the arm last wounded, by extensive nerve injury, gradually returned up to a certain point, where the improvement stopped and its condition has ever since remained nearly stationary. Though able to use it for many purposes, it remains much impaired, particularly in the fingers, which are still so devoid of sensation as to prevent or limit their use except as guided by the sight. As soon as I could manage to feed myself, and long before I could fasten my dress or trust myself on a horse, I reported for duty by letter and at the request of General John J. Peck, was assigned to command a brigade in his division, then engaged in defending Suffolk, Va., against the seige of Longstreet. In passing through Washington on the way to my new duties, I met General Sedgwick, just recovering like myself from his Antietam wound, who said he had been promised command of the Sixth Corps, and had written me at Philadelphia desiring me to take one of his brigades. Unfortunately it was too late, and I never saw that gallant soldier again. He was killed during an interval of that great battle, by the chance shot of a sharp-shooter, at Spottsylvania in 1864.

My new command had been recently organized as the 'Reserve Brigade,' and was composed of the 9th Vermont, 19th Wisconsin, 99th and 118th New York regiments, all good and veteran ones, though somewhat neglected in drill and unaccustomed to brigade organization. I found it holding an exposed position a long way in front of, and on a lower elevation than its camps, where it was partially protected by some slight earthworks, too much exposed to admit of more work being done on them at present. The pickets were sheltered in a line of shallow excavations still lower down the hill where they could only be relieved at night. The ground in rear of our line of battle being higher on the hillside, was so swept by the fire of the enemy's pickets, concealed in rifle-pits on the other side of the ravine, that it was a lively place for the officers who had frequently to traverse it. The position which was infinitely the most exposed part of the entire line of defense, could not be rectified at this point without giving up the ravine and so much ground as to expose important points, and we had therefore to make the best of it. The abominable condition was at length relieved by our assault and capture of Hill's Point, a vital part of Longstreet's line, which reduced the enemy to the alternative of retaking it, which was only possible with a greatly increased force and heavy loss, or raising the seige. They preferred the last and retreated, closely followed by us, to a defensive position on the line of the Blackwater, where we soon again confronted them. While in occupation of our new line an amusing incident occurred, unworthy of history but not perhaps out of place in this narrative.

A. E. S., a Virginian with whom I had formerly been on quite intimate terms in San Francisco, while on his way home prior to actual hostilities, had been arrested on the Isthmus by some over-zealous naval officer and sent prisoner to Washington on suspicion of being about to join the Confederate army. S. plead that he was unlawfully seized on his peaceful way from the loyal State of California, *via* the equally loyal State of New York to his lawful home in Virginia on private business, had committed no act of hostility to the U. S., and in the absence of proof to the contrary, was presumably a loyal citizen. As not a shadow of proof was forthcoming against these facts and presumptions, the legal position was unassailable, and after some months' detention he was released and sent through the various military channels and at length came to me, with orders to deliver him across the lines under flag of truce. Capt. F., a gallant young A. D. C. of mine, to whom was assigned this duty, with instructions not to make use of my name unnecessarily, placed the prisoner in a closed carriage and with an escort of a few troopers started on his errand.

The Blackwater is a deep sluggish stream flowing between a low closely-timbered bottom on the enemy's side, and a comparatively high bank on our side, clear of woods to the top of the hill a mile distant, where our pickets were disposed. When the small procession emerged into this open ground not long before dark on its way to the river, the enemy's pickets not immediately recognizing the white flag, opened fire, which increased in weight as their scattered pickets assembled, desiring to avoid unnecessary waste of life, F. proposed to the prisoner, that since he, S., must in any case risk the enemy's fire for a short time, he should take the carriage forward alone, giving his parole to return it. The character of these two men —both generous and brave—was inclined to punctilious exactness. S. moreover possessed a hot, aggressive temper not just then in its sweetest condition, while F., valuable and gallant as he was, had on occasions, certain ceremonious tendencies facetiously designated by his staff associates as 'the heavy military.' These were sure to crop out stiffly at formal military functions, such as parades, reviews, courts-martial, executions and the like. On receiving the above proposition which was sensible enough, since it would relieve the innocent escort of useless danger, while it involved not a particle of additional risk to the prisoner, S. rather airily replied, "Are not your orders to deliver me within the Confederate lines." "Yes, sir, certainly." "Well, sir, if you will say you are afraid to do that, I will accept your proposition." "Not at all sir; if you put it on that ground, I will see you delivered into the enemy's lines with every particle of ceremony you are entitled to." The firing soon ceased, after killing a trooper's horse and splintering the carriage once or twice, and on reaching the river, a scow was sent over by the Confederates for the carriage. But before embarking F. dismounted a couple of troopers and placed them inside the vehicle with these orders given in presence and hearing of the prisoner. "Draw and cock your pistols. Your instructions are to prevent the prisoner from leaving the carriage or communicating with anyone outside it on any pretext whatever, till further orders from me. Should he attempt either, you will immediately kill him without any discussion, and report. Do you understand the order?" "Yes, sir." "Repeat it." "Correct."

The flag was received by a Captain of pickets, who was all agog to learn the significance of a proceeding attended with such ceremony and precaution, but F. demanded audience of the Commanding Brigadier General, maintaining that he carried a B. G.'s flag, and would transact his business with no officer of less rank. In vain a sleepy Colonel was hunted up, who explained that his commanding officer, General Jenkins, was many miles distant, beyond a muddy cypress swamp almost impassable for wheels. F. was on his mettle, and was not to be budged by all the Colonels in the Confederacy. "Sir, you must either accept or decline my flag. If the latter, I will retire as I came. If the former, I will only communicate with the Commanding General in person." As the position, however wire-drawn, was correct enough to be defensible, the Colonel was by no means ready to refuse a message which bore such marks of importance, and a small cavalry escort was at last paraded, under whose charge F.'s carriage and party spent most of the night in ploughing through a fearful cypress swamp hitherto deemed impracticable for wheels, and toward morning were passed by the quarter-guard and reached Jenkins' quarters. That astonished officer hastily came out in his drawers to receive a dispatch duly heralded by wire, and surrounded with such precaution that it might be a proposition for peace, or any other fundamental subject. Who could tell? On delivering his message, F. of course removed the embargo on the captive, who bounced out in breathless rage, furiously denouncing his unheard-of treatment. Then F., with erect dignity and solemn gravity, proceeded to tell his side of the story, which, as Jenkins happened to be blessed with a fine sense of humor, nearly threw that officer into fits, leaving him scarcely breath enough to tell S. that as far as he could see, he only got the rigors of war he had himself required. But notwithstanding S.'s difficult temper and exacting disposition, he was a noble and gallant man, and at once entered the Confederate service, but was killed within a month in almost his first encounter.

Before I had been very long on duty at Suffolk I received from a number of distinguished citizens of Philadelphia a valuable token of their esteem and regard, which, coming from persons generally entertaining political opinions differing from my own and possessing their full share of the partisan excitement that raged much more fiercely at home than in the army, was not only graceful and liberal on their part, but was peculiarly grateful to one who had been so recently assailed on exclusively political and party grounds in the partisan press, and even in the Senate of the United States. This was a handsome and valuable General Officer's sword, flatteringly inscribed, and was accompanied by the following letter, to which appropriate reply was made.

Philadelphia, May 14, 1863.

DEAR GENERAL:

As the organs of your loyal fellow-citizens, who acknowledge, to use their own language, "the just claims to their gratitude of the brave men who hazard their lives to sustain the cause of the Union against the unholy rebellion by which it is assailed," and who recognize in you one of its most gallant defenders, we discharge with pride the duty assigned to us, of presenting to you on their behalf, the sword[21] which accompanies this letter "as a token of their respect and admiration."

Knowing as we do, that in assuming your place in the army of the Republic, you did so, meaning in the true spirit of a patriot soldier, to perform with alacrity whatever duties were required of you by the orders of those who alone are constitutionally invested with authority to direct our military operations for the preservation of the unity of our country, we have observed with much satisfaction that your courage and good conduct, rendering you so eminently worthy of promotion, have not been unrequited.

In this connection, it would be unjust to pass over without especial commendation, the California Regiment (71st Pennsylvania) with which your name has been from the first identified; whose brave men were always ready to follow in the path of danger where you led, and who, in enabling their commander to attain his present enviable distinction, have gained for themselves enduring renown.

Elevated as you have been to a higher command, we feel sure that however freely your blood has been shed on the memorable fields of Ball's Bluff and Antietam, there is still enough left in your veins to enable you to wield usefully in the righteous cause the weapon which, with earnest prayers for your honor and safety, we now place in your hands.

With the highest consideration and regard,

We remain

Your friends and fellow-citizens,

WM. D. LEWIS
A. E. BORIE
C. MACALESTER
SAMUEL L. SHOBER
O. W. DAVIS
C. P. BAYARD
Committee.

To GENERAL ISAAC J. WISTAR,
          Commanding the Reserve Brigade
                    Camp Suffolk, Va.

[21] This sword, with appurtenances, is deposited with The Wistar Institute of Anatomy.

Upon the evacuation of Suffolk some time during the summer, my brigade acting as rear guard, I took up the rails from many miles of railroad track and shipped them to the Quartermaster at Norfolk, pursuant to written orders. But having mislaid the order, it is doubtful with what success I could even now defend against a personal suit for that spoliation, since the statute of limitations does not run in favor of one outside the jurisdiction, and I was therefore for many years cautious of getting within the territorial power of Virginia Courts, but presume the facts have long since been forgotten or forgiven by the present generation.

Major-General Dix having during the same season assumed command of the Department of Eastern Virginia and North Carolina, soon after ordered my Brigade to Yorktown, the Headquarters of the military District of Eastern Virginia. It was quite time that some reforming and energetic hand should be laid upon that District, than which none could certainly be in much worse condition. I transported my Brigade of four regiments and a battery, on four steamers, and on calling to report arrival to the Brigadier-General in command, lately a western newspaper editor, I found him lying incapacitated in his quarters under the pious care of a pretty hard-looking staff, who called the affliction 'malaria,' a disease which seems to have much to answer for in morals, politics and war. The general condition of affairs was the most disgusting I have ever seen in a military post. The fortifications enclosed perhaps a couple of hundred acres, inside of which, besides the dirty, idle, and neglected troops, were gathered over 12,000 refugee negroes supported in idleness on Government rations, and lying about without order under any ragged shelter they could get, in every stage of filth, poverty, disease and death. The roadways, parade ground, gun platforms, and even the ditches and epaulements were encumbered by these poor wretches; the soldiery was ragged, filthy and idle, and unless all military signs were at fault, a raid by a handful of resolute and well-led men could have captured the place, with all its stores and its 3000 so-called troops, in a few minutes. The corruption underneath proved as bad as the more patent features of the all-pervading neglect and demoralization. The place was crowded with petty dealers calling themselves sutlers, whose trade across the lines received no pretense of supervision. Permits to take oysters from the private beds within our jurisdiction were sold to negroes for cash, of which there was no public or known accounting whatever. The thrifty Yankee serving as Post Quartermaster maintained 400 negroes on his pay roll, for whom he drew wages at the rate of eight dollars per month each, to handle supplies for a force not hitherto exceeding 3000 men besides the idle contra-bands. With strength enough to raid to the gates of Richmond and compel heavy detachments from the enemy's active armies to defend its back door, our troops were shut up in the two closed works of Fort Magruder and Yorktown, watched by a petty force, under a Captain, that they should have eaten up in a week.

Though nominally and legally placed under command of the creature who was responsible for all this, I sternly insisted on keeping my hard-worked Brigade clear of the mess; and taking post some miles in front of the place, allowed no interference, and permitted no person within its camp without my own pass, keeping my troops hard at work, picketing, patrolling and drilling. Finally, I made formal request through regular channels, for transfer with my Brigade to the Army of the Potomac, in place of which I was promptly ordered to assume command of the Military District, my predecessor being ordered to Washington, where he was soon lost sight of amid the crowd of politico-military patriots who sought to rearrange their disheveled plumage in that seat of Republican patriotism and purity. It was hard to know where to commence upon the Augean stables of the District of Eastern Virginia. As the whole mischief was not revealed at once, the first step was to clear out the fortified places and making then tenable by a minimum force, obtain use of a small movable column for aggressive purposes. For this purpose a large area of aban-doned fields, a few miles in the rear, was surveyed and laid out in two- and four-acre lots, with street and building lines; and all the able-bodied negroes set to work building log cabins of prescribed form and dimensions. To the government of this place, dubbed by the soldiers 'Slabtown,' was assigned a sergeant with a small force, under the supervision of an A. D. C. Oystering permits were sold by the Provost Marshal to these people; seeds and implements were obtained with the fund thus raised, and 'Slabtown' was soon in condition to contain all the refugees in the District.

The local troops, who had originally belonged to the 4th Corps, were reorganized and employed, with a portion of the contrabands, in policing and clearing up the fort and town, and when not thus usefully employed, were kept constantly at drill. Details of infantry were instructed in the working of the heavy guns, and troops so disposed and instructed that in a few minutes after an alarm from Headquarters every man was in his place on the ramparts or in the reserve. The Post Quartermaster's roll of 400 laborers was cut down to ten men, who, with details of troops on emergencies, were found amply sufficient for all purposes, notwithstanding the addition of my Brigade to the force supplied. Outlying posts were established, and an efficient system of infantry and cavalry patrols organized and constantly pushed farther towards the enemy's post at Bottom's Bridge, covering Richmond. The rogues who, under the name of sutlers, were driving a profitable trade across the lines in all sorts of articles contraband of war, were mostly sent out of the District, and an efficient Provost Guard was organized under Captain Brooks, a competent officer of zeal, force and integrity.

Though these and many other reformatory and military measures were necessarily carried on together, with some apparent, but no real confusion, in a very short time, our lines at Williamsburg were not only defensible against a much superior force, but the enemy's raiders were captured or driven out of the District, and either by occupation, patrols or expeditions in force, we held or substantially controlled the line of the Chickahominy from its mouth to Bottom's Bridge, within eight miles of Richmond, and were able to take an active offensive on both banks of York River.

Prior to, and in preparation for, General Dix's march on Richmond to relieve the pressure at Gettysburg, I was ordered to capture and hold the fortified post at West Point, the junction of the Pamunkey and Matapony, where these rivers unite to form the York. A sufficient number of steamers having been collected, the embarkation was so timed as to reach the place at one A.M. The wharves having been burned by the enemy, a picked force was landed in boats which drove back the enemy and deployed, to cover the landing. Houses were torn down for material and in a few hours a new wharf had arisen on the ruins of the old one, over which cavalry and artillery were successfully landed. A defensive line having been taken up across the point, a mile or two in front of the town, troops and impressed contrabands were set at work and within two days I was able to report it defensible by a small part of my force, leaving the remainder available for more active purposes. I therefore received orders to leave a sufficient force of infantry and guns to hold the place securely, and march to reinforce Dix, whose retreat on the south bank of the York to Yorktown was covered by this force, after which the garrison was withdrawn from West Point, and affairs resumed for awhile their former status.

Of course so much resolute clearing away of rubbish could not go on long without raising enemies and resistance, which though more or less annoying, I was quite prepared for. All the scamps collected in this snug harbor, both military and civil, with a wise discretion and enlightened regard for their own skins, confined their charges and imputations to the troublesome theme of my 'loyalty,' it being an axiom with the plundering scoundrels of that day that any coolness or deficiency in partisan Republican profession in itself constituted the most formidable kind of 'disloyalty.' To their minds the most 'truly loyal' man was he who asked fewest embarrassing questions, and their ideal patriot would be something like the late lamented Col. Yell of Arkansas, President of the Yellville bank of Yellville, of whom his sorrowing eulogist declared that, "our deceased friend though unable to account satisfactorily for the funds of that institution, yet showed by his remarks upon the 'busting' of the same, that his heart beat warmly for his native land."

I seldom took public notice of the weak expedients of the thieves and incapables who abused me after getting safely out

Genl. Custer's Head Quarters
West Point. Va. July 4. 1863
drawn by his
orderly Mart.

of my district, beyond grilling one occasionally, but it must be confessed that while in actual contact with the enemy in front, I had little patience with revenue-hunting rogues in the rear, and sometimes did hold myself justified in the use of extra-legal methods in extraordinary cases both military and civil. One of the former kind, which came near bringing me in collision with the legislative patriots at Washington, resulted from an effort to reform and improve the military service by applying to one of the incorrigibles, certain drastic remedies not specially provided for in the Articles of War. The rogue was turned in by his Colonel, who charged him with evading every duty, breaking all rules, being useless to the Government and a perpetual obstacle to discipline and good order, all of which was soon ascertained to be abundantly true. Now the Provost Guard was carefully organized of picked officers and men who had learned to know 'coffee boilers' and 'beats' at a glance, and possessed certain remedies which in the last resort sometimes cured, even after colonels and courts-martial had abandoned the patient as worthless and incurable. To it therefore the delinquent was sent, with an intimation of his character, the ineffectual efforts which had hitherto failed to make him useful to his country, and the hint that some improvement might be effected by a good private talking to from a couple of reliable corporals of the guard. I noticed from the Provost Guard returns next morning that the delinquent was 'in hospital; cause, a sore back,' and as hospital cases of all sorts were plenty, supposed the disease would receive due attention and thought no more of the matter.

But the patient was forwarded in due course to the general hospitals, first at Fortress Monroe, and afterward to Washington, where some surgeon, who had probably not served enough in the field to know the valuable hygienic and moral effects sometimes following a 'sore back,' discharged him from the service. Not long after I received a cypher message from the Department Commander that the man, together with his father, his M. C. and a couple of busybodies of the Sanitary Commission, had reached Fortress Monroe with passes from the Secretary of War and orders for me to arrest and forward such soldiers as they should identify in connection with a certain gross personal outrage committed on their suffering client. Of course a reply was telegraphed requesting they should be sent up at once in order that every practicable facility should be extended them. The Provost Marshal was at the same time directed to select two experienced soldiers of his guard for the special service of hunting down and arresting a certain troublesome guerrilla operating in the vicinity of our external lines, the men to start at once by night and if not successful by the expiration of ten days, to report then in cypher through the Colonel Commanding at Williamsburg, and there await further orders.

The Washington gentlemen duly arrived, and were of course assisted by an A. D. C. to search for the delinquents among all accessible troops, but unaccountably failed to identify the malefactors. They were then advised of the existence of sundry posts, guards and patrols in the vicinity of, and outside the military lines, for whose investigation authority would be furnished, on receiving a written acknowledgment that such dangerous quest was prosecuted by their own urgent desire against the opinions, warning and advice of the Commander of the District. But at this point the avengers—with great intelligence—weakened, and concluded to confine their researches to the safer territory inside the lines, which though it led to nothing, at least showed a commendable prudence, since though there was no means of knowing what might have been the course pursued by the two delinquents if arrested by civilians on the enemy's territory, there was reason to apprehend much from their energy, courage and manner of employment.

The District of Eastern Virginia had of course been nearly denuded of white males of suitable age for the Confederate army, nevertheless there remained a considerable population, including several hundred lunatics in the State Asylum at Williamsburg, among whom it was necessary to maintain order, and during the suspension of their ordinary resources, to preserve from absolute want. Such duties involved questions of municipal government and general policy, as well as the expenditure of government property for purposes authorized only by implication or not at all, where it was not difficult to fall into legal and other errors. Whether such an error was committed by me, or by the President of the United States in the following case, each reader may decide for himself.

A lady whose husband and sons were absent in the Confederacy and her pecuniary resources cut off, applied to the Commanding Officer at Willamsburg for leave to cross the lines into the Confederacy, taking her family and household effects "and a negro child six years old." The application came down endorsed, "Approved except as respects the negro child." Not wishing to decide the negro question myself, I forwarded it to Department Headquarters with the additional endorsement, "Approved, including the negro, since such a child, if left behind and separated from its natural protectors, would require dry nursing, for which I possess no soldiers properly fitted." The application was disapproved at Department Headquarters, and there the official part of the matter ended, but the negro question being at that time attended with much political excitement, some reporter at Fortress Monroe got hold of the correspondence, and I was soon in receipt from friends at home, of copies of a certain hyper-loyal eastern newspaper which, after printing the endorsements with a liberal addition of capitals, italics and exclamation points, devoted a column or two to violent abuse of myself as a traitor, a slave-hunter, kidnapper, and inhuman tyrant, who abused the power entrusted to him to hunt down, catch, and return, loyal and patriotic negroes to their cruel, bloodthirsty and disloyal owners. Of course I through the papers in the fire, but when soon after, the notorious Gen. B. F. Butler arrived at Fortress Monroe to succeed Foster in command of the Department, he also forwarded me a copy with an unofficial letter stating his pain at seeing the publication and that if I had a reply to offer, he would see it should receive proper publicity.

This proposition from a superior officer came much nearer to upsetting my temper than the libel itself, and I wrote an indignant reply, to the effect that while holding myself at all times ready to meet charges or explanations required by official superiors, I owed no duty to lying and irresponsible penny-a-liners, forced by their trade to invent such lies as might bring them the most pennies, and scorned to notice or reply to them, except by cutting off the rascal's ears if I could get hold of him. Butler who knew me very well, explained that I had misunderstood him; that he, Butler, wanted no explanation, but was only anxious on my account to give opportunity for public denial or explanation. Knowing his love of applause and notoriety I believed as much as I chose of this explanation, but nevertheless accepted the apology, and after giving some reasons which will readily occur to a humane person, added the following strictly legal one: viz. the President had by proclamation announced the abolition of slavery throughout the State of Virginia, expressly excepting the territory held therein by our military forces. Hence to send the negro from within the military lines where slavery had been recognized by the highest civil and military authority, to a point outside these lines where having been abolished, it no longer had a legal existence; was, in effect, sending the slave from slave territory to free territory, i.e., from slavery to freedom, unless indeed in the opinion of those disloyal persons who scoffed at the President's proclamation as equivalent to the pope's fulmination against the comet. This ended the discussion, though Butler afterwards told me in conversation that should my argument become public, he feared that prejudiced persons might regard my law as stronger than my 'loyalty.'

The district of country under my command having been set in order and being well-administered by active young subalterns detailed for the purpose, our troops were soon in position to beat up the enemy on his own ground, and some or all available troops were kept engaged in this work by expeditions of all arms, some of small consequence, and others taxing all the resources at my disposal. In October (1863) such an expedition was made in force, for the purpose of breaking up a body known as the Confederate Coast Guard, to destroy the extensive illicit trade and blockade-running of some of the maritime counties, and generally to annoy the enemy, and draw away detachments from his main armies. With these objects, a force of infantry and artillery was marched from Gloucester northward, to and across the Piankatank near its head, advancing its patrols to the Rappahannock. At the same time two regiments of cavalry, under Col. Spear, raked the Mathews County peninsula in its rear, while three gunboats assigned me by Admiral Lee prevented escape by water. Pretty much the whole of the Coast Guard besides a small regiment of cavalry and other prisoners were captured, many small vessels brought off or destroyed, and a considerable number of arms, cattle and horses taken and brought in. The success was so complete that it received honorable mention in the Annual Report of the General-in-Chief of the Army, and was transmitted to Congress by the Secretary of War.[22]

A small incident occurred on this expedition possessing some bearing on the value of negro testimony. At some small town an old fellow who kept a country store was brought up by some cavalry soldiers, on the charge of having in his shop a barrel of whiskey poisoned for the benefit of our soldiers. All the negroes in the place, male and female, crowded in to swear to the charge, but on cross-examination, seemed to have had the information only from each other. The man himself indignantly denied the charge, declared there was no poison in the town or neighborhood and the story was a baseless yarn got up by the negroes to make themselves agreeable and important to us, and finally offered to drink a tumbler-full himself, provided a guard should be assigned to protect him till he should recover his sobriety. This reasonable condition was soon arranged, and the whiskey consumed by the delinquent in the presence of his smiling family, after which the convinced cavalrymen did not require more than about ten minutes to empty the barrel.

During the winter of 1863–64 my force consisted of eight regiments of infantry, two of cavalry, and four batteries of artillery, which, though widely scattered, could generally be quickly concentrated for any movement which should serve at the same time to cover the positions at Williamsburg and Yorktown. The force had been hardly worked and a wide

[22] Message of the President of the United States and accompanying documents, to the two Houses of Congress at the commencement of the first session of the 38th Congress. Washington, Government Printing Office, 1863, pp. 22–3.

extent of country hitherto contributing men, horses and supplies to the Confederacy was more or less controlled by combined movements of cavalry and infantry so arranged that the
latter, while moving over less actual distances than the
cavalry, was always ready to afford it prompt and secure
support. By way of extending these methods, it seemed to
me that if a quick and secret concentration could be effected on
the Williamsburg peninsula, a surprise of Richmond itself,
by a sudden cavalry attack, might be possible. That city lay
about sixty miles beyond our military line, from the most
salient point of which a single road, midway between the York
and the James, led to New Kent Court House, where it branched
into several forks of which one led N.W. twenty-five miles, to
Hanover C. H., and another fifteen miles to Bottom's Bridge
on the Chickahominy, from which Richmond was less than ten
miles distant.

That city, though capable of quick reinforcements and
usually full of detached soldiers and convalescents, was held
by a small regular force. It was protected by redoubts, strong
but slenderly-manned; the citizens and government employees,
organized into infantry battalions, being principally relied on
for ordinary defense. A small force, rarely exceeding 1500
men, held Bottom's Bridge, to which they were pretty closely
confined by our patrols, but a strong Confederate Division
of the Army of Northern Virginia then lay in the vicinity
of Hanover C. H. Thus in case of disaster or delay to an
attacking force at Bottom's Bridge, or between that point
and Richmond, the enemy had upon the flank of such force,
and could readily place on its only practicable line of retreat
at New Kent, a larger force moved from Hanover, over a line
much better, and but little longer than that from Bottom's
Bridge to the same point. In view of these facts, the plan
submitted to Department Headquarters was as follows: While
obscuring the movement by a display of vigor on the Gloucester
peninsula, to effect a rapid concentration of a small column of
all arms in rear of the Williamsburg line. The infantry (two
brigades), preceded by a small cavalry advance for surprising
and capturing pickets, to march at 10 P.M., February 5th,

followed at daylight on the 6th by the entire force of cavalry reinforced to six regiments, or about 1500 men. One infantry brigade with most of the guns, to take position at New Kent, throwing out strong posts on all northern roads; the other brigade marching directly on Bottom's Bridge. The cavalry, after passing the infantry on the 6th and parking its reserve supplies in their charge at New Kent, to arrive at Bottom's Bridge, fifty miles distant from Williamsburg, at or before daybreak on the 7th, seize and repair the bridge, and leaving a small force to hold it till the infantry could come up, make a dash on Richmond, surprise its defences and enter the town. A minute schedule of detachments and duty for the two hours of possible occupation was carefully prepared, and numerous minor plans arranged for destroying public property and communications, cutting wires, etc. Each detachment after performing its allotted task would take care of itself the best it could, retreating by any route upon the infantry by that time arrived at Bottom's Bridge, and covered by it to New Kent, which would be firmly held long enough to cover an orderly retirement of the whole force on Williamsburg.

This plan with other minor features too numerous to relate here, was approved by General Butler and adopted by the War Department by whom it was also agreed that the Army of the Potomac under Meade, on the Rapidan, should make a simultaneous demonstration in its front. The concentration in rear of Williamsburg was pushed forward under cover of strong and enterprising patrols on both sides the York, but as the cavalry reinforcements and supplies necessarily arrived by water, it was impossible to conceal entirely the preparations going on within the lines, where some event of corresponding importance began to be eagerly looked for and discussed.

John Boyle, a soldier of a New York cavalry regiment, was at that time confined near Williamsburg under sentence of death for murder and was to be executed on February 7th. Some of the numerous camp rumors doubtless reached him, and on the night of the 2nd he escaped by the fault or connivance of a sentinel, who was promptly tried, convicted and shot; but Boyle remained at large and unaccounted for.

The movement took place as arranged, on the night of the 5th, the advance guard being sufficiently extended to surround the several outposts of the enemy posted between Williamsburg and New Kent, most of whose men were killed, captured or driven off on foot into the woods, all their horses being killed or secured. But the prisoners captured at different points and separately examined, all concurred in stating that Boyle, nearly exhausted by a close pursuit, had surrended to them on the night of the third, and had made such important statements that he had been expressed to Richmond by relays of horses. Had this important intelligence been sooner received it would have deferred the movement, since the mere knowledge by the enemy of an unusual concentration of troops at Williamsburg would naturally prompt them to hold with sufficient force either New Kent or Bottom's Bridge, and must have defeated the enterprise, whose single chance of success lay in surprising the only practicable crossing of the Chickahominy. In view however of the complicated arrangements made to cut wires, and especially of the auxiliary movement on the Rapidan to take place on the 6th, with which there was no possibility of immediate communication, it was decided to proceed.

At four A.M. on February 7th, the cavalry, composed of the 1st New York Mounted Rifles, the 5th and 11th Pennsylvania, the 1st District Cavalry and two other small regiments especially loaned me for the enterprise, after a march of fifty miles over winter roads, bivouacked near Bottom's Bridge to wait for daylight. Its pickets immediately encountered those of the enemy, prisoners from whom reported that the earthworks and redoubts on the Richmond side had been occupied by a large force the day before; that the bridge planks had been removed, trees felled into the stream and wired together, covering the whole front of the position. The only crossing was by a long causeway of approach constructed through a swamp, then impracticable, with a bridge over the stream at the center; the whole commanded by infantry and artillery in entrenched works on the further side; the Confederate General Hunton in command. These facts were verified by a reconnoissance at dawn, a simultaneous demonstration against the bridge serving to develop the enemy's artillery and reveal a large body of infantry in position. A passage could doubtless have been forced at some point above and the position turned, but instead of a ten-mile gallop to Richmond, the crossing and fighting, however, successful, must have consumed most of the day, long before the expiration of which the Richmond redoubts would have been fully manned, the town safe from a *coup de main* and the Hanover division moving on our rear.

There remained no object to be gained commensurate with the loss and jeopardy to be incurred by delay, and my orders were explicit—that if the *surprise* failed, the command was not to be risked for any new object. About 10 A.M., therefore, the necessary dispositions were made for a retreat on the infantry reserve at New Kent.

The enemy promptly crossed the river in pursuit, pressing the rear and flanks so closely that at Baltimore Cross Roads, a favorable position offering, it was determined to administer a check. The 118th New York, 9th Vermont and 11th Connecticut regiments of infantry, with two guns, after moving across the large open prairie at that place, were therefore halted and deployed to the rear in the woods. The rearguard— a detachment of the 11th Pennsylvania Cavalry—was here ably handled by Colonel Spear, securing ample time for these dispositions and then skillfully withdrawn. The enemy was effectively checked, pushed back with vigor, and cut off from his flanking detachments on both flanks. These, which had got well around to the Union rear, with whose flankers they were hotly engaged, were then attacked with superior force, broken, pursued and dispersed with loss. The command, suffering no further considerable molestation, was concentrated at New Kent the same evening, which place was held till all the wounded and prisoners had been forwarded and the cavalry dispatched to Williamsburg, the neighboring country, mostly forest affording no subsistence for man or beast. On the 8th the outposts were drawn in, and the infantry retired by easy marches to Williamsburg.

The demonstration of the Army of the Potomac was made by part of the Second Army Corps—in which my old regiment was included—on the 6th. It was embarrassed by difficult streams and bottomless mud, but contributed to retard the detachments of Confederate troops to New Kent, which might have made our retreat difficult and even disastrous.

Boyle escaped the hemp he so richly deserved and disappeared for many years, but was at last recognized and identified in the dead body of one of the victims of a great mine explosion in Colorado, January 24, 1884.

Thus failed an enterprise prepared with care in all its details, which had engaged the liveliest interest and expectations of those to whom it was confided, and which but for a minute accident which none could have foreseen, might have accomplished memorable results. Undoubtedly it was chargeable with a violation of standard principles, never to be lightly incurred, since it is but prudent to assume that an adversary will ordinarily meet one's unwarrantable risks and errors with the most appropriate measures. The Confederate division at Hanover Court House, either in consequence of our destruction of their telegraph line, or of the demonstrative movement of the Army of the Potomac, was not used in time to accomplish anything; but leaving that body entirely out of view, it is evident that had the Confederates thrown directly upon New Kent Court House by any of the upper roads the same Richmond force with which they reinforced Bottom's Bridge—contenting themselves with a small defensive force in the earthworks at the latter place—they had a good opportunity to cripple or crush the single brigade left in reserve at New Kent, and after thus occupying our only line of retreat at a vital point, might have driven our exhausted Bottom's Bridge detachment back on that place and destroyed or captured it. But though the defects of the plan which rendered such a catastrophe possible, were understood and foreseen, they were nevertheless accepted as a necessary feature, in view of certain considerations among which the following were prominent. *First:* The wires between Meadow Station and Richmond were cut by our spies on the night of the 6th. *Second:* Our reserve was only required to hold New Kent for twelve hours, that is, till night of the 7th. *Third:* The Confederates were nearly certain to neglect all speculative chances, in favor of a direct defence with their whole force, of a place on the shortest road to, and so dangerously near their Capital as Bottom's Bridge. *Finally:* The occupation of the Confederate Capital for even two hours, profitably and systematically used, would have been a fair equivalent for the loss of our entire expeditionary force.

The Department Commander did me the honor to indorse my official report as follows: (The report itself was printed by the Government in the *Rebellion Record,* series I, vol. xxxiii, pp. 146–8.)

Hdqrs. Dept. Va. and N. Carolina.
Fort Monroe, February 12, 1864.

Report approved. The operation was skillfully and brilliantly done. It gives the commanding general renewed confidence in General Wistar as commander of a division.

BENJN. F. BUTLER,
Major-General Commanding.

On the same date he wrote the following letter transmitting my report to the General-in-Chief of the Armies of the United States.

Hdqrs. 18th Army Corps.
Fort Monroe, February 12, 1864.

GENERAL:

I have the honor to forward to you, with commendation, the report (dated February 9th) of Brigadier-General Wistar of his brilliantly and ably-executed movement upon Richmond, which failed only from one of those fortutious circumstances against which no foresight can provide and no execution can overcome.

By the corruption and faithlessness of a sentinel, who is now being tried for the offense, a man condemned to death, but reprieved by the President, was allowed to escape within the enemy's lines, and there gave them such information as enabled them to meet our advance. This fact is acknowledged in two of the Richmond papers, the Examiner and the Sentinel, published the day after the attack, and is fully confirmed by the testimony before the Court-Martial, before which is being tried the man who permitted the escape. I beg leave to call your attention to the suggestion of General Wistar in his report, that the effect of the raid will be to hereafter keep at least as many Confederate troops around Richmond for its defense from any future movement of the Army of the Potomac as we have in this neighborhood.

I have the honor to be your obedient servant,

BENJ. F. BUTLER,
Major-General Commanding.

MAJOR-GENERAL HALLECK,
Commanding the Army.

The suggestion in my report alluded to by General Butler was as follows:

The whole result of the expedition, in addition to the prisoners captured and a few refugees, escaped Union prisoners, and negroes picked up and brought in, is the obvious demonstration that a small force in this vicinity, actively handled, can and should hold a much superior force of the enemy in the immediate vicinity of Richmond inactive, except for its defense.

CHAPTER XXI

Many less ambitious attempts made during the same winter, directed upon almost every point worth striking within a radius of a hundred miles or more, met with better results, among which not the least difficult and successful was an expedition directed upon Charles City C. H., for the purpose of capturing or dispersing a Confederate cavalry regiment posted at that place. This regiment was constantly raiding upon our pickets and patrols, generally advancing by way of Bottom's Bridge, and quickly retiring behind the Chickahominy when overmatched. The Court House was eight miles beyond, and nearly south of the crossing known as Jones', or the Forge Bridge. The bridge had been destroyed, but, in chasing their detachments over the river, our cavalry found near-by a ford often used by them and practicable for cavalry at ordinary stages of water. About 1200 cavalry moved out of our lines after dark, and marching by Slatersville, reached the Forge crossing at daylight and made a dash on the Court House, a small infantry column being placed at Slatersville by a rapid march, to cover and support. The cavalry having surprised and captured or dispersed the pickets at the Forge, crossed the river and after a rapid gallop reached and surrounded the Court House before seven A.M., securing every man in the enemy's camp who had not been killed, except three privates— a measure of success not often attained either on a large or small scale.

During this winter a military commission having been organized to sit at Norfolk to try a Fortress Monroe port captain for cheating the Government, the disagreeable duty of presiding over it fell to my lot, by direct assignment of the Secretary of

War. Fortunately I had first had time to get my District so well-organized, and to get together such a capable and reliable staff, that it did not suffer much during my necessary absence. The Commission sat over two weeks, without regard to hours, using every effort of its own and allowing every reasonable latitude to the Judge Advocate, in the hope of finding just occasion for making an example that might check this all-pervading vice. Sitting all day and much of the night on this business, a volume of testimony was accumulated quite sufficient to hang many of the noisiest loyalists in several of the great cities, but none of any great consequence against the particular rogue on trial. The only malfeasance positively fastened on him was a probable partnership with a sutler in North Carolina and the forwarding to him of merchandise on Government supply vessels, free of charge. Notwithstanding this failure of testimony, as there was little doubt of his general venality and corruption, we took advantage of the single act proved, to impose a fine of $5000, and a year's imprisonment. But in framing our report, which was unanimously signed, I took occasion to refer specifically to certain pages of the testimony transmitted, with a recommendation that several persons there implicated should be arrested and sent to us for trial. One of these, I remember, was a prominent and ultra-loyal member of the Union League Club of Philadelphia (over seven-eighths of whose members were said at one time to be contractors with the Government), who had chartered to the Government at the rate of $100 per day, an old, worn-out and leaky canal-boat for a 'rebel prison.'

The testimony showed that she would not have brought over $75 at a sale absolute; that she could not hold over twenty prisoners, with the necessary guards and attendants; that on the first night of her arrival in Hampton Roads she sank at her moorings; and that the owner drew $100 per day for a period of eight months, during the whole of which she lay at the bottom of the bay. We earnestly recommended that a chance should be given us at that particular patriot, and also at the Quartermaster who made the bargain and approved the payments, but their political opinions and bawling 'loyalty' were probably too correct and sound to permit the risking of their necks to the summary methods of military justice, as we never heard anything more of our report and its suggestions.

It is probable there was never a great war conducted by any civilized nation at once so extravagantly, inefficiently and corruptly as ours. In each of those respects the volunteer system itself, as put to use by us, is the worst and most wasteful that any ordinary ingenuity could devise. After extensive opportunities of observation, I believe it is speaking within bounds to say that a large proportion of the officers thus obtained are morally or physically worthless and must be sloughed off at the cost of great delay and expense to give ordinary efficiency to the remainder. The system of commissioning the promoters of enlistments in proportion to the numbers they obtain, or in accordance with the votes of those under their command, was not only fatal to all discipline, even with individuals otherwise fairly qualified, but brought into responsible positions a lot of rascals whose worthlessness paralyzed the army till means could be devised for weeding them out and filling their places with others more in accord with the views and necessities of the general officers responsible for their conduct.

Not long after Baker's death, President Lincoln, having heard of some acts or observations of mine on the weakness of our volunteer troops in regimental officers, invited me to a private audience, and on two occasions gave a considerable portion of his time and capacity to a discussion of the best means of remedying a difficulty which he had before heard of and which lay deep, because inherent in the original methods of organization. Great generals of course are *nascitur non fit,* but line officers, important as they are, can to a certain extent be improvised at will, and their excellence and value will much depend on the methods employed for selecting them from the mass of population about to essay its fighting qualities. Many of our regiments were doomed to inferiority before they left their native States, by the mode of enlisting men and electing officers, and when they approached the theatre of war and would have been of priceless value for instant use, their responsible places being already filled with incapables, precious time had to be wasted while some quick and ready method could be contrived for undoing what had been so badly done. When the State-raised regiments came suddenly under control of the General Government and were found to a great extent unfit for immediate use, there existed only two legal methods for correcting these inherent mischiefs of organization, both of which presented insuperable difficulties. Courts-martial could be assembled to try officers on specific charges, but besides the impolicy of discouraging volunteering by subjecting a large number of officers to trial on such indefinite charges as mere unfitness or incapacity, this plan, by taking useful officers away from their daily duties to constitute such tribunals, would for a time at least, aggravate the difficulty.

To use the President's power of arbitrary removal in such a vast number of cases, where judgment could only be based on the reports of others transmitted through many hands, themselves unknown, would be to invite intrigue, combinations and injustice, to discourage and discredit the volunteer system, to which, whether good or bad, the country was for the time committed, and to subject conscientious and self-respecting officers to such intolerable uncertainty of tenure and reputation as to drive out the good who were indispensable, rather than the bad whom it was desired to reach. Ultimately, and not a day too soon, the plan was devised by General McClellan and enacted into law, of appointing special commissions, before whom officers might be sent by their superiors for examination. Thus, while ostensibly examining on technical points, scope was given for the final decision to include those points of fitness and capacity for exercising authority, which though by no means the least essential qualities, are among the most difficult to deal with on formal charges and specifications.

Until this timely remedy was contrived and adopted, regimental commanders were put to all sorts of shifts to get rid of a certain kind of official rascals whose mere presence with their men was injurious and intolerable. I have myself had to drive such fellows away without a shadow of legal warrant, by simply putting them out of camp, threatening personal vengeance if they returned, and dropping them quietly (but illegally) from the rolls.

Of course nothing, not even waste of time or infirmity of purpose, can be more dangerous or more expensive to a non-military people required suddenly to exert its strength in war, than any kind of artificial or preventable inferiority of its troops; but next to such defects in the fighting ranks themselves, must be classed the injudicious methods and political appointments resorted to without any real necessity, for suddenly increasing to the enormous dimensions required, the general staff departments for arming, feeding, clothing and transporting the troops. I think no intelligent person who has had full opportunity of inside observation can avoid the conclusion—of course much more obvious after, than before—that a large part of the inefficiency, extravagance, waste, and even corruption in those Departments, which nearly ruined the North, and quite destroyed the South, might have been avoided; the mobility and power of the army doubled, and perhaps quite half the enormous and wholly unique cost of the war escaped, had there been an orderly, legal method, leisurely prepared in time of peace, for expanding these several business Departments on a sudden emergency, by a system of competitive test of persons, always ready for instant application. Of course in war, as in politics, the world is full of noisy humbugs who, if they can get themselves trusted with the public sledge-hammer, are capable of using it without immediately and visibly breaking their own heads, but something more than that ought to be expected and required from responsible statesmen, legislators, and executives, whose self-assumed business it is to organize the country's strength, administer its resources, and launch both against its enemies under trustworthy and competent superintendence.

During the last weeks of the winter of 1863-4, the enemy had been hunted up and pushed so often and so far, that there was little of suitable dimensions now left to strike at, within reasonable distance. It was generally understood that large movements and plenty of work would be undertaken when the weather and roads should become settled, and in the meantime without remitting the constant drilling and instruction of the troops, I applied myself to complete the various arrangements heretofore put in train for the orderly civil government of the District. Slabtown—if not exactly metropolitan—had become large and populous, and was clean, quiet, and to a considerable extent, self-supporting. It was well-policed by a small force of selected negroes, chosen by the Provost Marshal, and the most capable residents were from time to time placed on abandoned and unoccupied farming-lands outside the town. These were supplied with implements and seeds procured by aid of the 'Provost fund,' and also with such captured and inferior animals as were no longer capable of road work or useful for military purposes, under written agreements to deliver one-half their crops to the Government or its agents at the nearest place of shipment.

The Provost fund consisting of the proceeds of licenses and taxation, collected by the Provost Marshal and accounted for monthly to Department Headquarters, now yielded several thousand dollars a month, largely derived from the sale of licenses for fishing, oystering, trading and so forth. The orderly condition of the place and the prosperity of much of its large negro population had attracted from the enterprising people of New England, numerous cranks or self-styled missionaries of both sexes, who infested Slabtown in ever-increasing numbers, and as a rule, were by no means averse to extracting a pecuniary profit from their pious labors. Though some of these were unmitigated scamps, others no doubt really believed in the equality or superiority of the negro race, and that all that was necessary for the demonstration of that new-found fact, was to teach the darkey to sing hymns and read the newspapers, while supported at public expense, i.e., by the white laborer and taxpayer. As the delusion at first seemed harmless, and at all events, was none of my business, the missionaries were received and sent as fast as they arrived, to live among their chosen clients of Slabtown, and little attention was given them, till one day an investigating A. D. C. reported that a certain missionary named

C. had gotten nineteen negroes of both sexes and all ages tied up to trees, for refusing to let him re-marry them for a fee of twenty-five cents a pair.

Though the price did not seem unreasonable for a good article of connubial felicity, backed by a solid New England guarantee, it was but fair to the negroes to ascertain what sort of title they were getting; and when the reverend rogue was brought to book, it appeared he had convinced the poor darkeys that the principal thing required to make them equal to whites, was to be re-married by him for a cash consideration. Commencing with a five-dollar fee, he had for a time done a brisk and thriving business, but the price had gradually fallen with the increasing reluctance of the old black grandfathers and grandmothers to shell out their hard-earned cash, till even at the present modest rate, the demand had so declined that some forcible stimulation had become necessary. This thrifty moralist was of course expelled from the District and the negroes a second time emancipated, but his prayers must have exerted more influence with the Washington statesmen than in the quarter where they were more properly due, since he came back in a short time with an appointment as "Superintendent of Negro Affairs," and authority to disport himself among the negroes and their savings, at his will. As active military preparations for large operations had already commenced, there was then little time to devote to such predaceous insects and in the pressure of other business he was allowed to resume his residence at Slabtown on the promise not to meddle with the black men's pockets as long as I remained responsible as commander of the Military District. It was not till long after the vicinity had been evacuated by the advancing troops, that I learned through my successor, General Ord, that this reverend gentleman's pecuniary enterprises, thus deprived of salutary supervision, at last reached a stage which after exhausting the humble resources of the negroes, successfully attacked the coffers of the Government itself, by appropriating its share of the crops of its negro wards, or a large part of them.

In April, 1864, numerous regiments and batteries gathered from all parts of the Department, were sent me to be organized and Brigaded into the 18th Army Corps, which it was understood was to be commanded by the able and well-known General William F. Smith, then wearing his freshly-won Chattanooga laurels, at which place by rescuing the communications of the Western Army he had saved the army itself and thus rendered possible its subsequent success. Many of the regiments were old ones recently filled up with drafted or kidnapped men by certain iniquitous practices first made known to me by the following circumstance which, in the interests of humanity, one may hope could scarcely happen outside of a free (?) Republic. A New Hampshire regiment one night reported its arrival and was posted by one of the staff a couple of miles from the fort, to be inspected and provisionally brigaded next day. But early in the morning the Colonel personally reported that eighty of his men had deserted during the night! In reply to some sharp strictures on the quality and discipline of a regiment in which such things could happen, he explained that his command was an old and good one of long service, but having been reduced by various casualties to barely 150 men, had just been filled up with 600 drafted men. These were foreigners, mostly speaking foreign languages, who had been drugged and kidnapped in New York, there purchased by the 'quota agents' of his State, their muster papers regularly made out, then heavily ironed, confined in box cars, and shipped like cattle, to his regiment.

All this proved on inquiry to be true. One could not but sympathize with the poor wretches thus maltreated on their arrival in a land whither many of them had probably fled to escape a much milder military service at home; nevertheless their chains had been forged by experienced hands and were without a flaw. They came to me with all regular forms complete, as duly enlisted, sworn and mustered soldiers of their regiment, and I was bound by every consideration of oath and duty to treat them as such until discharged, regardless of their individual misfortunes. The deserters were of course trying to get to the enemy, but must all be retaken sooner or later by our pickets or patrols. Should their escapade be allowed to pass without special attention, as might have been possible under almost any other circumstances, the offense would be repeated indefinitely by them, as well as by the hundreds of similar unfortunates drafted like them into other regiments, and must at last be stopped at any cost, even by wholesale executions, if required.

It was therefore not merely in the interest of the Government, but of humanity as well, that I felt that such an example must be made of a few of those first caught as might serve to cut short the contagious and dangerous defection. The opportunity was not long delayed. Three poor devils were brought in that evening, immediately tried by special court-martial, found guilty, condemned to death, and sentenced to be shot at sunrise next morning, in presence of their regiment. I approved the conviction and sentence, as plainly authorized to do by the Sixty-fifth Article of War; but to avoid all question of authority, telegraphed the facts and my intention to execute the sentence to the Department-Commander at Fortress Monroe. General Butler wished the execution deferred till he could receive and examine the record, but feeling very clear both as respected my authority and duty, I declined to so do on the ground that the efficacy of the punishment as a deterring influence, lay mainly in its immediate infliction, and plainly stated that if restrained in this exercise of judgment, I should decline further responsibility for the troops in this condition, and would ask the favor of an immediate assignment to the Army of the Potomac. Butler then contented himself with requiring the record of conviction to be telegraphed him, which process went on through the remainder of the night and was still being conducted long after the culprits had ceased to exist.

One reason for such unamiable firmness in the matter, was the prevailing feeling that among so many newly-drafted reinforcements, the prisoners could not be publicly executed without insubordination and perhaps mutiny. Even so good an officer as the colonel of their regiment, while concurring in other respects, begged that the execution might be private, or at least not in presence of his regiment, which he feared might not be controllable. But his reason for privacy was mine for publicity, since the very existence of such doubts rendered it all the more imperative that the entire command should know by exhaustive public test, whether the Government with its officers, order and authority, was or was not stronger than the mutinous conscripts and drafted men, of whom the army was likely to become more and more composed.

The place of execution was selected near the center of a level plain south of the fortifications, extending from the high banks of the York estuary to a woods half a mile distant. Prior to the appointed hour, all troops having been first paraded in their respective camps, and the streets commanded by reliable artillery, the deserters' regiment was drawn up in line a few paces from the spot occupied by the prisoners, and a firing-party from their own regiment, closely watched by a picked detail of the provost guard. Opposite the flank of this regiment and at right angles with it, were posted two reliable regiments of my old brigade, one deployed in line of battle with a section of artillery in its center, the other in two columns each doubled on the center, in rear of the respective wings. A few squadrons of cavalry were drawn up at the edge of the woods, a quarter of a mile distant, a field battery, harnessed and mounted, was placed in position in the nearest bastion of the fort, and another was harnessed and standing ready on the road inside the nearest gate. It did not require a very experienced military eye to perceive that in case of any mutinous demonstration by the offending regiment, it could be mowed down by the enfilading fire of the regiment and guns on its flank, and if it broke, could be annihilated by the charge of the two infantry columns, and every straggler cut down or captured by the cavalry in rear. The disposition being effectually, and therefore mercifully made, the ceremony was conducted deliberately and with perfect regularity. The men fell dead at the first discharge, and were buried where they fell, not another sound being audible from first to last, but the necessary officers' orders, till quick time beaten by the drum corps announced the ceremony completed.

The results justified the painful harshness of this measure. All the other deserters were captured and brought in within a few days and received less severe punishment, and not another desertion occurred except on a single occasion some weeks afterwards, when thirty-four of the same class of men deserted from a Connecticut regiment while in action at Drury's Bluff, but were mostly killed by our fire while running for the enemy's line. To say nothing of the necessities of the service and the interest of the Government and country, I believe that many lives were saved by this timely severity, and have always felt fully justified in it, even regarded as a measure of humanity alone. But it was none the less an infamous outrage not only on the poor ignorant victims, but on commanding officers constrained to such painful measures, that these should be rendered necessary by the base acts of those quota-hunting villains in northern cities, who, if justice could have been done, would have first felt the halter. Smarting under this feeling I wrote an indignant but unofficial letter to Major-General Dix, then commanding at New York, setting forth the violence and fraud by which emigrants and other friendless persons were dragged against their will into the service, by outrages committed in New York, worse than any acts of the old British naval press-gangs, and the responsibilities thus imposed on commanding officers charged with the duty of receiving such so-called recruits.

This letter was published by the press of New York presumably with the consent of General Dix, and found its way into the English and Continental papers. Worse still, the Earl of Peterborough read it from his place in the House of Lords, as a statement by an "American officer somewhat less cruel and brutal than his fellows," of the modes by which the Americans forced innocent foreigners into their internecine quarrels, with a cruelty and disregard of human life and rights more infamous than any European despot had dared to practice during modern times, &c., &c. As all this came back in due course to the American papers, I expected to get a wooling from the War Department, but as I never heard from it on the subject, presume their attentions were bestowed on General Dix, through whose indiscretion—or humanity—my letter could alone have reached the printer.

Though the mixture of civil and military duties on the Virginia Peninsula had separated me for eight months from my comrades and friends in the Army of the Potomac, they were not otherwise disagreeable, except for the effect of that malarial region on my health. During this period I had suffered pretty much every variety of fever and diarrhea and pulled through them all with more or less residuum of damage. During a few months, chiefly in the previous autumn, three acres had been filled with the graves of soldiers of my command —which had scarcely at any time exceeded 6000 men—notwithstanding most of the regiments had been frequently interchanged with those from the more salubrious regions of the North Carolina Coast. Quinine was daily served at *reveille,* at first in whiskey and afterwards more surely and beneficially in coffee. Troops and quarters were constantly inspected and absolute cleanliness of camp, clothing and person rigidly enforced. The frosty weather of winter much improved the general health, but with the return of spring the old symptoms reappeared, and the organization of the 18th Army Corps was hailed by all ranks as evidence of approaching movement and change of scene.

I was myself relieved from command of the District by General Order of April 19th, 1864, and on the 21st was reassigned to the command of the Second Division 18th A. C. composed of my old brigade, now consisting of the 2nd and 12th New Hampshire, 11th Conn. and 148th New York regiments under Col. Stedman as Brigade Commander, and General Heckman's Brigade of the 9th New Jersey, 23rd, 25th and 27th Mass. On May 4th, the Division with the remainder of the Corps under command of Gen. W. F. Smith, sailed in transport steamers for the James River, where they were joined by the 10th Corps under General Gilmore, the whole constituting the newly organized Army of the James, commanded by Gen. B. F. Butler. During the night of the 5th, a landing was effected at Bermuda Hundred and the position at once entrenched. On the 6th, I was ordered by General Butler to make a reconnoissance with two regiments and if possible destroy the railroad between Petersburg and Richmond. This movement failed with loss, notwithstanding my best efforts, in consequence of the smallness of the force, which might just as well have been a Division, since the other troops were at the time unemployed, except in entrenching. Next day I was ordered to repeat the effort with a brigade, and after some sharp fighting about two miles of road was destroyed by throwing that much of the track, ties, rails and all, over an embankment; but being hard pressed by the enemy in nearly or quite equal force, no opportunity was afforded for burning ties and bending rails effectually without suffering greater loss than the occasion justified.

It was in this fight that I happened to notice personally the particulars of a remarkably sudden and impressive death. I was myself riding with the skirmish line some distance in advance of the line of battle, endeavoring to get some knowledge of the topography in front. The line of skirmishers had just emerged from a thick wood into a small road running parallel with it. The other side of the road was bounded by a high Virginia rail-fence, beyond which were some open fields with the railroad embankment on the far side. The embankment was at the moment rather weakly held by the enemy's infantry, but a battery at some distance to the right front, immediately opened a partially enfilading and rather destructive fire with shell, down the road. I called a soldier to throw off some rails that I might cross the fence, which stood on a high bank and was impracticable for a horse to jump from the road. The soldier had scarcely seized a rail for this purpose, when there was a sudden crash and blaze of fire, and I found myself covered with a shower of splinters and half-rotten wood. Right at my horse's feet lay the soldier, still enveloped in his blue overcoat and apparently uninjured, but a second glance showed that his head had vanished altogether, and in its place projected the long white bone of the neck—hot and smoking! A shell had struck and knocked to pieces the fence, and either the missile or some part of the fence had entirely carried away the soldier's head, the shell itself bursting on the opposite side of the road among the skirmishers, but without doing further mischief. No death could be more sudden or impressive to the bystander. The ominous and warning shriek or whistle of the shell was lost in the volume of infantry-fire about the place, and the victim could not have suffered a thrill of pain, or even a single instant of apprehension.

The same evening of this little success in breaking the rail-road, General Butler found it expedient to divulge to me a small scheme of his own affecting myself and others, which had no doubt long been a favorite with him, since it must have required at least a month of secret preparation. It eventually appeared that his main object was to get back under his command General Weitzel, a former and favorite instrument of his at New Orleans; and part of the original plan consisted in inducing me to give up my Division to that officer and accept command of the Third Division. This latter, however, though much stronger in numbers, was composed of negroes, dressed up like soldiers and euphemistically styled 'Colored Troops.' In numbers it was the strongest in the corps, never having suffered any considerable casualities; but having formerly had the assistance of one of its brigades in action, where it suddenly ran away before the charge of two small Confederate regiments, nearly causing my personal capture, I shared the opinion of most of the white soldiers, that while good at marching, and just then an interesting popular and Government pet and plaything, the 'Colored Troops' were not good to tie to in battle. After the above practical demonstration of their value, and sometime before the movement across the James, I had peremptorily declined Butler's proposal to take command of this colored Division, and when somewhat pressed, had by way of emphasis, declared my preference for a white brigade rather than a negro division, if necessary.

It had been, I suppose, at the instance of the Corps Commander General Smith, that I had been reassigned to command the Second Division after its reinforcement and reorganization, and my rank as fixed by date of commission, seemed to justify my regarding it as permanent, since a command at least equal, must have fallen to me in either of the larger armies. But Butler's little scheme, though rebuffed at the start, had been readjusted to meet all obstacles, and after a long period of secret nursing, had now reached a stage when it must necessarily be communicated both to General Smith and myself. After my refusal of the colored Division, it had been given to one Hinks, and Weitzel had been ordered to the 18th Corps from New Orleans, where he had been hitherto distinguished for political and civil, rather than military achievements. Butler now imparted this information, with the fact that Weitzel had reached Washington and was on his way thence and daily expected to arrive, when the only command suitable for his superior rank would be my Division, and the only thing left for me would be my old Brigade.

It was clearly too late for remonstrance here, but on the other hand, all the armies were now freshly reorganized and in active motion. It would require considerable time to get myself assigned to the Potomac, or any other army, and should I venture to leave the Army of the James now in actual contact with the enemy, I might have to sulk in Washington for a month or two during the most active part of the campaign, before the casualties of war should make room for my reassignment. Such a contingency was not to be entertained a moment, as the astute Butler had doubtless foreseen, and I therefore submitted with as good grace as I could assume, for the present.

General Weitzel arrived not long afterwards, and the change was effected while the army was actually engaged in front of Petersburg, as will presently appear. I retired from the Division which either directly or as District Commander I had commanded for several months, and had handled not discreditably on marches and in action, to the humbler responsibilities of my old Brigade. It is useless to deny that this injustice, skillfully and secretly committed by a wily politician, then at odds with almost every military man of repute in the army, and soon to make his military antics a laughing-stock to the country, galled considerably at the time. I think I may fairly remark that Butler, at least could not—and did not—make any pretext of deficiency on my part; for on that point he is fully committed by his official reports, over and over again, both before and after this event, some of which have been already quoted. Nevertheless, through these secret machinations, one of the best Divisions in the service, upon which I had labored assiduously for many months in anticipation of the campaign now opening, thus fell unearned to a follower of Butler's fortunes, of my own rank but antedating me slightly, whose best-known recommendation was his obedient usefulness to him in his persecution—and, as many have charged—plunder, of the non-combatant citizens and property-owners of New Orleans. The same considerations that forbade my withdrawal from the Army of the James at that juncture, rendered it equally or even more inexpedient to retire altogether from the service; and yet it was due more to the friendly sympathy and advice of my friends—especially General Smith, and Colonel Stedman—than to the strength of my own philosophy, that I was able to refrain from that ill-advised step. Stedman, in fact, suffered as much as myself, *pro tanto,* since my falling back to the Brigade, sent him back to his old regiment, at the head of which he soon after gloriously fell, sword in hand, in the act of leading it over the enemy's earthworks at Cold Harbor. He lived not to see that particular wrong righted, or even the final triumph of his cause, but long enough to be well-known and properly valued as an accomplished gentleman, a faithful friend, and one of the most gallant officers in the service of his country.

On the 8th of May, Butler having learned of the successful crossing of the James by the cavalry division under Kautz, left his colored division, about 5000 strong, in the Bermuda Hundred entrenchments, and marched on Petersburg with all the rest of the two Corps, then numbering in the ranks present for duty, about 22,000 men. No enemy was at first encountered, and the six miles of railroad was effectually destroyed, but the entire army was brought to a stand at the defensive line of Swift Creek, two miles in front of Petersburg, by the obstinate and skillful defense there made by a few Confederate regiments under Beauregard. At this place occurred an incident too obscure in magnitude and barren of results, to find any place in history, which, nevertheless cost the lives of some hundreds of brave men who marched gallantly to death in obedience to orders, the reason or object of which they could scarcely have understood themselves, certainly we did not. My Division, already deployed and standing in line, was suddenly assailed by a small column of five companies of South Carolina infantry, which suddenly charged from the woods but was, of course, almost to a man, destroyed. Not immediately perceiving any plan or object in such a desperate and hopeless movement, I rode out to the place, where these men fell, which, as our fire had been reserved for close quarters, was scarcely fifty yards from our line, but could find no officer unwounded or in condition to talk. The Lieutenant-Colonel in command having been killed coming up, the ranking officer present was Capt. Le Roy Hammond, who had himself received four bullets and was in a dying condition; all the other officers not killed on the spot, being in similar or worse condition. Officers and men alike, the former mostly sons of wealthy and historic South Carolina families, carried in their haversacks as their only rations, a scanty supply of raw corn just as shelled from the cob!

In the absence of more plausible explanation, it was inferred that the destruction of this small column had been risked in the desperate hope of striking my Division in the act of deployment, thus creating a confusion which might have justified Beauregard in sallying from the Swift Creek entrenchments with the whole of his small force. But the division having advanced in line, was already deployed, and whether or not the apparently desperate circumstances of the Confederates justified the attempt, it proved a failure that resulted in the entire destruction of the small assaulting column whose superb gallantry, though obscured and forgotten in the fame of larger and more prominent operations, well deserved a better fate.

Instead of throwing his vastly superior force instantly on the trifling opposition which the Confederate general was here able to offer, Butler at this critical moment permitted himself to be detained by a desultory combat, mostly confined to skirmish lines, which on my front was varied by a sharp fight in and around the Salem Church, the whole continuing till 4 A.M. on the 10th, when Weitzel arrived and replaced me in command of the Second Division. I was soon after directed to withdraw my Brigade from the line of battle by regiments, as relieved by Ames' Division of the 10th Corps, serve cartridges, form in marching order on the turnpike and await orders. These soon came, being to march up the road toward Richmond and reinforce Terry's Division of Gilmore's Corps, then covering our rear above Bermuda Hundred against an attack from Richmond, and said to be hard pressed by troops from that place. By this time the sun had become hot, the turnpike was white and glowing, the men had been in ranks, with more or less fighting, for twenty-four hours, and as I was enjoined to spare no time, it became a problem how to get the command moved over the eight miles that separated us from Terry, in the shortest time. I could think of no better plan than a modification of that adopted for crossing the Humboldt Desert in 1849, viz., to march half an hour and halt ten minutes till the ground could be covered. Scores of exhausted men dropped out from weakness or sunstroke, but as I was continually urged on by galloping staff officers from Terry, the march was remorselessly pushed, only to find that Terry was having no fight at all—not even as much as the skirmishing we had left—but was 'expecting' one.

It did not come to any great extent. One of his batteries was overrun and momentarily captured by the charge of a single Confederate regiment, but was immediately retaken by the voluntary charge of one of our regiments. I think the 13th Indiana. The same night Butler's troops all again camped within the Bermuda Hundred lines. On the 12th the same force again moved out, taking this time the contrary direction toward Richmond. By the evening of the 14th an advance of six or seven miles, mostly through dense woods, had been effected, every inch of ground having been hotly disputed by the enemy's skirmishers, sometimes only dislodged by vigorous attacks from our line of battle. The Army of the James here brought up in front, and within a few hundred yards, of a formidable line of earthworks extending from Drury's Bluff on James River a distance of several miles into the country, covering the several roads and railroads leading to Richmond, and now defended by an adequate force under Beauregard, constantly augmented by arrivals from Petersburg and more southern points, which our colored garrison at Bermuda Hundred directly on the flank and within two miles of their line of march from Peterburg, made no effort to prevent.

The Corps commanders advised an immediate assault, which was not approved by Butler, who had not yet arrived—and at no time did arrive—at the front. The troops having been placed in position on the general line of a small swampy rivulet at the edge of the slashed timber covering the *glacis,* to which it formed a strong *abattis,* protected themselves with a small breastwork of logs and earth, and during the night, by General Smith's orders, stretched telegraph wire from stump to stump through the tangled slashing in front of the position. For the easier handling of artillery, a corduroy road was constructed to firm ground in the rear, and with the exception of perpetual picket skirmishing and some artillery fire from the fort, the troops lay idle till early on the morning of the 16th, when the enemy made a sortie with his entire infantry force of three Divisions.

The extreme right of our line of battle was held by Heckman's brigade of Wistar's—now Weitzel's—Division, having my brigade next on its left, and on its right, some negro cavalry intended to cover its exposed flank by prolonging the general line across the meadows to James River, a distance of about two miles. During this night Heckman's pickets had lost touch with mine, and what proved of still more importance, with those of the two regiments of negro cavalry on his right. I was occupied with all my staff and orderlies the entire night, in trying to get the first gap rectified, but without success. In the first place, it was the duty of the Division General and not mine, to see to the continuity of his line, but though the defect was constantly reported to him through the night, it received no other attention from him, so far as I ever heard. In the next place, the business of rectifying this interval was difficult and exceedingly dangerous. The ground was densely covered with a 'slashing' of heavy white-oak timber, i.e., trees cut down two years before and left lying as they fell. This, though nearly impassable to marching troops, was filled with the enemy's sharpshooters, who concealed themselves readily among it, in rear as well as in front of our pickets, and made it hot, especially for the officers exploring for the purpose of rectifying the line.

About an hour before daylight on the 16th, the low swampy woods being filled with a dense fog, Ransom's Confederate Division advanced quickly and silently from the fort to turn Heckman's right, quickly dispersed the negro cavalry which offered little or no resistance, and struck and enveloped his uncovered flank. The brigade was a good one and made a desperate though disorderly resistance, but under the unfavorable condition of the circumstances, receiving neither warning nor support from the cavalry on its right, soon yielded to a well-prepared attack that reached its flank and rear almost simultaneously, and was entirely destroyed as a cohesive body, its general with all his staff and the greater part of the brigade being quickly surrounded and captured, after a heavy loss in killed and wounded. The swampy thicket being impracticable for horses, my staff officers, like myself, were on foot, and before I could get any accurate knowledge of the fight on my right, a long and heavy line of battle came charging down against my front. Owing to the darkness and fog, the distance between the fighting lines was reduced to a few yards and the firing was very destructive on both sides, but with the effective aid of the wire obstructions in our front, the attack was at length successfully repulsed. In consequence of the defeat of Heckman, it now became necessary as a condition of holding any part of our main line, to *crochet* to the right rear, first one, and then two, of my regiments, leaving but two on the original line.

The disposition had scarcely been made, both refused regiments being already heavily engaged on their new front, when a second front attack was vigorously made, but again repulsed with heavy loss and the capture by us of several hundred prisoners, who finding it impossible to get away, came in and surrendered and were sent to the rear. The firing on the right had now passed entirely around our extemporized right flank, and soon after, the recapture by the enemy in our rear of nearly all our hard-won prisoners, was reported to me at the same time that Lieut. Fairgrieve, A. D. C., came up to report his own personal capture and escape from the enemy, whose scattered and disorded masses already filled the woods in rear. Being apparently cut off from Headquarters, I had again stripped myself of staff officers to obtain information of the real condition of affairs on the right and rear, when a third dashing charge came upon our front, the enemy, under cover of smoke and fog, charging in close upon our retiring skirmishers, and getting up within a few feet of our line of battle. After hard fighting and severe loss on both sides, this attempt, like the others, was decisively repulsed, and was not repeated; their line retiring to cover of the slashed timber, from whence though a heavy fire was maintained, no further effort was made to close, nor any attempt to carry off their wounded from their distressing position between two fires.

It was about this time that an Aide of General Smith got through with an order for me to retire to a new position in rear and to the right of the wood, where a new line was being formed by him in open ground. But with every available man engaged, my right uncovered and crumbling away, and the enemy between myself and the designated point of retreat, this was not an easy thing to accomplish with success. The only way was to retire regiment by regiment, replacing each by a skirmish line, and trusting to events to get finally off the line without sacrificing the last. This was the method adopted, and as in such a dense, swampy thicket, it was impossible to retain control of anything when once out of sight, each Colonel was instructed to move off promptly as the order reached him, get quickly into column in condition to face to any front and fight his independent way to the rear, reporting directly to the Corps commander with whom only I was in any communication at all; having seen or heard nothing of Weitzel since the action commenced. Two of my four regiments had thus moved off, their places being so inadequately occupied by a skirmish line as to invite another attack in front, when a second order got through, directing me to disregard the first, and hold on, as Brooks of the 10th Corps, was about making an effort to reoccupy the place on my left, from which his Division had been driven.

But in addition to former difficulties, the enemy about this time had turned on us a heavy battery of twenty-pound Parrotts, captured from Brooks on the turnpike on our left, which mathematically enfiladed my line of battle, and would have been ruinously destructive if the guns had been better served. Whatever Brooks might ultimately accomplish, it was nevertheless plain that these two regiments of mine were at present the only ones remaining on any part of the line, with the enemy strong in front, both flanks entirely exposed, and even the woods in rear occupied more or less by a hostile force of unknown strength and position. I could not get back my two despatched regiments and it was no longer possible to recover the position vacated under the first order, and the second was therefore now impossible to execute. It was consequently determined to continue the evacuation first ordered, and the aide was sent back to announce the fact. The third regiment having been extricated and on its way to the rear, it was determined to charge and retake the captured battery, not so much to recover the guns, which probably could not be carried off, as to check the enemy and gain time and confidence for getting away with the last regiment. This was splendidly executed by Stedman with the 11th Connecticut, while the skirmish line was being drawn in from the right. The guns were retaken, and several of them spiked with horse-shoe nails found in the limber-boxes, after which, as there was no means of moving them, they were abandoned. General Smith was found about a mile to the right rear, with the new line skillfully formed in open ground and a strong position.

Thus ended for the time, one of the hardest fought combats of the war, in which two of Beauregard's three Divisions were thrown successively on Weitzel's single Division with the design of crushing our right, nearly all the fighting occurring after the destruction of Heckman's Brigade had reduced the Division to one Brigade. That Brigade had been fought from first to last without any communication whatever with Weitzel, whose personal position and occupation during the action remain unknown to me even at the present day, and yet the principal writers on the war, servilely following Humphreys—who was not present—have scarcely troubled themselves by even mentioning my name; probably because I was not a West Point officer! I have always flattered myself, and still believe, that if Weitzel had arrived to take my Division a month later than he did, Heckman's Brigade—which I knew well—would not have been surprised. It would have been effectually covered by a continuous picket line and by the time that line yielded, would have been quite ready to stand to its work. Long before the attack reached the left brigade there would have been ample time for any prompt and capable Division

General to detach from it to Heckman's flank and rear, and check or beat Ransom, only a small portion of whose troops at first enveloped Heckman's right and reached his rear. Had the right brigade maintained its line for even twenty minutes, which under such different circumstances should have presented no difficulty, the few Confederate regiments which had passed round its flank could have been easily checked by an alert Division Commander with another unengaged brigade to draw from; when an advance by Heckman *en echelon* from his right would have been perfectly safe, and must have cut Ransom's disordered Division in two and driven it back on its entrenchments with heavy loss of prisoners.

Though this view is my own, it has been concurred in by much more experienced judges, and be it as it may, the incontestable fact remains that the brigade scarcely mentioned by Humphreys and those who have slavishly followed him, was the last of both Corps to cling to the line of battle, from which it had repulsed three attacks, and whence it at last retired at leisure, in order, and under obedience to instructions.

General Smith had formed the new line with his accustomed skill, in a strong position with woods in rear and open ground in front, and artillery massed on higher ground in rear of his right. The losses of both sides having been heavy, no further hostile movement by either occurred till afternoon, when orders came from Butler, who remained at the Half-Way House, three miles in the rear, to send the best-conditioned brigade straight to the front to see what could be done toward bringing off the wounded, but with strict injunctions against bringing on another general action. This demonstration fell to my lot, and the brigade at once moved forward in order of battle, Smith's guns shelling the opposite woods over our heads. As our strong skirmish line entered the woods, it soon came into collision with the enemy, pushing him steadily back for near a mile, when his skirmishers, being strengthened, made a firm stand. Ours being in turn reinforced, drove them again, till the two lines both alternately and repeatedly reinforced, began to assume the dimensions and appearance of lines of battle. At length a considerable bunch of houses, barns, out-houses, and negro cabins, constituting an old-fashioned Virginia farm and affording a good point of defense, was occupied and obstinately held by the enemy, who even brought up guns to cover it. I also sent back for a couple of guns to open the way for assault, and the affair was in a fair way to swell to the dimensions of battle, when I was recalled and found that under cover of the forward movement, a general retreat had already commenced, to which my battle-worn brigade was assigned as rear-guard. There was no pursuit of any consequence, the enemy's loss in killed and wounded being quite equal to ours, and soon after dark the whole Army of the James was again assembled within the entrenchments of Bermuda Hundred, where as General Grant contemptuously stigmatized it, Butler proceeded to get himself and the remainder of his 30,000 men securely and permanently 'bottled up.' [23]

[23] General Wm. F. Smith, in his book entitled "From Chattanooga to Petersburg under Grant and Butler," 1893, has printed in Appendix No. 8, a letter from me dated January 23rd, 1893, which gives a more specific statement of some features of the action of Drury's Bluff.

CHAPTER XXII

After the considerable success at first attained by the Confederates in the severe and bloody action at Drury's Bluff, their failure to follow it up with real vigor during the several hours of almost entire suspension of arms that intervened between our retirement from the original line and the advance of my brigade in the afternoon, seemed not sufficiently accounted for by their mere losses in action, heavy as those undoubtedly were. It was known to us, both from prisoners and the Richmond papers, that President Davis was personally present at the affair, a fact scarcely tending to abate the well-known ardor and energy of the Confederate general, and the circumstances long remained unexplained. But soon after the termination of the war, my old California friend, Major William Addison, of the Confederate Army, furnished an intelligible and rather startling elucidation, since mainly confirmed by Confederate official reports.

Though belonging to the staff of Gen. A. P. Hill, he was that day, by special detail, serving on the staff of Confederate General Whiting. His statement was that early in the morning, immediately after their first success, fully half of Beauregard's troops were despatched under General W. to occupy a position in the woods on our left and rear, from which at the proper time, to cut off our retreat to Bermuda Hundred. When the attack was made by my brigade in the afternoon, the fighting was for a time severe, and the Confederate general probably taking the motive as more serious than intended, no doubt deemed his opportunity arrived, and sent orders to W. to launch his entire force upon our line of retreat and attack in rear while he should press us in front. But when this momentous order reached its destination, W., though brave, capable and effective under ordinary circumstances, was

457

not in physical condition to execute any movement; and his staff, after vainly trying to effect even a temporary restoration, were unwilling themselves to assume the direction of such an important operation. Thus at this critical juncture a long delay ensued, during which Butler, blissfully ignorant of the well-set trap yawning for his reception, retired unopposed to his entrenchments. Even Beauregard's own pressure on our front—now become the rear—was pushed with inexplicable moderation, the reason for which, thus explained, is now simple enough. He was momentarily expecting to hear the sounds of W.'s attack from the direction of Bermuda Hundred, which should give him the long-desired signal to rush in for all he was worth and reap the results of his skillfully devised plans.

General W. was, when in condition for work, a brave experienced and able officer of the old army, and severe as was the trial to Beauregard's philosophy, it is probable it would have been overlooked, but W. soon after fell in action at his unsuccessful defense of Fort Fisher, and the circumstance has received little public comment.

Personally, I had entered on this campaign against the remonstrances of my friends and the medical officers, and was in about as bad a state of health as was consistent with active work at all. Furthermore, as luck would have it, I had been subjected from the very first to almost constant exposure at all hours, with little opportunity for the indispensable necessities of food and rest, and had only been kept in the saddle by stimulating drugs of whose ultimate consequences, my brigade surgeon, Dr. Otis, had not left me ignorant. During the movment against Petersburg, I had my clothes off one night only, and in that against Drury's Bluff, not at all. The penalty justly to be expected, now appeared. The excitement of active field work was no sooner suspended, than the same alarming symptoms of fever and diarrhea which had kept our regimental and post hospitals overflowing on the Peninsula, seized upon me with overwhelming and ominous severity. In field hospital, notwithstanding such kind attentions as my staff and other friends were able to render, the condition grew steadily worse and I was informed that, whatever the issue,

I must not think of going into the field again for at least some months. All the doctors either instigated or backed Butler, who desired me to accept a long leave of absence, and even offered to, and did, purchase some of my horses. Thus at last, almost without knowledge or volition of my own, I found myself, in company with a steamer-load of wounded and sick of all ranks, on the way to General Hospital at Fortress Monroe, from which place I was in turn forwarded by the Medical Director to one of the great General Hospitals in Philadelphia.

But arrived in that city, whence at that season all my family and many of my intimate friends were absent, I was saved from the military hospitals, then in an overflowing condition, by the kindness of Thomas Kimber, an old Haverford College mate, whom I had scarcely seen since leaving there. Kimber was at this time president of several railroads, in the full tide of commercial success and might have reached almost any eminence in that line; but some years later deliberately abandoned all selfish personal interests in obedience to religious conviction, and became an able and distinguished preacher and writer in the Society of Friends. He was at this time residing on a fine estate that he had acquired in Delaware, and had recently added to his possessions a small property in the same vicinity, situated on the river of the same name, and containing the small but ancient manor-house of the alienated, much-divided, and long forgotten manor of Stockdale, reserved from sale for their own use by Penn and Carpenter, at the earliest settlement of the country. Into this house I was carried on a stretcher, and on the premises first known under such discouraging circumstances, I am now writing, having since lived there, more or less, during every summer season when not absent from the country. At a later period when I had learned from Kimber the history of the house, whose original builder, Carpenter, was a lineal ancestor of my mother, and saw the curious old Indian grants, signed with their 'totems,' or tribal or family symbols, I purchased the property, and have since from time to time enlarged and improved it, scrupulously preserving the integrity of the old manor-house, now surrounded by and embedded among modern additions.

At this place, not far from the station known as Claymont, 19 miles from the city, I lay ill several months, during which I also suffered a return of pain and trouble from the elbow wound received nearly three years previously, at Ball's Bluff. This was for several years the occasion of such excessive and almost continuous pain, that I should certainly have dispensed with the remains of the arm, but for the opinion of my father and his professional friends, Doctors J. Rhea Barton and George W. Norris, who agreed with him that the pain would in time be alleviated by natural process, as the lacerated nerves readjusted themselves; and that even in case of amputation, the stump would remain nearly or quite as sensitive. These views have proved to a certain extent just—since after several years of almost constant suffering, only rendered tolerable by the frequent use of hypodermic injections, the pain gradually became more and more intermittent, and for many years past has been comparatively moderate, with long intervals of immunity.

But in 1864, the prospect of health and prolonged life seemed remote, and, at all events, further exposure in the field was for the present out of the question, and near the close of that year I resigned my commission, and cast about for the means of livelihood at home. Since my last essay in civil life, my domestic responsibilities had of course been increased, while my means had been materially reduced by the legislative experiments of the Government itself. When I first embraced the military service I had invested what assets could be most quickly realized, in city mortgages, which, if moderate in returns, required little personal attention and seemed reasonably free from many of the ordinary vicissitudes of property. But under the inflation that followed the celebrated 'Legal Tender Act,' metallic and convertible currency was driven entirely from circulation, and the Government's paper money fell to a point marked by a gold premium at one time reaching nearly 300 per cent. A large majority of solvent debtors of course hastened to pay off their liabilities in the discredited medium, and my mortgages had thus, during my absence become converted into paper currency worth about a third of the value originally invested in them. It was the Government itself, that

I had worked and suffered for, that by ignorant and incompetent statesmanship rather than with any predatory intention, had done this wrong to me and others.

In 1865, strange as it may appear to some who may read this, canals still prominently contested with railroads the function of supplying public transportation, and looking about for occupation, and rejecting my old profession of the law as hardly worth recommencing for a third time, I observed that the old Union Canal Company which had claimed so much attention in its day, and in which most fortunes of old date even then continued to be interested, seemed even more discredited than was fairly consistent with its real capacity and resources. Its declining business, and the low price of its securities, seemed to my superficial view rather due to reparable causes, than to the slow but resistless progress in methods which we can now see had even then commenced in favor of railroads. The line of the work, connecting the fine basins of the Susquehanna and the Schuylkill, was unquestionably good, and its territory and connections, valuable, but it had never been able to surmount certain radical errors of design and construction.

Its summit level which supplied water to the others in both directions, had been placed at so high an elevation that it commanded little natural drainage, and that little had been entirely neglected, its original designers preferring to pump the required water to a vertical height of ninety-five feet, from the Swatara River. Even the water thus expensively obtained was badly utilized, since the level, passing through a cavernous limestone country, was very leaky, and wasted as much water as it conveyed for useful purposes.

After looking carefully over the ground, I felt satisfied these faults were still remediable, and in order to acquire control and opportunity, I at length effected an arrangement with four other persons to purchase together a large amount of the Canal Company's securities, calculating with that interest as a basis, to be able to influence a practical majority. The plan succeeded, and in due time I was elected President of the Company with a Board of Directors of my own selection, and went to work as earnestly as my crippled condition and impaired health permitted.

Two distinct problems were presented; first, to utilize all water-supply that could be got by gravity from higher territory; and second, by stopping the leakage, to make the entire quantity available. Lying north of Lebanon is a limited district of country locally known as the 'Gravel Ridge,' of uneven contour, but mostly of greater altitude than the limestone district on which the town is situated. After a minute preliminary examination of this tract—in which I received the able and gratuitous assistance of Thomas T. Wierman and James F. Smith, chief engineers, respectively, of the Canal Department of the Pennsylvania R. R. Company, and of the old Schuylkill Navigation Company—lines and levels were run upon it, and three reservoirs located to receive, store and distribute the natural precipitation, about three miles of conduit being required to connect them with each other and the summit level. But the estimates of cost exceeded two hundred thousand dollars, in addition to which, funds were urgently required to repair and restore the general canal-line, eighty-two miles long, and embracing, if I recollect right, seventy-two lift-locks, besides other expensive structures.

The Company had long been in pecuniary default; was without money, credit or security, and unable to borrow a dollar, without individual endorsement. But it still possessed the right of way formerly occupied by a branch canal twenty-two miles long, extending through the upper Swatara Valley from the western end of the summit level to Pinegrove, from which the canal works had been obliterated by the great freshet of 1862. The Reading R. R. Company had long entertained the idea of connecting their Lebanon Valley Road with the Schuylkill County part of their system by a short road passing through the same gap in the Blue Ridge, and had repeatedly introduced into the Legislature, bills for that purpose which had thus far been foiled or defeated by amendments prohibiting the proposed road from approaching the canal branch within some small specified distance. That apparently reasonable and innocent proviso, and the effect of moving back the line of the proposed road to the top of the Blue Ridge, at the narrow passage known as the Swatara Gap, and therefore rendered it impracticable. In the earnest search for ways and means, it now occurred to me that a sale of this old canal branch as a right of way, might be effected either to the Pennsylvania Company, which might thus connect its main line through a back door, as it were, with the anthracite district of Schuylkill County, or to the Reading Company, for making the connection they had formerly desired and closing a door of competition to its rivals.

With this view, I introduced myself to Mr. J. Edgar Thomson, President of the Pennsylvania, and submitted a proposal, but without success—he stating that while it seemed to offer them an appreciable advantage, he would prefer not to violate a certain tacit understanding existing between the two great roads, that neither should wantonly invade the other's proper territory. But with Mr. Charles E. Smith, President of the Reading, I had better success, and after tedious negotiation, effected with him a verbal sale to his Company for $250,000, one-fifth in cash, the remainder in four equal semiannual payments with interest, and the stipulation that a traffic connection between rail and canal at Jonestown should be made by their construction of the necessary schutes and appurtenances, and the perpetual maintenance of 'through' rates on all coal transferred at that point. But when this had been reduced to writing, I was obliged to omit, first the stipulation for interest on deferred payments, and then the agreement for interchange of traffic at Jonestown. When constrained by my increasing necessities to yield those points, Mr. St. George T. Campbell, counsel for the Reading Company, was still fertile in objections to the form of the paper, and conceiving myself treated by him on one occasion with personal insolence, I abruptly left his office and declined further interviews with him. At length through the interposition of Mr. Smith's assistant, John Tucker—whom I had formerly known as Assistant Secretary of War, Mr. F. B. Gowen, the Reading Company's counsel at Pottsville was sent for, and with him I had no difficulty in reaching a prompt agreement respecting the form of the contract. Nevertheless, weeks still passed by without Mr. Smith being able to bring himself to the point of signing the paper, which he himself had agreed to, his Directors authorized, and his own counsel approved.

Meanwhile, on faith of the expected funds, the constructions on the canal had been commenced and were in full progress, and my own personal means and credit were by this time strained to the utmost to provide the monthly payments required. As if the pressure was not already enough, two of the five co-purchasers of the canal securities became so alarmed, that to prevent their holdings from going in a body on the market, I was obliged to take or become responsible for them. I must have broken down entirely under these unexpected loads, but for an unusually easy money market, and a partial revival of confidence in Union Canal securities which enabled them to be borrowed upon, and even slowly and cautiously marketed. At length, when financial matters with me and the Company were approaching a crisis, occurred a certain famous falling-out between the two great corporations, respecting the movment upon the Pennsylvania lines of the Reading's Catawissa cars, several miles of which were refused transportation, and accumulated near Milton. Feeling by this time convinced that Smith was rather amusing himself with me to keep away other purchasers, than from any earnest desire to complete the transaction, I felt quite justified in devising some means of expediting his movements, and as the measure adopted not only relieved an embarrassment that was becoming intolerable, but indirectly brought about other results of considerable personal importance, they may be worth relating.

As soon as the railroad feud became pronounced and public, I called again on Mr. Thomson, and referring to that subject, inquired if, under the changed conditions, he now felt inclined to purchase. On receiving a negative reply, I informed him fully of the halting condition of my negotiation with Smith, and asked if for the purpose of aiding me, he would be willing to address me a note of two lines which should in no manner commit himself. "What is the note?" "Sir: If you are not yet positively committed respecting the sale of the Union Canal branch line, I would like to see you at your earliest convenience." With a faint and almost imperceptible smile, he at once acceded and handed me the note without another word, the commodity of speech being one which he never wasted. The same day I took pains to obtain a *casual* street meeting with one of the Reading directors who was personally intimate with Smith, and after some preliminary conversation, showed him the note in *confidence,* and asked if, under the circumstances, he considered me so far bound to Smith as to be under obligation to decline other overtures? I pointed out that such a note could not be absolutely neglected, and considering Smith's delay and indifference about signing, I was unable to say that I was positively committed with him, and would by no means be justified in declining to entertain other negotiations, &c., &c. But he was inclined to differ with me, and finally exacted a promise that I would at least see Mr. Smith and give him an opportunity to close, before responding to Thomson's note—a promise given with a sufficient amount of coyness, but considerable real alacrity. After allowing a few hours for this *confidential* interview to find its way to Mr. Smith, I called to see him and immediately perceived a surprising change of tone and manner. In place of treating me like a scheming adventurer with a nostrum to sell, he even inquired tenderly after my precious health, and went to the length of asking me to take a seat.

Neither Thomson's letter—nor even his name—was once mentioned, and finding my interlocutor now ready and anxious to close, I ventured on receding in exact proportion as he advanced, and did not quit him till both the interest payments and the traffic contract were restored to their original place in the transaction, which was re-drawn and signed the same day, and in due time fully executed. I hope and believe that few persons despise duplicity in general more than myself. It is usually the resource of a rogue or a coward, and those who habitually resort to it expose themselves to the suspicion of being ready to avail themselves of lying to promote it. In this case there was no lying, but it can not be denied there was a certain silent deception, only justifiable as a counter against the same weapon, which I was not the first to use, and which was likely to result in serious disaster to many others beside myself. I have always felt somewhat inclined to be ashamed of it, and have only related it to introduce and explain my subsequent intimate relations with Mr. Thomson.

The Union Canal storage reservoirs and conduits were completed and paid for, and proved as far as they went, an effectual and indispensable source of supply. The leaks in the summit level were discovered by strewing bran over the surface of the water admitted to quarter depth, and then effectually stopped with clay puddled by enclosing mules upon it and keeping them in lively motion. By means of regular and reliable movement, with low rates, a much larger traffic was obtained on the canal than it had ever before possessed, and the Lebanon Valley branch of the Reading R. R. felt the new competition so keenly that when I gave up the management of the property not long afterwards, a negotiation was already pending with them for its purchase, which was soon after completed and the canal abandoned as a line of transportation. Its securities had in the meantime considerably risen in value, and as I had purchased for control rather than profit, I succeeded in unloading those which I had voluntarily bought as well as those forced upon me; the entire transaction, large and onerous as it had been, netting a slight profit over the principal and interest involved, on a final settlement.

It was either just before or after I entered on that undertaking that I received a letter from Gen. Butler, then, I think, a member of Congress from Massachusetts, unfolding the scheme designed for the establishment of Soldiers' Homes, stating that he was or would be President of the Board of Governors; that the first Home would be immediately established somewhere in Ohio, as a central point, and inviting me to accept the position of Governor. Political positions and candidacies of various kinds had already been proposed to me from different quarters, and declined. Whatever attraction might exist in a noisy competition for the favor of an ignorant populace, must be much impaired by a sense of the incompetence, disorder, corruption and waste which seems everywhere to degrade the administration of public affairs under such a system. The intervention of an appointing power, itself selected and supported in the same manner, cannot much improve the result; and, moreover, one holding such heterodox views on the subject at present dear above all others to the rabble, could scarcely conceal his thoughts and receive their support with honesty. Besides, I preferred independence of opinion and action, and such occupation as tended to associations with educated and intelligent persons, rather than such miscellaneous scramble for the favor of the masses as is inseparable from a vulgar contest for votes.

I had, therefore, resolved to decline all temptations to a public life, and refused Butler's invitation on the simple plea that my attention had been directed to other and different objects. To this Butler replied that I could have little idea of what I was refusing. That I would practically have charge of the selection of the grounds, and the construction of extensive buildings, and would be but little interfered with in the inauguration of systematic government and discipline. Since Butler and I had scarcely ever got along together a single week without friction, I have never been able to understand why he sought to shower his favor on me on this occasion. Was it a scheme to get me under his control and shut my mouth on his financial adventures among the bankers, insurance companies, gas-works and other fiscal institutions of Norfolk? Or a conscientious effort to atone for his treatment at Petersburg, now that his own military exploits have become a laughing-stock? Or an honest appreciation of my fitness for the special purpose in view? I do not know, and probably shall never know, but with a certain amount of good nature, which others might call vanity, am willing to allow him credit for the last.

At the present time and for some years past, one of the least agreeable social features of our country is the want of regular training in some definite trade or industry which is the hard lot of a large proportion of native-born youth. No doubt so many causes conduce to this, that it would be mere empiricism to select one or two to bear the entire burden, though certainly a few seem to stand out pre-eminently. Semicollegiate education at the public expense, which tends to degrade manual labor, while substituting nothing better than scheming adventure; trades-unionism, which forbids or limits apprenticeship and competition; an ostentatious style of living, by the uncultivated prosperous; the influx of a bestial class of emigrants, with whom close association is distasteful to our own youth—all these contribute to the difficulty, but in addition to them, during the period succeeding the war, a large number of young men owed their want of industrial training to their absence from civil life and its instructions during the critical years of adolescence. In the volunteer army they had not only been unaccustomed to regular industry, but had been prematurely entrusted with minor titles, responsibilities and authority, and so indiscriminately bepraised by orators, press and politicians, that it was naturally hard for them to subside into insignificant drudgery on the collapse of the war. The successful politicians who, though rarely commanding much confidence in private life, are collectively and euphemistically termed 'the Government,' with their usual sagacity, increased and prolonged the difficulty by conferring so-called 'brevet' titles on all their political friends who took the trouble to ask for them, and fairly plastered the country with high-sounding and ridiculous titles, indicative of nothing real in the past, and therefore in themselves deceptive and demoralizing. The land has accordingly been ever since infested with 'Generals' who never commanded so much as a wagon train; 'Colonels' who had fought and bled only in the newspapers! and acres of Majors, Captains and so forth, who had been only useful in the telegraph or transportation service, or officious about 'Sanitary Commissions,' or in utilizing the 'soldier vote.'

It was not unnatural that men inexperienced in affairs and misled into false ideas of their own importance, should shrink from a return to common labor. Socialists and magazinists may rave of the beauty and dignity of labor, but they all take care to keep away from it themselves, and all men—whatever it suits them to profess—testify by their acts, a ready willingness to abandon its attractiveness to others, when they can. It remains a well-nigh universal fact that the successful men are not those who labor, but those who by intelligent combination and organization, control the labor of the masses. A cobbler who cobbles, is still a cobbler, whatever title he may hang up in his shop, and a hungry tailor gets no more for his coats, for being dubbed 'Colonel.' The hard truths underlying these considerations—though of course vigorously denied by all true patriots—did nevertheless at that period turn many disappointed persons to the possibilities of that easy, overpaid and specious pursuit, known in America as 'politics.' In a free country, anyone out of jail is good enough to serve the public. Neither training, talents nor character are essential for collecting the fees of office; and with the multitude, he who flatters and bawls the loudest is usually the fittest for their choice. In this trade, a pseudo-military title was at once a convenient distinction, and a badge of 'loyalty,' and hence for many years, and indeed to this day, the mob might select from an imposing array of rum-selling 'Generals' and pilfering 'Colonels' its favorite for any public function, from cleaning the gutters, to spouting patriotism in the Senate.

To avoid too much curiosity respecting such titles, and the peaceful and not too creditable exploits by which they were often won, quasi-military societies were formed for mutual assurance, admiration and support, such as Grand Armies, Loyal Legions, Sons of Veterans, and so forth, and at least the forms of grandiloquence kept alive by 'Camp fires,' Lodges, Grand Commanderies, and similar playthings. So far from real inquiry into titles and records, it has been a point of civility to give a true patriot a peg higher rank than he claimed, and the donkey whose incompetence, or worse, had injured the service and degraded his office, or the cheat who never was in real military service at all, readily got his own record endorsed by lying generously about those of his comrades. I have personally known the President of Councils in a neighboring city, who was dismissed from the service for stealing a horse; a high official of the G. A. R., who required much tough swearing to get the mark of 'Deserted' expunged from his official record; and a gay pensioner, whose only wound was a sabre-cut laid on by myself for mutiny before his first and final month in the service had expired.

In view of such circumstances, which cannot be justly called exaggerated, though with our easy-going American optimism we generally do not speak so plainly in public, the game of politics offered little attraction to anyone of sound information and independent thought. Whether as a vehicle of ambition or a means of support, it was mean and uncertain, beset with concealments and duplicity, surrounded with associations revolting to a person of taste, and entirely irreconcilable with

any independence of thought or action. Any promptings of that
sort of ambition that I may have ever entertained, readily gave
way to such convictions, and though many well-meant efforts
were from time to time applied to make use of any attractions I
might offer to the public as a candidate, they were put aside,
like General Butler's proposition, without difficulty, and I
have never felt an hour of regret.

For a considerable time after the war, the disposition of the
successful politicians being severe and sanguinary toward the
vanquished, it was supposed the regular army must be kept
up to a much larger force than previously—probably to fifty
regiments at least—and an appointment was proposed to me
that I was for a time tempted to accept, notwithstanding my
objections to the public service and the different course on
which I had already embarked. But though arms as a profession would at that time have been familiar and congenial,
the cold judgment which is not the least valuable heritage of
our Anglo-Saxon race, whispered two serious objections.
First, that no branch of regular Government service could
long be compatible with personal independence, and second,
that my crippled physical condition must painfully impair
the activity required for the infantry or cavalry command,
which alone I had a right to expect, in the absence of technical
military education. Had access to employment in civil life
been at this time absolutely barred, I am by no means sure
how far these sober views would have controlled my course,
especially when first smarting under the serious pecuniary
losses entailed by the 'Legal Tender Act.' But fortunately
such was not the case, and I escaped the rock of public life
upon which so many fair careers have been wrecked.

After the most pressing fiscal and physical difficulties of the
Union Canal Company had been got into a fair way of adjustment, and the business so carefully organized that it was
capable of supervision and general direction at the expense of
a small portion of my time, I accepted the presidency of a Zinc
Mining and Manufacturing Company, and after devoting some
time to its effective organization, still found myself with
surplus time and energies available for other purposes. About
this time I was offered by my friend, Theodore F. Randolph,

then president of the Morris and Essex Railroad Company, the general superintendency of that road, with a salary larger than both those I was already drawing. But as its acceptance would have required a residence either at New York, or at some point on the line, and necessarily broken up my connection with Philadelphia, domestic considerations constrained me to decline it. Randolph afterwards became Governor of New Jersey, and later a United States Senator from the same State. He was a well-educated and accomplished gentleman, an able man of affairs, and one of the most delightful companions I have ever known. At various times I travelled extensively with him in various parts of the United States, and our friendship and intimacy was maintained by frequent mutual visits till his death at his home in Morristown, N. J., in 1883. Mrs. Randolph was a granddaughter of Chief Justice Marshall, and quite as interesting in her own way as her excellent and distinguished husband.

As my connection with Randolph and his railroad carried me frequently to New York, I made the acquaintance there of a number of the large stock operators of that city, and at one time yielded much more than was wise to the fascination of their exciting but dangerous game. After some considerable experience in it, I record my deliberate opinion that nothing that is at all tolerated by the business world, is more demoralizing and dangerous, or more certain to lead ultimately to grief. It is demoralizing because it absorbs one's attention from all forms of steady industry; dangerous, because the amounts at risk are sure to exceed one's real capital and proper credit, and that, if persisted in long, it is a certain road to ruin, is matter of common observation. I am glad to say my eyes did not remain long closed to its spacious deceptions, and I therefore escaped disaster, but on the contrary, after being several times involved far beyond my means of payment, at last seized a moment when I was far ahead of the game to withdraw from it forever, and I have never since been tempted beyond actual means of payment. At the present time most of the large stock gambling is carried on at New York or Chicago. But at the time spoken of there were still some large and bold operators in Philadelphia, among whom was engineered, about the year 1867, one of the completest 'corners' that ever mystified and alarmed the 'street,' but which was nevertheless entirely frittered away and lost by want of bold measures at the critical moment.

I was at the time myself operating for a rise in the stock of the Philadelphia and Erie Railroad Company, and held a considerable quantity in possession or subject to call, when I was waited on by a large operator whom I will call K., who after displaying much curiosity respecting the amount of my holding, at last stated that he was one of a party who held 'calls' for more stock than there was in existence and available. After deducting the non-saleable stock then belonging to the Pennsylvania Railroad Company and to the cities of Philadelphia and Erie, it was shown that short sales had been made to the combination in excess of the entire available remainder, for which contracts or 'calls' were held upon responsible persons and firms. Nevertheless, as I had purchased on my own judgment and without knowledge of those facts, I declined to place my holdings in the pool, subject to their management, as desired, merely agreeing upon a general co-operation as long as the 'corner' should be managed to meet my views. But the event showed that those parties had fallen by accident on a larger and better thing than they were capable of managing.

The facts becoming partially known and the stock scarce and panicky, I urged them to stop talking, go to New York and borrow sufficient funds to make a simultaneous and general call of every share they were entitled to, which being impossible to supply, must have brought the matter to a crisis and produced an immediate settlement on the buyers' terms. This they repeatedly promised, but as constantly neglected, contenting themselves with local borrowings on the stock itself, and a series of small calls which were met by the 'shorts' borrowing from the lenders and each other. Becoming disgusted at this peddling method, by which they were in danger of frittering away the real advantages they possessed, I remonstrated in vain, but could not bring them to the decisive point. At last I called on the assembled party for precise information of their real plans, but was refused such information, on the ground that as I declined to deposit my stock in the pool I was not entitled to further knowledge of their position and designs. So far from being forced into the pool by this reticence, as intended, no course of theirs could have suited me better, since whatever implied obligation might have been previously claimed against me, was now incontestably dissolved by such concealment. I therefore retired before they had time to change their minds, went directly to my brokers, and ordered every share of my stock sold the same day to whatever depths the price might fall. The market of course yielded rapidly under such *bona fide* sales and actual deliveries, but I closed out every share, at a profit of many thousand dollars, before night, and so advised everyone, including the pool. Next day one of the party sold out heavily on his companions, the stock became plenty, and in a day or two the price had fallen from near par to about one-third of that amount, or perhaps less. The 'corner' which they had at one time really possessed, and needed only a fair degree of boldness to manage, was frittered away and lost, and the entire party, instead of reaping a fortune at one time actually within their reach, were ruined.

The New York and Erie stock was at that time a famous football in New York—Daniel Drew, first, and afterwards Fisk and Gould being in perpetual contention over it with the elder Vanderbilt and each other, and the numerous minor operators of Wall Street. Though considerably involved in it from time to time with little or no real knowledge, and sometimes placed in situations where, if compelled to realize, I must have lost everything, I ultimately gained great success in this stock, the identity and value of which, as in the case of many of the favorites of that day, has long since been swept away by financial reorganizations. While emerging from one of these struggles, on the summit of the wave I called seriously to mind the sharp lesson endured in Panama in 1850, and then and there resolved to quit forever this specious form of gambling. While such operations may be conducted without any moral wrong, since they assuredly possess certain broad distinctions from mere vulgar card gambling, yet they are over-exciting to the mind, tending to divert it from the regular pursuits of reputable industry, and brilliant as they seem, invariably end, sooner or later, in disaster and generally in personal discredit. Prudential reasons, alone, are therefore quite sufficient to warrant anyone in letting them severely alone, when once convinced that permanent, assured and respectable success in life can not be successfully based on any form of gambling.

In June, 1867, I was desired by Mr. John Edgar Thomson to meet a number of persons at his office. On this occasion there were present, among others, Thomas A. Scott, Simon Cameron, Ex-Gov. William F. Packer, Allison White, A. K. Cumming, John A. Gamble and others. Mr. Thomson desired to know what information I possessed respecting the West Branch and Susquehanna Canal, extending from Clark's Ferry on the Susquehanna, to Farrandsville on the West Branch, a distance of about 120 miles. I replied that I was well acquainted with its traffic connections and tonnage resources, but knew little of its physical condition. It was then asked how much time would be required to make a confidential examination of the facts and a reasonably full report on its physical and financial condition, commercial resources and value. To this, after some reflection, it was answered that such a report could be submitted within five days, provided the Pennsylvania R. R. Company's telegraph line, and its ticket agent at Middletown should be placed at my disposal.

This was done, and I telegraphed to Mr. H., my chief engineer at Lebanon, to take the first train to Middletown, prepared for a week's absence, and enquire of the ticket agent for specific telegraphic instructions. By this method all publicity was avoided, and it was only among entire strangers, both to him and to me, at Middletown, that the actual mission could be disclosed, if disclosed at all. He was directed to go by train to Clark's Ferry thence a walk in one day, by the towpath, to Northumberland, and from that place mail his report of the first day's examination. The following day to repeat the examination and report from Williamsport, and on the third evening from Farrandsville or Lock Haven. Although, in view of the distances, such examination could be but superficial, it nevertheless supplied H. with three pretty good days' work, notwithstanding he was an expert canal engineer, already possessed much knowledge respecting the line, and knew how most quickly to acquire more. As these daily reports came in, they were collated and connected, complete commercial, financial and tonnage statements were added, and at the time promised, Mr. Thomson received the most comprehensive report the time admitted of, and possessed the elements of a better knowledge of the property than had probably ever been in the hands of its own managers.

Two or three weeks passed without anything more on the subject, and I myself was so ignorant of Mr. Thomson's real object, that I was simply speculating on the probable dimensions of the check he would send me for the service, when I was again sent for and informed by Mr. Thomson that his Company had purchased a majority of the Canal Company's stock, to be paid for in bonds of the Pennsylvania Canal Company, the latter being a new corporation recently chartered to purchase from the Pennsylvania Railroad Company the main line of canal, extending from Columbia to Hollidaysburg, formerly acquired by the Railroad by purchase from the State, and connecting with the line now acquired at Clark's Ferry.

Both companies were to be reorganized with a combined mileage of over 300 miles, and I was invited to assume the Presidency. Of all conjectures on the subject, this—owing to various circumstances too numerous to relate here—had been the last to occur to me, and I was somewhat taken by surprise. My reply was that if the line thus constituted was to be used merely as a pack-horse for the Railroad, there could be little use for anything more than a simple engineer organization to restore and preserve its physical condition, but if the management was to enjoy real commercial independence with reference only to its own capacity for business and profit, I thought there was in it a fair career for anyone, and I would be glad to undertake it.

The matter was thus arranged and in the course of a year or two, the two Canals, pursuant to appropriate legislation and financial adjustment, were merged into a single corporation. Subsequently, in order to consolidate and acquire a firm hold of the anthracite coal trade from the Wyoming and Lykens districts, the Wyoming Valley Canal Co., and the Wiconisco

Canal Co. were merged in the same corporation under the common corporate name of the Pennsylvania Canal Company, of which I have ever since continued to be President, though not without earnest efforts during later years, to be relieved, without injuring the interests or the partial prejudices of my friends. Prior to the year 1869, I had urged upon Mr. Thomson the policy of procuring legislation prohibiting or limiting the ownership of coal-producing lands by transporting corporations, but by that time the acquisition of such property by the several railroads leading to New York, threatened to absorb and permanently control all the production of the Wyoming District, and the proposed restrictive legislation having been neglected, it became plain to me that unless we should also acquire control of such lands, the entire coal tonnage of the canal line would be irretrievably lost and the value of the line destroyed.

I therefore felt constrained, under these new circumstances, to reverse my former counsel and recommend similar purchases on behalf of our own transportation interests. With the approval of Mr. Thomson, to whom only the project was confided, refusals of numerous parcels of land in the lower part of the Wyoming coal field contiguous to the canal, amounting in the aggregate to over 6000 acres were obtained; the parcels being in such strategic locations with relation to each other as to dominate the intermediate tracts and deter other large corporate purchasers. These lands were purchased—with more or less opposition from other directors, suppressed under the skillful advice of Thomson—and the enterprise organized into a corporation since known as the Susquehanna Coal Company. Possessing but trifling cash capital, such use was made of its stock, bonds and credit, together with those of the Canal Company and some guarantees of the Pennsylvania Railroad Company, that the lands were obtained and held, more than two millions of dollars invested in the construction of productive improvements, and an annual productive capacity of two million tons gradually acquired. For some years, I frequently stood, personally, upon the Company's paper for much larger amounts than I was worth, and was obliged to use the entire capital and credit of its sales agents at New York, Boston, Philadelphia, Baltimore, Chicago, and minor points, and it would be difficult to convey to others an adequate idea of the financial struggles incident to this heavy burden, between the years of 1869 and 1875. Mr. Thomson was my only real confidant, others being for a long period so timid and doubtful that a part only of the difficulties could be imparted to them, but from him of course there were no reticences, and to this day I look back with ever-increasing admiration at the imperturbable courage and equability of his character—never betraying the slightest excitement himself, and always skillful to moderate the ill-advised elation of others when things went well, and to hold up one's sinking spirits when all seemed lost.

The ultimate success of this Company has been wonderful, if not unique. It may be said to have started on credit and really earned its own capital, or most of it; gradually paid off from earnings, the whole of its floating and much of its funded debt; acquired a large amount of other valuable property, and now possesses in its treasury, cash, or investments immediately convertible, equal to its entire capital stock, after yielding for many years annual dividends, mostly of ten per cent. I have in late years purchased for its sinking fund, at 120 per cent, large amounts of its bonds originally placed, with difficulty, at 65, and would gladly buy them all in if they could be had, but unfortunately at the time of their isssue in 1871, the prevailing object was to defer their maturity as long as possible, and they do not mature till A. D. 1911. In addition to the above pecuniary success of this Company itself, and what is of far greater importance, it has for many years past supplied to the Pennsylvania Railroad and Canal Lines an annual tonnage ranging from one and a half to two million tons for transportation to nearly all parts of the United States, and for exportation.

CHAPTER XXIII

INCIDENTS AND REFLECTIONS IN CONCLUSION

John Edgar Thomson, without whose tranquil courage, calm resolution and transcendent skill in administration such results as those briefly and inadequately sketched in the last chapter could never have been attained, was one of the most remarkable and useful men that this country, so fertile in practical talent, has ever produced. It is easy enough for those in whom judgment has not been warped by prejudice or fear to see and appreciate successful results, but only to a minute fraction can ever be known the laborious and painful character of the long and weary processes by which alone they can be designed, prepared and finally achieved. There is a certain cheap reputation for prudence and conservatism always easy to obtain by criticising the active spirits of the day, and shaking one's head at projects too large for immediate general comprehension. An impulsive temperament, impatient of artificial and unnecessary obstacles, is often prone to resent them by arguments and measures which, though just may be ill-timed or inexpedient. Thomson's experience and knowledge of men, no less than his calm mental processes and changeless imperturbability of temperament, not only kept him free from such errors, but could not fail to moderate the faults of his associates less endowed by nature with those priceless qualities.

The life and work of this great man would be a complete history of modern transportation in America. The period of his life—February 10, 1808, to May 27, 1874—covered the transition from pack-horses and Conestoga wagons, through the intermediate expedients of turnpikes and canals, to the complete and perfect work of railway lines thousands of miles long, and utilizing such vast aggregations of labor, capital and credit as were previously unknown in the private affairs of men. Shallow politicians and village demagogues may fret their brief hour on the stage, in railing at those great fruits of corporate association, but every well-informed and thoughtful person knows that by diffusing population and bringing new comforts to every hearth, they have beneficially influenced private and family life far beyond the most optimistic conceptions of our predecessors of even one or two generations. They have absolutely created modern travel and transportation, the two greatest factors in existing life, and have thus immeasureably improved domestic resources and comfort. They have scattered over an entire continent the scanty population previously confined to its shores and navigable waterways, and revolutionized the values of all commodities, including the fixed surface of the earth itself. By augmenting the capacity of the country to sustain population, they have practically made two blades of grass grow where one grew before. Politically, they have—without impairing the content which the world's experience proves can only reside in local government—welded together a mass of isolated states of no great separate importance, into the mightiest confederacy the world has ever known, and seem to suggest possibilities of terminating the strife of nations by combining in friendly federal relations all the warring peoples of the earth.

Mr. Thomson was descended from an ancient Quaker family well known in Delaware County since the first settlement of the country. Bred to the profession of surveying and engineering, whose precise drafts and unyielding figures tend rather to narrow and restrict the mental horizon, his generous talents readily soared above such limitations, and while retaining the professional judgment and exact methods to which he had been trained, his mind quickly embraced all the defects and possibilities of the great and complex subject of transportation.

What the development of this science—so eminently important to our wide American domain—has accomplished during a single lifetime, for the diffusion, comfort and multiplication of mankind, can best be realized by such as reflect, that it now costs less time and money to move a given quantity of merchandise from ocean to ocean, than it cost sixty years ago to carry it from Harrisburg to Philadelphia; and that thousands of persons are now constantly traversing, in a few days and at trifling expense, the same vast distance, where at a still more recent period, months and even years were required for the purpose, where failure and death lurked at every step, and where none even ventured but the young, the vigorous and the brave.

Thomson lost his parents at an early age, and his first professional successes were achieved without patronage or assistance. He was, successively, engineer on the State Railroad, the Camden and Amboy, the Georgia Central and was finally elected, in 1847, chief engineer of the Pennsylvania, and in 1852, its president, which position he retained till his death. As its engineer he solved the hitherto impracticable problem of carrying it across the Alleghenies, and as president he was the author and steady promoter of the construction and acquisition of the thousands of miles of ultra-montane connections which have made it the greatest line in the world, given wealth to its proprietors and patrons, and built up to imperial dimensions the great Commonwealth in which it possesses its seat and capital. Since his day, no doubt Paul may have planted and Apollos watered with skill and success, but it was his eye of faith that first discerned the measureless potencies lying hid in the misty future, and his courage, energy, foresight and unceasing labors that secured them for his state and city.

Strong, resolute and fixed in purpose, he was peculiarly simple, unostentatious, and reserved in manner. His judgments were deliberate and his words few, but he was an attentive and able listener and neglected no argument worthy of notice on either side. So slowly were his conclusions formed as sometimes to try the patience of more ardent spirits; but once fixed, they remained unchangeable and were but consolidated and strengthened under opposition and hostility. He was slow to give his confidence to individuals, but once given, he was a rock of refuge to his friends, abounding with trust, confidence and support that never wavered, and impregnable to the influence of open or secret animosities. He rarely made

Isaac J Wistar

mistakes himself, but was full of charity for others, and never reproached his friends for errors of judgment. Unlike many others with somewhat similar opportunities, he was careless of his private fortune, which was left very much to the care of his secretary and personal assistants. All his time, labor and thought were given to his great work, his sole amusement or relaxation being found in his domestic relations. Exerting during many years a potential voice in public affairs, it was never used for his personal advantage. While making others Senators and Governors, he persistently refused official preferment for himself, and usually gave similar advice to his personal friends. Personally, I owe to him more than any other, my steadiness of purpose in avoiding public or political life, which of course abounded with temptations and opportunities for such as had attained any promience in the war.

Though numerous short biographical sketches of this great man have been published, and no history of the public works and material prosperity of Pennsylvania, or even of the United States, can ever be complete or intelligible without a record of his influence, his complete life should be written by some competent biographer, for Pennsylvania has given birth to few men whose career has exerted such beneficial and enduring results upon her fortunes, or whose private character would better repay assiduous study and preservation. Neither can we forget that his priceless services were rendered to his country at the nick of time, for the more we regard them the more fixed must be our conclusion that had he come upon the stage of action before the railroad system was invented, or after its main channels were established, the loss to this Commonwealth and its inhabitants would have been far greater than if a large percentage of all her modern politicians and legislators had perished at their birth.

These remarks have been purposely confined to Thomson's work and public career, because if one who so loved and revered him should trust himself to attempt a description of his personal qualities, he would be in danger of falling into what others might regard as indiscriminate eulogy. No words could convey to those who knew him not, an adequate idea of the respect and affection which he inspired in those who possessed his confidence and friendship. To them his death, at the untimely age of sixty-six, was a memorable loss, leaving a void reparable by no lapse of time or subsequent event.

The Pennsylvania Railroad Company had at various times and in several localities acquired other anthracite property for the protection of its tonnage, held in nearly every variety of tenure—by direct ownership in fee or for years, by control of capital stock, by pecuniary advances and through the medium of allied corporations. The great competitive struggle for concentration and cheapness which has been everywhere such a distinctive feature of the last half of the present century, has been nowhere more conspicuous than with the railroads and the numerous subsidiary interests which naturally become grouped about them. It is the same tendency which displaying itself in every productive process of modern times, has in a single generation multiplied many times the dimensions of factories, the application of artificial power, and the capacity of transporting agencies; and in the older communities, at least, has directed almost the entire increase of population into cities and towns.

By such natural process the various coal-carrying canals and coal-mining interests of the Pennsylvania Company, variously acquired, and hitherto heterogeneously organized and managed, were by or before the year 1879, brought together under a single management, thus rendering it practicable, while greatly reducing the aggregate expenditure, to command the best technical and expert capacity for the increase of production and corresponding cheapening of cost. Though the unyielding character of laws and charters still required separate corporate structures, rights, and powers, yet by assimilating all that was not merely formal, and extending to many corporate entities the same *personnel* of officials and directors, the main economic purpose was effected; and notwithstanding the unavoidable sacrifice of small private interests and the jealous suspicions of the ignorant portion of the populace, there can be no doubt that the general public interests have in that manner been efficiently promoted. These particular coal enterprises, though in many corporate forms, with property distributed through numerous counties, and inseparably connected with subordinate bridge, land, water, timber and other companies, thus came to fall under my direction, requiring of course careful and systematic organization to avoid an intolerable overtaxing of individual time and capacity.

But both before and since that consummation, I have found time to do something toward maintaining and increasing acquaintance with my own and adjacent countries by occasional travel. It was I think in the winter season of 1869–70, that my wife and I sailed from New York to Havana, and after some interesting travel in that Island took passage thence *via* Yucatan for Vera Cruz, on the British *S. S. Corsica*—which ill-fated vessel on her return voyage to Southampton *via* Havana and St. Thomas, foundered at sea, losing her captain and most of her crew. From Vera Cruz we proceeded by the newly-completed English railway—then the only one in Mexico —to the capital where a brief study of the still-prevailing feudal manners and institutions of the country proved extremely interesting. These had then been little changed by the influx of foreign ideas and persons so common since the construction of the American railway connections. As my wife and myself could together manage the French and German, besides some Spanish, it was not a matter of much moment to us that English was then little known or used, though some other strange social features were of no mean importance to strangers. The brigand system—for instance— was then in its most flourishing condition. Two car-loads of infantry were attached to each railway train from Vera Cruz, and a squadron of cavalry was in line at each station on the arrival of the train. There was difficulty in getting police permission to take a carriage even as far from the capital as Chapultepec and Tacubaya without an expensive military guard. The usual escort of a gentleman taking an afternoon ride in the vicinity of the city, was a half-dozen or more armed retainers, and the only American we saw in the city was a young man just arrived from Acapulco, who in that moderate distance had been robbed four times and arrived coatless and bootless, though the brigands had refrained from stealing the animals which were the property of the *arriero;* their policy being to stand well with the native peasantry. We returned by the same route *via* Pueblo and Vera Cruz, to New Orleans.

Later in the same year, in company with T. F. Randolph, then Governor of New Jersey, and two other gentlemen, I made an extensive tour through our own Southern States to acquire personal knowledge of their political condition, and the progress of the so-called 'reconstruction.' Carpet-bagging and negro domination were then in full career, and presented phenomena which will scarcely be credited in a more sober future age. In South Carolina both houses of the legislature were almost entirely negro, manipulated and led by a few rascally New England whites for purposes exclusively of plunder. Pending the passage of a bill, these rogues with rolls of money openly displayed, circulated among the black 'statesmen,' driving their bargains with little attempt at concealment, after the completion of which process, the Speaker considerately rang his little bell, the house came to order and the vote thus openly purchased was taken and recorded! The system would have been ludicrous, if it had been less destructive. Under it nearly all property was destroyed or stolen, and State debts incurred for ridiculous purposes, and to absurd amounts; the State of North Carolina, under pretense of supporting a negro militia, adding thirteen millions to its debt in one year, an amount probably much exceeding the value of all taxable property in the State, at the time.

The Supreme Court of South Carolina, which did us the honor of adjourning to receive a visit from us, was composed of a Jew, a negro, and a Yankee—the last of whom has since served a term in the Massachusetts penitentiary for introducing his methods too rashly among the property holders of that Commonwealth, which by no means accepts for itself the good things it had provided for South Carolina. Before that learned and august tribunal, we heard Mr. Memminger, Judge Campbell and other great lawyers of national reputation, arguing a case involving the law of contingent remainder, affecting the estates of a family celebrated in the history of the country. The negro—who impressed one as the most honest of the lot—admitted in conversation that he knew no law and understood nothing of the cases he was called on to decide, and would like to resign, if permitted by his party managers. In Atlanta, our visit to my old comrade, General Terry, Commander of the Military District, was rudely interrupted by the carpet-bag Governor, one Bullock, who, with a half dozen negro 'Senators' at his heels, made no scruple of riding rough-shod over the General, whose official position obliged him to receive, and to a certain extent obey these creatures, with the respect due the titles they had assumed, and which they could not have maintained an hour but for the Federal troops corruptly used to keep up the farce. This ludicrous but vicious system was maintained by the corrupt Grant administration during the eight years of his term by the end of which, little stealable property remained available. The State debts fastened upon the people by unlimited issues of bonds, often sold at auction by the carpet-bag State officials for any price they would bring, could be increased no farther; and on the disappearance of Grant from public life, the system perished, mainly for want of any more plunder to sustain it.

General history—false and misleading as it notoriously is— will no doubt ultimately shed some real light on the character of Grant's administration, but a single incident of it, which personally concerned myself, may be related here. Prior to the public exposure and retirement of Belknap, the pilfering Secretary of War, and his fellows, a certain subservient and unscrupulous politician occupied the position of Secretary of the Treasury, and had ordered the imposition of lighthouse, hospital, and other marine taxes on canal boats. I was at the time managing both the Pennsylvania and the Delaware and Raritan Canals, whose boats were seized in large numbers, in pursuance of this new legal construction. In vain we bonded the boats and contested the question in the courts of the despoiling power itself, where we invariably recovered judgments in our favor, every one of which remained and still remain in force, unappealed. The persecution continued until some three hundred of our boats, besides those of other navigation companies, were under bond at one time, our boatmen alarmed and demoralized, and the business likely to be ruined. When I showed the Secretary that our contention was supported not only by the uniform decisions of the U. S. Admiralty Courts, but by an unbroken series of legal constructions by the Treasury Department of every former Federal administration, he had the impudence to reply that his Department had rules of its own and paid little attention to the Courts. As nothing could be expected from an official who ranked himself above the laws and judiciary of the government that employed him, I therefore determined to appeal to the President himself, as the sworn defender and executor of Federal laws.

General Grant was at this time residing at Long Branch, in a cottage not long before presented to him by certain Philadelphia satellites and office-seekers, and owned another one close by which had been given him by other emulous New York persons of the same class. Arrived at Long Branch, I met with Senator Frelinghuysen of N. J., who though a Republican and a friend of Grant, was a gentleman and an eminent lawyer, and who at my request agreed to accompany me and assist—if required—at the discussion. Grant, who had not forgotten me, received us in the drawing-room, politely introduced us to the members of his family who were present, and soon handed us cigars and invited us to adjourn to the piazza outside. Here a full statement was made, and having amply explained the subject and asked for an appropriate executive order upon the Secretary, I awaited the decision. A short silence ensued, which was at length broken by Grant, substantially in these words: "General Wistar, have you any friends in Philadelphia who would buy that cottage across the road? I have no use for it myself, and am very anxious to dispose of it." Of course I was extremely shocked at the construction naturally inferable from this frank proposition, and did not fail to take leave at once and express my feelings to my companion. But the Senator insisted that the remark was due to nothing worse than artless simplicity; that not understanding or feeling interested in the legal question presented, the great man's mind had wandered to the subject most interesting to himself at the moment, and had betrayed his thoughts in a manner as artless as it was natural. It may have been so; I do not presume to make any comments, but surely do no one any wrong in simply giving the facts exactly as they occurred. Nothing more was ever heard from Grant on the boat subject, and I was ultimately obliged, with the aid of the several interests affected, to get an Act of Congress passed, declaratory of the century of uniform interpretation of law on the subject, in order to protect the canal boats, and the boatmen their persecuted lessees, in the legal rights solemnly pronounced in their favor by every known authority during three generations.

In the year 1875, the city of Denver having become an important place, I felt desirous of seeing it once more and comparing its condition with the untrodden wilderness I had known in 1849, and the wagon camp of 1859. With two young friends I therefore visited it, by way of the Kansas Pacific Railroad, in September, and spent a month in travelling to the various points of interest in what had now become the State of Colorado. Denver had already grown to be a large city, with every sign of permanence and prosperity. We visited Pueblo, Colorado Springs, where the *Fontaine qui bouille* bursts forth from the mountains, and many other prominent places in southern Colorado; and afterwards the Parks, Georgetown, and other points in the north. At Georgetown I met by accident in the street, a captain (Crawford) of my old regiment, now a prosperous civil and mechanical engineer, who kindly devoted himself to our amusement, and accompanied us to various points of interest. From the summit of the range back of Idaho Springs, some considerable distance above the timber-line, I took a small pine seedling from an elevation said to be 12,000 feet above the sea, planted it carefully in a cigar box, and carried it home to my summer residence at Claymont on the banks of the Delaware, a few feet above tide level. This seedling lived, but failed to grow—for a period of about ten years, when, recovering from the shock of such a violent removal, it commenced a fairly vigorous growth, and is now ten feet high and in healthy condition. It has been identified by my distinguished botanical friend, Josiah Hoopes, as *Pinus Ponderosa Scopularia,* and I strongly suspect is the only tree in America that has successfully changed its altitude in the neighborhood of 12,000 feet, i.e., from an arctic to a temperate climate.[24]

In the year 1877, occurred the disastrous labor riots, which threatened property in many localities but especially in Pennsylvania, where the ignorant prejudices of the rabble became especially excited against the railroads, whose property was destroyed to the extent of several million dollars, particularly at Pittsburg where the mob defeated the militia, and for some days virtually held possession of the city. Governor Hartranft came to Philadelphia and called on me to inquire if I would raise an effective force in the cause of order. I expressed a confident opinion that it would be quite practicable within a day or two to raise all the force required, officer it with experienced officers, and suppress the riot in twenty-four hours after arrival at Pittsburg, and proposed to undertake the responsibility myself, if he would first perform his own part of the duty. "My duty? What do you mean? I am ready to do anything in reason." "Well, Governor, I have worked hard all my life, and have accumulated a little property, not much, but of some importance to myself. If I go to Pittsburg, I don't propose to put down the riot by coaxing, but by force; and as matters now stand, the relations of every loafer who gets himself killed would be bringing suits against me for the rest of my natural life. Do your own share. Declare martial law, so as to protect your military agents, and I will take a sufficient force to Pittsburg, prohibit all street assemblages, require the surrender of all fire-arms, fire on every unlawfully assembled squad, and after a reasonable time, hang on the spot, every man taken with prohibited arms in his possession. Give me lawful authority and a safe legal *status,* and I will guarantee you such order in Pittsburg that, in twenty-four hours after my arrival, no prayer-meeting could be more orderly and law-abiding. But you must accept the fact that at the stage where things have arrived, order will cost blood, and blood must be shed.''

[24] This tree died without visible cause, in 1896, having attained a height of twelve feet and produced seed.

The Governor had been a soldier himself and knew the truth and sense of all this, as well as anyone, but he had since fallen into the ways of politicians, and preferred a politician's method. He shrank from and declined the responsibility of declaring martial law, which of course would suspend the civil laws and vest plenary power in the military commander, and I declined to undertake the job with my hands tied. I obtained a company of U. S. regulars under a smart young captain and had it located at the mining properties in my charge, where there had been signs of disorder, but where all now remained serene, and concluded I could stand the riot as long as the State authorities could. Ultimately the thing wore itself out after considerable desultory and useless loss of life and the destruction of a vast amount of property, a large part of which was due to the feebleness, and political cowardice of the persons selected by popular vote to maintain public order and protect private rights.

In 1878, accompanied only by my wife and a courier, I travelled extensively in Europe, and not then knowing whether another opportunity would present, moved rapidly on a carefully prepared schedule so as to get at least a superficial view of most of the principal countries and capitals. We traversed Great Britain from Cornwall to Inverness, gave some time to Ireland, and visited France, Holland, Prussia, Baden, Saxony, Bavaria, Austria, Switzerland and northern Italy, devoting five months to travelling, and getting a fine confusion of ideas. Nevertheless, I believe it is not on the whole a bad plan for a busy person to run hastily over a great deal of ground the first time, and then return on later occasions for a more detailed examination. Of course, however, such rapid visits would be useless for any practical purpose, unless preceded—as in our case—by carefully arranged prior studies of the places visited, and their distinguishing features.

It was, I think, about 1879–80, that I was tempted for the first, and I hope the last time, to attempt some practical benefit—by political means—for the community in which I lived. As already intimated, I had hitherto constantly declined not merely the several offices and candidacies proposed to me, but all active participation in controversial politics, beyond some occasional writing for the better portion of the periodical press; and, entertaining certain unfavorable prepossessions respecting the favorite American panacea of universal or 'manhood' suffrage, could scarcely have asked with honesty for any 'gift of the people' or other personal advantage based on the stupid foundation of miscellaneous voting. I have perhaps already sufficiently expressed my contempt for the fallacies of general suffrage in municipal affairs, i.e., the judgment of the ignorant and non-taxpaying classes respecting the proper expenditure of other people's money, and concerning the qualifications of the publicists, judges, engineers, and other professional experts required for the proper transaction of the public business. But at the time referred to, both public and private interests seemed so seriously menaced by the character of the municipal nominations on both sides, that I was induced to join in the call for, and attendance at a public Democratic meeting, outside of and hostile to the regular party organization. Of course the Republicans, who possessed a large and reliable majority in the city, might abuse their control of the machine by demanding the party vote for anyone agreeable or serviceable to the wire pullers, without regard to character or qualifications. But it was intolerable that the opposition should desert its function of tempting thoughtful voters from the majority by well-chosen nominations, and for corrupt considerations, put up persons so obnoxious as to compel even the most liberal of the majority to adhere to their own bad ticket.

At this assembly of the disaffected, I had some indignant remarks to make, which were well received and supported, and the meeting directed the formation of a standing executive committee of one member from each ward, which soon became locally famous as the 'Committee of Thirty-One,' of which I became permanent Chairman. Samuel G. King, a man of no great force or capacity, but personally honest, and the best Democrat that seemed available at the moment, was nominated by us as Democratic and People's candidate for Mayor, and after a hot canvass was actually elected by a large majority, a considerable proportion of the entire Republican vote of the city having either voted for him, or, in his interest, refrained from voting. Most of the money contributed for this canvass, and much of the laborious part of the work, came from persons like myself, of no very rigid party connections, and free from personal or political designs of their own. A large amount was raised and deposited in a Trust Company, all disbursements were made by check, a minute statement of account was rendered, being the first in the history of Pennsylvania politics so far as I know, and a considerable unused balance was ultimately paid over to the Republican 'Committee of One Hundred,' organized on their side, for a somewhat similar purpose.

Some optimist who still retains a modicum of confidence in popular methods might perhaps ask, "Since a few public-spirited persons accomplished a substantial benefit for the community on this occasion, why cannot such always be done, by proper association of the young, active and patriotic?" Alas! the answer must be, that success on this occasion was only rendered possible by the most barefaced and unusual impudence of the party in power, the almost universal remonstrance of the press, and the consequent fostering of a public excitement which, though ephemeral, as such spurts always are, was for the moment strong enough to overcome that form of political stupidity known as party 'consistency' or 'fidelity!' Such revolts, being conducted by persons whose time and capacity are otherwise occupied, are necessarily spasmodic and therefore unreliable and but partially effective, and even then can only accomplish beneficial results when a worse than ordinary blunder has been committed by the vulgar rogues who habitually get control of the machine, and under republican forms and nomenclature, wield a despotic, corrupt and selfish power for themselves.

In a mere business career pursued for private advantage, there can be little worthy of commemoration, and perhaps even less to interest others. In our country all are obliged to watch and labor for the protection of what they possess, or the support and comfort of themselves and families, and presumably all do their best under the common pressure of individual interests and family affection. I may therefore be excused from going further into such matters, or referring to the numerous affairs of others, which, much against my own wishes, have from time to time fallen under my management, but as railroad construction and financial readjustment have influenced many private fortunes and concerned the public interest in many localities, I am induced to give a brief account of one of these, in which circumstances compelled me to take a principal part.

The Texas and Pacific Railroad Company, composed of several short lines formerly consolidated by Thomas A. Scott, and of extensions and connections constructed by him, was in 1884, controlled by the celebrated New York millionaire, Jay Gould, who not long prior to Scott's death had purchased his interest, including a controlling majority of the stock. It embraced 1500 miles of road, extending from New Orleans, through Shreevesport, Marshall, Dallas and Fort Worth to El Paso, on the Rio Grande, together with intermediate lines and branches covering the largest and best parts of central and eastern Texas. It was separately mortgaged in three divisions of nearly similar mileage, but very unequal value, which may be called for brevity the Eastern, Middle and Western. Of these, the Western failed to earn current expenses, the Eastern barely earned them, and the Middle earned its expenses and a small surplus in excess of the annual charges on its own mortgages. In the year named the road defaulted on all its mortgages, and offered proposals to its creditors which were very distasteful to those best secured. These were, of course, the holders of bonds secured on the Middle Division, mostly residents of Philadelphia, who were invited to submit to nearly the same sacrifices as the holders of securities of the non-earning divisions. Of the approximate total of about thirty-four million dollars of mortgage bonds, about fourteen millions were secured on the Middle Division, and mostly held in Philadelphia. By many of these holders, I was solicited to call a meeting of the Philadelphia bond creditors to adopt measures for a defensive organization to protect their interests. This was done, and after an explanatory speech, a Managing Committee was chosen, of which I was elected Chairman. Amended proposals for reorganization were made by us, and resisted by the New York holders, also represented by their respective Committee. Negotiation proving unsuccessful, our Committee called for the deposit with it of all the securities of its constituents and supporters, and soon controlled by actual possession nearly all the bonds secured on the Middle Division. The several opposition committees representing the bond-holders of the land grant, and of the two less valuable divisions respectively, in addition to a fifth committee of stock-holders, finding their several schemes of readjustment at the expense of the Middle Division creditors, thus effectively blocked, then proceeded to organize a strong bankers' syndicate, to buy out the latter, or a majority of them, and thus remove or overcome their opposition. Though our Committee—which throughout the contest became generally known as the 'Wistar Committee'—held possession of these bonds, as before stated, it had, for the purpose of facilitating transfers of ownership, issued negotiable certificates to the several depositors; and its opponents, once possessed of these, might with reason urge upon the Court, that though the Wistar Committee held the bonds, they as purchasers of the beneficial interest represented by the certificates, possessed the real rights of the depositors, including the very important right to name the Judicial Receiver, and thus control future proceedings, both legal and financial. In order to protect the large body of our certificate holders who had not sold and did not wish to sell, it therefore became necessary for us either to contest the possession of the certificates by rival purchases of our own, or to be crowded out altogether and submit to having our Middle Division—almost the only real security—administered and perhaps plundered for the benefit of the other claimants.

A large money-lending firm of Philadelphia and New York, operating in both cities and professing to influence through their customers a large number of the Middle Division bonds, had been minutely consulted and kept informed by us from the beginning, with the clear understanding of receiving their assistance and support. But as they had demanded the enormous fee of $100,000 to act as our depositary, we had obtained competitive bids and contracted the same service for $12,000, to the Farmers' Loan and Trust Company of New

York, the lowest bidder. This disappointment, though so plainly in the interest of our depositors alienated the firm referred to, of which the first intimation that reached us, was their earnest and ill-concealed effort to purchase against us, on behalf of the hostile New York Committees. Had they candidly announced to us their resentment and proposed defection, it is quite possible that in view of the value of their adherence, our Committee might have felt constrained to yield much, perhaps even to the extent of admitting them to the coveted agency on some terms limiting their charges and protecting the depositors from any excessive voracity. But this selfish and secret desertion to the enemy left to us only the alternative of open war, with the weapons chosen by themselves, or ignominious surrender of the interests confided to us. General John Markoe (the same whose charge with A and D Companies of the 71st, broke and captured prisoners from the 8th Virginia at Ball's Bluff), William D. Winsor, and John N. Hutchinson, constituting with myself a majority of our Committee, promptly chose the first; and with this view, I immediately repaired to New York where I first sought the aid of Mr. Gould, a large holder of bonds as well as stock, who had already assented to our plan of readjustment. But unfortunately, that able and experienced financier was absent on his yacht, beyond reach of telegraph. Arrangements were therefore quickly made with several prominent New York Trust Companies to borrow large amounts of money, on the deposit of the bonds as fast as they might be purchased, reinforced with what private collateral security I could muster. Half a million were purchased the first day, over a million on the second, and nearly two millions, on the third day, the market rates rapidly advancing, when our treacherous opponents deserted their new allies and resold their own purchases to our brokers, having thus accomplished the nimble feat of betraying both their old and new associates twice, in the compass of a single week! Among the predatory private 'bankers' that infest our large money markets I am told that sort of thing is considered a smart stroke of business, though even the famous Dalgetty would probably have found a more appropriate name for it.

Mr. Gould, at length learning of the conflict through the newspapers, hurried home about this time and gave us his powerful and unwavering support; and in view of the denunciation often lavished upon him, it is but fair to add that through the weary years of contest and litigation that ensued, he proved invariably staunch and true, requiring from first to last nothing from us but a fair adherence to the obligations we had publicly assumed. In the secure possession of substantially all the bonds secured on the profitable portion of the property, our Committee was not long in obtaining the general adherence of all parties to its plan of readjustment, after which we were enabled to resell all our purchases at a moderate loss which, by terms of the agreement was assessed upon, and paid by those whose eccentricities had occasioned it. A long though formal litigation and receivership ensued, the mortgages were all foreclosed, and the property sold to our Committee. But as all parties ultimately came to our terms and surrendered their securities to us, we never obtained a confirmation of the sale, being in due time able to cancel all liens by means of new mortgages; raise a cash amount of several million dollars, chiefly by contributions from the stockholders; restore the road and equipment to a better condition than it had ever before known, and hand over the property sound and solvent to its stockholders, who, notwithstanding their vigorous, if not bitter original opposition, have ever since done me the honor— much against my preferences—of retaining me in the Board of Direction.

As by these rather irregular efforts of memory, I recall so many circumstances from the obscure and half-forgotten past, I must not omit some things not yet entirely passed, and especially the pleasure and improvement I have for many years derived from my dearly-prized connection with the Biological Club. This was—and I am glad to say, still is—a social organization of limited number, meeting at a fortnightly dinner for purely social intercourse and conversation, under the widest conditions of mutual confidence and freedom. Entire unanimity has always been required for every affirmative act, and a deliberate and judicious care been invariably exerted to maintain the membership, without regard to wealth or display, from persons unanimously judged eminent in some intellectual pursuit, mainly those connected with Natural History or Physical Science. Professor Joseph Leidy, universally beloved for his personal qualities, and famous among the learned of all lands for the unsurpassed value of his researches, was the President for over thirty years, till his death in 1891. The other members have comprised men distinguished in nearly every branch of knowledge, and few scientific questions could be propounded in the Club without finding at least one expert of authority, capable of giving the best elucidation as yet reached by modern learning. It was not long after the war that I was admitted to this Association, and I have never ceased to derive from it a solid enjoyment surpassed by no other connection of the kind. A list of the members, past and present, would include many of those most eminent in their day in all the learned institutions of the city, and some whose distinction has extended far beyond the boundaries of their native land.

I passed a part of the winter of 1883–84 in the Bermuda Islands, which was not unprofitably occupied in observing the physical and geological, and even the political peculiarities of that interesting group, respecting each of which topics I had afterwards something to remark in the periodical press. I had even commenced the preparation of a geological section and physical history of the Islands to read before the Academy, but finding the thoughts and studies of Professor Heilprin bent on the same interesting subjects, yielded the matter to him, on his undertaking to visit, investigate, and write, himself. That promise he has handsomely fulfilled by his excellent work entitled "The Bermuda Islands: A Contribution to the Physical History and Zoology of the Somer's Archipelago, with an Examination of the Structure of Coral Reefs." Philadelphia, 1889. That excellent performance nevertheless still leaves for a future student the interesting subject of the political organization, public revenue, and municipal administration of the colony under a suffrage, limited only by a moderate property qualification. The peculiar interest of this lies in the fact that although sixty per cent of the total population of 14,650 are colored, the number of legal voters is reduced by a sixty-pound freehold qualification, to 864, or less than six per cent of the whole, thus ensuring in fact, as might have been antecedently inferred, honest, intelligent and cheap administration, coupled with the entire content of the governed. How to extend to larger populations some such system, combining the assured liberty of the individual and his unchecked freedom to accumulate and rise if he can, with the intelligence and integrity thus far only to be found in a small portion of the mass, is the great future problem for Anglo-Saxon statesmen on both sides the ocean.

In company with my wife and some younger members of the family, I spent part of the year 1888 in European travelling, which afforded an opportunity of obtaining information on several interesting subjects. Among these was the most approved form and arrangement of modern Zoological Gardens and Museums of Natural History, in both of which I had become particularly interested as a Director in the Philadelphia Zoological Society, and a member of the Board of Trustees of the Building Fund of the Academy of Natural Sciences of Philadelphia, of which Institution I have at this writing just been elected President. Another subject of examination was the organization and appliances for municipal engineering and administration; and a third was the organization, discipline, instruction, mobilization and supply of great modern armies, especially those of England, Germany and France. A large part of the time not thus occupied, was devoted to travel in the Alpine regions of Austria, Switzerland and Italy, for which purpose a four-horse vehicle was obtained and suitably provided, in which we crossed most of the great passes that I had not previously visited, including the Stelvio, Maloja, Julier, Furka, Splügen and St. Gothard. These, with those visited in 1878, give one a fairly extensive knowledge of the scenery, character and history of the principal Alpine passes.

During the summer of 1890 we visited, in a large party, with all the comfortable appliances of modern travel, the famous glaciers of Alaska, touching at several points ground traversed by me forty years before, in what had then been far in the heart of an unknown and primeval wilderness. Our journey was by the Canadian Pacific to Vancouver, thence by steamer to Victoria and the various posts in Alaska, back to Seattle and Tacoma, thence to Portland and home through the Yellowstone Park, by the Northern Pacific Railway. The contrast between then and now, between the exhilarating and noble freedom of the primitive wilderness, and the rather vulgar triumphs of recent civilization, were intensely interesting to me; but it is hopeless to attempt to convey the feeling to another. One's recollections of the persons and conditions of the strange and distant past, tinged with a melancholy realism by the inevitable reflection, that the first are gone forever and the last changed beyond recognition, can hardly be realized or even understood by another mind, however sympathetic. As our noisy train rushed headlong through the echoing chasms of the mountains, the rocky pinnacles and snow-clad summits still stood piercing the sky, the same as for ages past and perhaps for cycles yet to come, but far away behind them and beyond ken of the holiday tourist, how faithfully I remembered the steep and narrow cañons with their foaming torrents and roaring cascades, up which the lonely trapper once led his pack-horses, surrounded by privation and danger and separated by a year's travel or more, from the then distant invasion of the settler. Rolling over and down the wild pass of the Wapta—once the home of the bloody Surcees and Blackfeet—following down the one almost continuous cataract of that rushing stream, passing by the sunny Shuswaps, and down the fertile and now well-settled bottoms of the Thompson, I strove in vain to identify the once lonely spot, where in the shadows of the great range, and in mortal fear of its inhabitants, we had swum that noble river, pushing before us the frail and hastily-made raft which, carrying all our worldly effects and dragging us with it far down the swirling current, was at last safely landed several miles below the starting-point.

The long and awful cañon of the lower Frazer, then for the most part only accessible to the solitary eagle, now carried clinging to its mountain walls, a wagon-road on one side and a railroad on the other. The primitive H. B. stockade of Victoria, with the Indian canoes hauled up on its rocky beach, now had become a great city, full of splendid buildings, crowded by fashionable residents, infested with millionaires, and girt with long lines of tall ships and stately steamers. The half-dozen trading cabins strung along between the falls of the Willamette and the H. B. farm and stockade at Multnomah Island, had grown to a town of 40,000 people, with electric lights and railways, cable roads and miles of tall and solid wharves and buildings. On Puget Sound, the lonely fishing village, where the kindly old Seattle strove to shelter his tribe from the fierce Hydahs and Queen Charlotte Islanders, and win the friendship of the white man, had totally disappeared; and on its metamorphosed site, extending far back upon the hills, had risen a city as modern-looking as New York, its long wharves lined with ships and steamers, and its steep streets crowded with gaunt and sharp-eyed Yankees, perpetually haggling—even in the sight and presence of the glorious summit of Ranier—over the mean insignificance of their corner lots.

Strange as it all was, the mighty transformation was anything but exhilarating to the spirits. Not one inhabitant could I find that had even seen the place, till twenty years or more after I had left it. In vain I inquired for some stray survivor of the friendly natives with whom I might have mustered enough of their once well-known language, to have learned the fate of the individuals I remembered. All, all were gone, mostly exterminated by the white man's contact, and the wretched remnant herded up on some distant inland reservation, to be robbed and starved at leisure by the statesmen and politicians of our great and glorious (?) Republic. Fort Vancouver had become a great United States military post, where my old army friend, General Gibbon was in command. Fort Steilacome had long been abandoned by its former owners; the great Multnomah grain farm was inhabited by miscellaneous American settlers, and even at the British town of Victoria, when I inquired for the H. B. representatives, in hopes of finding some well-remembered old mountain chief, I was introduced to a lot of sleek and dapper young London clerks, selling their haberdashery over counters like any other shopkeepers! Far, far toward the Arctic, must one now go who seeks yet to find the H. B. in its glory, and its bold chiefs and hardy servants engaged as in the days of yore. As for finding those grim relics of mountain chivalry in our sleek and prosperous modern towns—as well look for an old man-of-war's man in a canal boat; a dashing cavalry leader in the village police; a Highland chieftain in the slums of Glasgow.

But though one may at times be tempted to indulge in sober reflections, in coming thus upon unforeseen transformations and suddenly realizing the complete disappearance of old customs and old friends, it is but folly for any of us deliberately to regret the past. Man still advances, still multiplies, still increases his knowledge and extends his dominion over Nature. Spite of all his follies, ignorance and prejudices—obstinately perpetuated through the ages by the most venerable and powerful institutions he has at any period been able to construct—the race does constantly, notwithstanding perpetual jolts and interruptions, move forward to a broader knowledge and a wiser life. It is not by the memories of any individual, or the misleading comparison of year with year, but by that of generation with generation or century with century, that we are to comprehend this positive and as yet unchanging fact.

When—if ever—such progress shall be visibly and permanently checked; when all lands shall be filled with a hungry and hopeless population; when the fuel and minerals and fertility accumulated for us through innumerable ages shall be at last exhausted; when the sun's fructifying heat shall wane, and the conditions of Nature on which we now implicitly rely, shall have been modified or impaired, then, and not till then, may our remote successors begin to fear a stationary or retrograde condition, and may with reason look back with regret to the better days that will have passed for them.

But surely such regret would be folly for us who daily behold our ever-widening control over the riches of Nature, bringing results which tend to increase the happiness of our lot and to augment the multitudes destined to enjoy it. No! there is nothing even in our declining years and waning powers that should tempt us to prefer the past. Our remote future as individuals may not yet have been satisfactorily revealed to us, but the earthly destiny of our race as a whole, is most assuredly marked out by its constant and marvelous progress in the past. As I now lay down the pen, probably not to be resumed, I feel more than ever confident, that while much still remains to be gained in respect of the social and political welfare of our kind, it is sure to come as other knowledge and improvement have come; and our distant posterity will one day enjoy conditions as superior to ours, as these surpass the lot of our savage progenitors of the remote geologic eras of the past.

The Wistar Institute of Anatomy and Biology
Woodland Avenue and 36th Street, Philadelphia

APPENDIX

THE WISTAR INSTITUTE OF ANATOMY AND BIOLOGY [1]

MILTON J. GREENMAN

The name of Isaac J. Wistar will ever be associated with the progress of American science, not only by reason of his princely gift to anatomy, but also on account of his personal interest in the various scientific organizations with which, during the later years of his life, he was connected. His autobiography touches some of the details of his varied activities and inadvertently develops some of the personal qualities which were so admirable. The autobiography, however, does not deal with his interest in the institution to which he gave so liberally of his time and fortune.

Those who enjoyed the privilege of knowing General Wistar intimately loved him for his force, his independence, his deep human sympathies and the qualities which are combined in the true friend.

During the last twelve years of his life he was interested in and more or less actively engaged in placing upon a firm financial basis the institution bearing his family name: The Wistar Institute of Anatomy and Biology.

This Institute owes its origin in 1808 to Dr. Caspar Wistar (1761–1818), great uncle of Gen. Isaac J. Wistar who, eighty-five years later, gave to anatomical science this most generous endowment to perpetuate the memory of one of America's first and most distinguished anatomists.

Dr. Caspar Wistar, a Philadelphian by birth, was a graduate of the University of Pennsylvania and took his degree of Doctor of Medicine in Edinburgh in 1786, where he had been closely associated with Doctor Cullen and Dr. Charles Stewart. While in Edinburgh, he was honored by election to the Presidency of the Royal Medical Society of Edinburgh for two successive years, and in consequence of his broad interest in comparative anatomy he was elected to the Presidency of the Edinburgh "Society for the Further Investigation of Natural History."

---

[1] This sketch of The Wistar Institute was prepared as an Appendix to the Autobiography of General Wistar at the request of the Publication Committee.

During Doctor Wistar's four years' study abroad, he came under the influence of the celebrated teachers of anatomy in both Edinburgh and London. Here he became familiar with those methods of imparting anatomical knowledge which were employed by the Hunters and Monroes, and on his return began his teaching in 1792 as Adjunct Professor of Anatomy with Dr. William Shippen at the University of Pennsylvania.

Doctor Wistar was actively engaged in the practice of medicine; his attractive personality together with his skill brought him a large practice. His hospitality, his sympathy, the modest firmness with which he held to his own conclusions and the scrupulous integrity with which he performed his duty won for him many friends. We have left to us still in Philadelphia the 'Wistar Party,' an organization for the diffusion of "true and elegant, yet simple and unambitious hospitality," a derivation of Doctor Wistar's Sunday evening parties.

In 1808, following the death of Doctor Shippen, Wistar was elected to the Professorship of Anatomy in the medical school of the University of Pennsylvania. His work as a student in the Edinburgh and London schools and his desire to perfect his anatomical demonstrations while Adjunct Professor, had led him to a keen appreciation of John Hunter's methods and gradually, during the years which followed, he accumulated an extensive series of dissections and preparations useful in the teaching of Anatomy.

Doctor Wistar's benevolence and charity and his active interest in the promotion of his science brought him into numerous positions of importance.

In 1787 he was appointed physician to the Philadelphia Dispensary. In 1789 he was elected Professor of Chemistry in the College of Philadelphia, a rival institution of the University of Pennsylvania. He accepted this position largely to bring about the union of the two institutions, an act which was finally consummated. In 1793 he was elected physician to the Pennsylvania Hospital, a position which he resigned in 1810 much to the regret of the managers of the hospital. In 1794 he was appointed censor of the College of Physicians, a position which he held until his death. He was president of the American Philosophical Society at the time of his death in 1818.

Doctor Wistar was a man of classical learning and well versed in the science of botany, of mineralogy and of chemistry, but his active interests were in anatomy. His work as a teacher and as an investigator did much to bring the science of anatomy to the high standard which it enjoyed in the early days of Pennsylvania's Medical School. He wrote the first American system of Human Anatomy, an excellent work which passed through several editions. His name is inseparably connected with the spheno-turbinal bones, the development of which was more completely described by him (Trans. Amer. Phil. Soc., 1818). The original drawings of these bones, made for publication, are now preserved at The Wistar Institute, as are many of his dissections and other objects relating to his work.

Doctor Wistar's stimulating influence in his chosen field of science brought large classes to his lectures and demonstrations.

The anatomical preparations which Doctor Wistar accumulated during his active career in the University of Pennsylvania as Adjunct Professor of Anatomy from 1792 till 1808 and as Professor of Anatomy from 1808 till 1818, were used by him in his lectures and demonstrations.

Following his death, in 1818, this collection was presented by his widow, Mrs. Elizabeth Mifflin Wistar, to the University of Pennsylvania where through the activities and generosity of succeeding incumbents of the Chair of Anatomy, Physick, Horner and Leidy, the collection was increased in extent and value. In 1892 the so-called Wistar or Wistar and Horner Museum was incorporated under a new name as *The Wistar Institute of Anatomy and Biology*. A new building and endowment for maintenance were provided by Gen. Isaac J. Wistar.

The immediate stimulus for such a step came from the fact that the Wistar Museum, then used chiefly by Prof. Joseph Leidy in his lectures on anatomy, was without that continuous financial support which was needed to increase the collection and to replace and maintain the specimens it contained.

Dr. James Tyson, Dean of the Medical School of the University of Pennsylvania at the time, interested a number of men in the support of this Museum, among them was General Wistar, who took more than ordinary interst in the Museum with the result that a trust fund of about $20,000 was created on July 20, 1891, by General Wistar for the support of the Museum.

General Wistar had always been interested in natural history. This inclination had led him to take active part in the affairs of the Academy of Natural Sciences of Philadelphia of which he was at this time President.

Having vested $20,000, in a trust fund for the care of the Wistar Museum, his interest in this museum, through the influence of Dr. William Pepper, no doubt, and from the fact that Caspar Wistar was his great uncle, became more intense and he decided to do something further. Accordingly, in less than a year from the date of the foundation of the original trust, The Wistar Institute of Anatomy and Biology was incorporated, April, 1892.

The Board of Managers for the first year was composed of the following members:[2]

WILLIAM PEPPER	HENRY C. McCOOK
ISAAC J. WISTAR	WILLIAM SELLERS
S. WEIR MITCHELL	ARTHUR V. MEIGS
SAMUEL DICKSON	JOHN MARKOE
CHARLES C. HARRISON	

The University of Pennsylvania presented a plot of ground on 36th Street between Woodland Avenue and Spruce Street and General Wistar erected thereon a fireproof museum building at a cost of $125,000. The University of Pennsylvania then presented the original Wistar Museum and on May 21, 1894, the new Institute was formally opened.

While inseparably connected with the University of Pennsylvania, the Institute was organized as an independent institution under a charter from the Commonwealth of Pennsylvania. Its organization requires that the Trustees of the University of Pennsylvania shall annually elect its board of nine managers, that one of these managers shall be the eldest and nearest male lineal heir of Caspar Wistar (1801–1867), father of the donor, Gen. Isaac. J. Wistar, and that two of the said board shall be representatives from the Academy of Natural Sciences of Philadelphia.

The purposes of the Institute are stated in the Trust Deed of October 1, 1898 as follows:

The main and principal object of the Institute shall be the safe preservation, intelligent arrangement, and free exhibition of the Anatomical Museum originally commenced by Prof. Caspar Wistar and now in possession of the said Wistar Institute, and its increase and extension to a complete collection of all objects and preparations useful in the higher and advanced study of Biology, of Human, Comparative and Pathological Anatomy, and of the historical development of the present organs and structure of Man, and it shall not be used to replace, modify or interfere with such elementary instruction on those or any other subjects as is or may be given at the University of Pennsylvania or other schools and colleges, but in order further to promote such advanced researches and studies, the Board of Managers may, when consistent with the financial resources of the Institute, establish systems of lectures on the above-named subjects for the instruction of postgraduate and advanced students only, especially as illustrated by Museum preparations, to be delivered on its premises by its Director, Fellows and others, and may also, when deemed by them expedient, institute and conduct a publication, periodical or otherwise, of its

[2] The present Board of Managers is composed of: Dr. Samuel S. Fels, Mr. Jansen Haines, Mr. E. B. Morris, Jr., Mr. Arthur E. Newbold, Dr. William Procter, Mr. Frederic Rosengarten, Dr. George E. deSchweinitz, Dr. Alfred Stengel (President).

lectures, catalogues, scientific proceedings and contributions, and may originate any other work for the research in, or increase of original scientific knowledge of the said several subjects and those kindred to them, at the same time devising and enforcing a competent and strict censorship of the material of such publications, and the scope and scientific value of such work. But since owing to the ample facilities already supplied from various sources for the publication by scientific men of their observations and discoveries, such publications are apt to be considerably in advance of proved facts and well established knowledge, therefore all work and expenditure of the Institute for publishing purposes shall always be secondary and entirely subordinate to the principal object which is and shall always continue to be to accumulate the most complete and perfectly displayed Anatomical Museum that can be devised, keeping the same always fully up to the latest and best methods of preparation and exhibition. While the Museum shall, under suitable regulations, be free for the inspection of the public, and especially of all teachers and students, the object of the laboratories and workrooms and of any lectures or instructions to be given at the Institute shall be for the improvement and research of postgraduate or advanced students and of searchers after new and original knowledge, and neither the Institute, its premises or property shall be used to replace or supersede such elementary instruction of undergraduate students as now does, or hereafter may fairly pertain to the ordinary or necessary curriculum of the University.

The rapid increase in the number of medical schools in this country from the time of Dr. Caspar Wistar to that of Dr. Joseph Leidy, established as many were for pecuniary profits, tended to a lowering of the standards of admission. Anatomy during this period remained subservient to surgery, being frequently utilized as the stepping stone to the Chair of Surgery. Its preservation and advancement as a science was accomplished chiefly by men active in comparative anatomy rather than by the professors of anatomy in medical schools.

At the time of the opening of The Wistar Institute, men like Harrison Allen, Cope, Leidy, Marsh and Ryder were actively working in the broader field of comparative anatomy and were rapidly regaining for anatomy a position as an independent discipline.

The influence of these men, all personal friends of General Wistar, is strongly reflected in the statement of the purposes of the Institute.

General Wistar appreciated the value of comparative morphology in the development of anatomy, the necessity of abundance of material, ample laboratory facilities and above all, the stimulus for capable young men to enter upon this field of science.

Dr. Harrison Allen, for many years had advocated the introduction of comparative anatomy and comparative pathology into the medical curriculum. He was Professor of Medical Zoölogy and Comparative Anatomy in the University of Pennsylvania from 1865 to 1879 and did much to advance the knowledge of the subject. It was largely through his influence that General Wistar fixed the purposes of The Wistar Institute upon that broad scientific basis and limited its activities to advanced work in anatomy and allied subjects.

The formal opening of The Wistar Institute occurred on May 21, 1894. The principal addresses were made by Dr. William Pepper, Provost of the University of Pennsylvania; Dr. William Osler, Professor of Medicine in the Johns Hopkins University and Dr. Harrison Allen, the first Director of the Institute.

It is worthy to note that the Wistar Museum was the first anatomical museum and The Wistar Institute is the first anatomical research institution to be established in this country.

Provost Pepper, with characteristic enthusiasm in his opening address predicted a great work for this unique Institute and called attention to the advantage of concentration and liberal coöperation of scientific institutes even when financial and organic integrity are scrupulously maintained. Undoubtedly Pepper, with his generous breadth of view had scented the development which was about to take place in American anatomy and felt that an institute, whose resources were to aid in this development, would very soon settle into its proper field of usefulness, do credit to its founders and form one of the units in his ideal university which should be an aggregation of institutes and agencies more or less independently governed, for the promotion of research and the acquisition and diffusion of knowledge.

Dr. Harrison Allen, the first Director of the Institute was in active medical practice, but notwithstanding this fact, Doctor Allen for many years had been an enthusiastic investigator in comparative anatomy, the cultivation of which science he considered inseparably connected with that of medicine. He was of the opinion that the study of anatomy in relation to its ancient mistress medicine, should be identical with its study in relation to a scheme of evolution of organic forms.

Doctor Allen had for years maintained most advanced views as to the importance of scientific anatomy as compared with so-called practical anatomy and although he resigned as Director of The Wistar Institute on July 2, of the same year (1894), he nevertheless left his impression upon the future development of the institute which today is following his suggestions almost as closely as if he were still its Director.

Nor could an ideal institute be developed without a very substantial and considerable material foundation.

After General Wistar had erected a fireproof museum and laboratory building at a cost of $125,000 on ground presented by the University of Pennsylvania, he created substantial trust funds for the support of the Institute. These funds were increased from time to time by General Wistar.

Through the liberality of General Wistar, the Institute now has ground for expansion and an increasing endowment which permits it to maintain a museum and research staff of sufficient proportions to accomplish much in its special field.

During the early days following the incorporation of the Institute, General Wistar took a most active interest in every detail. It was his custom to make weekly visits to the Institute, usually on Sunday mornings, when he reviewed the work of the week or discussed with the Assistant Director, the needs of the Institute. It was on these Sunday morning visits that the future of the Institute was most frequently discussed and gradually General Wistar became aware of the necessity of greater income so that with a larger staff the Institute might make an impression upon the progress of American anatomy.

Dr. Horace Jayne succeeded Dr. Harrison Allen as Director of The Wistar Institute in 1894.

Doctor Jayne's work in biology had brought him into prominence as an investigator. His activities in organizing the first biological department of the University of Pennsylvania and his generosity in providing a building for this department indicates the type of work which he enjoyed and in which he was so successful. As Director of The Wistar Institute, he took active interest in the building up of the museum and through his generosity and influence with others continued to add to the collection much valuable material for the study of comparative anatomy.

The library needed attention and with characteristic generosity Doctor Jayne presented his complete anatomical library to the Institute. This made a most attractive beginning especially in sets of zoölogical periodicals.

During the ten years of Doctor Jayne's administration, the museum received the chief attention. The casing of materials, their orderly and accessible arrangement were serious problems. Only foreign museums had thus far enjoyed the advantages of modern museum equipment. The disadvantages of the wooden case were overcome by adopting the steel and glass cases for all forms of exhibition. This type of museum case was not to be purchased in the American markets. Therefore, new cases were devised, various forms of storage, exhibition jars and laboratory equipment were invented. A machine shop was installed for the production of such cases and other museum and laboratory devices as could not be purchased, and thus The Wistar Institute was the first museum in America to produce a satisfactory metal-glass museum case.

During this period of museum growth, while the amount of material had quadrupled, the laboratories had received some attention and a number of investigators had found it advantageous to pursue their researches at The Wistar Institute.

In December, 1904, Dr. Horace Jayne resigned as Director of the Institute and in January, 1905, Dr. Milton J. Greenman, who had acted as Assistant Director from the time of the opening of the Institute, was elected Director.

During the early period of the Institute's existence marked changes had taken place in the methods of biological research. Experimental work with living forms came to be an interesting and fruitful field of research; cytology developed as an important and extensive special field in zoölogy; heredity received greater attention, the chemistry of organic substances came into much greater importance in the interpretation of vital phenomena; biological investigation was advancing from the qualitative to the quantitative type.

About this time the necessity for greater coöperation in anatomical work was recognized by Professor His in Germany in his suggestion of a central anatomical institute for embryology and by Professor Flechsig in his outline of a central anatomical institute for neurology. Through the efforts of the International Association of Academies, the Brain Commission was organized, its object being to stimulate coöperative work on the structure and function of the brain. In America, through the influence of the American Association of Anatomists, the Society of American Zoologists and various other organizations, new life had been instilled into biological science and American anatomy had not only regained its place of a century previous, but was also making rapid advances.

It seemed now that the Institute should take a more active part in the productive scientific work of the country. With its physical equipment, its modest yet increasing income, its organization, sufficiently independent to do national coöperative work, yet with an advantageous University connection, and a keen progressive Board of Managers headed by Mr. Charles C. Harrison who had succeeded Dr. William Pepper as President in 1898, it seemed well worth while to call together a number of representative anatomists and zoölogists to discuss the scientific policy of the Institute and determine what type of work and along what lines the Institute could most advantageously expend its energies.

In a letter addressed to the Director, General Wistar said: "I fully agree, viz: (1) that The Wistar Institute Museum should be designed for the use of investigators, rather than a mere gaping public. In doing so, you would incidentally and necessarily supply all that is necessary for undergraduate students, outside of the regular Chair of Anatomy. (2) I think that after the preparation you have already made, by conferring with leading anatomists, an expenditure of a few hundred dollars to assemble and entertain a meeting of such men in April, would be of advantage to the Institute; its objects and public value. (3) I think the President has authority to order such expenditures and to invite, or authorize you to invite the anatomists you have named, and I will strongly recommend him to do so.''

Consequently, on April 11 to 13, 1905, a Conference of American Anatomists was held at the Institute and as a result a permanent Advisory Board was organized and arrangements made for holding yearly meetings in Philadelphia. This board was at that time composed of the following men:[3]

Prof. L. F. Barker	Dr. G. Carl Huber
Dr. E. G. Conklin	Dr. F. P. Mall
Dr. H. H. Donaldson	Dr. C. S. Minot
Prof. S. H. Gage	Dr. G. A. Piersol
Dr. G. S. Huntington	Dr. J. P. McMurrich

Dr. M. J. Greenman was elected to this board in 1911.

Committees were appointed to establish relations with other scientific bodies with the object of promoting coöperative work and establishing The Wistar Institute as a central anatomical institute.

A definite scientific policy was outlined and neurology, comparative anatomy and embryology were designated as the research fields in which the Institute should take active part.[4]

While such a procedure was at that time without precedent, its results rendered it one of the most important events in the history of the Institute. The impetus which it has given to the scientific work of the Institute cannot well be estimated.

Owing to the modest sum available at that time for current expenses, the Institute's energies were at first expended in developing the work in Neurology by appointing Dr. Henry H. Donaldson as Professor of Neurology, and a small staff of trained assistants.

In 1906, The Wistar Institute was designated by the Brain Commission, a Commission appointed by the International Association of Academies, as the American Central Institute for Brain Investigation, the object of this Commission being to encourage and direct coöperative work in the study of the brain.

Since 1906, some 250 human brains have been collected for this work; of these fifteen or more are from distinguished individuals who have left their brains to science.

The next step in the development of the Institute was to establish a publication. It was apparent that the usefulness and strength of a central anatomical Institute lay in its connections and coöperation

[3] The present Advisory Board is composed of: Dr. L. F. Barker, Dr. E. G. Conklin, Dr. H. H. Donaldson, Prof. S. H. Gage, Dr. S. Hatai, Dr. R. G. Harrison, Dr. C. M. Jackson, Dr. H. D. King, Dr. C. E. McClung, Dr. J. P. McMurrich, Dr. W. C. Rose, Dr. C. R. Stockard.

[4] Nutrition added in 1936.

with other institutions. It was proposed, therefore, to continue the publication of the Journal of Morphology as a periodical of The Wistar Institute.

This journal, founded in 1887 by Prof. Charles O. Whitman, had established for itself an enviable reputation for the excellence of its contributions, but had suspended publication in 1902 for lack of funds. After a conference with Professor Whitman and others interested in this journal and the Institute, this journal was assigned to The Wistar Institute and the publication was re-established in February, 1908, when Vol. 19, No. 1 appeared under The Wistar Institute imprint.

The re-establishment of the Journal of Morphology led to the consideration of the advisability of publishing The Journal of Comparative Neurology, The American Journal of Anatomy and The Anatomical Record, the latter two journals being closely allied with the American Association of Anatomists, and finally The Journal of Experimental Zoology, all well established independent journals financed and edited by scientific men.

The guarantee of permanency which the Institute's imprint would give to these journals, the financial advantages of management in one central office, instead of five, and the relief of busy scientific men from many routine editorial duties were arguments in favor of combining the five journals under The Wistar Institute's control.

The five journals were acquired by the Institute on a somewhat tentative plan lest the experiment should prove a failure and it might be desirable to inaugurate some other form of control and management.

The editorial board of each journal was accepted as it had formerly been constituted, only a few changes being made by the editors themselves. These journals had in each case a paid subscription list, but not one was entirely self-supporting.

At that time the Institute was permitted to expend only a little more than one-half of its income, and therefore, it was necessary to secure financial aid to carry on the journal enterprise. To meet this exigency, Dr. Horace Jayne, formerly Director of the Institute, generously assisted in the editorial management and paid the deficit incurred for two successive years.

In 1909 with greater available income, the Institute assumed the entire financial responsibility of the journals.

The results of this combination of publications under one management were first, to increase the distribution of the publications to libraries and institutions, incidentally increasing the financial support of the journals and second, to reduce the cost of manufacture, the reduction accomplished in manufacturing costs, by the scheme of central management, being more than sufficient to pay the entire cost of the staff required to conduct the publications. In addition, there has been improvement in typography, in paper, in the promptness of issue and an increase in the amount of material published.

For the Institute, these publications furnish an outlet for the work of its laboratories and bring it into relations with a large group of investigators scattered throughout the country, while the scientific work of the Institute is carried into practically every research anatomical laboratory of the world. Furthermore, the Institute is promoting anatomical science in a most substantial manner.

From 1905 to the present time, the Institute has maintained an active staff of investigators composed of Professors, Instructors and Fellows. The Professors and Instructors are persons of similar qualifications to those of men in corresponding university positions. Fellows vary in grade so that the title does not indicate any fixed degree of achievement. The Fellowships of the Institute are provided for in the Deeds of Trust, while the Professorships and the Instructorships have been created by action of the Board of Managers. Fellows are usually men who come to the Institute for limited periods, devoting their time to research and to the work of the museum and eventually receiving teaching or research appointments elsewhere.

The chief energies and resources of the Institute since 1905, have been expended in establishing the research work while the museum has become the depository of materials having scientific interest. This has necessitated a considerable equipment in the laboratories, including microscopes, microtomes, ovens, refrigerator and many special devices. The Institute is now well equipped for its work.

That the research has been successfully established is best shown by the papers, too technical to mention here, which have emanated from the Institute's laboratories.

It has been asserted that institute work differs from the work of a university laboratory in one essential respect, namely, that a research institute staff is more or less permanent from year to year while the majority of a university staff composed of the Professor and a group of graduate students is changing every year. The Institute, therefore, is able to undertake an investigation requiring several years to complete without the disadvantage of having to train a new group of assistants at frequent periods. Then, too, a research institute may direct all its force for a time onto one or two fields of research requiring intensive work and extensive funds, while rarely can a university laboratory divert any great amount of energy and funds to one problem. It is here that not only The Wistar Institute, but every research institute may hope to prove its usefulness.

It has been stated further, that the existence of the research institute in America today is due chiefly to the inability of universities to promote research in their laboratories as a training and culture as well as for its practical good. The research institute is in a sense on trial as an independent organization. The present tendency seems to be for the establishment of institutes for limited fields of work.

There is a group of men who regard the position of a teaching professor as the most desirable for the production of good scientific work. They tell us that contact with students is a stimulus to better work and that the investigator in a research institute becomes self-centered, extravagant of time and funds and loses much which comes of contact with the untrained student. It seems to the writer that there is much force in all these statements, but that the real question is a question of individuality. Many men do excellent research in a teaching position, while another group is better fitted for the research institute and need no student stimulus to produce good work.

At The Wistar Institute it is quite certain that the work of Professor Donaldson on the growth of the nervous system is unique in its conception and in its results. Probably no American anatomist has so deliberately planned and so persistently followed a single subject, with its closely allied branches, as Professor Donaldson has followed the problem of growth of the nervous system. Continuous, connected and correlated work of this type means progress in anatomy.

His results have added much luster to the reputation of The Wistar Institute and his example of scientific exactness has influenced the entire staff. Closely associated with Professor Donaldson has been Dr. S. Hatai whose assistance in the neurological work has been invaluable.

The experimental study of living animals has been actively pursued in much of the work done by the Institute's staff. For this purpose a large colony of albino rats is now maintained at the Institute to supply research materials. As a result of the intensive character of investigations by the Institute staff there now exists more data bearing upon the life history of this mammal than upon that of any other form, man not excepted. This fact together with certain characteristics of the species render the albino rat a most useful laboratory animal. It is easy to handle, readily kept and is omnivorous. It is almost unique in that it represents a domesticated variety, the wild ancestor of which may be easily obtained the world over. Its span of life is about three years. It breeds at three months and during all seasons; has a gestation period of 21–22 days and casts seven young in a litter—which are very immature—a most useful character.

Reared under uniform conditions, the albino rat becomes a standard form suitable for the most accurate experimental purposes. Age, body length, weight of body, of brain and other organs, number of fibers in peripheral nerves all bear a certain relation, so that any modification of food, environment or any treatment the animal receives may show a deviation from normal in one or more of these factors. For accurate experiments on living animals, it is sometimes necessary and always advisable to use a portion of one litter for experiment and the other half of the litter as controls for the experimented half. In this manner the slightest deviation from normal may be detected.

The Institute now maintains probably one of the largest and undoubtedly one of the most successful animal colonies in the country. It requires a great deal of care and constant vigilance to maintain a healthy breeding colony of small mammals. To Dr. J. M. Stotsenburg, whose methods and skill have produced this unique colony, the Institute is indebted for its best research material.

The animal colony now occupies a building about thirty feet by ninety feet, three stories in height, well equipped with sanitary cages and the requisite devices for the production of healthy animals under uniform conditions of food and environment.[5]

In addition to its own laboratories, the Institute furnishes a large number of animals to coöperating laboratories throughout the country with the object of encouraging research upon a single form so that results from the various laboratories may be correlated with greater accuracy.

During the past ten years from 1905 to 1914, inclusive, the working force of the Institute has doubled. The laboratories are now producing on an average, one scientific publication per month throughout the year. A number of advanced workers on anatomy have found it advantageous to conduct their researches in the laboratories, which are always open to men who are prepared to utilize the facilities, and several graduate students from other institutions are usually found in the Institute's laboratories each doing research work for his doctor's degree.

During the decade just passed, the working library of the Institute has grown with the work in the laboratories and under the careful management of Miss Clara N. Perine now contains 2466 bound volumes and 3015 pamphlets [6] carefully catalogued according to the latest scientific methods, and an author-subject index to the literature on microscopy, anatomy and physiology of 140,000 cards.

In addition to this purely anatomical library, the Institute received by General Wistar's Will his private library which contains about 4000 bound volumes also catalogued, and in addition many letters and documents relating to the early history of this country.

The museum during the same period has accumulated considerable material for future study and at the close of 1914 the work here has been resumed with the purpose of continuing in an active manner

[5] A new animal colony building of fireproof construction was completed in 1921—a gift from Dr. Samuel S. Fels.

[6] 10,564 bound volumes; 37,398 pamphlets (1937).

the development of a synthetic museum of comparative anatomy. The number of preparations has increased from 3000 at the opening of the Institute to 15,300 at the end of 1914.[7]

A large number of the finest preparations in the original museum were never transferred to the Institute, but were loaned to the Medical School of the University of Pennsylvania for teaching purposes. Many of the older dissections have passed their usefulness and are gradually being replaced by better and more permanent preparations. Some of these are interesting historically, having been prepared by Dr. Caspar Wistar himself while another class of material, pathological in character, is interesting because it indicates the advent of modern surgery in overcoming the conditions which these specimens exhibit.

During the existence of the present Institute, many interesting human skulls and skeletons, representing race types, have been collected and a large series of skeletons of other mammals have been accumulated. Several hundred human brains, many of the highest type have been secured. The museum also possesses a large series of birds, reptiles and mammals from Borneo and its neighboring islands.

The future development of the museum will depend upon the research conducted in the laboratories.

Materials having research interest and value will be added and the museum will present nature's original record of the investigator's published work.

In human anatomy an elaborate series of educational exhibits has been prepared on the structure of the skull. This series is in use almost continuously by medical and dental students who visit the museum. The teratological collection is the most extensive in the country. The embryological collection of sectioned and mounted embryos ready for study is growing rapidly. This collection will form one stage in the synthetic museum of comparative anatomy.

The close of 1914 will see the Annex completed and facilities added for photography, plaster casting and model making. There will be additional laboratory space, just now very much needed. The Annex will also provide a seminar room, committee rooms, storage rooms and a number of minor facilities for the work of the Institute.

The Wistar Institute, the first of its kind to be established in this country, takes its rank with institutions of similar character like the Senckenbergische Institut in Frankfurt A/M, the Naples Zoölogical Station, the Institute Solvay in Brussels and with the later institutions like the Pasteur Institute, the Rockefeller Institute and the Carnegie Institution of Washington.

[7] 17,585 preparations (1937).   November 20, 1914.

ADDENDUM [8]

Since 1914, the improvements and developments of The Wistar Institute of Anatomy and Biology have been many.

Under the guidance of the late Dr. Milton J. Greenman, Director from 1905 until his passing in April 1937, The Wistar Institute has become a noted research institution with a unique biological farm for experimental work, a place for breeding many varieties of standardized animals, and a valuable printing department for publication of the leading biological journals.

In 1923, the Board of Managers authorized the establishment of a Press, so that all the mechanical details of composition, presswork, binding, etc., could be done on the premises of The Wistar Institute with its own equipment.

The evolution of The Wistar Institute Press has been rapid, for within 10 years, it was found necessary to seek larger accommodations in order to handle the increase of biological research presented for publication. Therefore, the Board of Managers authorized the erection of the basement floor of a new building where the Press was established in larger and more suitable quarters.

The following journals are published by The Wistar Institute Press:

JOURNAL OF MORPHOLOGY
THE JOURNAL OF COMPARATIVE NEUROLOGY
THE AMERICAL JOURNAL OF ANATOMY
THE ANATOMICAL RECORD
THE JOURNAL OF EXPERIMENTAL ZOÖLOGY
AMERICAN JOURNAL OF PHYSICAL ANTHROPOLOGY
JOURNAL OF CELLULAR AND COMPARATIVE PHYSIOLOGY
THE JOURNAL OF NUTRITION
AMERICAN ANATOMICAL MEMOIRS
PUBLICATIONS OF THE BIOLOGICAL SURVEY OF THE
    MOUNT DESERT REGION

To this number of journals has been added a Bibliographic Service, which issues authors' abstracts of papers well in advance of their appearance in the journals.

In 1928, Effingham B. Morris, LL.D., a kinsman of General Wistar, and the late President of the Institute, presented to the Institute a farm of 150 acres, together with complete farm equipment of buildings, livestock and funds for securing the necessary equipment to begin the scientific work, and for reconstructing the old brick farmhouse as a residence for scientific investigators and laboratory guests whose work would require their constant presence on the farm.

[8] Addendum prepared by Edmond J. Farris.

The acquisition of The Effingham B. Morris Biological Farm adds to The Wistar Institute equipment ideal opportunities for solving some of the problems presented. In dealing with certain types of fresh water organisms and with small mammals, not to mention the study of plant life, the Institute is now able to take the laboratory out to nature, rather than follow the usual course of bringing nature into the laboratory.

The farm is located about thirty miles from the Philadelphia laboratory of the Institute in a region that presents a favorable retreat for many forms of terrestrial and fresh water organisms.

An aquarium building or Spring House Laboratory with outdoor pools was completed in 1929 and research work was begun at once in the laboratory; following this three residence buildings, a rat colony building, an opossum colony building, and other necessary structures were built. The Old Farm House was completely restored and equipped with modern conveniences for the comfort of investigators.

In closing, it may be stated that the aims, intentions, and purposes which Gen. Isaac J. Wistar had in view in establishing The Wistar Institute of Anatomy and Biology have developed with marked success. Not only has a fine museum been maintained, but The Wistar Institute has become a unique research unit, where standardized animals are raised, where food is grown for the animals at its biological farm, and where original results of experimental findings are published by means of The Wistar Institute Press and publications.

INDEX

519